Nonprofit Fundraising Strategy

A Guide to Ethical Decision
Making and Regulation for
Nonprofit Organizations

JANICE GOW PETTEY

EDITOR

WILEY

For general information on our other products and services or for technical support, please contact our Customer Care Department within the United States at (800) 762-2974, outside the United States at (317) 572-3993 or fax (317) 572-4002.

Wiley also publishes its books in a variety of electronic formats. Some content that appears in print may not be available in electronic books. For more information about Wiley products, visit our web site at www.wiley.com.

Library of Congress Cataloging-in-Publication Data:

Pettey, Janice Gow.
    Nonprofit fundraising strategy : a guide to ethical decision making and regulation for nonprofit organizations / Janice Gow Pettey.
        pages cm. – (The AFP fund development series)
    Includes index.
    ISBN 978-1-118-48757-0 (hbk.) – ISBN 978-1-118-61421-1 (ebk) – ISBN 978-1-118-61405-1 (ebk) – ISBN 978-1-118-61490-7 (ebk) 1. Fund raising. 2. Nonprofit organizations–Finance. I. Title.
    HG177.P486 2013
    658.15′224–dc23
                                                                            2012048296

The AFP Fund Development Series

The AFP Fund Development Series is intended to provide fund development professionals and volunteers, including board members (and others interested in the nonprofit sector), with top-quality publications that help advance philanthropy as voluntary action for the public good. Our goal is to provide practical, timely guidance and information on fundraising, charitable giving, and related subjects. The Association of Fundraising Professionals (AFP) and Wiley each bring to this innovative collaboration unique and important resources that result in a whole greater than the sum of its parts. For information on other books in the series, please visit www.afpnet.org.

THE ASSOCIATION OF FUNDRAISING PROFESSIONALS

The Association of Fundraising Professionals (AFP) represents over 30,000 members in more than 207 chapters throughout the United States, Canada, Mexico, and China, working to advance philanthropy through advocacy, research, education, and certification programs.

The association fosters development and growth of fundraising professionals and promotes high ethical standards in the fundraising profession. For more information or to join the world's largest association of fundraising professionals, visit www.afpnet.org.

Contents

Acknowledgments

I am grateful for the following colleagues who are contributing authors: Sam Gough, Jim Greenfield, Bob Herman, Barb Levy, Dianne Lister, Paulette Maehara, Paul Marcus, Paul Pribennow, Carleen Rhodes, Jerry Rohrbach, Gene Scanlan, William Schambra, Bruce Sievers, Gene Tempel, Andrew Watt, Bob Fogal, Audrey Kintzi, Bob Shoemake, Owen Watkins, and Cathy Williams. Without them this book would not exist.

Cathy Williams deserves special thanks for assisting in the editing of this book. My thanks to the Publishing Advisory Council for their attentiveness and support, and to the team of editors at Wiley—Susan McDermott, Claire New, and Jennifer MacDonald. To the wonderful staff at AFP, Andrew Watt, Rhonda Starr, Rebecca Knight, thank you for your support in this endeavor.

Serving as Chair of AFP's Ethics Committee was one of the most enriching volunteer experiences of my career and I am indebted to my colleagues on the committee for their support of ethics education for our profession.

To my husband, Marv, our sons and daughter-in-law, thank you for your constant support.

About the Editor

Janice Gow Pettey, EdD, CFRE, is the editor of *Nonprofit Fundraising Strategy: A Guide to Ethical Decision Making and Regulation for Nonprofit Organizations*. She is chair emeritus of AFP's International Ethics Committee and served on the committee for ten years. An acknowledged authority on the topics of diversity and ethics, Janice has taught and presented on ethics and diversity on three continents and many states. She has served as an expert witness on nonprofit ethics on a federal case and she has been interviewed by the *International Herald Tribune, San Francisco Chronicle, Chronicle of Philanthropy*, and the *Sacramento Bee*. Her award-winning book, *Cultivating Diversity in Fundraising*, was published by John Wiley & Sons in 2002. She has written numerous articles, which have been published in various journals and other print media.

She is the Vice President for Resource Development at the Asia Foundation and is the founder of J.G. Pettey & Associates, a consulting firm based in San Francisco. Janice is the recipient of a lifetime achievement in philanthropy award from the Golden Gate chapter of the Association of Fundraising Professionals.

Janice is an adjunct professor at the University of San Francisco, where she teaches courses in fundraising, strategic planning, and board governance. She is also on the faculty of the Fund Raising School, housed at the Center on Philanthropy, Indiana University.

She is a former Peace Corps volunteer, having served in Korea as a public health specialist. She earned a B.A. degree in literature from Park College and a master's in Nonprofit Management from Regis University. She earned her EdD from the University of San Francisco. Janice and her husband live in San Francisco. They have three sons.

CONTRIBUTING AUTHORS

Robert Fogal

Samuel N. Gough, Jr., CFRE

James M. Greenfield, ACFRE, FAHP

Robert D. Herman

Audrey Kintzi

Barbara A. Levy, ACFRE

Dianne Lister, LLB, CFRE

Paulette V. Maehara, CFRE, CAE

Paul Marcus, LLB, CFRE

Robert L. Payton

Janice Gow Pettey, EdD, CFRE

Paul C. Pribbenow, PhD, CFRE

Carleen K. Rhodes, CFRE

Jerry Rohrbach, CFRE, ChFC

Eugene A. Scanlan

William A. Schambra

Robert Shoemake

Bruce Sievers, PhD

Eugene R. Tempel, EdD

Owen Watkins

Andrew Watt, FInstF

Cathlene Williams, PhD

Foreword

The first edition of *Ethical Fundraising* was published in 2008. I doubt that many of us who were involved in Janice Gow Pettey's endeavor saw much significance in that. Hindsight adds a different perspective to the picture.

In 2008, the world stood on the edge of a financial precipice. As I write these words we are in the final countdown to a U.S. presidential election. The fate of the candidates will be determined on how they are perceived to have addressed the consequences of that financial collapse and how they propose to help all of us move forward.

Over the last four years government funding has been slashed. The social compact between governments and citizens around the world has, sometimes, been viewed as a luxury. Corporate support for the work of our communities has diminished and consequently the demand for what we do has never been greater.

All of the organizations that we work for, in health, education, community development, social impact and the arts have one thing in common: we work to create an environment in which all of us can be proud to live, side by side, with our fellow human beings.

So no one can say we're not under pressure to deliver. And people under pressure, organizations under pressure, need to deliver results—and deliver them fast. And at that point there can be an overwhelming temptation to take short cuts, precisely because the need for what we do is so great.

Taking the fastest route comes with risk. Risk to reputation, financial risk, and above all, risk to our beneficiaries. It is that last risk that needs to be at the forefront of our minds. If we fail, for whatever reason, so we fail those we serve.

Our reputation is a fragile thing built on trust—a bond between us and the philanthropic communities who trust us to deliver on their vision, using their resources. Once destroyed, that trust is overwhelmingly difficult to rebuild. So what can we do to mitigate that risk?

In my mind, there are three things critical to that bond; trust, confidence, and accountability. All of them rest on one platform—Ethics. An ethical framework for what we do is non-negotiable. The stakes are too high for us to fail to understand that. We are entrusted with implementing a vision of the world as a just, equitable and inspiring place for all and to risk failure is not an option.

So why ethics? Working within an ethical framework commits us, publicly, to certain values; it builds trust in our integrity; it builds confidence in our ability to support the work our organizations are committed to do; and it demonstrates that we are committed to communicating our impact—and what it took to deliver it.

These factors are critical to building an integrated platform for change. Without them the bond between all of us who work for change would be weaker, our relationships less clearly defined and our ability to serve impaired.

We don't have to talk ethics to support this. We do have to live ethics, understand ethics, to demonstrate leadership through the example we set. And that's where *Nonprofit Fundraising Strategy* comes in.

Under Janice's leadership, this team of authors has addressed the context and framework of ethics. They put the issues under a microscope that we don't normally apply and help us to understand those things that we normally take for granted. They help us to understand the concerns of the world around us, the impact of impropriety, the impact of our approach, how perceptions are formed and trust built—above all, the context for the decisions we make.

The knowledge and understanding of the contributors to this book is formidable. To have that knowledge at our disposal provides us with a phenomenal tool to help us as we help others.

On behalf of all those who read this book, I need to thank those contributors and above all, thank Janice for her commitment to this project. Without the investment she has made, this updated edition would not have seen the light of day. This is a resource that we should all keep constantly to hand. It's a source of inspiration and understanding; it's also a supremely practical tool for all of us who place ethics at the heart of everything we do.

Andrew Watt
President and CEO, AFP
November 2012

Preface: Ethical Will

REMARKS BY DR. ROBERT L. PAYTON
(FROM THE 2005 AFP THINK TANK ON ETHICS)*

W hen I turned 75 a few years ago, I decided that I was certifiably
old and therefore, arguably, *wise*, and that if I had anything to pass
along to a successor generation I should attend to it. It then occurred
to me that I could use as a starting point an idea that I came upon more
than 20 years ago. It was in a book entitled *So That Your Values Live
On*, about the ancient Jewish tradition of the "ethical will." The ethical
will is a document analogous to the will with which one designates the
disposition of one's goods and property and other material of economic
value. The ethical will summarizes the disposition—passing on of the
stewardship—of one's *moral* values.

I've been working on that document for a long time. I won't bore
you with it here. (But I may try to bore you with it somewhere else.)
These remarks will reflect on the *professional* values I most want to pass
on to a successor generation, to you and to those who follow you. To
sharpen the focus I will try to compress the philosophy of philanthropy
that I've been working on for 50 years into reflections on the ethics of
fundraising. To show respect for my elders, I will use the framework

---

*Robert L. Payton, born August 23, 1926, in South Bend, IN, passed away on
May 19, 2011. Philanthropist; first-ever professor of philanthropic studies; founding
director of the Center on Philanthropy at Indiana University; author; foundation
executive; university president; U.S. Ambassador; WWII veteran. Above all, a
remarkable public teacher, inspiring action through books, ideas, talk.

of the three-sector society that was given to us 30 years ago by some very wise people—John Gardner, Brian O'Connell, John Simon, Cathy McDermott, Virginia Hodgkinson, and many others, including a fundraising practitioner and teacher named Henry Rosso.

"Ethics and Civil Society," which was the way the topic was proposed to me, will be examined here as the morality of fundraising. "Ethics and Civil Society" casts the topic in elevated language; "the morality of fundraising" is intended to bring the subject back down to earth, "into the trenches," as people used to say who remembered World War I. That image of fundraising is of a struggle that is grubby, grimy, tough, and very determined.

The first image loses touch with the reality of the hard work and commitment that fundraising requires. The second image loses touch with the nobility of the causes that fundraising serves. We seem to shift or stumble or stagger from one to the other, or we choose images of ourselves either as *hard-headed* or *visionary, practical* or *idealistic*—given that we must be both.

When we set out to bring the study of philanthropy into the university as a serious academic subject, we had to decide where it belonged. Most were of the opinion that philanthropy should be studied as "nonprofit management" and that as such it belonged in the business school or the school of public administration. Some of us were convinced that the roots of the subject were to be found in philosophy and history and literature and economics and sociology and that the study of philanthropy should be integrated into the liberal arts.

The educational philosophy I inherited contended that specialized studies were greatly strengthened by being based on two years or even four years of general education. It didn't matter whether you wanted to specialize in medicine or engineering or law or social work or music or television; you would be better at it if you had a grasp of what they called at the University of Chicago "the organization, methods, and principles of knowledge." I bought that philosophy lock, stock, and barrel; hook, line, and sinker.

To move from the University of Chicago in 1950 to the Association of Fundraising Professionals in 2005 is not a long or mysterious journey.

My professional life took me from publishing to public relations to higher education to diplomacy to philanthropy—five or six *careers* over a working lifetime, as began to be the norm of my generation and will be part of yours. My preparation was a *liberal* and *general* education: I was supposed to be able to respond to opportunities that I had never anticipated. None of the endless waves of new technologies was going to leave me redundant and out of work or unemployable.

Over the course of my career I found myself doing all sorts of things I hadn't been trained to do. One of those was fundraising. It just happened. The grand ideas and prestigious institutions I served were not sustained by hope and glory only; they needed *money*.

Over the course of many years I came to share the prejudice against money that characterizes so many academics and other intellectuals. I found in working for the State Department and for Exxon Corporation that people in business and government are *more mature* in their attitudes toward money than are college and university faculty members. There are reasons for that. The most familiar one goes back at least to the 1930s: that faculty disputes over salaries are so bitter because the stakes are so low. People in the fields where I was educated—in the humanities and social sciences—disdained the search for funds but envied their colleagues who had funds for research and travel and books and graduate students and other things among the precious goods of higher education. Too many failed to see the connection.

Philanthropy, to quote myself, involves high ideals and low technique. (And to quote George Bernard Shaw: "I often quote myself. It adds spice to my conversation.") The challenge to fundraising and to fundraisers is to integrate the two without compromising the integrity of either one.

Much of fundraising strikes me as stupefyingly dull work. I tended to neglect that part. I was inspired and sustained by ideas and ideals, and I was convinced that fundraising research rotted the mind as well as the soul. I still carry some of that prejudice, which is why I was never as good at fundraising as I wanted to be or should have been.

"Ethics is the science of morals," according to Fowler's *Modern English Usage*, and "morals are the practice of ethics." Ethics is a *science*—that is, it is grounded in *theory*. Fundraising is based on that theory but manifest in *practice*.

There are many moral people, including many fundraisers, who have no interest in ethics, who don't read very widely, and who assume that their moral compass is as accurate as anyone else's. I wish them well when the day comes that two of their guiding principles are in conflict, or when their boss expects them to "go along" with a decision to honor a donor of questionable repute. Or when they, as fundraisers, *recommend* that a person of questionable repute be awarded an honorary degree.

I've "been there, done that," as they say. I've been lost more than once in the fog of my own rhetoric. "Trimming," it used to be called, or "cutting corners." Those terms go back a long way. Our moral problems are neither new nor unique.

I'll conclude with some reflections on the other term of this topic: the notion of "civil society." I confess at the outset that "civil society," like "third sector" and many other terms, was not part of my vocabulary until 30 years ago, even though Hegel and a few other ponderous intellectuals were deep into it more than a century before. Many fundraisers know only about the third sector and have read little about the processes that have created the "space" for *voluntary action for the public good*, for the organizations and policies that have made modern fundraising practice possible and effective. The historical origins of "501(c)(3)," for example, or of tax exemption and tax deduction are taken for granted as if they came into our lives *at night*. I asked the same question three decades ago: Why is it that American society relies so extensively on voluntary initiatives to do the public business? Fundraisers have no better excuse than anyone else to be ignorant or neglectful of their heritage.

If you share my view of why philanthropy is America's most distinctive virtue and see philanthropy as central to our health and survival as a free and open and democratic society, then you must see fundraising as central to civil society and fundraisers as people engaged in work that is as important to us as government or the marketplace. Without the third sector, we're a society without a moral compass; without fundraising, we're without a third sector.

I suggest that you try to draft an ethical will: What values do you most want to live on? Write a professional version and a personal version as well; write one that you might discuss with a colleague and another that you might discuss with your spouse or your children. The professional version that I'm working on attempts to ground the study of philanthropy in the liberal arts.

I've had greater response to a question I posed 20 years ago at a meeting of the Independent Sector than to anything I've ever written: *Do you live* for *philanthropy, or do you live* off *philanthropy?* It's a hard question. It's only with the help of the liberal arts that one can find an answer. Your answer belongs in your ethical will.

Some of your work may in fact be stupefyingly dull at times, even to you, but it's important. Most of us don't realize it, but we're all profoundly in your debt.

Robert L. Payton
August 2005

Introduction

This book explores the importance of ethics to the fundraising profession and addresses the ethical decisions boards and fundraisers make and the ethical dilemmas they face. It is intended to be a resource for nonprofits large and small, young and mature, local and international.

Nonprofit Fundraising Strategy offers explanations of common ethical fundraising challenges along with practical case studies to stimulate thought and discussion. The case studies were developed by the AFP Ethics Committee as an educational tool for members and chapters.

Bob Payton (1926–2011), mentor and teacher to many fundraisers, wrote "Ethical Will" for the Association of Fundraising Professionals (AFP) Ethics Think Tank in 2005. He kindly provided permission for the paper to be reprinted here, and this thoughtful essay sets the tone for the book.

This book contains 21 chapters and three appendixes, which help readers use an ethical lens in strategic fundraising and are set forth as follows:

- Chapter 1, "Fundraisers and the Good Life" by Paul Pribbenow, defines virtues and discusses obstacles to living the good life.
- Chapter 2 by Dianne Lister presents the appearance of impropriety and conflict of interest from organizational and individual perspectives. Lister demonstrates how the appearance of impropriety can eventually lead to conflicts of interest.
- Chapter 3 by Jim Greenfield presents the rights of donors. Donor intent as a right addresses the issue of public confidence and trust in nonprofits.
- Chapter 4 on privacy and fundraising is written by Gene Scanlan. From prospect research to gift restrictions, Scanlan acknowledges

that privacy is not a straightforward issue in an increasingly donor-centered fundraising environment.

- Chapter 5 by Gene Tempel presents the ethical dilemma of tainted money.
- Chapter 6 by Paulette Maehara presents compensation as an ethical dilemma. Maehara discusses the major issues surrounding compensation and AFP's response to them.
- Chapter 7, "Using Donations as Intended" by Paul Marcus, covers stewardship from cultivation to acknowledgment.
- Chapter 8 by Jerry Rohrbach presents "Ethical Considerations of Making the Ask," using the universal principles of honesty, respect, integrity, empathy, and transparency as guidelines for donor stewardship.
- Chapter 9, "Honesty and Full Disclosure" by Sam Gough, presents food for thought on how fundraisers define honesty. Transparency is the hallmark of full disclosure, yet there are valid concerns around what limits exist on the public's right to know.
- Chapter 10 by Barbara Levy provides a useful resource for fundraisers looking to develop a plan for ethical leadership.
- Chapter 11 provides a comprehensive overview of ethics from a global perspective from Andrew Watt. Watt suggests the framework of self-regulation as an autonomous model and presents the International Statement of Ethical Principles in Fundraising.
- Owen Watkins writes about the ethical responsibilities of businesses in the fundraising sector in Chapter 12.
- In Chapter 13 Janice Gow Pettey offers two frameworks for making ethical fundraising decisions and presents various organization codes, creeds, and standards supporting ethical decision making.
- In Chapter 14 Paul Pribbenow offers a reflection on the moral framework of philanthropy as a vocation or calling.
- In Chapter 15, Bob Shoemake presents the AFP Ethics Assessment Inventory.
- Audrey Kintzi and Cathlene Williams coauthor Chapter 16 on regulation, ethics, and philanthropy.

- Bob Fogal writes about leadership, governance, and giving in Chapter 17.
- And for Chapters 18 through 21, information is presented from the 2005 Association of Fundraising Professionals (AFP) conference discussing ethical issues affecting the work of philanthropic fundraising from the following presenters:
  - Bruce Sievers, Chapter 18, and Carleen Rhodes, Chapter 19, write about the ethical considerations for funders.
  - And Bob Herman, Chapter 20, and William Schambra, Chapter 21, write about the regulation of the nonprofit sector and restoring public confidence, respectively.

The book then concludes with three appendixes offering readers organization codes of ethics and standards, websites for international fundraising codes of ethics, and the Statement of Values and Standards for Excellence at the Tucson Symphony Society.

CASE STUDIES

The Association of Fundraising Professionals (AFP) has developed fundraising cases as a tool for ethics education. Throughout the book you will find cases that relate to the topic of the chapter in which they are found. The answers given at the end of each case relate to AFP's Code of Ethical Principles and Standards. AFP has granted permission for the use of the cases. AFP's Ethics Committee has provided answers to the case questions using the AFP Code of Ethics and Professional Standards as a guide. For general discussion, readers may choose to use the cases without the questions and answers.

CHAPTER 1

Fundraisers and the Good Life

PAUL C. PRIBBENOW, PhD, CFRE

Some 20 years ago, I sat in a Chicago hotel conference room taking the required examination in order to earn my Certified Fundraising Executive (CFRE) designation. It was a multiple-choice test, intended to measure my understanding of the core areas of fundraising knowledge and practice. I remember vividly the question near the end of the exam that posed this situation: "You are the director of development for a small social service agency in Chicago. You receive a call from the board member who chairs your development committee offering you tickets to the Cubs game that evening. What do you do?"

There were four options from which to choose—and there was a right answer according to the code of ethics—but all I remember is thinking how much I loved baseball. I began to think back on my growing up in Wisconsin and how my dad would take my brothers and me to Milwaukee to watch Major League Baseball games. I remembered fun car rides together, baseball park concessions, and the thrill of seeing big league ballplayers up close. Those memories were about family, about rich and valuable learning experiences, about joy and fun. Those memories were about my moral life.

I chose one of the multiple-choice answers—hopefully the right one, which is that I could not accept the tickets for my own use (though there are ways to accept them on behalf of clients or for the good of the organization)—but what I realized in that moment was that too often we focus our moral reflection and decision-making primarily on the dilemmas we face in our life and work, rather than on all of the ways in which our values help to create what I want to call "the good life." Too often, we focus on preventing misbehavior rather than inspiring the richness and joy of the good life.

Why is this? I think it is arguable that one reason for our often punitive focus in ethical deliberation is that the world is a complex and messy place, and the fact is that human beings don't really like the messiness. We want answers, we want conflicts resolved, we want to believe that if we simply apply the right principle to the dilemmas we face, we will have our answer and resolution. I get that. There are many days on which I would give anything for the right answer to life's big (and small) questions.

As fundraisers, we face this messiness daily. Our work involves relationships, keeping confidences, serving as links between institutions and individuals, and perhaps most vexing of all, money. And for a whole lot of reasons, it is simply easier for us to believe that we need answers to the ethical challenges we face.

At the same time, I would argue that the nature of our work as fundraisers actually places us in situations and relationships where the overriding ethical consideration is not misbehavior, but the value-laden decisions that donors and volunteers make to further causes they are passionate about by giving of their time, talent, and resources. What a privilege it is to be in those situations and relationships! What a noble profession we have chosen, where we are witness to remarkable acts of generosity and vision and commitment! What a privilege and obligation we have in our professional work to help our donors and volunteers give voice to their values! University of San Francisco professor Michael O'Neill has gone so far as to claim that fundraisers must be moral trainers because we are with people when they are making moral decisions.[1] Now, that is the good life!

So, our dilemma in thinking about our moral lives is also messy. We are human beings and we crave order and resolution. We also often crave having someone else tell us what is right and wrong. (As an ethicist, I often find myself consulting on the moral dilemmas folks face, and I am quick to remind them that, though I might offer an opinion about how to respond, my primary duty is to help them think through on their own or with peers what is the right thing to do.)

Our humanness is extended by the fact that our primary work as fundraisers involves dealing with other humans in often intimate and personal ways, thus leading to even more complexity and vulnerability in our moral lives.

Our responses as a fundraising profession to these challenges for our ethical reflection and decision making are instructive. More than 50 years ago, when our first professional associations were being formed, our focus was on drawing together the disparate threads of our professional community—recall that the first professional fundraisers often came out of advertising or journalism or community organizing. In those early days, the issues facing the profession were more about identity and public perceptions of the work of fundraisers.

As the profession evolved—and the numbers of self-described professional fundraisers increased—it became important to begin to codify the ethical values and standards that governed the behavior of fundraisers and that also depicted our commitments to being accountable to the various publics we served (organizations, communities, and the wider society). The work of some of our most wise and experienced colleagues to craft a code of ethical principles and standards for the National Society of Fundraising Executives (NSFRE)—now the Association of Fundraising Professionals (AFP)—is a model of professional reflection and self-regulation. The AFP Code has gone through many changes during the past 50 years, but it remains a comprehensive and compelling statement of our common values and aspirations as a profession.[2]

The issue is, of course, that when you make the effort to write down such a code of ethics, it can take on a life of its own (think of Moses and the Ten Commandments!). Given our human and professional inclinations, codes of ethics can quickly become primarily the law that helps us respond to misbehavior rather than a statement of the sort of moral aspirations we share for our work and the world.

Over my 30-year career as a fundraiser, I have watched my colleagues become more and more focused on applying the Code to solve ethical dilemmas. I lead workshops where we review ethical cases and the climax is often giving participants the right answer to the multiple-choice questions. Despite my efforts—and those of many like-minded colleagues—to expand the moral conversation to helping colleagues develop ethical reflection skills and to point to the promise of the good life, we often revert to the legalistic parsing of the dilemmas we face.

But the times are changing! A few years ago the AFP Ethics Committee dedicated itself to developing resources for ethical reflection and decision making that are designed to support this more expansive vision of the moral life for fundraisers. And the timing makes sense, I think, in the context of the evolution of our profession. Our fiftieth anniversary as a professional association in 2010 provided an occasion to say that our important and groundbreaking work on ethics over the decades had now led us to understand the need to help our colleagues not only respond to ethical dilemmas, but to focus as well on their ethical growth and development as professionals. This represents a sea change for our association and profession. The launching of the AFP Ethics Assessment Inventory (EAI) in 2011 created a forum for both individual and common reflection on our moral aspirations, the sorts of people we hoped to be, and on what I might call our public character as professionals and a profession.

What does this mean? What difference will it make to focus on ethical growth as opposed to solving ethical dilemmas? What is the good life for fundraisers—other than following the rules and doing the right thing?

Good questions—and to answer them we need to go back a few millennia to learn from the ancient philosopher Aristotle, whose entire view of ethics is linked to the concept of the good life.[3]

Not to get too wonky, but just a little bit of philosophy helps. Aristotle believed that the good life is linked to how we define our *telos*, our ultimate end. For Aristotle, the proper end of human beings is happiness. But this is not happiness in our usual twenty-first century way of defining it—the stuff we possess, the relationships we enjoy, the success we achieve. Rather, happiness for Aristotle is something that comes from within, it comes from our making choices that promote our true nature. For humans, these choices are linked to our particular powers—powers of intelligence and will, the power to make choices, and develop good habits. The good life, therefore, is directly linked to the development of good, moral habits (what are called virtues) and the turning away from bad habits (what are called vices).

The good life, then—at least according to Aristotle, who many of us think got it right—is about the appropriate ordering of our virtues and the resisting of vice. We achieve the good life when we find harmony and peace, controlling our human appetites and perfecting our human powers through the virtues. Perhaps you've heard of the four principal (or cardinal) virtues: prudence, justice, fortitude, and temperance. The good life is defined by our capacities to make choices that order these virtues in our thinking and acting, and to develop the habits of living that lead to good character and order.

There is much more nuance and complexity in Aristotle's ethical philosophy, but I would argue that his vision of the good life is precisely what we are trying to promote for fundraisers as they navigate their ethical lives. We want fundraisers to have the support and resources they need to reflect on their experience, to make choices that bring order to their lives, to develop good and virtuous moral habits, and ultimately to be perceived by others as individuals (and a professional community) seeking to live the good life.

Our good colleague, Albert Anderson, writing in his *Ethics for Fundraisers*, challenged all of us to find in Aristotle the means to consider how "achieving moral excellence begins as a natural bent to gain happiness mainly by discovering and developing a pattern of actions shaped by self-conscious choices that draw the line between too much and too little, the excessive and deficient..."[4] Hardly an easy undertaking— having someone give us the right answer seems so much more expedient in the midst of my busy life—but surely one worth aspiring to as our fundraising profession continues to evolve in its important public work to support social causes and values.

So what does the good life look like for fundraisers—other than meeting goals and closing gifts? The research undertaken in the development of the EAI offers us a beginning point to answer this question.

As detailed elsewhere, the EAI project began by asking fundraisers this question: "Think of an AFP colleague whom you consider to be highly ethical. Describe the behaviors of that person that led you to this conclusion."[5] The 2,528 answers received were sorted and categorized by a group of our peers, and ultimately six responses were recommended as of the highest order. We might look at these six characteristics of ethical fundraisers as our professional virtues.

We claim that: "An ethical fundraiser aspires to: *Observe* and *adhere* to the AFP Code of Ethical Principles and Standards (and other relevant laws and regulations); Build personal confidence and public support by being *trustworthy* in all circumstances; Practice *honesty* in relationships; Be *accountable* for professional, organizational and public behavior; Seek to be *transparent* and forthcoming in all dealings; and, Be *courageous* in serving the public trust."

Here then are six virtues, if you will, of the ethical fundraiser. Here is the basis for good, moral habits. Here is the stuff of a good life for fundraisers. We observe the rules. We are trustworthy, honest, accountable, and transparent. And we are courageous. The issues are how we define these virtues, how we respond to the challenges to living this way as professionals, and how we support each other in making the choices and developing the habits that bring order and harmony to our professional lives.

Allow me to take each of these three issues in turn as the foundation for understanding fundraisers and the good life.

DEFINING THE VIRTUES

First, defining the virtues. I want to commend my colleague, Robert Shoemake from the Center for Ethical Business Cultures at the University of St. Thomas, whose article in this volume provides an overview of how the EAI was developed. Once the six characteristics of ethical fundraisers were identified, Shoemake understood the need to provide an initial definition of those characteristics. In what follows, I borrow from his definitional work[6] as the starting point for defining the virtues associated with ethical fundraisers. Though Shoemake offered his definitions in alphabetical order, I want to argue that there is a certain rank order to the virtues that is important for understanding their integrated role in defining the good life for fundraisers.

Adherence (or Observance)

This is the baseline for a moral life—following the rules and living as if they matter. Ethical fundraisers act according to the highest standards of the profession, not because they have to but because they know it is the right thing to do. The importance of adherence as a virtue is not so much the legal aspects of observing the AFP Code of Ethical Principles and Standards—as important as such observance is—it is the understanding that the Code and Standards reflect a positive depiction of the sort of profession we aspire to be and the sort of world in which we want to live. In other words, what is important in adherence is not simply that I don't do something because the Code says so. For example, the Code says don't take donor lists from one organization to another when you change jobs. I would go further to say that the virtue of adherence says that I so understand and respect the need for healthy organizations, and I appreciate how transience in jobs can potentially threaten organization well-being, that I would do anything in my power to protect the needs of the organization I am leaving. My career decision does not override the need to honor organizational mission and public trust.

Trustworthy

Trust is at the heart of the relationships that fundraisers create and sustain in support of mission-based organizations. We all know what damage can be done to otherwise good and noble work by breaking trust with the mission, values, and constituencies we serve. There are countless examples in our society of individuals manipulating a relationship for their own benefit, and thereby calling into question the trustworthiness of an entire organization (and occasionally, the entire philanthropic sector). I believe that the concept of trust and trustworthiness has various components: it is about trust in competence (and thus, the need for fundraisers to be technically rigorous); trust in interpersonal relationships (and thus, fundraisers must be particularly careful of relationship boundaries); and trust in organizational integrity (and thus, fundraisers must hold their organizations to a high standard in trustworthy policies and procedures). Trust also impels us to attend to relationships on various levels—from individual relationships, to organizational ties, to the public good and trust. No one individual or organization is perfect, so trust can be strained if not broken, in the course of our hectic and complex daily lives. At the end of the day, broken trust may demand another moral skill that seems in short supply—the ability to ask for and offer forgiveness.

Accountable

This seems so obvious, but often runs counter to the demands of the marketplace and the world in which we live. Fundraisers have multiple accountabilities—in fact, part of the distinctive aspect of our professional work is that we reside on the boundaries of an organization, linking its mission and programs with donors and volunteers and their values and commitments. I think of fundraisers as having a role as consciences of the philanthropic community, being willing to ask tough questions and hold all parties accountable for their responsibilities and actions. We must honor organizational mission and strategy, of course. We also must honor donor intent and interests. We live in a society in which most people wait for accountability to be demanded, rather than pursuing it proactively. As a virtue, accountability demands of fundraisers intentionality for taking responsibility, not waiting to be asked. For example, a recent situation in my organization called into question whether or not we were honoring donor intent in our handling of various restricted funds. When this issue was called to our attention by fundraising staff and others, we were challenged as an organization to take responsibility for circumstances in which we had been lax and to establish policies and procedures to live up to a higher standard. That is pursuing accountability, rather than waiting for it to be imposed.

Honesty and Integrity

Honesty in our various dealings is always the moral path, and integrity in our relationships is grounded in both trust and honesty. Speaking the truth in the midst of a gift negotiation may be difficult to do. We've all been there in situations where a gift seems so close and when the donor asks that tough question about the program's impact or outcomes, we are tempted to fudge the results and slant the truth. In the end, if honesty is not practiced in all of our dealings, then we will live a lie—whether a small or big lie—and ultimately know that the integrity of our relationships is fragile. Many of us know that public perceptions of fundraisers are sometimes stereotypical—watch your pocketbook when the fundraiser is around, or don't tell that person on the plane next to you that you are a fundraiser for fear they'll clam up. We must overcome these stereotypes, not by continuing to skirt the truth with some self-justification, but by practicing the virtue of honesty in all we do. No matter what the stereotypes may depict, ours is noble work, helping to support worthy organizations and causes, and we are a privileged profession, witnesses to and facilitators of moral acts of generosity and vision. What reason do we have to be less than truthful? Ultimately, a lack of honesty insinuates itself into the very fabric of our communities, leading to a breakdown in the integrity of our mission and work. That is too high a price to pay for not telling the truth, as it undermines the public trust and values.

Transparent

This is rather a "buzz" concept these days, but the fact that it ended up as one of the six virtues of ethical fundraisers strikes me as meaningful and provocative. This is about accountability, honesty, and trustworthiness, of course (this begins to show how these six virtues are interrelated), but it points to an even more demanding standard. Stephen Carter, a Yale law professor, has written about the demands of moral life by outlining three steps needed to live with integrity. First, you must reflect on the values and issues raised by a moral situation. Second, you must act based on your reflections. And third, you must be willing to stand up at the end of the day and be accountable for both your reflection and action— even when it didn't go well. This, for me, is the sort of claim that transparency makes upon ethical fundraisers. Yes, we should be open and clear in our communications and procedures. Yes, we should respect the wishes of donors, providing accurate and complete information about our organization. But more than that, we should live as professionals who have nothing to hide and who understand that as public servants, we have a special obligation to live our lives out in the open, to not hide behind whatever boundaries or policies or social norms that might otherwise provide cover. Ethical fundraisers are an open book because their work serves the public.

Courage

The final virtue of ethical fundraisers is perhaps the most provocative and unexpected, but in the end, it seems almost commonsensical that those of us called to this work—this work in service to the public trust, this work guided by the values and virtues described herein—will be in many cases, living and working against the grain of the world's norms and expectations. And that takes a huge amount of courage. Following the rules, telling the truth, being open and accountable, and building and sustaining trust in all our dealings, sets the bar high for our professional lives. As a long-time member of the AFP Ethics Committee, I have witnessed case after case of our professional colleagues succumbing to the temptations and demands of the business of our lives—temptations to skirt the truth and manipulate relationships; demands to meet goals and close gifts; expectations to do what is needed to succeed, not what is right and good. Thus, the claims of moral courage may be the highest standard of all, tying together the other virtues to offer a pathway to the good life. No one said it would be easy, only that it was the right thing to do, the right way to live.

OBSTACLES TO LIVING THE GOOD LIFE

With these brief definitions of the virtues of ethical fundraisers in mind, our second challenge is to name the obstacles to living the good life. And they are myriad. Allow me to suggest three primary challenges we face in our lives as fundraisers that seem to me central to our ethical work ahead.

1. **No one taught us how to do this work**. I'm not joking. Perhaps the core challenge to pursuing the good life in our professional work is that we live in a society where we are expected to just get the job done, and there are fewer and fewer opportunities to learn a different path. Perhaps you took a required ethics course in college—or maybe you went to a parochial school where ethics training was part of the culture—or maybe you grew up in a family that took the time to think together about what is important and how we should behave. But more and more, it is the case that we have few training opportunities to practice ethical reflection and virtuous living. I often find myself leading ethics workshops with experienced fundraisers who have never taken the time to think through an ethical situation, to imagine different ways of responding to the situation, and to consider the implications of their actions (or lack thereof). These are good people, good professionals, who often fall into the trap of choosing the expedient or worse, simply because they've always done it that way. Living the good life—thinking about it and making the right choices—takes practice.

2. **Our professional work is often judged by external standards, not internal rewards**. The historic genius of the professions in America is the dynamic between expertise and serving the common good. At their best, professionals understand that they have a technical expertise that is needed by patients or clients or students—or the wider public. They are given a privileged status in society because of this expertise and are expected to live up to a higher standard because of it. Part of that higher standard is the obligation to give back to society, to use your expertise in service to the world, even to take on public leadership. When this dynamic between expertise and service is in balance, professionals find their happiness in the intrinsic rewards they receive, by the sense that they are doing what they are called to do—this is what Aristotle meant by the good life. When, however, as is more and more the case, professionals are defined more by the economic goods their work engenders than by those intrinsic rewards, it is hard to live

a good life. Meeting the bottom line, beating the competition, securing the perks of success in an upwardly mobile career—these are external rewards and standards that are often sources of temptation to cut corners, to manipulate relationships, to do whatever it takes to get more. The good life is difficult to navigate when the standards of success are more about vice than virtue.

3. **Our professional work revolves around relationships and resources that often entangle us in the most intimate aspects of peoples' lives**. Robert Payton once suggested that one of the central challenges for fundraisers is that "the currency of our work is often 'currency.'"[7] When we work with donors and volunteers giving so deeply of themselves with time and talent and financial resources, we are drawn into a web of social and psychological dynamics that can be very difficult to navigate. Some of the most vexing ethical dilemmas we face in our work are related to what we know about peoples' lives (think about confidentiality), how we maintain appropriate boundaries in our relationships (think about getting too close to a prospective donor, or coming to think we ought to live in his/her world), and how we balance the needs of our organizations with the needs of donors and volunteers (think of honoring intent or not telling the truth about our organization's fallacies). It is hard to pursue the good life when the very nature of our work places us in situations where our decisions and actions are inextricably bound up with someone else's values and gifts. Virtue requires moderation between extremes. Our professional work often situates us amidst extreme circumstances—and it is hard to avoid the force with which those extremes pull us away from the moral path.

These, then, are simply a few of the obstacles to fundraisers living a good life. But if it was easy, then I wouldn't be writing this essay, and we wouldn't need ethics training or inventories or books. I think it is important for all of us to take a deep breath and admit vulnerability when it comes to the ethical challenges ahead. Humility may be the most helpful virtue we learn to practice. We'll make mistakes. We'll take two steps back after one forward. We'll be tempted to do just what it takes. And we'll enjoy the rewards we reap from our work, even if they come with a price.

But there are things we can do if we genuinely hope to grow as ethical fundraisers and pursue the good life.

GROWING AS ETHICAL FUNDRAISERS

First, we can find opportunities to *practice* ethical reflection and living the good life. I often tell students not to take on the entire challenge at one sitting. Begin with the EAI and be honest with your answers. When you see your results, reflect on what they may tell you about your own values and those of your organization. Create opportunities to engage in conversation with professional colleagues—either in your workplace or through our professional associations—about ethical situations (not necessarily dilemmas you face) but also how you are perceived by peers, what you hope to accomplish in your professional life, and what sort of world you'd like to live in. Talk about how much you like baseball, even as you consider whether or not you should take the baseball tickets you've been offered. And consider how in your own professional life you might do a better job of following the rules: being trustworthy, honest, accountable, and transparent; and perhaps taking a courageous stand on something that you've always thought you should. Practice is the only path to the good life.

Second, we can *create communities of moral deliberation* in the organizations we serve. The good life is not possible without a network of support for the choices you make and the virtues you seek to live out. I have written elsewhere of specific strategies to create these communities of moral deliberation[8]—involve your colleagues in crafting an organizational ethics statement or use a tool such as administrative case rounds or clearness committees to create safe places for ethics conversations. The point is that this cannot be solitary work. This is why the EAI asks you to share your perceptions of your own ethical situation, as well as that of the organization you serve. The organization in which you work is not the only community of which you are a part. Other so-called communities of memory—family, religious community, school, neighborhood, and professional association—all play a role in your life and offer important resources for learning about and practicing the good life.

Finally, we can remember that *the work we do as professional fundraisers is a form of public service*[9]; that is, we serve the public trust by engaging people and raising funds in support of the missions of our organizations—missions that reflect the most deeply held values of our society. Whether education, the arts, social service, health care, the environment, or faith-based communities, each of the organizations we serve seeks through its mission-based work to be a force for good in society. We have the privilege to serve those missions with our professional expertise and personal commitment. Our organizations deserve our very best—both technically and ethically. Our noble work on behalf of organizational missions calls us to a higher standard, a standard that I have chosen to call the good life.

We have choices. What will you choose? The good life awaits.

ABOUT THE AUTHOR

Paul C. Pribbenow, PhD, CFRE, is the tenth president of Augsburg College (MN) and is chairman emeritus of the Association of Fundraising Professionals Ethics Committee and Research Council.

NOTES

1. Michael O'Neill, "Fundraising as an Ethical Act," *Ethics in Fundraising: Putting Values into Practice, New Directions for Philanthropic Fundraising* 6 (Winter 1994): 3–13.
2. Association of Fundraising Professionals, AFP Code of Ethical Principles and Standards, Arlington, VA. First drafted in 1964 and updated regularly.

3. Aristotle, "The Nichomachean Ethics," in *The Basic Works of Aristotle,* Richard McKeon, ed. (New York: Random House, 1941), 927–1112.

4. Albert, Anderson, *Ethics for Fundraisers* (Bloomington and Indianapolis, IN: Indiana University Press, 1996), 7.

5. Robert Shoemake, "Assessing Your Ethical Performance," *Advancing Philanthropy* (September/October 2011): 14–18.

6. Ibid.

7. Robert L. Payton, *Philanthropy: Voluntary Action for the Public Good* (New York: American Council on Education and Macmillan, 1988).

8. Paul C. Pribbenow, "Growing Our Ethical Skills," *Philanthropy Journal* (July 12, 2011), www.philanthropyjournal.org/resources/fundraisinggiving/growing-our-ethical-skills.

9. Paul Pribbenow, "Fundraising as Public Service: Renewing the Moral Meaning of the Profession," *Ethics in Fundraising: Putting Values into Practice. New Directions for Philanthropic Fundraising* 6 (Winter 1994): 27–48.

CHAPTER 2

The Appearance of Impropriety

DIANNE LISTER, LLB, CFRE

S candals are reported with numbing frequency in the corporate, public, and not-for-profit worlds. While some ethical and legal transgressions are blatantly clear, more nuanced judgment and cultural interpretation is required when we assess behavior that is deemed questionable or inappropriate.

The term "appearance of impropriety" arises in the field of applied ethics. Some professional groups, such as the judiciary, explicitly state that members must avoid even the appearance of impropriety. The aspiration for untainted appearances is very old; what is new is the scope and force with which it is now applied to everyday living. Joseph Fulda[1] argues that the Biblical aspiration ("And ye shall be pure before God and man") cannot and ought not to be the standard of morality by which secular society judges its members.

Synonyms for impropriety span a broad range: immodesty, indecency, rudeness, incongruity, impudence, unseemliness, incorrectness, or an erroneous or unsuitable expression or act. For the purposes of this discussion, impropriety must be something that a subset of society deems inappropriate, not merely a handful of individuals; there must be a community standard breached.

The concept of avoiding even the *appearance* of impropriety is often linked to a potential or perceived conflict based on personal self-interest, but it is broader and less well defined in application. This chapter focuses on reputation management—how the appearance of impropriety is linked to other standards of professional practice for professional fundraisers and their organizations and whether there is a case to be made for private and occupational morality. The reader is asked to consider whether the appearance-of-impropriety standard is a "garbage standard" as argued by America's preeminent legal ethics professor, Geoffrey C. Hazard Jr.,[2] or this concept indeed applies within mission-based organizations.

THE LINK BETWEEN ETHICS AND FIDUCIARY DUTY

Defining ethics is complicated. Some philosophers have attempted to make ethics objective and universal, while others claim moral decision making is a lonely, intuitive, and wholly individual business of making fundamental choices. Some individuals anchor their ethics in religion; others believe morality is an odd mixture of received tradition and personal opinion. During the past 50 years, ethics has moved from the academic realm of the theoretical to the need for applied, day-to-day guidance in such fields as health care, law, business and, more recently, the environment and biotechnology. The Association of Fundraising Professionals (AFP) was the first international organization for professional fundraisers in the world to create a code of ethics in 1964.

For the purposes of this chapter, we are using the definition from Michael Josephson of the Josephson Institute of Ethics:

> Ethics is a code of conduct, based on moral duties and obligations, which indicates how we should behave. Ethics deals with the ability to distinguish right from wrong and with the commitment to do right.

The complexity of understanding ethics increases when we consider mission-based organizations. In contrast to corporations, which focus on generating profits and increasing shareholder value through the creation of goods and services, mission-based organizations contribute to the common good, and focus on strengthening civil society and creating social value. They achieve their missions by promoting and upholding public trust. They are accountable to multiple stakeholders.

Most mission-based organizations work to serve charitable purposes and, across North America, they are accorded special tax privileges as charities. Few charitable organizations are self-funded, and most require private, philanthropic funds to run their operations and programs. Philanthropy sits outside of the economic marketplace; a donation can be defined as a voluntary gift made with no expectation of benefit.

The dynamics employed to identify prospective donors, educate them about organizations' missions, and solicit funding must be done in a clear and transparent way that honors the principles in the Donor Bill of Rights and Codes of Ethics of such professional organizations as AFP, the Canadian Association of Gift Planners, and the Institute of Fundraising (United Kingdom), to name a few. In addition to codes of ethics and standards of practice that bind individual practitioners, organizations such as Imagine Canada have created codes specifically to be adopted by resolution of the boards of charitable organizations to govern the behavior and practices of directors.[3]

Fiduciaries are understood to be those to whom property or power is entrusted for the benefit of another. Under the useful glare of the public microscope, the boards of directors, chief executive officers, and professional fundraisers must have a heightened understanding of their roles as fiduciaries and the particular role that ethics plays within their organizations.

REPUTATION MANAGEMENT AND IMPROPRIETY

Once integrity goes, the rest is a piece of cake.

—J. R. EWING, from 1978 CBS hit series, *Dallas*

In her book *Ethical Decision Making in Fund Raising*, Marilyn Fischer discusses what is required to act with integrity.[4] One needs independent judgment, responsibility, and moral courage. Ms. Fischer refers to Plato's

The Republic: "[Moral courage] is the part which causes us to call an individual brave, when his spirit preserves in the midst of pain and pleasure his belief in the declarations of reason as to what he should fear and what he should not."

A good reputation is often linked with integrity. The reputation of an organization and of its individual players is its most valuable asset and its highest risk. Upholding the highest standards of ethical conduct and decision making makes good moral and business sense for mission-based organizations.

While most associations for professional fundraisers include references in their codes of ethics to acting with integrity, honesty, and truthfulness, the Code of Conduct for the Fundraising Institute of New Zealand refers explicitly to reputation in its first principle:

> PROFESSIONAL CONDUCT: Members shall at all times conduct themselves with complete integrity. They shall respect the dignity of their profession and ensure that their actions enhance the reputation of themselves and their Institute.[5]

AFP's Code of Ethical Principles and Standards does not explicitly refer to reputation. Its only reference to "ethical impropriety" is Standard No. 3:

> 3. Members shall effectively disclose all potential and actual conflicts of interest; such disclosure does not preclude nor imply ethical impropriety.

However, there are several sections that could, if violated, lead one to the conclusion that there was real or perceived impropriety, and thus potential reputational damage. Under the aspiration section of the AFP Code, is stated (in part) the following (emphasis added to those sections that can be linked to reputation and fiduciary duties).

AFP members aspire to:

- Practice their profession with integrity, honesty, truthfulness and adherence to the *absolute obligation to safeguard the public trust.*
- Act according to the highest goals and visions of their *organizations, profession, clients and conscience.*[6]

- Inspire others through their own sense of dedication and *high purpose.*
- Avoid even the appearance of … *professional misconduct.*
- Bring credit to the fundraising profession by their *public demeanour.*

The related Standards, which fall under the general umbrella of reputation, include Standards Nos. 1, 2, 3, 4, which address issues of not causing harm to the organization or clients of the profession; avoiding conflict of interest situations; and not exploiting relationships with donors, prospects, volunteers, or employees for the benefit of the member or the member's organization.

Within the world of mission-based organizations, some strenuously argue that avoiding the appearance of impropriety is an important standard inasmuch as it protects an organization's reputation. In contrast, others insist that the opportunity for subjective judgment—if not outright abuse by the accuser—limits the personal freedom of individuals. This tension comes to a head in considering whether a professional fundraiser or board member of a charitable organization can offset any reputational damage as a consequence of his or her behavior by claiming the actions were those of a private citizen.

CONFLICT OF INTEREST AND THE APPEARANCE OF IMPROPRIETY

A conflict of interest is a situation in which someone in a position of trust has competing professional or personal interests. This is particularly of interest to directors of boards of charities and not-for-profit organizations who, under some legal jurisdictions, are "trustees" at law, as well as acting as guardians of the reputation of institutions.

Such competing interests can make it difficult to fulfill an individual's duties impartially. A conflict of interest exists even if no unethical or improper act results from it. A conflict of interest can create an appearance of impropriety that can undermine confidence in the person, profession, or court system. A conflict can be mitigated by third-party verification or third-party evaluation, but it still exists. One might claim that even if the conflict is mitigated, the air of appearance of impropriety lingers.

Most organizational codes of conduct or rules governing conflict of interest describe how and when to declare conflicts of interest and how the individual ought to act in the specific circumstances.

For example, let us assume Susan Lewis is a board member of a children's hospital. Her son, James, is the owner of a company competing for the architectural design for a new wing of the hospital, and the value of the contract is $1 million. The board will make the ultimate decision. There is no adjudication panel. Susan would need to declare a potential conflict and recuse herself from the vote. This action would need to be recorded in the minutes and the public record of the decision.

Let's change the scenario. James is bidding for business to supply computer software. The purchasing manager, Vladimir Gandsky, has issued a request for a proposal, indicating that the budget is $200,000, and this information is posted on the hospital's website. The administrative staff of the hospital will make the final decision with no board consultation. Susan finds out at a weekend dinner party that her son will be bidding on the business.

Is there an ethical duty for Susan to alert the purchasing manager that her son is a principal of one of the companies bidding on the project? Would it make any difference if Susan and Vladimir were long-time members of a weekly book club? What if Susan sat on the Human Resources Committee that approved bonuses for senior staff, including Vladimir?

CASE STUDY   LIKE MOTHER, LIKE SON

As the chief development officer for a youth organization, you learn from a donor that the son of the chair of your board has been calling donors to the organization to solicit business for his investment company.

A. What should you do?
    1. Inform the chair of the board that the AFP Code of Ethical Principles and Standards forbids this practice and it must stop

2. Ask your CEO to advise the chair of the board that this practice must stop
3. Inform your CEO that the AFP Code does not speak to this practice
4. Keep quiet
5. Other

Answer: 5. Other. Nothing improper is necessarily going on here. The whole situation could be a coincidence. However, consistent with Standard No. 2, it would be advisable for you to advise your CEO that the activities of the son of the board chair could give an appearance of impropriety or misconduct and that, consequently, it might be advisable to have her son cease soliciting business for his investment company from donors.

B. Suppose that investigation reveals that the son obtained the list of donors from the printed program of your organization's recent recognition dinner. Would this practice be acceptable under the AFP Code?
   1. Yes
   2. No
   3. It depends
   4. Don't know

Answer: 1. Yes. The information contained in the program cannot be considered privileged or confidential information, given that it was publicly available information (Standard No. 18).

C. Suppose your investigation reveals that the board chair has been giving the names of donors and acquaintances to her son to help the son get his business started. What should you do?
   1. Inform the board chair that the AFP Code of Ethical Principles and Standards forbids this practice and it must stop
   2. Ask your CEO to advise the board chair that this practice must stop
   3. Inform your CEO that the AFP Code does not speak to this practice

(Continued)

4. Keep quiet
5. Other

Answer: 2. Ask your CEO to advise the board chair that this practice must stop. Providing her son with the names of donors to the organization is proscribed by the AFP Code (Standard No. 17) and must stop.

One can see that there are no hard-and-fast rules when it comes to perceived conflicts of interest or appearance of impropriety; sometimes the "smell test" is the best guide. A simple check is to imagine how this information, if reported on the front page of the local newspaper, would affect other stakeholders of the organization. Would other suppliers complain about the process? Would donors cancel their pledge commitments? Would potential volunteers feel wary about being engaged with this organization? Would employees feel embarrassed or upset by the media story?

THE CONTINUUM OF SUSPECT BEHAVIOR

Let us move out of the relatively clear situation of conflicts of interest and dive into the murkier waters of impropriety. Consider the following scenarios as we test the behavioral continuum. At one end is illegal activity; the opposite end relates to behavior that falls within the private domain.

Background Facts

Tom Tenacious is a young bachelor and the vice president of external relations and advancement for a university in a midsize city. He has been asked by the university's nominating committee and its president to approach a recently published author, Rosie Romantic, who is an alumna from the 1980s, to join the board of governors. It is an expectation of all board members that they make a gift to the university. The bonus component of Tom's compensation relates in part to achieving certain revenue goals.

The board wants to address the gender imbalance on the board and add luster to its ranks. The president of the university sits on the panel of a national award that recognizes literary talent, and Rosie's book has been short-listed for the competition. Rosie has recently and acrimoniously separated from her partner, who is a reporter for the city's newspaper, the *Daily Tattler*.

Scenario A   Tom arranges to meet Rosie for dinner at a local restaurant. He is enchanted with her, and after too many glasses of wine, he escorts her to the parking lot. Rosie reaches into her purse and hands Tom an autographed copy of her new book. He misinterprets this gesture and makes a sexual overture. Rosie bursts into tears and threatens to call the president and take this "to the papers." A crowd gathers.

Scenario B   Tom arranges to meet Rosie for dinner at a local restaurant. Rosie knows Tom finds her attractive. She wants Tom to influence the president's vote on the national literary award committee; she argues if she wins, then it is a big coup for the university to have her on the board. She does not agree immediately to come on to the board, and Tom takes her out for dinner on four subsequent occasions, charging the meals and alcohol to the university's charge account. He promises to speak with the president, noting that Rosie has a great chance of winning the top prize even without his conversation. A reporter for the society column in the *Daily Tattler* snaps a shot of the couple leaving one of the city's more upscale restaurants and writes: "Rosie Romantic seen on the arm of Tom Tenacious at the Lulu Lounge, again."

Scenario C   Tom arranges to meet Rosie for coffee with the chair of the English Department on campus. Tom finds her attractive but sticks to the task of testing her interest in joining the board. Rosie mentions that the president sits on the national literary award committee. Tom confirms but offers no further comment. Two weeks later, Rosie indicates she does not wish to join the board. A month later, she wins second place in the national literary awards. Six months later, Tom invites her out for dinner socially. A relationship develops. While discreet, they are not secretive. The *Daily Tattler* features a story on Rosie Romantic, with a comment, "Rosie has been seen around town frequently with young Tom Tenacious."

In Scenario A, Tom has, at the minimum, behaved inappropriately and may have committed the criminal offense of sexual harassment. Other questionable matters include whether he ought to have been drinking alcohol on a business meeting. In many institutions, alcohol cannot be expensed as a "cost of doing business." Was the restaurant lavish, or was it comparable to venues normally used on university business? The consequences of impropriety relate not only to the individuals directly involved, but spill over and may affect the employer's reputation. It is not accurate to claim that impropriety is experienced only by the involved parties. An individual can be offended; the community will judge the behavior as unacceptable if it has crossed the threshold of impropriety. Tom's overtures were not welcomed by Rosie. Others witnessed the incident. If this is reported in the media, Tom has potentially compromised the university and may damage its reputation. Predictable consequences for the university range from losing funding from donors who feel a loss of trust in the leadership of the institution, to hurting enrollment numbers if parents or students feel the administration is morally adrift, to causing employees to be upset by the actions of a colleague who represents their institution.

In Scenario B, there is no illegal behavior. However, there is an appearance of impropriety even if other individuals are not aware of the content of the conversations between Tom and Rosie. This is due to questionable frequency of the meetings and the fact that they do not take place within a space that clearly relates to university business.

Tom fails the fiduciary test. Tom ought to have ended the exploration of Rosie's board candidacy after the first meeting and apprised the president of Rosie's questionable ethics. Instead, Tom pursues the meetings with Rosie out of his own personal interest and at the expense of the university. Moreover, the situation is compounded by Tom's promising to speak with the president to influence an outcome for Rosie. Tom is misusing his position as an employee of the university and risking the reputation of the university through his behavior. The reputational damage is amplified by the media's reporting to the broader community about Tom's behavior.

In Scenario C, Tom has acted appropriately in his role as a senior executive of the university. The case is designed to pose the question: Do employees and board members of charitable organizations carry the responsibility to protect the reputation of their charitable organizations under all circumstances? Is there a distinction between occupational and personal ethics? Has the reputation of the university been negatively affected by Tom's liaison? If so, who decides?

A TEST FOR IMPROPRIETY BEYOND CONFLICT OF INTEREST

Once a reputation has been sullied, it is difficult if not impossible to regain the trust and confidence of others. This is true whether we consider the reputation of individuals or the organizations with which people are affiliated. The reputational stakes are raised when the organization is a not-for-profit charitable entity with a mission to improve society and build healthy and viable communities. There is a direct correlation between scandals affecting charities and the ability to maintain donor confidence and recruit and retain leadership volunteers.

CASE STUDY   TO ACCEPT OR NOT TO ACCEPT

You are a new director of development for a social sector organization, and you find that your organization does not have a policy regarding acceptance of gifts by the development staff. You decide you want to establish a gift policy that will be acceptable under the AFP Code of Ethical Principles and Standards.

(Continued)

A. Under the AFP Code, which of the following policies would be acceptable?
   1. No member of the development staff may accept more than a token gift from a donor, prospective donor, sponsor, or advertiser who became known to the member as a consequence of a member's current or past employment.
   2. No member of the development staff may accept a gift from a donor, prospective donor, sponsor, or advertiser under any circumstances.
   3. Gifts of more than a token gift from a donor, prospective donor, sponsor, or advertiser must be disclosed to the CEO and the board.
   4. Gifts of more than a token gift from a donor, prospective donor, sponsor, or advertiser will be considered on a case-by-case basis and must be approved by the CEO.

Answer: 1, 3, and 4 would be acceptable. Standard No. 3 requires AFP members to disclose all potential or actual conflict of interest, and a gift from a donor represents at least a potential conflict of interest. Answers 1, 3, and 4 would be acceptable because they each include a requirement of disclosure.

B. What would be a more workable gift policy that would be acceptable under the AFP Code?

Answer: A more workable policy would include a specific definition of an acceptable "token gift" —for example, a specific dollar amount—and would specify the criteria to be considered by the CEO and the board. It would also address whether or not a larger-than-token gift to a fundraiser would be acceptable (e.g., a gift from a donor who is a relative or a long-term friend).

C. Suppose an elderly major donor has bought you a gold ring as a thank-you gift for helping arrange a planned gift of $1 million to your organization. You know the donor and know that the donor would probably be offended if you turned down the gift. According to the AFP Code, what should you do?
   1. Thank the donor and explain that the AFP Code forbids accepting gifts from donors

2. Thank the donor and explain that AFP Code requires that all gifts must be disclosed to the CEO and the board, and you may not be able to accept
3. Accept the gift
4. Use your best judgment (the Code is silent on the subject)
5. Other (specify)

Answer: Number 2 is the best answer—thank the donor and explain that the AFP Code requires that all gifts must be disclosed to the board. Standard No. 3 of the Code only requires AFP members to disclose all potential and actual conflicts of interest. It does not specify disclosure to the board, but, as the governing body of the organization, the board is the appropriate entity for the disclosure.

Standard No. 4 also applies. It states that members shall not exploit any relationship with a donor, prospect, volunteer, or employee to the benefit of the member or the member's organization. One reason for the disclosure requirement in Standard No. 3 is to ensure that no one exploits a relationship.

Answer number 1 is incorrect because the AFP Code does not impose an absolute prohibition on gifts from donors. At the same time, answer number 3 is incorrect because the Code requires disclosure of a gift (as the source of a potential conflict of interest), and answer number 4 is incorrect because the Code is NOT silent on the subject.

Examples of situations which could cause someone else to claim there is an appearance of impropriety, offensiveness, or unsuitability include the following:

- The use of undue influence in respect of the power dynamics between the individuals involved (for example, an elderly senior who is lonely, and an aggressive fundraiser who feels compelled to meet an ambitious annual revenue goal).
- Sexual innuendo in the workplace (this can include inappropriate dress, language, or behavior).

- Disrespectful language (a board member commenting that a professional fundraiser on staff needs to "wring the money out of that prospect").
- Lack of knowledge of, and sensitivity toward, diverse communities.

Ultimately there is no definitive test for impropriety. Acting appropriately turns on personal values and ethical decision making applied in a consistent and transparent manner. It is about exercising judgment, discretion, good manners, and tolerance; being aware of potential or perceived conflicts of interest; and demonstrating the moral courage to "do the right thing."

A WORD ABOUT DIVERSITY

Community approval of behavior can occur only if there are shared cultural values. In the increasingly diverse and multicultural and multi-religious communities in which fundraising is practiced, it is important to encourage empathy in order to treat all people with dignity and respect. By respecting worldviews and understanding cultural beliefs, it becomes possible to calibrate appropriate behavior and avoid the appearance of impropriety.

Marilyn Fischer encourages professional fundraisers and board members of charitable organizations to foster diversity.[7] "We demonstrate respect for people's fundamental moral worth through paying attention to the particularities of their individual lives as situated within their cultural context.... [C]ultural differences among different groups are real, yet within a given cultural group there is enormous individual variation. We should always hesitate to judge individuals on the basis of group membership alone, yet we should hesitate to say 'that is just a matter of individual personality' as if cultural differences were insignificant."

COMMON RATIONALIZATIONS

In his article entitled "Obstacles to Ethical Decision-Making: Rationalizations,"[8] Michael Josephson refers to several situations where rationalizations may raise the appearance of impropriety:

- **All for a good cause.** People are especially vulnerable to rationalizations when they seek to advance a noble aim. "It's all for a good cause" is a seductive rationale that loosens interpretations of deception, concealment, conflicts of interest, favoritism, and violations of established rules and procedures.
- **It doesn't hurt anyone.** Used to excuse misconduct, this rationalization falsely holds that one can violate ethical principles so long as there is no clear and immediate harm to others. It treats ethical obligations simply as factors to be considered in decision making rather than as ground rules. Problem areas include asking for or giving special favors to family, friends, or public officials; disclosing nonpublic information to benefit others; and using one's position for personal advantage.
- **I've got it coming.** People who feel they are overworked or underpaid rationalize that minor "perks"—such as acceptance of favors, discounts, or gratuities—are nothing more than fair compensation for services rendered. This is also used as an excuse to abuse sick time, insurance claims, overtime, personal phone calls, or personal use of office supplies.
- **I can still be objective.** This rationalization can be a potential concern for senior decision-making executives and board members where gratitude, friendship, and the anticipation of future favors may affect judgment.

In Defense of Impropriety

Can senior public figures in a charitable organization ever successfully defend themselves from the claims of reputational damage caused to their organization as a result of their private actions? Is there a distinct boundary that separates occupational ethics and personal ethics?

To paraphrase Pierre Elliott Trudeau, then Justice Minister for Canada, who declared in 1967, "there is no place for the state in the bedrooms of the nation": Is there a place for our professional associations in the private lives of fundraisers, senior executives, and board members?

In the 1998 United States case of *Johnston v. Koppes*,[9] the court held that a supervisor could not sanction a government lawyer-employee from private policy positions that she was advocating. The court drew a distinction between professional capacity and private capacity and noted: "the appearance of impropriety is too vague and *ad hominem* to be a real rule in itself. When dealing with ethical principles . . . we cannot paint with broad strokes. The lines are fine and must be marked." Some commentators have argued that an action is either improper or not and that the appearance of impropriety standard is a "garbage standard" because it fosters instinctive and ad hoc claims. Such unsubstantiated claims may lead to abuse where the goal is to taint reputation.

Joseph Fulda[10] writes: "Our heightened concern with appearances detracts from genuinely moral concerns and shifts the burden of proof to the accused, and erodes basic yearnings for privacy, naturalness and freedom." While this appears to be the right balance between an individual's actions and how these actions are judged by the community, matters are not so simple in all contexts. As we have seen, in the interesting field of ethics as it applies to professional fundraising executives, we are not being judged in a court of law but rather in the court of public opinion. The jurors are donors, volunteers, colleagues, and members of the community.

The New Zealand Code of Ethics does not limit the application of the standard that relates to professional conduct. Rather, it states members shall *at all times* conduct themselves with complete integrity. While one would always wish to be seen to be acting with integrity, the question remains whether the private lives of professional fundraising executives and volunteer leaders can remain distinct and separate from their public personas.

ABOUT THE AUTHOR

Dianne Lister, LLB, CFRE, is the president and executive director of the Royal Ontario Museum Board of Governors. Ms. Lister earned an Honors BA in English Literature from Trent University (1976) and an LLB from Osgoode Hall Law School (1980) in Toronto. She has attended the MIT–Harvard Program on Mediation, and is a well-known speaker and facilitator.

Ms. Lister has served on the board of Cedara Software Corporation and as trustee of the Ivy Funds. She served as the inaugural Chair of the Board of the Association for Fundraising Professionals Canadian Council. Dianne currently sits on the international AFP Ethics Committee. Ms. Lister was the first Canadian to receive the "International Outstanding Fundraising Executive of the Year" Award (2001) given by the AFP organization. In 2004, she received the AMS/John Hodgson Award for outstanding leadership from the Ontario Bar Association, Charity and Not-for-Profit Law Section.

Ms. Lister continues to hold professional memberships in the Law Society of Upper Canada, the Canadian and Ontario Bar Associations, and the Ethics Practitioners' Association of Canada.

NOTES

1. Joseph Fulda, "The Appearance of Impropriety" (Academic Sexual Correctness, California State University at Long Beach, October 1997), www.csulb.edu/~asc/post16.html.
2. Trustee Professor of Law, University of Pennsylvania Law School, as reported by Professor Ronald D. Rotunda in *Hofstra Law Review* 33:114.
3. Imagine Canada's Standards Program, www.imaginecanada.ca/node/297.
4. Marilyn Fischer, *Ethical Decision Making in Fund Raising* (New York: John Wiley & Sons, 2000).
5. "Promoting Fundraising Excellence," Fundraising Institute of New Zealand, www.finz.org.nz/ScriptContent/Index.cfm.
6. W. E. Maxwell, Chair, Ethics Practitioners' Association of Canada, links the ethical behavior and performance of a professional, working within an organization, with the potential for conflicts of values. "Ethics is the demonstration of behaviors in a whole spectrum of performance based on an individual's personal, corporate and professional values. Conflicts between the

three sets of values lead to situations which test the application of those values to performance and accountability issues."

7. Fischer, *Ethical Decision Making in Fund Raising*, 208–210.

8. Michael Josephson, "Obstacles to Ethical Decision-Making: Rationalizations," Josephson Institute of Ethics, www.josephsoninstitute.org.

9. *Johnston v. Koppes*, 850 F.2d 594 (9th Cir. 1988).

10. See note 1.

CHAPTER 3

Rights of Donors

JAMES M. GREENFIELD, ACFRE, FAHP

There is as much greatness of mind in acknowledging a good turn, as in doing it.

—SENECA (4 BC–AD 65)[1]

Imagine this: A donor responds to a direct mail appeal for an emergency fund drive, sends in a check for $100, but receives no response. Now, what does the donor think? And, what should officials at the emergency fund drive have done?

Clearly, sending some form of acknowledgment was the correct thing to do. But this lack of even a minimal response happens all too often, with the result that donors experience a loss of trust and develop a negative attitude about giving to charitable causes. In one sense, this is a fundraising error—not in the solicitation phase but in the proper conduct of gift acknowledgment. But, in a larger sense, this is a nonprofit organization error for failure to require, as a matter of board-level policy, a level of respect and appreciation for every donor and of every gift.

> In the voluntary business that is philanthropy, donors support specific causes or institutions with their contributions. The level of trust that these endeavors require is extensive—trust primarily by the donor in the organization requesting funds.[2]

Donors have rights, beginning with respect for their generous actions. They deserve the right to be thanked, be it a postcard, receipt, letter, telephone call, or email message. Being thanked is less about the form than the act itself. And, as this chapter explains, the method of acknowledgment and how soon the donor receives it can make all the difference in building a respectful and trusting relationship for the future with each donor. "In simplistic terms, any action that violates or threatens to violate an institutional relationship with a donor or prospective donor is a breach of ethics."[3]

IS IT DONOR RELATIONS OR DONORS' RIGHTS?

In all of fundraising, it is imperative that building lasting relationships with donors is "job one." Nonprofit staff including fundraisers will come and go; donors remain, as do organizations. How long donors stay involved and how long they keep giving is related directly to the time and effort given to support the ongoing relationship. Donors are about more than a gift of money each year; they are a reliable resource of financial security to the organization, year after year. But that is the case only if they receive proper attention, beginning with respect for their generosity each and every time they make any type of gift, whether of their time, talent, or treasure. "Remain sensitive to the needs, requests, and desires of your donors, and adapt your program accordingly. Such special effort will go a long way toward encouraging initial contributions and ensuring continued allegiance over time."[4]

Call it "donor loyalty," and you have to work hard to install and keep it. "Does loyalty really matter? As long as we can keep recruiting new donors, does it matter how many of them will offer a second and subsequent gift? After all, if we are always able to find new supports, we will still be hitting our income targets, won't we? Loyalty does matter, however, because organizations have to spend a lot of time and effort to find new major donors."[5] And, one of the proven methods to build relationships and increase loyalty with donors is through recognition.

Stop and think about it—recognition is easy. Call it "making nice." If you were the recipient of a personal gift of money, you should feel appreciative toward those who gave you the money. You also should feel obligated to thank them for their gift. Nonprofit organizations correctly spend time developing donor recognition plans and programs to be ready with a consistent, fair, and equitable method that expresses sincere appreciation to donors for their generosity. Donor recognition and its companion, donor relations, begin with the very first gift and may continue for the lifetime of the donor. How long they continue depends almost entirely on the organization and its efforts to maintain positive contact with donors and to strengthen and expand their involvement and commitment to the organization and its cause. Recognition is but one tool to use; it is centered on respect for donors, each and every one, and their potential for additional support. "We look both at the immediate impact and at the longer-term results, introducing the concept of donor lifetime value."[6]

Pomona College in California has the following mission statement for its Office of Donor Relations: "Pomona College affords its donors access to information about the College's management and use of the funds that they have contributed. To that end, the College is a responsible steward, provides annual reports to its individual, corporate, and foundation donors about fund balances, usage, as well as investment performance."[7]

Recognition can take many forms, such as donor clubs with their lists of benefits and privileges that also serve as enticements for continued giving. Recognition can take the form of visible lists of donors' names published in the organization's newsletters, magazines, annual reports, and on its website. Recognition can be in the form of plaques, portraits, and donor walls that also graduate to the level of permanent visibility. All these forms are intended to convey to donors an honest appreciation for their generosity. It, also, is intended to facilitate gift renewal and serve as an example to encourage others to give.

What does recognition have to do with the rights of donors? In many ways, recognition is the official form and method of a nonprofit organization's fulfillment of its mandate to treat donors respectfully. However, some donors do not wish any form of recognition, even to the point of asking for anonymous status. All such requests must be honored in full, of course. But what rights do even these anonymous donors also possess?

CASE STUDY
DONOR, DONOR, WHO HAS
THE DONOR?

Nat Networthy is the chief development officer for an organization whose board wants it to get in on fundraising via the Internet. He contacts an Internet company that offers what seems to be a fair deal for facilitating and processing donations via the World Wide Web. Nat would like to get a list of his donors for recognition and further cultivation, but in reading the company's proposed terms and conditions he finds that all donor information will remain the property of the Internet company.

A. Would this arrangement be acceptable under the AFP Code of Ethical Principles and Standards?
   1. Yes
   2. No
   3. It depends
   4. Don't know

Answer: 1. Yes; nothing in the Code prohibits ownership of donor information by an Internet company; however, in his contract with the company Nat should make sure that the company would use the information in accordance with the AFP Code. This includes ensuring that all solicitation materials are accurate and correctly reflect the organization's mission and use of solicited funds (Standard No. 12), that contributions are used in accordance with donors' intentions (Standard No. 14), that financial reports are timely and accurate (Standard No. 15), that donor information is not disclosed to unauthorized parties (Standards No. 10 and 17), and that donor information gathered for Nat's organization is not used on behalf of other organizations (Standard No. 18).

B. Suppose the terms and conditions say that the Internet company keeps confidential all information on donors, including their credit card numbers. Would that be acceptable under the AFP Code?
   1. Yes
   2. No

3. It depends
4. Don't know

Answer: 1. Yes, because this would not disclose privileged or confidential information to unauthorized parties (Standards No. 10 and 17). It would be up to Nat to decide whether or not to obtain some of the donor information for his own organization, in which case he would have to negotiate a change to the company's terms and conditions in his contract.

C. Suppose the terms and conditions say that for an additional fee, Nat's organization can receive the names and addresses of all donors to the organization. Would this arrangement pass muster under the AFP Code?
   1. Yes
   2. No
   3. It depends
   4. Don't know

Answer: It depends on whether or not the company promised confidentiality to the contributors. If the company promised complete confidentiality, this arrangement would be a violation of Standards No. 10 and 17, since Nat, himself, would be an unauthorized party. If the company did not promise confidentiality or if it first obtained donor permission to disclose information to Nat, then nothing in the AFP Code would prohibit such disclosure.

A DONOR BILL OF RIGHTS

In the late 1980s, four trade organizations representing professional fundraising practitioners began to develop a set of principles known today as A Donor Bill of Rights. Their goals included "to assist donors in making decisions about charities, believing informed decision making would assist donors and charities in forging stronger, more productive relationships that would ultimately benefit the recipients of charitable support."[8] Participants included volunteer leaders and professional staff of the American Association of Fund Raising Counsel (AAFRC) (now the Giving Institute), the Association for Healthcare Philanthropy (AHP), the Council for Advancement and Support of Education (CASE), and the Association of Fundraising Professionals (AFP). The value of this covenant, which has been endorsed by nonprofits everywhere, is "[a] united public voice for fund raising and philanthropy fundamental for the strength and health of the field. Professional organizations must continue to help practitioners understand and implement ethical standards of practice and treatment of donors."[9] Further, "the bill emphasizes disclosure, social responsibility, two-way communication, truth, and interdependency.... Its 10 tenets, in many ways, are stronger than the codes of ethics of the individual associations.... It identifies philanthropy as an American tradition of giving and sharing. It acknowledges the dual levels of accountability to the 'general public,' as well as to the specific publics of donors and prospective donors. Finally, it advances self-regulation by assuming that charitable organizations must continually demonstrate their worthiness of confidence and trust."[10] The preamble for A Donor Bill of Rights captures all the reasons for this good effort:

> Philanthropy is based on voluntary action for the common good. It is a tradition of giving and sharing that is primary to the quality of life. To assure that philanthropy merits the respect and trust of the general public, and that donors and prospective donors can have full confidence in the not-for-profit organizations and causes they are asked to support, we declare that all donors have these rights.

The tenets in A Donor Bill of Rights (see Exhibit 3.1) specify 10 moral principles and establish a covenant donors should expect every nonprofit organization to observe in their behalf, as follows:

> I. To be informed of the organization's mission, of the way the organization intends to use donated resources, and of its capacity to use donations effectively for their intended purposes.

The purpose is full disclosure to donors of how their funds will be used to meet mission objectives based on prior year results and sound

EXHIBIT 3.1   **A DONOR BILL OF RIGHTS**

A Donor Bill of Rights

PHILANTHROPY is based on voluntary action for the common good. It is a tradition of giving and sharing that is primary to the quality of life. To assure that philanthropy merits the respect and trust of the general public, and that donors and prospective donors can have full confidence in the not-for-profit organizations and causes they are asked to support, we declare that all donors have these rights:

I.

To be informed of the organization's mission, of the way the organization intends to use donated resources, and of its capacity to use donations effectively for their intended purposes.

II.

To be informed of the identity of those serving on the organization's governing board, and to expect the board to exercise prudent judgment in its stewardship responsibilities.

III.

To have access to the organization's most recent financial statements.

IV.

To be assured their gifts will be used for the purposes for which they were given.

V.

To receive appropriate acknowledgment and recognition.

VI.

To be assured that information about their donations is handled with respect and with confidentiality to the extent provided by law.

VII.

To expect that all relationships with individuals representing organizations of interest to the donor will be professional in nature.

VIII.

To be informed whether those seeking donations are volunteers, employees of the organization or hired solicitors.

IX.

To have the opportunity for their names to be deleted from mailing lists that an organization may intend to share.

X.

To feel free to ask questions when making a donation and to receive prompt, truthful and forthright answers.

DEVELOPED BY
AMERICAN ASSOCIATION OF FUND RAISING COUNSEL (AAFRC)
ASSOCIATION FOR HEALTHCARE PHILANTHROPY (AHP)
COUNCIL FOR ADVANCEMENT AND SUPPORT OF EDUCATION (CASE)
ASSOCIATION OF FUNDRAISING PROFESSIONALS (AFP)

ENDORSED BY
(IN FORMATION)
INDEPENDENT SECTOR
NATIONAL CATHOLIC DEVELOPMENT CONFERENCE (NCDC)
NATIONAL COMMITTEE ON PLANNED GIVING (NCPG)
COUNCIL FOR RESOURCE DEVELOPMENT (CRD)
UNITED WAY OF AMERICA

Please help us distribute this widely.

plans for the future. Mission is the guiding statement for donor decision making and expresses the purposes donors' gifts will serve, such as direct services to others or advocacy of the cause. The cause is the attraction that donors exercise with their support—that's the covenant between donor and nonprofit. The traditional "case statement" used in solicitations for annual, capital, or planned giving purposes usually contains details that answer to these needs.

> II. To be informed of the identity of those serving on the organization's governing board, and to expect the board to exercise prudent judgment in its stewardship responsibilities.

Providing the roster of board members on all its publications and solicitation materials (letterhead, brochures, website, etc.) will satisfy this "right," but names alone may be insufficient. Adding board position, employer, and city and state of residence offers more complete details for donors and prospects to assess. In addition, while the duties and responsibilities of board members are broad and legally enforceable, evidence of routine practices (e.g., board size and terms, frequency of board meetings, committee structure, etc.) along with principles of governance (e.g., conflict of interest policy) also should be disclosed. Stewardship of any nonprofit organization is a large and demanding task and includes all of the following:

1. Determine the Organization's Mission and Purpose
2. Select the Chief Executive
3. Provide Proper Financial Oversight
4. Ensure Adequate Resources
5. Ensure Legal and Ethical Integrity and Maintain Accountability
6. Ensure Effective Organizational Planning
7. Recruit and Orient New Board Members and Assess Board Performance
8. Enhance the Organization's Public Standing
9. Determine, Monitor, and Strengthen the Organization's Programs and Services
10. Support the Chief Executive and Assess His or Her Performance.[11]

III. To have access to the organization's most recent financial statements.

This tenet applies to annual budgets, audited financial statements, and IRS Form 990 Annual Information Return, all of which are public documents. Federal law requires copies of these documents for the most immediate three years to be provided upon request at any time along with the organization's original application for tax-exempt status (IRS Form 1023). Any donor requesting these documents is acting as an "investor" who is seeking to understand the capability of the organization to manage its fiscal affairs competently before making a decision to share personal funds and/or assets (i.e., real estate, stocks and bonds, personal property, etc.). The organization also should offer to discuss its financial reports and should be available to answer questions about their contents.

IV. To be assured their gifts will be used for the purposes for which they are given.

This "right" speaks directly to the donor's issue of public confidence and trust in what we say and what we do with a donor's money. "It is always harmful to divert charitable assets from their intended purposes; it is wrong for the poor or sick consigned to an organization's care to be abused or neglected; it is immoral for the administrators of philanthropic institutions to enrich themselves; it is tragic for wasteful and inefficient uses of scarce charitable resources to be tolerated."[12]

This covenant is the bond of trust invested in the organization's faithful adherence to using all donor funds exactly as stated in its appeal. More importantly, if a donor specifies a purpose for use of funds that the organization accepts, it cannot change its use without the express written consent of the donor. "These restricted funds must be spent for their designated purpose. Nothing is more certain to damage a nonprofit organization's ability to attract funds than for it to be found using restricted funds for purposes other than those specified by the donor. An organization that receives restricted gifts must account for the funds carefully so that it can prove their use for the purpose intended."[13]

The rise in the number of donor-advised funds is a direct consequence of donors' concerns that their wishes will be observed faithfully; to that end, they attached strings to reinforce this bond.

V. To receive appropriate acknowledgment and recognition.

As discussed previously in this chapter, receipt of each and every gift requires a timely acknowledgment. At the same time, each gift opens the opportunity to develop a binding relationship with donors. Recognition elements such as benefits and privileges can be added that are guided carefully by board-approved written policies and procedures appropriate to the size and purpose of the gift, donor history of giving, how all other donors are treated, and other factors. "It is of the utmost importance to thank every donor, accurately and promptly, for every contribution, as well as to ensure that donations are recorded in such a way that donors are able to take any tax advantages that accrue to them for their gifts."[14] Much more is possible so long as it is appropriate. The guiding principle is the relationship. How can the recipient organization cultivate its donors to expand their involvement? What are the elements of donor satisfaction?

This can be achieved in several ways, including

- Strive to satisfy current donors. Satisfying current donors is critical, because dissatisfied donors are highly likely to spread negative word of mouth on the charity network and to discourage other prospective donors.
- Undertake a program of asking donors for regular feedback on how they view relationships with the nonprofit and how satisfied they are.
- Create a response management program to act on all negative feedback received. Experience with affluent individuals in other settings indicates that it is possible to turn dissatisfied people into loyalists again if the response to a complaint is appropriate and thorough. Given the high costs of new donor development, even extreme efforts to protect the donor base are usually worthwhile.[15]

VI. To be assured that information about their donations is handled
with respect and with confidentiality to the extent provided by law.

The bond of trust between donors and their chosen charities includes
the presumption that all these transactions are personal, private acts
involving money and are not for public disclosure. It is common
practice by nonprofit organizations to publish rosters of donors and
prepare forms of visible displays (i.e., donor walls) that list donors by a
range or size of gifts, usually with congratulatory labels such as "Patron"
or "Benefactor." With this knowledge, donor decisions to make gifts
can be presumed to reflect their acceptance of this practice, except when
they request their gift be anonymous. On another front, in the United
States, there is an IRS requirement that organizations must report all
gifts by name of donor and amount if $5,000 or more as part of their
annual IRS Form 990 return. However, the IRS does not release this
list, nor is it to be included in any distribution of this tax form by the
organization.

VII. To expect that all relationships with individuals representing
organizations of interest to the donor will be professional in nature.

Respect each donor and treat him or her accordingly. Donors represent not only a reliable fiscal resource but also the potential to support
the organization and its mission, vision, and values. Examples include
advocacy of the cause, attendance at benefit events and public affairs,
voluntary service, and more—all based on their personal interest and
commitment that may rise to the role of board membership and other
leadership services over time. To achieve any of these enhanced levels of
relationships, there must be consistent and respectful communications.

The type and level of communication will be a function of the nature
of the relationship between the fundraiser and the donor. A number
of elements must characterize this relationship:

- There must be mutual trust between individuals.
- The relationship also depends on respect.

- The relationship must be sincere.
- The fundraiser must give something as well as receive something.[16]

VIII. To be informed whether those seeking donations are volunteers, employees of the organization or hired solicitors.

Donors must be informed at the time of each solicitation of who is making this request and what their position with the nonprofit organization is. Volunteers and employees are unpaid for their help in solicitation. This tenet is in response to the several states that have fundraising and solicitation regulations requiring registration and public reports by hired solicitors, be they commercial fundraisers, paid solicitors, or in other categories. The donor's concern is linked to the solicitor's compensation, which often is tied to the gift amount and has been the source of many abuses and fraudulent practices. Several state laws and regulations require these for-profit firms to have a signed contract with a nonprofit prior to soliciting the public, approval by the state authority (usually the office of the Attorney General), and the requirement to provide a full report of funds raised, expenses, and net proceeds delivered to the charity. Organizations that hire paid solicitors must be vigilant and observe strict ethical and professional practices in these matters and use only a fee-for-service basis for their compensation to avoid any impropriety and resulting media attention.

IX. To have the opportunity for their names to be deleted from mailing lists that an organization may intend to share.

One of the great benefits that donors and organizations share is open communications. Donors expect to receive newsletters, magazines, annual reports, and other information from the organizations they support, which also is important to the charity in maintaining and enhancing the involvement and relationship with its donors. However, the practice of exchanging, renting, or selling lists of donors is used by some organizations to expand their donor base. Any organization that observes these practices must offer their donors the option to have their names, addresses, and other information deleted from these lists and withheld from any such exchange.

You are the chief development officer of a nonprofit organization. A charity portal Internet company ("CharitiesRus.com") contacts with you with the following offer: For $2 per name, the Prospect Research department of the company will send to you each month the names and addresses of donors who have contributed $100 or more via the company's website to organizations similar to yours.

A. Would this arrangement be acceptable under the AFP Code of Ethical Principles and Standards?
   1. Yes
   2. No
   3. It depends
   4. Don't know

Answer: 2. No; Standard No. 18 states that all donor or prospect information created on behalf of an organization is the property of that organization and shall not be transferred or utilized except on behalf of that organization. To use on behalf of your organization the names and addresses of donors to other organizations without their prior permission would be a violation of Standard No. 18.

B. Suppose that, instead of the foregoing plan, the Internet company offers to send you the names and addresses of contributors to other similar organizations without charge if you will list your organization on the company's website and pay its normal fee for processing contributions. Would this plan be acceptable under the AFP Code?
   1. Yes
   2. No
   3. It depends
   4. Don't know

Answer: 2. No; the principle of Standard No. 18 stands, whether or not you pay for the information.

C. Suppose the Internet company offers simply to send you a monthly list of the names and addresses of contributors to your organization for your own donor-recognition and

(Continued)

prospecting purposes, if you will list your organization on the company's website and pay its normal fee for processing contributions. Would this plan pass muster under the AFP Code?

1. Yes
2. No
3. It depends
4. Don't know

Answer: 1. Yes; nothing in the AFP Code prohibits your organization's receiving the names and address of its donors and paying a normal processing fee, so long as the processing fee is not based on a percentage of the funds raised.

X. To feel free to ask questions when making a donation and to receive prompt, truthful and forthright answers.

The act of solicitation implies disclosure of several details: why the funds are needed, how they will be used, when they will be used, what are the intended outcomes, actual results achieved, and more. Solicitation materials and solicitors should be prepared to offer this information first and should also be prepared to respond with any added details the donor requests. This tenet, among all the others, speaks directly to the need for transparency as well as to open and full disclosure by nonprofit organizations as a matter of principle and daily practice by all its representatives. Open communications is the recommended practice at all times so that "you build loyalty to your organization by focusing on the ways in which you effectively manage gifts to deliver the highest possible program return on the investment, but you provide the true return on values when the donor sees how her investment is affecting larger community or global issues."[17]

STEWARDSHIP OF DONORS' RIGHTS

The maintenance of relations with donors has evolved well beyond "thank you" letters and other forms of appreciation at the time of the gift. Donor stewardship is a lifelong investment built on mutual respect. Although most organizations continue to pay close attention to their donors, their sheer numbers and the continuous pursuit of new donors to meet every increasing fundraising goal can result in treating donors more as part of a group than as individuals. The text of A Donor Bill of Rights includes options for donors to ask questions, request reports, and inquire after the results of their giving. Many nonprofits, being proactive about accountability to donors and anticipating these requests, voluntarily communicate often about their activities and invite inquiries on all phases of their operations. The benefits and privileges accorded donors, in large part as recognition, plus a schedule of frequent communications are designed to enhance the relationship and seek even greater involvement by donors in what is intended, active engagement with "their" favorite charity. At all times, however, nonprofits also must maintain appropriate levels of security regarding details of a donor's giving history. They also must assure donors of full privacy regarding their generosity. Although security and privacy were not specified directly in A Donor Bill of Rights, both should be assumed to flow naturally from its mandates (see also Chapter 4 on privacy).

Adrian Sargeant has conducted extensive research on donor loyalty and has developed a formula to calculate the lifetime value of a donor or constituent group.[18] His goal is to provide a methodology to achieve effective donor retention strategies for maximizing the worth of a donor. Donors have expectations about their gift decisions even if they are unaware of the 10 tenets of A Donor Bill of Rights. Nonprofit organizations need to move beyond good acknowledgment practices and appropriate recognition policies. Accountability in meeting the rights of donors must be measured beyond counting the number and variety of their gifts along with preprogrammed responses. In the final analysis, it is the donors' opinions that provides the most direct advice on how they wish to be treated. Ken Burnett has written about the duties and responsibilities of nonprofits in their relationships with donors. In his latest, *The Zen of Fundraising: 89 Timeless Ideas to Strengthen and Develop Your Donor Relationships*, he reveals an informal survey among donors, asking the major reasons for why they give. Their answers are as follows:

- I want to be recognized and valued for my gift.
- I want to feel good about giving.
- I want to know how my money will be used and what difference it will make.
- I want to be inspired.
- I want to feel involved, a part of something.
- I want to be impressed, so I can tell others about the cause and recruit them to support it.
- I want you to ask my opinion.
- I want to know that you listen to me.[19]

CONCLUSION

The great beauty of A Donor Bill of Rights is its clear language. In this era of increasing attention to accountability by nonprofits for all their actions, it is equally important to retain close attention to the rights of all donors. Donors are the best friends any nonprofit organization can hope to have. Perhaps if donors are treated as friends in the way each of us would like to be treated, we will honor their support and merit their confidence and trust. Because, in the end, that is the covenant—to use their gifts to do good works that benefit others.

ABOUT THE AUTHOR

James M. Greenfield, ACFRE, FAHP, served a 40-year career as a fundraising executive at three universities and five hospitals, prior to retirement in February 2001, as executive director, Hoag Hospital Foundation in Newport Beach, CA. During this career, he started several fundraising programs from scratch, including University Hospital/ Boston University Medical Center, New England Baptist Hospital, and the Cleveland Clinic Foundation. He is the author and editor of eight books and 40 articles and chapters on fundraising management.

He continues as a frequent conference speaker and trainer for The Fund
Raising School, along with serving the nonprofit sector with fundraising
and management consulting services.

NOTES

1. Seneca, *De Beneficiis in Moral Essays*, Vol. III. This text on gift-giving is
   "still arguably the wisest and most exhaustive analysis of the subject" says
   James Allen Smith in his chapter "In Search of an Ethic of Giving" from
   Taking Philanthropy Seriously: Beyond Noble Intentions to Responsible Giving
   (Bloomington, IN: Indiana University Press, 2006), 13.
2. Duane L. Day, *The Effective Advancement Professional: Management Principles and
   Practices* (Gaithersburg, MD: Aspen 1998), 220.
3. Christina A. Pulawski, "The Effects of Technological Advances on the
   Ethics of Gathering Information in Support of Fundraising," in *The Impact of
   Technology on Fundraising, New Directions for Philanthropic Fundraising, No. 25*
   (San Francisco: Jossey-Bass Publishers, Fall 1999), 73.
4. Kent E. Dove, *Conducting a Successful Fundraising Program: A Comprehensive
   Guide and Resource* (San Francisco: Jossey-Bass, 2001), 158.
5. Adrian Sargeant and Elaine Jay, *Building Donor Loyalty: The Fundraiser's Guide
   to Increasing Lifetime Value* (San Francisco: Jossey-Bass, 2004), 1.
6. Ibid.
7. Pomona College website. See www.pomona.edu/donorrelations/.
8. William C. McGinly, President, Association for Healthcare Philanthropy in
   November 9, 1993, news release entitled "Rights of Charitable Donors
   Reinforced."
9. Margaret A. Duronio and Eugene R. Tempel, *Fund Raisers: Their Careers,
   Stories, Concerns, and Accomplishments* (San Francisco: Jossey-Bass, 1997),
   2006.
10. Kathleen S. Kelley, *Effective Fund-Raising Management* (Mahwah, NJ: Lawrence
    Erlbaum Associates, 1998), 307.
11. Richard T. Ingram, *Ten Basic Responsibilities of Nonprofit Boards* (Washington,
    DC: BoardSource, 2003), 25.
12. James Allen Smith, "In Search of an Ethic of Giving," in *Taking Philanthropy
    Seriously: Beyond Noble Intentions to Responsible Giving* (Bloomington, IN:
    Indiana University Press, 2006), 18.

13. Andrew S. Lang, *Financial Responsibilities of Nonprofit Boards* (Washington, DC: BoardSource, 2003).

14. Dove, *Conducting a Successful Fundraising Program*, 158.

15. Russ Allen Prince and Karen Maru File, *The Seven Faces of Philanthropy* (San Francisco: Jossey-Bass, 1994), 127.

16. Gary A. Tobin, "Between the Lines: Intricacies of Major Donor Communication," in *Communicating Effectively with Major Donors, No. 10* (San Francisco: Jossey-Bass, Winter 1995), 75–76.

17. Kay Sprinkel Grace and Alan L. Wendroff, *High Impact Philanthropy: How Donors, Boards, and Nonprofit Organizations Can Transform Communities* (New York: John Wiley & Sons, Inc., 2001), 153.

18. Adrian Sargeant and Elaine Jay, *Building Donor Loyalty: The Fundraiser's Guide to Increasing Lifetime Value* (San Francisco: Jossey-Bass, 2004), 161–179.

19. Ken Burnett, *The Zen of Fundraising: 890 Timeless Ideas to Strengthen and Develop Your Donor Relationships* (San Francisco: Jossey-Bass, 2006), 32.

CHAPTER 4

Public Privacy: An Exploration of Issues of Privacy and Fundraising

EUGENE A. SCANLAN

Nor has he spent his life badly who has passed it in privacy.

—MARCUS TULLIUS CICERO

We deal with a right of privacy older than the Bill of Rights—older than our political parties, older than our school system.

—WILLIAM O. DOUGLAS

Privacy is what might be called a "slippery" concept. There may be "rights" to privacy spelled out in laws at different levels of government. Court cases may define how to interpret these laws and the needs of the "public" versus an individual's "rights." And one person's definition and personal boundaries of privacy may be quite different from another person's. Legal definitions of and limits to privacy are undergoing constant revisions as courts are faced with cases of privacy versus the need to know, especially where information can become critical to possibly saving lives.

There is also the ethics of privacy, confidentiality, and the right of the individual to set limits on information and its dissemination. Both legally and ethically, the issue of privacy and its uses are not very clear, especially when expectations of privacy conflict with the "need to know." This chapter raises many questions, not always providing clear answers, and will examine the issue of privacy as it applies to fundraising, information, and donor relations. At the end of the chapter some specific recommendations are offered for consideration.

I was meeting with the Executive Director of a large national health association, which was a client of mine. We were discussing how gifts would be handled and processed at the association, which had never undertaken any significant fundraising effort and had received almost no gifts or grants. The conversation went something like this:

> Executive Director: "I'm really concerned about who here knows who gave to us and how much each donor gave."
>
> Me: "That's a common concern at many organizations."
>
> Executive Director: "I want as few people as possible here to have this information."
>
> Me: "There are ways that can be done. Information on amounts given especially can be restricted to a few people here."
>
> Executive Director: (thinking) "I really don't want to know myself how much any individual gave."
>
> Me: "That's possible, although it might be helpful for you to know, especially about the larger gifts."
>
> Executive Director: (after a long, thoughtful pause) "In fact, I don't want anybody at all in the association to know who gave and how much!"
>
> Me: "Ummm—now you have a problem."

Issues of privacy and discussion of these issues have become more intense ever since the attacks of September 11, 2001. The media continues its extensive coverage of the debate over personal privacy versus national safety and the "need to know." A partial list of the topics of the broad debate would include

- Government monitoring of phone conversations and email.
- Government opening and reading of regular mail.
- Uses by cities and other government agencies of video surveillance cameras in public areas.
- Review by government agencies of library materials read by individuals.
- Uses and distribution of patient information, medical records, and other health information about individuals.
- "Profiling" of individuals based on appearance, possible ethnic background, and/or religious beliefs.
- Searches at airports and other transportation centers.
- Monitoring of computer search and materials selection habits of individuals.
- "Warrantless" searches and seizures of property and individuals.
- A law enforcement agency publicly designating someone "a person of interest" without filing formal charges against him or her.
- Uses and theft by "hackers" or others of personal information, including financial and credit information and other "private" information—so-called identity theft.
- Media investigations and coverage of "high-profile" individuals.
- Postings of information, often without the knowledge of those affected by it, on the web.
- Conversations and records of attorneys and their clients, counselors, and media reporters.
- Individual discussions with lawyers, priests, ministers, rabbis, and psychiatrists or psychologists.
- Access to any information an individual wants to keep from public scrutiny.

Should the Executive Director know who contributed and how much each person gave to his organization? To those of us in the profession the obvious answer is "yes," and we might even add, "it's essential." To the Executive Director at this particular organization the answer was not as obvious. It is likely that both his own cultural traditions and the culture of the organization, which received almost no contributed funds, made the question very real and the answer counterintuitive. His desire not to know may appear to run counter to "best practices," but it reflected a deep and genuine concern for the privacy of the individual donor and donor information.

THE "RIGHT" TO PRIVACY

Is there really a "right" to privacy? What is, can be, or should be "public" information? Where do the "public" interests and needs intersect with the "right" to privacy? And who is the "public"? A review of the Constitution of the United States shows there is no mention of the word or concept of privacy. The Bill of Rights, however, does deal with some issues related to privacy. A brief survey by this non-attorney indicates the most relevant amendments of the Bill of Rights are:

Amendment I
Congress shall make no law respecting an establishment of religion, or prohibiting the free exercise thereof; or abridging the freedom of speech, or of the press; or the right of the people peaceably to assemble, and to petition the government for a redress of grievances.

Amendment IV
The right of the people to be secure in their persons, houses, papers, and effects, against unreasonable searches and seizures, shall not be violated, and no warrants shall issue, but upon probable cause, supported by oath or affirmation, and particularly describing the place to be searched, and the persons or things to be seized.

Amendment V
No person shall be held to answer for a capital, or otherwise infamous crime, unless on a presentment or indictment of a grand jury, except in cases arising in the land or naval forces, or in the militia, when in actual service in time of war or public danger; nor shall any person

be subject for the same offense to be twice put in jeopardy of life or limb; nor shall be compelled in any criminal case to be a witness against himself, nor be deprived of life, liberty, or property, without due process of law; nor shall private property be taken for public use, without just compensation.

Amendment IX

The enumeration in the Constitution, of certain rights, shall not be construed to deny or disparage others retained by the people.

At various times in our history these key amendments have been interpreted narrowly to give the government broad powers over individuals' property, including both physical property and information, or they have been interpreted broadly to protect individuals and the privacy of their property and information. Amendment IX, in particular, has been variously interpreted to cover a broad range of rights of individuals, including privacy.

Legislation such as the still-controversial PATRIOT Act and court decisions at all levels, up to and including the Supreme Court, continue both to determine and to test the limits of privacy versus the perceived needs of the public and the greater good. The issue of where to draw the line between privacy of self, property, and information, and the requirements of public and governmental agencies, especially when cast in terms of the "greater good" or protection of the national interests, will probably never be resolved. "Privacy," as both a broad concept and a guide to specific actions, remains a fluid and evolving concept.

THE INTERNET EXPLOSION

The advent of Google and other sophisticated web-based search engines, and the continued rapid growth of the Internet and its continually growing use by individuals and organizations of all types, including the nonprofit sector, have combined to provide an often surprising and sometimes worrisome ability to access information about individuals, groups, formal organizations, and relationships. As an example, I was once asked by a client to see if I could use online resources to determine the possible gift capacity of a board member who had been giving relatively small (four-figure) gifts to the organization. Fortunately his name was not a common one and a quick online search revealed a press release from his undergraduate college whose capital campaign he was heading; he had made a lead gift of $1 million U.S. to the campaign. Should this information have been so public and readily available? Was he consulted about the press release before it was posted on the college's website? Twenty years ago the college would probably have posted the information in an alumni publication, and possibly sent it to the local press. Now anyone anywhere could quickly find it and use it—or even misuse it.

As test of your personal privacy, carry out the vanity exercise of putting your own name into Google and seeing what comes up about you. First, look at all the links that have nothing to do with you. Could someone mistake the information there as being relevant to you? In my case, am I really capable of inspecting and appraising yachts before they are sold to new owners? Second, look at the links, if any, that are relevant to you. You might be surprised where you show up. Do they provide information you would consider private? Is the information given accurate? Has the information been posted with your consent or, better, by you? Or where did it come from? I once did a Google search on my brother's name and found a picture of him posted on the web; the picture had been taken at a conference where he was a presenter. When I told him about this, he was surprised, as no one had asked him about posting the picture or told him it would be posted. This was not a major violation of his personal privacy, but supposing the picture had been taken, unknown to him, in another not so professional setting and posted on the web. Then what about his right to privacy?

More and more nonprofits are using the web to post not only organizational information but often detailed information, such as biographies of board members and staff, donor information that includes levels of giving and often specific amounts for significant gifts, profiles of donors and those intending to make planned gifts, information and sometimes links to clients and alumni, along with other information that would previously have been unavailable, had only limited distribution, or been known only within the institution. Again, there may be privacy issues with this explosion of information on the web. Is information posted that the individual it refers to might consider private? Did the individuals involved review the information before it was posted? Did they even know it would be posted? Does the information that might appear innocuous on the surface actually provide doorways to other, possibly more sensitive information or details of people's lives that could be used or misused by others?

PRIVACY AND SECURITY

Some people—for example, CEOs of major companies or other high profile individuals—might be very concerned about information about where they live, how many children they have, where the children go to school, or other details that could be harmful if in the wrong hands. Security for such people has become a major concern, especially since 9/11. Companies, in attempts to protect the privacy and security of individuals, may deliberately limit contact and other information concerning their senior executives.

But what about the average person? Should we, as professional fundraisers and consultants, be any less concerned about each individual and his or her information, no matter what the source? When we say to an individual that personal information, contributions records and amounts, opinions and ideas collected in feasibility study interviews, background information, email addresses, phone numbers, home and business information, and the like is personal and confidential, what do we mean? How will the information be disseminated or withheld within the organization, outside the organization, on the web, or to the media?

And what about those within our organizations—staff, board members, and other volunteers? Do they know and understand what is private information and what is not? Those that have access to donor information, prospect lists, board information, or other information may or may not know the limits on conveying these to others, either formally or informally. It is easy, especially in an informal situation, to let slip some small item that can violate someone's sense of privacy.

A colleague of mine and I conducted a series of feasibility study interviews, always carried out "in confidence," and were reporting our results to the board of the organization. At one point a board member made a comment during the meeting, and my colleague responded "But you said in your interview X, Y, and Z!" The board member's immediate comment? "I thought you said these interviews were done in confidence." My colleague had to apologize; I'm not sure we ever regained the trust of that board member.

Anyone with a credit card, an insurance policy, or other similar arrangements is likely to receive a statement of the company's policy on the privacy of information. Enter a doctor's office or a hospital and it is likely that you will be asked to sign a statement that you have reviewed their information privacy policy, or at least received a copy of the policy. But, in many cases, the nonprofit sector does not yet show consistent behavior and common purpose in respecting the right to privacy.

DONORS' RIGHTS, FUNDRAISERS' RESPONSIBILITIES

The Association of Fundraising Professionals (AFP) has long promulgated the Donor Bill of Rights, referred to in Chapter 3. Relevant sections of the Donor Bill of Rights include:

> VI. To be assured that information about their donation is handled with respect and with confidentiality to the extent provided by law.
>
> VII. To expect that all relationships with individuals representing organizations of interest to the donor will be professional in nature.
>
> IX. To have the opportunity for their names to be deleted from mailing lists that an organization may intend to share.

The Code of Ethical Principles and Standards for professional fundraisers, also cited elsewhere in this book and developed by the AFP, includes the following expected behavior related to privacy for members:

> demonstrate concern for the interests and well being of individuals affected by their actions; value the privacy, freedom of choice and interests of all those affected by their actions.

Going back much further, the original Greek version of the Hippo-cratic Oath, when speaking of the privacy of patients, states,

And about whatever I may see or hear in treatment, or even without treatment, in the life of human beings—things that should not ever be blurted out outside—I will remain silent, holding such things to be unutterable [sacred, not to be divulged].[1]

THE DILEMMA OF PRIVACY

Keeping information private and setting the limits of privacy pose ethical and potential legal dilemmas. Although, as was indicated at its beginning, this chapter is not about the legal right to privacy, a right that is under considerable debate at all levels as we have seen, it is about the ethics of privacy. And this is where we encounter a major dilemma. Funds given to nonprofits by donors, whether they are given by organized philanthropy (corporations, foundations, and corporate foundations) or from individuals, must be both acknowledged and recorded. And they also must be reported, including providing information to other staff, boards of directors or trustees, possibly auditors, and definitely to outside agencies, such as state agencies and the Internal Revenue Service through the IRS 990 form.

The dilemma is the conflict between the right to privacy and the need to know. Referring to the conversation that started off this chapter, one can see this dilemma clearly expressed. The amount of the donor's gift, the form of the gift (check, stock, real property, etc.), any restrictions or conditions, the date received, pledge conditions if any, the source, and the source's contact information are probably the minimum pieces of information that might need to be shared with others in your orga-nization. How widely should they be shared, and who within your organization needs to know these pieces of information? Are there poli-cies and controls in place to ensure that only those who need to know will receive the information? And what about donors who give anony-mous gifts? Such donors may pose even more of a problem as knowledge of the source of the gift may need to be even more tightly controlled.

PROSPECTING FOR DONORS

Many nonprofits carry out either formal or informal prospecting sessions when there is a planned campaign or major gift effort. A typical prospecting session might involve several board members or other volunteers, a few staff members, and possibly a consultant sitting around a table discussing each prospect and his or her potential for a major gift. Information on past giving, involvement with the organization, and other background information (professional and personal in many cases) about each individual might be given to the group in written form or verbally, usually by a development staff member. The group's members are asked to provide any other information that might be useful in rating each prospect's potential gift level.

CASE STUDY   SHARE AND SHARE ALIKE

Two small arts organizations each have struggled to generate sufficient public awareness for a communitywide annual fund campaign. The director of development of one organization suggests that if the organizations pool their resources, they can maximize their visibility in the community, minimize their individual costs, and increase their chances for a successful campaign.

A. If the two organizations worked from their own donor lists, would this arrangement be acceptable under the AFP Code of Ethical Principles and Standards?
  1. Yes
  2. No
  3. It depends
  4. Don't know

Answer: 1. Yes. Two organizations may have a joint campaign and solicit from their own lists as long as each organization has the same clearly defined regulations, guidelines, policies, and procedures.

B. If the two organizations pooled their lists and hired a telemarketing firm to conduct a joint campaign, would this arrangement be acceptable under the AFP Code of Ethical Principles and Standards?

1. Yes
2. No
3. It depends
4. Don't know

Answer: 3. It depends. It is the responsibility of the member organizations to "respect the wishes and needs of constituents, and do nothing that would negatively impact their social, professional or economic well-being" (Guideline 1.c), so the organizations must approach the joint campaign with caution. They must "effectively disclose all potential and actual conflicts of interest" (Standard No. 3). Therefore, the Code would allow this joint campaign as long as the constituents are clearly informed about the relationship between the two organizations.

C. If the two organizations each solicited from their own lists in a joint campaign, would this arrangement be acceptable under the AFP Code of Ethical Principles and Standards?

   1. Yes
   2. No
   3. It depends
   4. Don't know

Answer: 1. Yes. The donor also must be clearly informed about the destination of the gift. According to Standard No. 12, the organizations must "take care to ensure that all solicitation materials are accurate and correctly reflect their organization's mission and use of solicited funds." This is particularly important in a joint campaign, because constituents need to understand the nature of the campaign and which organization they are supporting. Standard No. 14 further reinforces this principle: "Members shall take care to ensure that contributions are used in accordance with donors' intentions." The organizations also should follow Standard No. 15 Guidelines regarding written policies for endowment funds, annual reporting, planned gifts, donor recognition, investments, and administration of restricted funds.

(Continued)

D. Would it be permissible under the Code for organizations to work together in a fundraising drive?
1. Yes
2. No
3. It depends
4. Don't know

Answer: 3. It depends. If there is disclosure to constituents, organizations may be able to work together in a fundraising drive. Standard No. 19 states that "members shall give donors and clients the opportunity to have their names removed from lists that are sold to, rented to, or exchanged with other organizations." The organizations must have a clear, stated policy that they will not share donor information. If the organizations did share lists, without disclosure to donors, it would be a violation of Standard No. 17: "Members shall not disclose privileged or confidential information to unauthorized parties" and Standard No. 18: "Members shall adhere to the principle that all donor and prospect information created by, or on behalf of, an organization or a client is the property of that organization and shall not be transferred or utilized except on behalf of that organization."

Guidelines about what types of information should not be revealed may or may not be stated at the start of a session. If there are no stated guidelines, information on each prospect might be presented that crosses the line and violates confidentiality and the privacy of the person under discussion. But these days what is "public" information and what is "private" information? Here are some examples of information that may—or may not—cross the line:

- **Example 1.** An attorney on the prospecting group says he just drew up an estate plan for the individual under discussion, and recommends seeking a seven-figure gift.
- **Example 2.** A car dealer on the prospecting group says the person under discussion just purchased a car "that cost more than $150,000."

- **Example 3.** A neighbor of the individual under discussion said that in a conversation over the backyard fence the person said he had just purchased a second home that cost over $1 million.
- **Example 4.** Information from the Internet indicates that the person may be one of two anonymous donors (each of whom gave $1 million), to the donors' college campaign fund. The development staff concluded this because the person is both chair of the board and is chairing the campaign, but her gift is not listed elsewhere under major gifts.
- **Example 5.** Online research by development staff indicates that the person under discussion is one of the top five major stockholders in a company that does over $1 billion per year in business.
- **Example 6.** A banker on the prospecting group says that she is aware that the individual has several large accounts at the bank.
- **Example 7.** A business associate of the person states that he has inside information that the individual is planning on selling the very successful company he owns, and it will have a very high value.
- **Example 8.** Another neighbor says he has been in the person's home several times and observed a "magnificent and probably very valuable" collection of rare Asian art.
- **Example 9.** A member of the group questions what is the "real" source of a person's wealth and indicates that the wealth may not have been entirely obtained through legitimate businesses.
- **Example 10.** A friend of the person, a long-time donor, said that she is a widow with no children and may be suffering from a terminal illness.

As a development professional how would you respond to each of these pieces of information if they were offered in a prospecting session? Which ones do you think crossed the line and violated the person's privacy and confidentiality of information? Which can be considered "public" information, and which should be excluded from any further discussion?

The AFP Donor Bill of Rights, cited previously, pledges that donors

VI. . . . be assured that information about their donation is handled with respect and with confidentiality to the extent provided by law.

In addition, the AFP Code of Ethical Principles and Standards, as cited previously, states that members will

> ... demonstrate concern for the interests and well being of individuals affected by their actions; value the privacy, freedom of choice and interests of all those affected by their actions.

In each example given in the preceding text, has information about the individual (not just his or her donation) been handled with respect and confidentiality? Has the group valued the "privacy, freedom of choice, and interests" of each person under discussion? Should, in each example, the information be used in the rating of the prospects? Or, for each example, should the group be told that such information is not appropriate for its discussion? Have any ethical lines been crossed? And if so, in which examples?

As may already be obvious, the privacy issue and its relation to the ethics of fundraising are not as clear-cut as some of the other issues discussed in this book and elsewhere, such as misstatement or misuse of funds given, providing false or misleading information about an organization to donors or potential donors, not fully informing donors of major challenges affecting the organization, or similar concerns. Privacy may mean very different things to each individual, and information that one person might consider harmful to his or her personal life, security, or other matters may be considered public and not a concern by others.

DONORS AND DONOR INTEREST

Organizations typically list donors in categories based on the size of their gifts, and may highlight individual major donors with profiles, interviews, awards, and the like; these may be included in publications, events materials, or online documents. Unless a donor directly indicates he or she wants to be "anonymous" (see the following section) or at least not listed, most organizations assume they do not need specific clearance from each donor to include them on lists or to feature them. But occasionally a donor might object after the fact, or a listing might include someone who had directly said he or she did not want to be listed.

Some individuals—and some cultures—consider giving a very private matter and any form of recognition as counter to the spirit of giving.

Some donors may want to be listed as giving, but may not want any indication of the size of their gift published or shown. Others may have specific and special preferences for uses by the organization of information about their giving. Some may want their gift pledges kept in confidence, and want to be listed only when their pledges have been fulfilled completely. For some donors these may be privacy issues, but for others there may be no issues at all.

Ethically, the best approach is to offer each and every donor, no matter how large or small the possible gift, the option, when the gift is being considered, to choose to be listed or not, as well as how to be listed, whether or not to be included in a given level, and the other choices discussed previously. This can be done as part of a simple gift response card for most routine gifts. For more complicated gifts, it might be necessary to have a detailed letter of agreement or other written arrangements, with both parties—the organization's representative and the individual(s) involved—signing the document. In some cases, such as the transfer of real property, there may need to be legal documents agreed to by both parties, or other specialized documentation. In each case, the organization should clearly understand and have in writing the wishes of the donor in terms of listings and recognition. In every case, options should be offered to ensure the privacy of the donor as the first priority, with the second priority being meeting the needs of the organization.

GIFT RESTRICTIONS

Donors and potential donors, especially those giving substantial gifts, may want to include restrictions on the uses of the funds when given. Restrictions may be discussed with the organization as part of the gift negotiating process, or may just be included when the gift is made. Some donors may want to protect the privacy of these restrictions or of the discussions about them with the organization. In the case of the gift restrictions themselves, these may need to be reviewed by a committee or the full board of the organization before they are accepted; the organization's accounting/business operation will also need to ensure that funds are treated as restricted and are accounted for separately from unrestricted and general operating funds.

Some gift restrictions, if accepted, might become controversial if widely known; any controversy might be considered an infringement on the privacy of the donor, especially if the controversy moves beyond the organization and into the public arena. Organizations, when reviewing possible gift restrictions offered by donors, should take into consideration this and the other possibilities where the integrity and reputation of the organization itself may be harmed by acceptance of the gift and its restrictions. Does the donor have the right to keep gift restrictions private? Can the donor separate the gift itself from any restrictions in terms of listings and public recognition? Can there be unwritten agreements in addition to any written agreements pertaining to gift restrictions?

For example, a donor has decided to endow a chair at a university. In discussions with the university's president and its vice president for development, the donor says that he wants an unwritten and private agreement among the three of them that he will have veto power over anyone under consideration for appointment to the chair. He insists that he must consult with the president about any candidate, and, if this condition is not agreed to by the president, he will not make the gift.

By accepting these conditions the university is also accepting that the unwritten agreement will be kept private. Should it do this? Is even the discussion itself something that should be accepted as private and confidential, regardless of whether or not the conditions are accepted? When, if ever, should a "private and confidential" conversation such as this be made more public?

DONOR WISHES ABOUT PRIVACY OF INFORMATION

In addition to the listings and recognition issues that have been discussed, there are other considerations related to donors, donor prospects, and their privacy. The most obvious is the variety of "Do not" lists. While the formal "Do not call" list applies to corporate telemarketers, the nonprofit sector is not yet affected by this legislation. However, many nonprofits maintain a variety of "Do not" lists and offer their donors, volunteers, and others the option of being placed on these various lists. Examples of "Do not" lists include

- Do not call to solicit.
- Do not email to solicit.
- Do not send more than one annual solicitation letter.
- Do not send newsletters, only the Annual Report.
- Do not contact between December 1 and March 31.
- Do not list in published materials.
- Do not contact.

In such cases, donors themselves are often offered choices by the organization and can opt out of regular solicitation or contact processes, thus protecting their privacy at the level they wish. For some organizations, the "Do not contact" list may include people who make regular gifts on their own initiative rather than responding to appeals. In terms of the ethics of donor privacy, it is entirely appropriate that donors be given options about how they may be contacted.

An additional concern is to clarify *where* the donor may or may not be contacted. Should calls and emails be sent to the donor's office or home? Where should the organization's mail be sent? If there are to be meetings with the donor, does he or she prefer not to hold them at the office or the home? Are there good—or bad—times for the donor in terms of meetings and direct personal contact? Each person has the right to define some limits on the nature and location of contacts, and ethically the organization should honor these as much as possible.

Previously, listings of donors, gift levels and amounts, gift restrictions, and other privacy issues were discussed. Limits on contact and "Do not" lists were discussed in the immediately preceding text. One particular issue that also needs discussion is the anonymous donor. Just how anonymous can an anonymous donor be, and who needs to know the identity of the individual? Except in the case of a person leaving a suitcase full of cash on the doorstep of an organization, or a gift being conveyed to an organization through a third party, there is probably no truly anonymous donor. Just as in the conversation at the beginning of this chapter, someone inside the organization needs to know the identity of the "anonymous" donor. Checks or gifts in other forms need to be processed and acknowledged, tracking information needs to be kept, and other measures that involve the identity of the individual or organization need to be taken. Somewhere, somehow, the anonymous donor must be a known donor. And yet the donor's wishes must be respected insofar as is possible.

CONTROVERSIAL DONORS

The opposite of the anonymous donor may well be the donor who is too well known, possibly for the wrong reasons. Having grown up in New Jersey, I was aware from a fairly young age that there were people in our area, some of them very generous, who did not exactly have strong, positive images. Unless they actually ended up in jail (and some did), they were a part of the community. But there were always the rumors about what they "really" did to earn a living. Often the stories were never confirmed, but sometimes the media or other sources made charges, uncovered the "dirt," or at least claimed to have done so. Legal action may not have resulted, but the individual involved would subsequently have been tainted with, minimally, a controversial reputation.

As donors, these same people could be very generous. But their private and business lives received more attention than those of others, even if there was no proof of actual wrongdoing. Accepting a gift from them, revealing the source of the gift (both the individual and the payer), and any other actions the organization might take could possibly damage the organization and violate some of the sense of privacy of the individual. Turning down the gift, or keeping the individual "anonymous" might have the same impact. What should the organization say and do to ensure these things don't happen? What are the ethics of accepting gifts from people who may have controversial reputations, especially if there is not specific proof of wrongdoing? What should the organization say to the individual involved? Where does the speculation end and the person's right to privacy begin?

INSIDE YOUR ORGANIZATION

Any organization has both formal and informal channels of communication. The formal channels are often proscribed by policies and procedures, codes of conduct, personnel policies, and the organization's reporting and staff structure. The informal channels are much more difficult to control and monitor and thus can be a major weak point when issues of privacy and its protection are involved. The key questions are "Who needs to know?" and "What needs to be known?"

Development offices will most likely need to know who gave, what was the nature of the gift (check, stocks, etc.), what was the amount of the gift or pledge, and what were any restrictions. They will also probably need to know about any special arrangements, such as the donor's preferences for listing, contact, recognition, or other donor-indicated instructions.

Senior staff may need to know about major gifts, results of gift solicitations they participated in, gifts from people identified as special supporters of the organization (such as those who have indicated the organization is in their estate plans), and major gift donors. Accounting/business staff will need to know and process incoming gifts, ensure restricted funds are recorded and utilized for the purposes intended, account for the use of all funds, and ensure proper acknowledgments meeting IRS requirements are sent, even if they don't send them out themselves. Accounting/business offices may actually receive and process incoming gifts and thus may have to report these to the development office and others.

Program staff may need to know about funds received and restricted to their specific program or its components. Data entry staff, whether in the development office or the business/accounting office, will need to enter and process the information. Board and volunteer committee members may need to know as a follow-up for solicitation calls they participated in or for financial and development office reporting purposes.

When you review the above list, it probably becomes obvious that many people within an organization may need to know about gifts, sources, and conditions or restrictions. Even attempts, through policies and procedures, to limit information and protect the privacy of individuals and other possible or actual sources of support might be overwhelmed by the more informal channels of communication. "Gossip" and casual conversations can be the means by which personal information that may be private and confidential is given to others. Data entry people on coffee breaks might discuss information about a particular donor with a program staff member. The Executive Director may have lunch with a board member, who may ask for or provide some personal information about a donor. In these and other cases has the confidentiality of information been breached? Has the privacy of the individual been violated? Where does the "need to know" stop within your organization?

DONOR RECOGNITION

Most donors like—or at least don't mind—being recognized for their support and involvement with a nonprofit organization. But some may want to limit their recognition or avoid it altogether. The latter are usually donors who specify they want to be anonymous, but this may not always be the case. Does a donor have a right to be public about his or her gift to an organization but private when it comes to recognition? A donor may not mind being listed at a particular level of giving in published information, but may object to being recognized at an event held by the organization, such as an annual gala or other "public" event. There may be a variety of reasons for this choice, and the donor may or may not reveal the particular reason he or she has for not wanting to be so honored. Some people may prefer to be very private and don't want to be publicly recognized in front of others. Their reasons may be very personal, and their decision may need to be accepted without any further explanation on their part being expected.

Personal and possibly cultural beliefs might also affect the types of awards that can or will be accepted by donors. These beliefs might be very private and not understood by others, but may cause embarrassment or anger if a gift or award is presented that is not in keeping with these beliefs. Some Asian cultures, for example, have very formalized cultural traditions about giving and receiving gifts. Certain types of gifts may not be considered acceptable by some individuals because of their personal, religious or cultural beliefs. Some gifts may be seen as violating a donor's beliefs about modesty, costs of such gifts, or other principles.

So even the act of providing an appropriate level of donor recognition, a "best practice" in the fundraising profession, may be seen as violating the privacy of an individual.

DATABASES

Standard fundraising software programs or custom-designed programs are widely used in the nonprofit sector to track prospects, donors, gift requests pending, gifts received, pledges and payments made, mailings, solicitations, formal proposals, sponsorships, event information and attendance, and a wealth of other information. All of this information is readily available to those who know how to access it and to others who may want access. Access may be limited to certain development staff, or the information may be more widely available to several staff members, such as those in the business/accounting area.

Access to this information may actually be wider than desired, especially if certain security measures are not in place to prevent access by those not authorized to have it. The result can be that information considered confidential and personal can become compromised.

For example, an office I worked in maintained considerable information about clients of the consulting firm, including some details of donors for a major event that was managed by the office. The office had a window facing into an inside hallway and a set of Venetian blinds on the window. Staff working in the office would keep the blinds up most of the time. One staff member noticed that when he arrived in the morning, the blinds were pulled down. After some checking, it was determined that one of the cleaning staff was pulling the blinds at night so that he could use the computers to access the Internet. There were no security codes or access protection on the computers. While the intent was not malicious, the private information was readily accessible.

For another example, a recent news story highlighted how some hotel office centers had computers with hidden software. This software enabled others to receive the credit card and access codes of people using these computers for online stock trading, and thus gain access to their accounts. One person reported entering his account and watching as someone unknown sold off all of his holdings.

Donor records may include many personal details and information that, in the wrong hands, could be used for invading the privacy of individuals and doing harm to them and their personal lives or professions. Records, unless they are password protected, may be easily accessible. Even passwords can be compromised; news articles have highlighted how users often create passwords based on their first or last name, a partner's name, or some other word that is easily figured out by others. Sometimes a few users will share the same password, just to make things "easier" for everyone. Thus internal record security can be compromised, even with the use of passwords and other security measures.

The greater danger may well come from those outside the organization who want to obtain access to the information in the databases. As software protection becomes more sophisticated, it appears that these "hackers" also become more sophisticated in the ways they devise to attack and either destroy or gain access to private information in computer databases. This chapter is not intended as a guide to dealing with these attacks but should be a reminder that the privacy of individual information in fundraising databases may be accessed and used in damaging ways. Each organization needs to protect the privacy not only of its staff and board members, both of whom may have personal information on organizational databases, but of its donors, volunteers, and prospects. The maximum possible security measures and security software should be used, and all employees should have a clear understanding of how to avoid hacker attacks into databases as well as websites and "phishing" emails seeking personal information under the guise of prizes, cash transfers, "personal account" warnings, and the like. These can be carried out in very sophisticated ways and appear completely legitimate, such as your bank seemingly asking you to verify account information.

SOME PRINCIPLES

Privacy, as was stated previously, is not an easy and straightforward issue. As professional fundraisers, we are continually striving to become more donor centered and to always keep in mind the values, needs, and individuality of each donor, prospect, and volunteer. At the same time, we must try to balance this approach with the needs of our organizations and our desire for a successful fundraising program. The fact that there is both a Code of Ethics and a Donor Bill of Rights supported by the Association of Fundraising Professionals reflects this dual emphasis.

We must also keep in mind that the legal definitions of privacy are under ongoing scrutiny and are constantly changing as the "need to know," however defined, conflicts with "the right to privacy." Privacy was once easily defined in terms of the walls of your home or residence, your person, your beliefs and acquaintances, and your conversations and correspondence. This is no longer the case. All of these may be open to investigation if they are judged to pose an actual or even potential threat to the safety and lives of others.

In the past, within some limits, individuals were able to define what they considered private information and what they chose to reveal. To a large extent, this option has become even more limited, and others can and do define what the individual can and cannot consider private. The 9/11 attacks and subsequent events are part of the reason for this change, but there are other reasons, such as the rapidly growing use and abuse of technology, and especially the development of sophisticated search engines, databases, and other information sources that were simply not available 15 years ago.

From the preceding discussion, it is possible to define a few general ethical principles that might be considered by organizations, professional fundraisers, and others in the sector. These principles are not intended as legal guidelines, only as ethical guidelines, and are proposed as follows:

- Each individual, regardless of whether he or she is a donor, a volunteer, or a prospect, has the right to define, except as required by applicable laws, the limits of information, both written and verbal, he or she will provide to an organization.
- Each individual has the right to determine, except as required by applicable laws, what specific information may be made public beyond the internal operations and leadership of the organization.

- Each organization has the obligation to define the necessary information it needs from each donor, prospect, or volunteer to meet its information and reporting needs, how this information will be kept, and who will have access to it within the organization.
- Each organization should have available for any individual or other organization a written statement of what information it needs to meet its internal and reporting requirements, how this information is kept, how accessible it is, and the individual's rights to privacy of personal information.
- Each organization has the responsibility of determining what information from the donor, volunteer, or prospect may be presented beyond the staff and leadership of the organization and adhering to the wishes of each individual involved.
- Each organization must take steps to ensure that the wishes of each donor, volunteer, and prospect in regard to his or her information and its privacy and confidentiality are carried out to the best of the ability of each staff member, board member, and other volunteers.
- Each organization should fully inform all staff members, leadership, and volunteers of its information privacy policies and procedures, the rights of individuals and other organizations to have their information protected, and steps taken to control access to this information.
- Each organization should fully inform all staff members, leadership, and volunteers of the need not to share either formally or informally the personal, private, and/or confidential information of individuals or other organizations outside the bounds of the organization unless required to do so by the applicable laws or by legal action.

About the Author

Eugene A. Scanlan, a published author, is the president of eScanlan Company, a nonprofit management consulting firm he founded in 2001; he has since worked with a number of local, regional, national, and international clients. Prior to founding his firm, he spent 18 years as vice president and senior vice president of The Alford Group, Inc., a national consulting firm. He has also served as a foundation program officer and fiscal manager at The Chicago Community Trust, the foundation officer for The Brookings Institution, the Director of Development for Defenders of Wildlife, and as an independent consultant to several organizations. In addition, Mr. Scanlan holds several academic appointments, including serving as Adjunct Associate Professor at the University of Maryland University College; Associate Professorial Lecturer in International Affairs, Elliott School of International Affairs, George Washington University; and as a member of the Advisory Council for the George Mason University Nonprofit Management Program. He chaired the Association of Fundraising Professionals' (AFP) Research Council, served on the Steering Committee for the Professional Advancement Division, and recently served as a board member of AFP's DC chapter. He received the 2003 Professional Fundraiser of the Year award for the DC chapter of AFP.

NOTE

1. Heinrich Von Staden, "In a Pure and Holy Way: Personal and Professional Conduct in the Hippocratic Oath," *Journal of the History of Medicine and Allied Sciences* 51 (1996), 406–408.

CHAPTER 5

Tainted Money

EUGENE R. TEMPEL, EdD

This book deals with the importance of ethics to the fundraising profession and addresses the ethical decisions fundraisers make and the ethical dilemmas they might face. This chapter deals with "tainted money." Just as in other ethical areas, there are decisions that can be guided by the Association of Fundraising Professionals (AFP) Code of Ethical Principles and Standard[1] and others that are more complex and require deeper reflection, discussion, and guidance than a code of ethics can provide. This chapter defines tainted money and lays out the complexity of tainted-money issues fundraisers and their organizations might face. Finally, it provides ways for fundraisers to examine the most complex tainted-money issues and provides advice and counsel to their organizations in solving them.

Ordinary definitions are useful in understanding concepts. The *American Heritage Dictionary* lists two of the definitions of the verb *taint* as (1) "to stain the honor of someone or something" and (4) "to imbue with principles contrary to contain implicit moral or other prescriptions." The first definition listed for the noun *taint* is "A moral defect considered as a stain or spot." We can apply these concepts to contributions to our organizations.

Tainted money refers to funds contributed to an organization that may raise questions of propriety among the organization's constituents and stakeholders because of the source of the funds or circumstances surrounding the contribution. Typically, tainted money issues call into question the organization's integrity, the manner in which it acts out, acts on, or practices the values it promotes. Integrity is the most important ethical value that our constituents look for in us and, by extension, in our organizations. Simply put, integrity is acting out our beliefs, doing as we say. Our constituents and stakeholders, our donors, and clients want to see us and our organizations "walk the talk." They want to see our organizations act in ways that reflect their missions, their purposes, and their values.

There are different types of contributions that might be regarded as somehow "tainted" and different ways of responding to them. Some types are more complex than others and require a greater degree of analysis and decision making related to accepting or declining a gift. Other cases are more straightforward and easier for organizations to resolve.

In this chapter we'll discuss the types of tainted money by using examples, apply standards of the AFP Code of Ethical Principles and Standards to the tainted-money issue, and use publicly reported cases to help us solve more complicated, less clear-cut tainted-money situations.

DEFINITIONS OF TAINTED MONEY

As was discussed in the introduction, there are different types of tainted money. Alternatively, money contributed to our organizations might be unacceptable for different reasons. In this section we will examine these different types of tainted money.

One of the aphorisms about tainted money that is common among fundraisers is, "The problem with tainted money is t'aint enough." And ethicists have wrestled with a figurative Rorschach test on the tainted-money issue. At one moment or in one situation we might answer one way, at another a different way. Isn't it better to use tainted money to do good in society than to have it available for the potential of furthering unethical activity or activity in conflict with our values? But does our accepting tainted money cleanse the money in such a way that illegal or unethical behavior of the donor becomes acceptable? Resolving issues related to tainted money is vexing.

Let's discuss the easiest first. The most obvious type of tainted money is illegal money. Illegal money is simply money obtained through illegal activity: the sale of illicit drugs, stealing, or white-collar crimes committed by an individual or corporation. A nonprofit organization should never knowingly accept illegal money. Nonprofit organizations have an important responsibility to uphold the law. We are stewards of the public trust. Involvement in illegal activity not only harms trust in individual organizations but impacts the sector as a whole.

Standard No. 5 of the AFP Code of Ethical Principles and Standards commits us to "comply with all applicable local, state, provincial, and federal civil and criminal laws." That expectation is extended to our organizations as well. In its preamble the Code states that members aspire to "practice their profession with integrity, honesty, truthfulness and adherence to the absolute obligation to safeguard the public trust." Like other ethical issues, dealing with tainted money ultimately impacts the public trust in nonprofit organizations. Here is one area where the AFP Code of Ethical Principles and Standards helps us provide solid guidance to our organizations. Nonprofits should not knowingly accept these contributions. And we have the clout of a 30,000-member organization, its ethics committee, and sanctions to help enforce our responsibility.

It is more challenging for nonprofit organizations to deal with issues involving funds that seem legal when they are received but turn out to be illegal through later revelations. For example, what about a major gift from an individual who is later convicted of fraud or income tax evasion? Should the organization return the funds? What if the funds have already been spent? These are questions that we'll discuss later in the chapter.

As reported in the *New York Times*, when Representative Randy Cunningham pled guilty to taking bribes in 2005, more than a dozen of his fellow Congressional lawmakers decided to donate money they had received from him to charity. Cunningham, who took $2.4 million in bribes to assist in securing military contractors for government work, had given these colleagues money from both a campaign account and a political action committee. Seeking to discard the now-tainted political donations by contributing them to nonprofit organizations, these lawmakers effectively created a whole new category of tainted-money issues.[2]

There can be issues in the circumstances surrounding a gift of legitimate money that make it a legally based, tainted-money issue. These are regulations that deal with "insider dealing" in nonprofit organizations. For example, if a donor makes a gift with the expectation of some advantage from the organization in doing business, it would be a clear violation of the "Intermediate Sanctions" laws.[3] We'll deal with guidance that the Intermediate Sanctions provide further on in this chapter.

There are other issues that challenge the legality of a gift. If a donor makes a gift—for example, an endowed chair—but insists on naming the chair holder, that would be a violation of the definition of a gift because the donor maintains interest in the use of the funds. The situation impacts the integrity of an organization in two ways: in addition to violating the charitable gift definition, it also violates values that the nonprofit organization promotes—fairness, independence, and academic integrity.

While illegal money is the most obvious type of tainted money, it is generally not the most common. Most cases of tainted money are less easily defined as such and more difficult to resolve. They include legal tainted money that compromises the organization's integrity, money that conflicts with the organization's values, and money that becomes tainted by a donor's actions after the gift is made or by information about the donor or the funds after a gift is made. Additionally, money can be considered tainted because of the source of funds or the circumstances surrounding the donation, the commitment required of the recipient of the donation, or a clash between the values of the donor and the values of the nonprofit.

A common form of tainted money is a contribution that is a direct assault on the organization's integrity. In this case the positive value of the organization is in effect used to offset direct conflict with the negative act, or behavior of the donor or contributing organization. For example, if our task as an environmental organization is to help clean up the environment, then accepting a contribution from a corporation that has a reputation for harming the environment is a direct assault on our integrity. It calls into question what our purpose is, whether our value of the environment is really more important than other financial considerations. If our purpose is to provide a support structure for families and children suffering from substance abuse, then accepting funds from corporations that produce or sell alcohol would directly impact our integrity. Because there is an established link between alcohol abuse and spousal abuse, the money is tainted because our two organizations are working in opposition. In both cases the values upon which the organization's mission is based are called into question by its actions. In neither case is the organization seen as "walking the talk."

Value conflicts can be more subtle. While they ultimately might impact our integrity, value conflicts must be carefully analyzed to determine if they create tainted-money situations. How do we as professional fundraisers advise an environmental organization on accepting a major contribution from an individual who drives a large SUV? It's not illegal or generally unethical to drive a gas guzzler or fly a private jet, but both activities might be in conflict with the values of the organization. Again, an organization concerned with preserving the environment might be advocating for each of us to leave a minimal footprint. So accepting a major contribution from a donor who lacks integrity on this issue might challenge the integrity of our organization. Value conflicts between a donor and the organization generally are on the line when the donor's values impact the values of the organization through the contribution—for example, when a university that stands for open exploration of new ideas in search of knowledge and truth agrees to promote a particular ideology in return for a gift. Or when the organization is asked to use the goodwill it generates with the public through the values it promotes to support the values of the donor (i.e., a theater dedicated to highest-quality artistic production endorses the donor's lower-quality, commercial productions).

There have been numerous incidents of tainted money reported in the media during the past several years. They illustrate how nonprofits seek to resolve tainted-money issues, the role that key stakeholders in nonprofits play in the decision, and the impact that tainted money can have on an organization.

An article appearing in the *Philanthropy News Digest*[4] in 2007 noted a conflict of values between Stanford University and a corporate donor, ExxonMobil. Stanford University had entered into a $100 million research partnership with ExxonMobil that the oil and gas company had been publicizing in an advertising campaign. The initiative was to find technologies that reduce greenhouse gas emissions while delivering more energy. According to the account, Stanford alumnus Steve Bing rescinded a $2.5 million pledge when he became aware of the partnership. Bing, a movie producer and environmental activist, saw the relationship as antithetical to his own philanthropic values. Jennifer Washburn, a researcher tracking relationships between universities and corporate donors, claims that Stanford allowed corporate donors to exploit its name in the campaign: "Stanford really allowed ExxonMobil to exploit Stanford's academic brand name." University officials denied the claim, stating they were proud of their collaboration with "a variety of private and nonprofit organizations" in their effort to seek solutions to environmental and energy problems. But this situation illustrates that the values and beliefs of one donor might be in conflict with the behavior of another and that key stakeholders' values conflicts can result in a tainted-money situation.

This is one of those cases of values conflict. Was there a real breach of ethics here? Was the money really tainted? How might this issue have been resolved? Might Stanford have communicated intentionally with its donors, alumni, and the public about why it accepted the contribution from ExxonMobil and what it hoped to accomplish with the contribution? In situations like this, organizations might negotiate the extent to which a contribution can be used to promote the donor corporation. Finally, a large complex university dedicated to the development of new knowledge is likely to have ongoing one-time projects that may be in conflict with some of its diverse stakeholders. Openness, transparency, and forthrightness may be the best way to deal with the situation.

The University of Iowa College of Public Health faculty voted to decline a gift from the Wellmark Foundation in July 2007. Eighty percent of the college's budget is funded by research, and half of faculty salaries are funded by research dollars, reported the *Cedar Rapids Gazette*.[5] The Wellmark Foundation wanted to give the university $15 million to name the college after the Wellmark health care insurance company. The faculty felt that accepting the gift and naming the college after the state's largest health care insurance provider could jeopardize its prominent reputation for independence in research and affect how research funding is viewed by the public. Those involved believed the business interests of the insurance company might cause a perception of dishonesty, compromise, or unfairness at the school. Because the bottom line of the company may have created the perception of a conflict with the top line mission of the school, the money was viewed as tainted.

According to the *New York Times*,[6] in February 2005, Maggie's Center, a British cancer charity, turned down a £10,000 donation raised through a benefit event, "Jerry Springer: The Opera." A conservative UK religious organization, Christian Voice, had pressured the charity to decline the gift because it disapproved of the performance. The organization deemed the donation tainted money because of the way in which it was raised. Christian Voice had been protesting airing the act on a BBC television broadcast. Maggie's Center explained their decision to decline the gift: "Maggie's exists to help cancer sufferers, their families, friends, and carers, and to risk causing offense seemed unnecessary." The company which produced the musical said they would make the donation to another charity. This is another example of conflict between key stakeholders. The values Jerry Springer represents are not in direct conflict with a cancer patient, as would be, for example, an organization like a cigarette company. But the Springer values did conflict with those of another key stakeholder.

The complexity of the values conflict basis for tainted money is further illustrated by the fact that one can get general agreement that money given by a particular donor to one organization might be considered tainted but not tainted if given to another. Which charity might accept funds from Jerry Springer? Capital funds for a homeless shelter from a tobacco company might not be considered tainted whereas the same gift to the "Campaign for Tobacco-Free Teens" or Maggie's Center might.

The Salvation Army in Florida turned down a gift of $100,000 from a lottery winner because gambling conflicts with its core values, and it often has to counsel families who are homeless because of gambling. But Habitat for Humanity and the Rotary Club of Marco Island both accepted gifts from the same donor.[7]

Cases such as these also reveal the trade-offs involved in tainted money. Generally there are services not provided when gifts are declined. Tainted-money questions are important for us to answer in the most thoughtful way because much is at stake. Bob Payton taught me a wise adage: "There are no ethical answers, only ethical questions."[8] There are a number of questions that we as fundraisers can ask to help clarify tainted-money issues.

First, will taking money from a donor provide short-term benefits to our clients but risk long-term damage to the reputation of our organization and decrease services to our clients in the long run? If we turn down the money, what will be the short-term impact? What services will we not be able to offer?

What are the various ways in which accepting a potentially tainted gift can affect the organization? Would the gift offend key stakeholders and damage long-term relationships with other donors? Would it have an impact on our ability to deliver services in which our clients would have confidence?

But other more vexing, more complex, ethical questions also arise. For example, who are we to judge donor motivations or sources of wealth? Or even more difficult, how much time must pass before tainted money is no longer tainted?

And then, of course, we get back to the Rorschach test questions again. If we do not accept tainted money, does it continue to circulate and promote negative values in the economy or society when our organization could have provided some public or societal good? Or if we do accept it, are we in effect "cleaning" the money, using the good reputation and the positive image of our organizations to help promote a positive image for the donor or funder?

In concluding a chapter on tainted money in *The New Idolatry* in 1905, Gladden writes:

> Really—must it be said?—money is not the first requisite of a great church or a great college. Some things are more important. Is it not well for churches and colleges to ask themselves what these things are? What shall it profit a church or a college if it shall gain the whole world and lose its own life?[9]

At the heart of tainted-money issues is, in fact, the potential impact on our values, our mission, and our reputation because of values and circumstances related to the donor, the funding source of the gift itself. How we resolve these issues has an impact on the future of our organizations.

THE AFP CODE OF ETHICAL PRINCIPLES AND STANDARDS AND TAINTED MONEY

So in this complex world of tainted money how do we find guidance and assistance to help us fulfill our professional responsibilities? We should begin with the AFP Code of Ethical Principles and Standards. Codes of ethics represent agreement among professionals on minimum ethical standards of conduct or behavior that guide their work. The AFP Code applies directly to our work as professional fundraisers as well as to the organizations we represent. As professionals, we sign a pledge to uphold these standards. In this section we examine various standards in the Code of Ethics that provide guidance to us on matters of tainted money.

First we look at all the standards that might apply and then examine ways each applicable standard might guide us. Of the 24 standards in the Code, five provide guidance on tainted money issues. Four of the five are listed as "Professional Obligations." They are as follows:

- **Standard No. 1.** Members should not engage in activities that harm the members' organization, clients, or profession.

- **Standard No. 2.** Members shall not engage in activities that conflict with their fiduciary, ethical, and legal obligations to their organization and their clients.
- **Standard No. 3.** Members shall effectively disclose all potential and actual conflicts of interest; such disclosure does not preclude or imply ethical impropriety.
- **Standard No. 5.** Members shall comply with all applicable local, state, provincial, and federal civil and criminal laws.

One standard from "Solicitation and Use of Philanthropic Funds" also applies:

- **Standard No. 13.** Members shall take care to ensure that donors receive informed accurate and ethical advice about the value and tax implications of contributions.

These standards typically apply to us as fundraisers. But the intentions of these principles also provide us guidance in dealing with tainted-money issues and in helping inform donors and our organizations.

The easiest standard to apply is Standard No. 5, which challenges us to comply with all laws. As discussed previously, when questions of legality are involved, most tainted-money questions can be answered using this standard of the Code. Accepting money that is illegally begotten might implicate us in the illegal activity. Issuing a receipt for a gift in one year for a gift in another year is fraudulent. It has the potential to violate tax regulations. Agreeing to hold a piece of real estate beyond the date at which the sale price has a potential impact on the value of the tax deduction the donor can claim potentially is conspiring in a scheme to avoid taxes (Standard No. 13 also applies here). Accepting a gift from a donor and agreeing to support a particular political candidate violates the Section 501(c)(3) Internal Revenue Service Code that defines organizations eligible to receive deductible charitable gifts. Aiding a donor in overvaluing a gift to the organization ultimately is conspiring to defraud the federal government of taxes.

As part of our commitment to uphold all applicable state, local, and federal laws, we should be aware of what is called "Intermediate

Sanctions." Intermediate sanctions are so called because they are a series of laws enforced by the Internal Revenue Service that allow it to impose fines and require repayments. It can take these actions if organizations are in violation of these laws instead of taking the ultimate step, revoking the Section 501(c)(3) status of the organization, the only legal recourse prior to these new laws.

Intermediate sanctions are contained in Section 4958 of the Internal Revenue Code. An excellent set of guidelines for applying those regulations exist on the Independent Sector website at www .independentsector. org/uploads/Accountability_Documents/sarbanes _oxley_implications.pdf The regulations are designed to address inappropriate private or personal benefits that an individual or organization might receive from relationships with nonprofit organizations. The regulations made into a potential violation of the law transactions that previously may have been of a questionable ethical nature. Certain gifts can now be clearly defined as tainted money because they violate the intermediate sanctions. The sanctions apply to anyone in a position to influence the organization's decision making. That includes major donors. For example, a major donor to an organization may be awarded a noncompetitive contract for services, (e.g., printing, design work, construction or consulting), where the cost of the services provided turns out to be more than the value of the services delivered. Both those who benefit from and those who knowingly help approve such contracts (this could include volunteer board members) are subject to heavy penalties.

Standard No. 5 provides guidance for us to deal with any contribution that is tainted because of the legality of the funds being contributed or any circumstance surrounding the transactions that make the transaction itself illegal. An old saying in ethical circles applies here: Everything illegal is unethical. Although philosophers and activists might debate this as oversimplified, Standard No. 5 and this old saying provide good guidance. The other side of this saying is that not everything unethical is illegal. And that is where things become more complex.

The four other standards from the Member Obligations section of the Code provide some guidance for us in dealing with the more complex and difficult decisions that arise from those transactions that might not be illegal but might be unethical—those transactions that have the potential to do harm because they involve "tainted" money. Standard No. 2 takes us right back to personal responsibility to uphold the law. Any behavior on our part that violates the law is a violation of Standard No. 2. Standard No. 2 reminds us of our obligation, for example, not to change the date of a gift receipt from one tax year to another. Doing so not only makes tainted money of the gift but is also activity that conflicts with our legal obligation.

CASE STUDY   THE BIG BAD DONOR

A city hospital desperately needs a critical care wing. The nearest facility is 250 miles away, and patients needing critical care often do not survive the trip. Shortly after the hospital board announces a capital campaign, a local businessperson offers to donate the entire cost of the new wing, provided the hospital names the wing after him.

A. Suppose the donor is known as an underworld figure who allegedly makes his money from drug trafficking. Would it be a violation of the AFP Code of Ethical Principles and Standards to accept the money?
   1. Yes
   2. No
   3. It depends
   4. Don't know

Answer: 3. It depends; "allegedly" is an important word in the scenario—organizations and individual fundraisers are not judge and jury. Hospital leadership (staff and board) need to determine whether the nature of the transgression is in conflict with the organization's mission to the extent that acceptance of the gift would do harm to the organization. If the individual is found guilty and if the organization concludes that the nature of the transgression conflicts sufficiently with its mission, then acceptance of the gift could be construed as a violation of Standard No. 1. The naming issue is only marginally relevant. In the spirit of transparency, the real issue is whether the organization wants any relationship with the potential benefactor, publicized or otherwise.

B. Suppose the donor in question actually went to jail for drug trafficking, served his time, and is now "legit." Would it be a violation of the AFP Code to accept the money?
   1. Yes
   2. No
   3. It depends
   4. Don't know

Answer: 3. It depends; much of the reasoning noted above for the first question applies here as well. The organization needs to ask itself whether it believes a convicted felon can be rehabilitated. Organizations should be hesitant to sit in judgment of (potential) benefactors.

C. Suppose the donor is willing to forget putting his name on the building but will give the money only if he is named to the hospital board. Should you accept the money?
   1. Yes
   2. No
   3. It depends
   4. Don't know

Answer: 2. No, Standards No. 1 and No. 2 seem relevant here. Boards of nonprofit organizations have developed **policies** and practices for inviting people to board service. Individuals ought not to be able to "butt" their way onto boards.

In Standard No. 1 we commit not to engage in activities that harm our organizations, clients, or the profession. We cannot allow our search for funds to compromise important missions or feel pressure to solicit gifts or accept funds that might be tainted. If we can see clearly that a gift conflicts directly with our organization's mission or its values, our obligation is to turn it down. This assumes that we can easily identify cases as having that kind of conflict. Typically, these are the gifts discussed previously as having a direct impact on the integrity of our organizations. Gifts from alcohol companies for a battered women's shelter or from a tobacco company for a children's anti-tobacco program fall into this category. When we know that the contribution might do the organization harm, that it might have negative impact on the reputation of our organization, it is our professional obligation not to solicit the gift, not to accept the gift on the organization's behalf, and to counsel the organization not to accept the gift. In fact, it is in these cases that organizational policies might be developed to help us.

Standard No. 2 includes a focus on our fiduciary and ethical obligations as well as our legal obligations. In this case, tainted money issues can arise related to third-party organizations that are assigned to help carry out fiduciary responsibilities—that is, to administer a trust on behalf of our organizations. We have an obligation to make certain that these third parties do not have values that conflict with our organization or have relationships with the donor that could create conflicts that would be less apparent than if a gift were made directly to our organizations. The potential for having money become tainted may jeopardize our organization, and Standard No. 2 commits us to exercise due diligence on relationships with donors and outside partners to make certain to the best of our ability that the relationship will be positive and that it will not do the organization harm.

Standard No. 3 deals with conflicts of interest. This standard applies to conflicts of interest we as fundraisers have in relation to a gift that is being solicited or in other transactions that the organization is pursuing, such as, for example, a potential contract with one of our relatives. By raising the issue of conflict of interest to the level of a standard in the code of ethics, we have another plank in our platform of guidance on tainted-money issues. As noted previously, some tainted-money issues are related to conflicts of interest that involve the donor and the gift. Situations in which the donor expects to influence the mission of the organization (determine the orchestra's selections, or the theatre's play selections, receive favorable treatment for a friend or relative) are all conflicts of interest that create tainted-money situations. Standard No. 3 provides us some help in counseling our organization and potential donors about the impact that the gift might have on the reputation of the donor and the organization.

The AFP guidelines on Standard No. 3 include Intermediate Sanctions. The guidelines state:

> f. Members understand the provisions of the IRS "Intermediate Sanctions" regulations in the US, or their equivalent in other countries, that apply to persons associated with nonprofit organizations who might also benefit from business or commercial arrangements with the organization.

This interpretation of Standard No. 3 provides us with guidance in dealing with tainted-money issues based on conflicts of interest or personal "inurement."

Standard No. 13 deals directly with our responsibility to provide donors with accurate and ethical advice. And although the standard is directed toward value and tax implications of potential contributions, we can also apply this standard to a range of tainted money issues. This standard of the Code also applies to the simple act of providing donors with advice about tax deductibility for such items as raffle tickets, dinners, or other special event tickets or auction bids. An organization that doesn't follow legal requirements will cause tainted-money issues itself. And there are new requirements for us to follow in reporting the receipt of noncash gifts to the IRS in the Pension Act of 2006. We must make certain that we do not damage our organization's reputation by creating the perception that we may overvalue noncash gifts or create legal issues by failing to report noncash gifts as required by the IRS, both of which create tainted money.

Certainly we should apply Standard No. 13 to value and tax implications issues. As discussed in the section on Standard 5, gifts that are overvalued and for which a tax savings scheme is the primary motivation have the potential to violate the tax code and are tainted by the violation. But Standard No. 13 can also provide us guidance in informing our organization and potential donors of issues related to ethical situations that might impact the way a gift is harmful to the organization. The application of this standard is helpful in gaining the confidence that is required for us to provide appropriate counsel to a donor or to our organizations that may have an inclination to make or accept a potentially tainted gift.

There are other standards that might provide guidance on tainted-money situations as well. For example, Standard No. 4 involves exploiting personal relationships for the benefit of the member or the member's organization. One of the unethical practices cited in Standard No. 4 is

> Manipulating a donor or prospect who is vulnerable because of age, handicap, infirmity, illness or emotional or physical impairment or dependence to arrange his or her affairs so that the member or member's organization becomes a beneficiary of the individual's estate or financial support plans.

This activity is considered unethical by a variety of professional organizations. It violates the public trust. It calls into question our concern for others. It creates tainted money because it is "predatory" fundraising that will harm the organization's relationship with current donors and its ability to engage new donors.

Standard No. 14 also relates to tainted money. It relates to our obligation to use funds in accordance with the donor's wishes. Standard No. 14 provides guidance in two ways. First it is the obligation to carry out the obligations we accept. If those obligations are burdensome or create tainted-money situations, we will place our organizations in difficult situations. If the organization accepts funds that are restricted or burdensome or even funds tainted by the circumstances of the gift without the intention of fully meeting the obligation, it violates this standard. Second, if we or our organizations do not follow the guidance of this standard, we create tainted-money situations through loss of confidence by donors and the public. Any money not applied as agreed by the organizations and the donor is tainted.

TAINTED-MONEY DILEMMAS   95

TAINTED-MONEY DILEMMAS

The AFP Code of Ethical Principles and Standards provides guidance on some tainted-money issues, especially those involving legal issues. It also challenges us to the highest levels of professional and ethical behavior to inspire and ensure the public trust. And it challenges us to be knowledgeable and to counsel and inform our organizations to make the right decisions. More complex tainted-money situations require understanding and decision-making, policies and communication with key stakeholders and the public. As discussed previously in this chapter, most legally based tainted-money issues organizations face can be solved as wrong-or-right, yes-or-no decisions. In this section we examine several publicly reported cases related to tainted-money issues to focus on decision making related to tainted money; policy recommendations are considered in the last section of the chapter.

The case of a contribution by rapper Master P reported in the New Orleans *Times-Picayune* provides opportunity for discussion of many of the issues related to complex tainted-money situations.

The prospective gift from Master P to the St. Monica Catholic Elementary School definitely created an ethical dilemma. As discussed in other chapters of this book, in an ethical dilemma, two positive values are in conflict. Most complex tainted-money issues involve a conflict between our organization's integrity on one side and values such as fairness, concern for others, our services to clients, and prudent application of resources on the other. The question usually is related to the potential impact on our organization's integrity and the impact on public trust as compared with the public benefit a gift might have. Often, we may be faced with a situation like that illustrated in a recent Dilbert cartoon in which the boss expresses concern that in order to remedy too much goodwill on the balance sheet, an anonymous buyer has offered a million dollars for the right to decrease the company's goodwill. Except that an organization, especially a nonprofit organization, cannot have too much goodwill. And if we decrease our goodwill, we risk damaging the public trust.

The ethical dilemmas that are involved in tainted-money issues are typically choices between two goods and are likely to be viewed differently by different stakeholders. Often the overarching questions posed earlier in the chapter come into consideration. If we don't take tainted money, does it continue to contribute to the economy in some other way? If we take the money, will we be in effect "cleansing" it? If we don't take the money, what services will we not be able to provide?

How does one deal with the dilemmas? In the section "Illegal Acts, Unethical Behavior and Ethical Dilemmas" in *Obedience to the Unenforceable*, Independent Sector says

> We offer no answers to ethical dilemmas because organizations must struggle with such decisions on their own. Rich benefits will devolve from the process each organization follows in explanation of its own values, ethical behaviors and practices. (p. 21)

How then should we approach dealing with ethical dilemmas related to tainted money? Briefly Michael Josephson recommends the following process:

1. Identify values involved.
2. Identify and consult key stakeholders.
3. Determine what's best for the most stakeholders in the long run.
4. Implement.
5. Monitor and modify.[10]

Remember, an ethical dilemma is a situation where there are competing goods and competing values, such as integrity and our concern for others. Key stakeholders might include staff, board members, community leaders, donors, and current and future clients. A key to Josephson's approach is to monitor the way a decision is received by constituents and be prepared to modify the decision if there are unanticipated consequences.

Albert Anderson[11] asks a set of questions that provide a slightly different perspective:

1. What seem(s) to be the ethical issue(s)—that is, what does one judge to be right or wrong in this situation?

2. Which option(s) would seem to make the situation right—that is, what ought we to do?

3. Which ethical principle(s), and ultimately which governing framework, would justify the action(s)?

There are, of course, other models and approaches. But we will advance our discussion of the Master P gift using these models.

First, the gift from Percy "Master P" Miller to St. Monica's does not involve any legal issues. Nor does the gift violate any code of ethics. It does, however, raise questions about values that are in conflict. What seem to be the ethical issues that make this a tainted-money situation?

On one hand we have St. Monica's School. The school is sponsored by the Catholic Church and the Archdiocese of New Orleans. The school teaches Christian values along with the typical academic subjects. Among those values is respect for others. The school would include in showing respect for others not using language that would degrade others. On the other hand, we have Master P. Master P, according to the article, made his money in a genre known as "gangsta rap." His No Limit label was said at the time to be the nation's most successful marketer of gangsta rap, sexually explicit lyrics that tell the tales of living in tough, violent neighborhoods. The lyrics are often disrespectful of and degrading to women. The lyrics in Master P's songs seem to be in direct conflict with the values St. Monica's tries to instill in its students.

On the surface, the money is tainted by the conflict of values between the Catholic Church and the school and the lyrics and performances by which the money to make the gift was secured. This conflict in values challenges the integrity of the church and the school. So accepting money earned in this way, even though it was earned through legal activity, would call into question the integrity of the school and the Catholic Church. Having a policy never to accept money from any source that represents values in conflict with the values of the school or church would make this a very easy decision.

But ethical dilemmas are more complicated. Other values come into play. It turns out that Master P is an alumnus of St. Monica's School and consequently has some direct knowledge of the contributions that the school can make. The report also says that the school is a "safe harbor" for poor children. Like other Catholic schools in urban areas across the country, it may have been the last hope for many young people in the area to succeed scholastically. And the report adds that the school was scheduled to close after many years of struggle.

There are additional values are involved in this situation. The school was providing a public good. No doubt it was demonstrating a basic concern for others. Another basic value would be fairness, making sure that there is a level playing field, that no matter what the child's circumstances, he or she has a chance to succeed. In fact, St. Monica's likely was helping kids growing up to succeed in the mean rough neighborhoods described in Master P's songs. They were likely teaching them respect, concern for others, fairness, and other values that might have a positive impact on society.

What then if the school were to close? What would be lost? What services would no longer be provided? What would happen to the children who are enrolled in the school?

So we have a dilemma. On the one hand, a choice might be to act in an ethical manner to preserve the integrity of St. Monica's School. On the other hand, we also have an obligation to fulfill an important mission in the neighborhood. There are two competing goods. How do we judge what might be right or wrong in this situation? Would it be wrong to accept the money? Would it be wrong to allow the school to close?

Who are the stakeholders in this dilemma? Certainly the children and the Catholic Church, including the local archbishop. In addition, there are local Catholics, donors to the Catholic Church, parents and grandparents of the children, and teachers and administrators at the school. These key stakeholders might have different answers to these questions. There might be Catholics who would be upset by acceptance of the gift and other Catholics upset by the closing of the school.

What would help make the situation right? How do we gauge the attitudes among our key stakeholders? The news article reports that the Roman Catholic Church applied a deliberate process to deal with the dilemma. They asked two basic questions:

1. Would taking this money amount to cooperating with evil?
2. Would taking the money stir such a scandal that the church's mission would be damaged?

Two moral theologians were involved in the discussion with the archbishop and with the donor. They were essentially searching for things that might make the situation right, what might be best for stakeholders in the long run, what principles might be involved to make a decision on the gift.

In the end the advisors on this case said that the gift passed on both counts. A key factor cited was Miller's assurance that he was moving beyond gangsta rap and was developing new lines of income in clothing and professional sports. He also contended that the gangsta rap was only a persona and did not reflect his true character. So one might say that in discussing the case the decision makers discovered information that might have changed circumstances related to the ethics decision. There was less concern in the end that accepting the gift was cooperating with evil. They also determined that there would be little impact on the mission of the church.

On another level what was best for the most stakeholders in the long run was to accept the gift and keep St. Monica's School open. The good accomplished through the programs of the school in the eyes of the decision makers was more significant than the potential harm. The archbishop made the right decision if one views public response as a key indicator. The *Times Picayune* reported very little public response.

The practical discussion of tainted money in the article touches on a number of other dilemmas that we encounter. One is the question of whether money considered tainted in one organization is also tainted in another. And one principle we can consider is whether or not there is a values conflict. One can find almost universal agreement that Mother Teresa could accept funds from *almost* any source without damaging her reputation. Perhaps her mission, focused on such basic needs, did indeed make the source of her funds irrelevant. Furthermore, she probably was not in a position with the work she did to "cleanse" the reputation of someone who offered ill-gotten gains. Her work probably avoided the second overarching question asked earlier: Does accepting the money help make the source legitimate?

A well-publicized case in Minnesota also illustrates the difficulty of this dilemma. A group of female strip club entertainers had a legitimate car wash and contributed the $1,000 raised to support the sports program at a high school near St. Paul. The high school turned down the gift presumably because of the conflict of values between the strip club's entertainment and the values promoted by the high school and its sports programs. A recommendation that the gift be made to the Booster Club did not alter the tainted-money situation. The Booster Club represented the same values as the sports program. The high school's decision not to accept the gift seems fairly straightforward.

But the story reported that a priest in St. Paul said he would gladly accept the gift in support of his mission to serve inner-city kids. From his perspective, like Mother Teresa's, his mission was so essential to basic needs that the source of funds was almost irrelevant. For him, resolving this dilemma was just as easy as reaching the opposite decision was for the high school.

In the New Orleans *Times Picayune* story the issue of association and the conflict that occurs though association was addressed as a factor. A seminary development officer says that as a practical matter institutions don't seek gifts from people with different values. Peggy Outon takes this to another level: "When I ask for money, I'm entering into an implicit contract with the donor. If I'm not proud of who that person is, of supporting them in whatever way I need to, then I don't want to be associated with them." A key principle here is the complementary values between the organization and the donor. It reflects one of the questions in the Master P case: Would accepting the gift be associating with evil?

If association with conflicting values is one of the principles useful in deciding dilemmas related to tainted money, does anonymity make a difference? The integrity of an organization can be damaged by associating with funding sources that conflict with its values or by accepting gifts that are direct assaults on its integrity. As reported in the *St. Petersburg Times* and previously mentioned in this chapter, the Salvation Army in Naples, Florida declined a $100,000 gift from a Florida lottery winner because gambling conflicts with its core values. According to the *Times*, Major Damon, who declined the gift, was variously applauded and belittled by others around the country. But what if the gift had been anonymous? What if the donor had placed $10,000 in 10 different kettles during the holiday fund drive? Presumably the Salvation Army would not have known the source and there would have been no tainted-money issues.[12]

Some other issues raised in the *Times Picayune* story are worth mentioning. One is the notion that there is such a strong sense of poverty, such a need for funds in most nonprofits that they don't have the luxury of engaging in ethical dilemmas. Like St. Monica's School, the nonprofit may be in such a desperate financial situation and the value of continued service to clients is so critical to the public good that the risk to the organization's integrity from tainted money becomes irrelevant. That still doesn't mean the organization should knowingly accept illegal money.

Some organizations believe they "clean" money in service to humanity. That's perhaps what Mother Teresa did. It brings us back to the questions posed in the previous section: Is it better to use tainted money to accomplish some good in society rather than leaving it to circulate in the economy in other, potentially harmful ways?

The story also mentions the case of Michael Milken, the "junk bond" lender who was convicted of securities fraud and spent time in prison. Today it is almost a badge of honor to have a grant from the Milken Foundation. There is very little (perhaps no) risk of loss of reputation or assault on mission integrity in accepting a grant from the Milken Foundation. This example deals with the question of whether the passing of time "cleans" tainted money. A corollary question might be: Do the actions of the potential donor over time change the circumstances so that the gift is no longer tainted? If one serves time in prison for an illegal act, carries out service to the community, lectures publicly about the damage one's actions have done to society and the importance of having ethical standards in one's life, does that change the circumstances sufficiently to remove any taint? Probably in many organizations' decision making related to tainted money dilemmas, this would be an important consideration.

There are still some questions we posed earlier that we have not answered. What if the gift accepted by an organization that seemed to be legal, that was not tainted at the time it was accepted, turned out later to be illegally begotten or tainted because of the source? What if the money had already been spent? Think of all the gifts that had been made by officers of Enron who were later found guilty of conspiracy, securities and wire fraud, and insider trading.

In *Nonprofits and Morals*[13] Dorff examines a case quite like this. Investment banker Ivan Boesky made a pledge to the Jewish Theological Society of America prior to his indictment and conviction on securities fraud charges. The issue for the Jewish Theological Seminary is the transmission of values, principles, and tradition deeply embedded in the Jewish religion and Jewish culture. Part of Boesky's pledge to the seminary had been paid and expended for a new library building, which bore the Boesky family's name. Should the money already received have been returned? Should the seminary accept additional contributions from Boesky? In the end, the seminary did not return the money already received and spent, but also would not accept additional contributions from Boesky. Dorff explains how the seminary reached its decision using principles from Jewish tradition. The principles are instructive to nonprofits generally, and his discussion of this case, the Milken case, and the Philip Morris case (pp. 107–113) are useful reading for developing principled decision making related to tainted-money questions.

The Jewish Seminary was lucky on one count. Before he was indicted, Boesky called the institution and suggested the family name be removed from the building so that dilemma was not left for the institution to resolve. But a variety of principles from Jewish tradition helped the board of directors reach the decision they did about the two questions remaining. Such principles as "the moral idealism of the prophets" and the moral integrity of the institution supported the concept of returning the money already paid. Jewish concepts for distinguishing between the nature of guilt and innocence reflected in an indictment versus a conviction are explained. And Maimonides's concept that one should not accept anything that is or might be stolen came into the discussion. Dorff's summary of how the questions were answered is helpful to us:

> [P]eople differed in how to interpret and apply the law to this case, with some emphasizing the laws that exempt unknowing recipients of stolen property from any liability and others focusing on Maimonides's warning against accepting anything that even *appeared* tainted. Others were interested in what Jewish law had to say, but were even more motivated by the Prophets' call to moral idealism and by the important principle in Jewish law and tradition holding that one's actions should not desecrate the reputation of God and the Jewish people (*hillul ha-shem*) and should instead sanctify God's name (*kiddush ha-shem*). The result the Seminary reached combined these approaches by differentiating between the money that had already been collected and used, which it would not return, and the remaining portion of Mr. Boesky's pledge that it would not accept even if he could pay it after the indictment.

Most organizations would probably come to the same conclusion as did the Jewish Theological Seminary. In accepting the money in the first place we were acting according to our values. Returning money is difficult. If it is spent we must have reserves or raise money to cover the cost. If there is an unpaid pledge toward a constructed facility and we do not accept further payments, we will still be faced with uncovered construction costs.

If the donor doesn't suggest removing the name from a facility or program as Boesky did, we are still faced with that dilemma. What if the pledge was entirely paid? Integrity and promise keeping become conflicting values. There is still a Kenneth L. Lay Chair of Economics at the University of Missouri. Examining the real situations of other institutions, creating hypothetical situations and case studies and discussing them, we can discover principles to guide our decision making.

POLICIES AND PROCEDURES FOR DEALING WITH TAINTED MONEY

We have to operate under the assumption that we as professionals and the organizations we represent will be faced with tainted-money issues. Our responsibility as professionals is to help our organizations deal with these issues. And even if our organization operates with such poverty or fulfills such a basic human need that the source is irrelevant, it is best to have policies and procedures for reaching decisions about tainted money and communicating those decisions to key stakeholders and the public.

Organizations should establish policies and procedures in an environment when they are free to think through the issues, free of a real case that might impact their decision making.

Organizations should recognize that most of the tainted-money issues they will face are ethical dilemmas in which there are competing goods instead of simple right or wrong decisions. Our policies and procedures must be developed to take into account the importance of judgment on the issues in the decision-making process.

In developing policies and procedures we should first discuss the guidance we can receive from codes of ethics that we and our organization have pledged to follow. As discussed earlier, the preamble to the AFP Code of Ethical Principles and Standards Nos. 1, 2, 3, 5, and 13 provide guidance. So do Standards No. 8, 9, and 10 from the Partnership for Philanthropic Planning's "Model Standards of Practice for the Charitable Gift Planner."[14] The Code of Ethics from the Council for Advancement and Support of Education, the Association of Healthcare Philanthropy, the Association of American Museums, the American Symphony Orchestra League, and various nonprofit and subsector associations might provide guidance as well. The principles from any code that apply to tainted money should form the foundation for the organization's policies.

Organizations should also establish a policy related to money that is known to have been illegally earned. In most cases our organizations will not have a dilemma related to money tainted through legal issues.

But even if we are "Mother Teresa," we should have a policy explaining why we can accept money tainted by questions of legality.

Organizations should decide whether there are principles that guide decision making that they will not violate. For example they may have values that are so important to what they do that some gifts are always unacceptable (e.g., the Naples, Florida, Salvation Army).

Guiding principles and policies can also be developed from the values and mission of the organization and other cultural or religious values that help guide the organization.

Initial guidelines should include policies for permanently naming buildings and programs and should take into consideration potential conflicts of interest and future embarrassment to the institution. We should help our organizations establish policies and guidelines on which issues can be decided by staff and by what level staff, how decisions are reviewed by staff, and which decisions related to tainted-money issues are made by the board. Once it has been determined which issues can be decided by staff, the boards of nonprofits should determine how boards of directors or trustees will consider other tainted-money dilemmas. Establishing a special committee of the board or a special subcommittee of the development committee is a good practice. Some boards have gift acceptance committees that evaluate a variety of issues related to major gifts. This committee can be charged to deal with tainted-money dilemmas as part of its function.

The major advantage of having a special committee to focus on tainted-money dilemmas is that members can prepare themselves well to perform expertly when the time comes. They can review periodically the principles, policies, and procedures. They can review tainted-money cases that arise in other organizations to test their own decision-making process. And they can prepare themselves through readings and briefings to stay current on contemporary issues. The process should still end with a recommendation to the full board and a decision on the issue made by board action so that there is organizational commitment behind the decision.

Communication is a key to dealing with tainted-money issues. Communication with the donor or funder is the first important step. Open and honest communication with a potential donor by knowledgeable staff and other leaders is essential. Thanking the donor for the offer and explaining the organization's decision-making process on gifts of this nature give the organization an opportunity for review and to avoid raising expectations with the donor. If circumstances permit, the donor can be invited to meet with the appropriate committee or with members of the board to discuss the gift and its implication for the organization. This is an opportunity to review the criteria and circumstances of the gift and any changes in understanding and requirements that would aid in solving any tainted money dilemmas. If it is not possible to accept a gift because of institutional values, the organization can be helpful in suggesting other good causes that might not have the same conflict.

Communicating with key stakeholders and the public is equally important. If an organization decides not to accept a gift, issues of privacy may mean the entire matter is kept confidential. If the organization decides after deliberation to accept a gift that might raise questions, securing permission from the donor to explain its decision to the public will help build confidence and trust in the organization and bring credit to the donor. In the case of Master P's gift to St. Monica's School, the Archdiocese of New Orleans explained its reasoning to the public. As in all matters of ethics, transparency in matters related to tainted money is essential in building public trust. We must remember that, although we are private organizations with rights of privacy, we serve the public good, and the public has expectations that we will act in a manner that builds public trust. Whatever our decisions related to tainted money, transparency, explanation, and communication help build the public trust.

CONCLUSION

Tainted money is an ethical issue that every organization needs to be prepared to deal with. Many of us might think that we or the organizations we represent will not be impacted by tainted money. After all we don't deliberately seek tainted money. James Lee said in the

Times Picayune story that, "As a practical matter, institutions don't seek gifts from people with different values."

But we might seek gifts that later become tainted. Or we might be approached about gifts that challenge our integrity, conflict with our values, or damage our goodwill. It may be as small as the $1,000 raised by the strip club entertainers at a legitimate car wash or as complex as the Master P gift to St. Monica's School. So we have a professional responsibility to prepare ourselves and the organizations we represent to deal with tainted-money issues before we confront them. We should understand the complexity of tainted money issues and how the AFP Code of Ethical Principles and Standards can provide us guidance on dealing with them. We should help our organizations define what is tainted money for individual organizations based on their unique values and culture. This will lead us to some general principles and policies for dealing with tainted money and a process for deciding the issues. Every organization should develop policies and a process for dealing with the tainted-money issues that are more complex, that are true ethical dilemmas, and that truly are conflicts between two goods.

Nonprofit organizations serve the public good. In "Obedience to the Unenforceable: Ethics and the Nation's Voluntary and Philanthropic Community," Independent Sector says, "Those who presume to serve the public good assume a public trust."[15] Those who wish to uphold or embrace the public trust must hold themselves to the higher standards the public expects of nonprofit organizations. How we deal with tainted money ultimately impacts the public trust.

ABOUT THE AUTHOR

Eugene R. Tempel, EdD, is founding dean of the School of Philanthropy at Indiana University. Dr. Tempel's career includes more than two decades of administration, teaching, and fundraising in higher education. He previously served as vice chancellor of Indiana University–Purdue University Indianapolis and as vice president of the Indiana University Foundation. He is the author and coauthor of several books, including *Fund Raisers: Their Careers, Stories, Concerns and Accomplishments*, which he coauthored with Margaret A. Duronio, and *Hank Rosso's Achieving Excellence in Fund Raising*, 2nd edition, for which he was editor and author of three of the chapters. He has held numerous leadership positions with the Association of Fundraising Professionals, currently serving as Immediate Past Chair of the Ethics Committee. *The NonProfit Times* has annually selected him as one of the 50 most influential leaders in the nonprofit sector, and the late Indiana Governor Frank O'Bannon named him a Sagamore of the Wabash in 2002. In 2007, he received the prestigious James L. Fisher Award for distinguished service to education from the Council for Advancement and Support of Education.

NOTES

1. Association of Fundraising Professionals, "AFP Code of Ethical Principles and Standards," www.afpnet.org/files/ContentDocuments/CodeOfEthicsLong.pdf.
2. "Bidding Goodbye to Tainted Money," *New York Times*, December 2, 2005.
3. Independent Sector, "Intermediate Sanctions," www.independentsector.org/PDFs/sanctions.pdf.
4. "Donor Rescinds $2.5 Million Gift to Stanford Over ExxonMobil Ads," *Philanthropy News Digest*, March 14, 2007.
5. Diane Heldt, "Faculty Says No to Naming UI College after Wellmark," *Cedar Rapids Gazette*, July 5, 2007.
6. Pam Kent, "Arts, Briefly; British Charity Rejects 'Jerry Springer' Opera Donation," *New York Times*, February 22, 2005.
7. Sharon Tubbs, "Churches at Odds Over Gifts from Gamblers," *St. Petersburg Times*, June 10, 2003.
8. R. L. Payton, *Philanthropy: Voluntary Action for the Public Good* (New York: American Council on Education/Macmillan Publishing, 1988).
9. Washington Gladden, *The New Idolatry and Other Discussions* (New York: McClure, Phillips Co., 1905), 29.
10. Michael Josephson, *Making Ethical Decisions* (Marina del Rey, CA: The Josephson Institute, 1992, 1993).
11. Albert Anderson, *Ethics for Fundraisers* (Bloomington and Indianapolis: Indiana University Press, 1996), 76.

12. Sharon Tubbs, "Churches at Odds Over Gifts from Gamblers," *St. Petersburg Times*, June 10, 2003.

13. Elliott N. Dorff, "Nonprofits and Morals: Jewish Perspectives and Methods for Resolving Some Commonly Occurring Moral Issues," in *Good Intentions: Moral Obstacles & Opportunities*, ed. David H. Smith (Bloomington and Indianapolis: Indiana University Press, 2005), 103–126.

14. Partnership for Philanthropic Planning, "Model Standards of Practice for the Charitable Gift Planner," 1991, revised 1999, www.pppnet.org/ethics/model_standards.html.

15. Independent Sector, "Obedience to the Unenforceable: Ethics and the Nation's Voluntary and Philanthropic Community," 1991, revised 2002, www.independentsector.org/uploads/Accountability_Documents/obedience_to_unenforceable.pdf.

CHAPTER 6

Compensation

PAULETTE V. MAEHARA, CFRE, CAE

IMPACT OF PROFESSIONAL ETHICS AND STANDARDS

Compensation practices and levels for development professionals have changed significantly during the past 25 years. Several converging factors have accounted for this evolution: changing donor demographics, the growth of the nonprofit sector, the promulgation of ethical codes for the profession, and the recognition of the importance of stewardship and donor-centric relationship building.

The nonprofit community in North America has grown tremendously during the past 10 years or so. In the United States, the number of nonprofits has grown from 1.20 million in 1999 to more than 1.43 million in 2009, including just over 1 million Section 501(c)(3) charities.[1] In Canada, there are an estimated 165,000 nonprofits and charities.[2]

Because of this growth, competition for funds has become extremely fierce. More nonprofit organizations than ever are soliciting funds from the public. As a result, fundraisers of all experience levels are in great demand, especially those with specific skill sets such as major gifts.

Many organizations have sought to enhance their overall compensation practice by conducting annual or biannual salary surveys of like organizations, increasing salaries and benefits to compensate for high-stress environments and to retain competent and skilled staff. Identical trends are evident in the fundraising profession, with development professionals enjoying significant gains in both salary and benefits.[3]

During the 11 years that the Association of Fundraising Professionals (AFP), formerly the National Society of Fund Raising Executives (NSFRE), has conducted the annual *Compensation and Benefits Study*, average salaries reported by U.S. respondents increased from $61,233 in 2001 to $75,595 in 2011, a 23 percent increase. In Canada, the average salary reported in 2001 was CAN$67,600, while the average salary reported in 2011 was CAN$78,067—a 15 percent increase.

CASE STUDY   **SCALING THE CAPITAL STEPS**

You are considering a position with a nonprofit organization as the director of an upcoming capital campaign. The CEO offers you a salary and an annual incentive bonus "in steps" if the campaign meets certain milestones. The salary he offers is a little less than you hoped for, but the bonus would be 25 percent of your annual salary if the campaign reaches its first-year goal, 25 percent if the campaign reaches its second-year goal, and 50 percent if the campaign reaches its third-year goal.

A. Would you be violating the AFP Code of Ethical Principles and Standards if you accepted this compensation package?
   1. Yes
   2. No
   3. It depends
   4. Don't know

Answer: 1. Yes, 25 percent of your first year salary is a specific number, let's say $10,000. That number is a percentage of the first-year goal, perhaps $700,000. By tying the bonus in this fashion only to the amount of funds raised, the practice violates Standard No. 21.

B. Suppose the CEO said you will be required to keep the bonus arrangement confidential because the organization has a policy of keeping the terms of individual employment confidential. Only one or two other managers in the organization have bonus provisions in their employment contracts; in fact, only two other managers besides the CEO have employment contracts. Would you be violating the AFP Code if you accepted this condition?

1. Yes
2. No
3. It depends
4. Don't

Answer: 1. Yes; Standard No. 22 requires that bonuses be in accord with prevailing practices within the members' own organization.

C. Suppose the CEO offered to base the bonus each year on the amount as well as the number of gifts and pledges in the campaign. Would you be violation the AFP Code if you accepted this plan?

1. Yes
2. No
3. It depends
4. Don't know

Answer: 3. It depends; the proposed arrangement begins to include a number of nonfinancial quantifiable factors. The more the arrangement focuses on nonfinancials, the better. However, regardless of the formula, the arrangement must be in accord with the prevailing practices of the organization.

A common misconception about fundraising salaries is that they are in some way tied to a percentage of dollars raised. Many nonprofit board members, especially those with backgrounds in the for-profit sector, believe that this method of compensation is not only acceptable but also desirable because it serves as an incentive for individual fundraisers to raise more money. Percentage-based compensation was a common practice 25 years ago, but with the creation of standards of professional practice, the use of compensation based on a percentage of dollars raised has declined.[4]

The AFP Code of Ethical Principles and Standards of Professional Practice was adopted in 1960 and is the oldest actively enforced fundraising code in the world. The standards related to compensation were added to the Code in 1984, and the association's leaders later developed a position paper on percentage compensation in 1992.[5] This long-held and fundamental tenet of AFP has significantly changed compensation practices for fundraising professionals, not only for their work obtaining charitable gifts, but also for their efforts focused on non-gift revenues (cause-related marketing, corporate sponsorships, raffle tickets, to name a few). In 2003, the AFP Ethics Committee conducted a survey on compensation practices for fundraisers. Two-thirds of survey respondents indicated that they spend up to 25 percent or more of their time engaged in the generation of non-gift revenues for their organizations. More than 88 percent of respondents stated that they were compensated through a flat fee or salary alone for generating non-gift revenues. When asked whether fundraisers should be allowed to receive commission- or percentage-based compensation from charitable gifts that they generate, nearly 82 percent of those participating in the survey disagreed or strongly disagreed that fundraisers should receive such compensation.[6] These statistics reflect the significant impact of the AFP compensation standards and promulgation of the AFP code of ethics across North America and around the world.

CASE STUDY   BONUS POINTS

You are the director of development of a biomedical research organization. The organization's board decides to establish a bonus plan for all senior managers, based on performance of responsibilities. Your bonus is to be 10 percent of your annual salary if you bring in 10 new corporate sponsorships and another 10 percent of your annual salary if you bring in at least 10 major gifts of $10,000 or more.

A. Would this bonus plan be acceptable under the AFP Code of Ethical Principles and Standards?
   1. Yes
   2. No
   3. It depends
   4. Don't know

Answer: 1. Yes. The AFP Code provides that members may accept performance-based compensation, such as bonuses, provided such bonuses are *not* based on a percentage of contributions (Standard No. 22). In this case, the bonus is a fixed amount, and it is based on the number of sponsorships and major gifts that you bring in, not a percentage of the amount of the contributions.

B. Suppose that instead of the foregoing plan, the size of the bonus was based on your performance in three areas:
   - Number of new volunteers recruited
   - Number of new major gifts received
   - Exceeding the amount raised the previous year in the organization's annual fund

   Could such a bonus plan be acceptable under the AFP Code?
   1. Yes
   2. No
   3. It depends
   4. Don't know

Answer: 1. Yes, as there is no violation of Standard No. 22. This is an example of a performance-based compensation plan that provides financial and nonfinancial indicators that are acceptable under the Code.

C. Suppose that the bonus was a fixed amount (5 percent of your base salary) and was based on achieving three performance targets:
   - Recruiting 50 new volunteers
   - Successfully soliciting 10 new major gifts
   - Growing the organization's annual fund receipts from the previous year

   Would this bonus plan pass muster under the AFP Code?
   1. Yes
   2. No
   3. It depends
   4. Don't know

Answer: 1. Yes. There is no violation of the Code (Standard No.v22), and the criteria are not based on a percentage of contributions.

The essence of the association's prohibition of compensation based on a percentage of funds raised is rooted in the fundamental purpose of the nonprofit sector: to serve the public. AFP holds that percentage-based compensation can encourage abuses, imperils the integrity of the voluntary sector, and undermines the very philanthropic values on which the voluntary sector is based. Individuals serving a charity for compensation must accept the principle that charitable purpose, not self-gain, is paramount. If this principle is violated and percentage-based compensation is accepted:

- Charitable mission can become secondary to self-gain.
- Donor trust can be unalterably damaged.
- There is incentive for self-dealing to prevail over donors' best interests.

In addition, percentage-based compensation, however administered, can produce reward without merit. Fundraising is a long-term process of cultivation that often involves many staff members—not just one person—working together. However, the use of percentage-based compensation ignores that process, focusing instead on just one gift at one moment in time, which may or may not be detrimental to the long-term health of the organization or indicative of the work the fundraiser has put into making the solicitation and receiving the contribution.

The Giving Institute (formerly the American Association Fundraising Counsel, AAFRC), a Chicago, IL–based trade association for fundraising consulting firms, prohibits its member firms from charging fees based on a percentage of dollars raised.[7] The Giving Institute, which represents 34 fundraising consulting firms that work with thousands of organizations worldwide, recommends charging a flat fee or hourly fees for service.

There are numerous standards and codes of ethics developed by other umbrella and specialty organizations that serve the nonprofit and fundraising communities. Many discourage the use of percentage-based compensation, but fall short of prohibiting the practice. These organizations are fearful of violating antitrust legislation in the United States that could result in possible restraint of trade.

A large nonprofit institution has recruited you to be the chief development officer and director of volunteers. The institution offers you a compensation plan consisting of a base salary, a variable bonus based on your performance in several areas of the job, and the institution's standard employee benefits package. The amount of the variable bonus will be based on the number of personal solicitations for major gifts you make, the number of planned gifts that your department writes, and the number of active volunteers the department recruits during the year, plus a percentage of the revenue from all sponsorships.

A. Would a compensation plan of this type pass muster under the AFP Code of Ethical Principles and Standards?
   1. Yes
   2. No
   3. It depends
   4. Don't know

Answer: 2. No; Standard No. 21 states that members shall not accept compensation or enter into a contract that is based on a percentage of contributions; nor shall they accept finder's fees or contingent fees. Standard No. 24 states the members shall not pay finder's fees, commissions, or percentage compensation based on contributions, and shall take care to discourage their organizations from making such payments.

B. Suppose the compensation plan consisted of a salary plus a percentage of all revenue produced from sponsorships and fee-for-service activities. Would this compensation plan be acceptable under the AFP Code?
   1. Yes
   2. No
   3. It depends
   4. Don't know

Answer: 2. No; Standard No. 21 states that members shall not accept compensation or enter into a contract that is based

(Continued)

on a percentage of contributions; nor shall they accept finder's fees or contingent fees. Standard No. 24 states the members shall not pay, finder's fees, commissions or percentage compensation based on contributions, and shall take care to discourage their organizations from making such payments.

C. Suppose the compensation plan consisted of a salary plus a bonus of $5,000 if the annual fund reaches goal and, if the annual fund exceeds goal, a bonus of $1,000 for each percentage point by which it exceeds goal. Would this compensation plan be in accord with the AFP Code?
1. Yes
2. No
3. It depends
4. Don't know

Answer: 2. No; Standard No. 21 states that members shall not accept compensation or enter into a contract that is based on a percentage of contributions; nor shall they accept finder's fees or contingent fees. Standard No. 24 states the members shall not pay finder's fees, commissions, or percentage compensation based on contributions, and shall take care to discourage their organizations from making such payments.

In 1989, as a result of a legal opinion (the Federal Trade Commission found a corporation had violated Section 5 of the Federal Trade Commission Act by restraining compensation related to restricting usage of contingent fees and commissions), AFP modified its standards on compensation to read "Members should refrain from. . . ."[8] This new language softened AFP's stance on percentage-based compensation, merely encouraging members not to engage in such arrangements. AFP members were outraged by this radical change in the association's code of ethics and raised such an outcry that in 1991 the prohibition on percentage-based compensation was added back to the standards. The prohibition remains in place today. These compensation standards receive the most questions by members, the public, and government officials.

Acceptable Compensation and Incentives

Most fundraising consultants or grant writers charge a fee that is typically based on a number of factors, including the value of their expertise and experience, market factors, and the time needed to complete the task. These three factors enable fundraisers to establish a market rate for their services.

The most common question posed by a board member or CEO is how to compensate such fundraising professionals if the organization is new and lacks the necessary start-up money to pay a salary. One of the key reasons some organizations use percentage-based compensation is because it "shares the risk" of fundraising costs. These organizations do not have the funds to pay fundraisers up front, especially with the risk of not getting the money back through their fundraising. By allowing fundraisers to keep a percentage of funds raised, organizations share the risks with them.

However, if the organization lacks the money, there are other ways to compensate a fundraiser that allow for "risk sharing" and are not based on a percentage of dollars raised. Asking fundraising professionals to defer their compensation until their organizations have raised enough money or paying fundraisers in installment payments over time involves sharing risk without resorting to percentage-based compensation. AFP has not conducted research on how many professionals are willing to work under these circumstances, but those who have a personal affinity for or a special connection with a cause may be willing to accept such risk-sharing arrangements.

CASE STUDY   REWARDING EXCELLENCE

Sally has done such an outstanding job as CEO in building the financial support for her environmental organization that the board of directors thinks she should be rewarded. In executive session, they vote unanimously to raise Sally's salary by 25 percent.

(Continued)

A. Would this arrangement be acceptable under the AFP Code of Ethical Principles and Standards?
   1. Yes
   2. No
   3. It depends
   4. Don't know

Answer: 1. Yes. There is nothing in the case to suggest that the increase is tied to the raising of a specific number of dollars. Sally is being recognized for "building the financial support" of her organization. That recognition may include improved communications, cultivation, entrepreneurial activities, and so on. The raise in no way violates any aspect of the AFP Code.

B. If the reward were a one-time bonus instead of a salary increase, would the ethical situation be any different?
   1. Yes
   2. No
   3. It depends
   4. Don't know

Answer: 3. It depends. The ethical situation related to the bonus may be problematic if Sally has been singled out for such a bonus. Standard No. 22 of the AFP Code says: "Members may accept performance-based compensation, such as bonuses, provided such bonuses are in accord with prevailing practices within the members' own organizations, and are not based on a percentage of contributions." Thus, if Sally's bonus reflects prevailing practices within her organization, there appears to be no cause for ethical concerns.

Another frequently asked question concerns incentives or bonus compensation for fundraising professionals. Because of the shortage of fundraising professionals, many organizations use incentives or bonus compensation as a retention and acquisition strategy. In 2001, the average number of respondents to the AFP Compensation and Benefits Study who reported receiving incentive compensation was 22.4 percent overall in the United States and 21 percent in Canada. The percentage of respondents who reported receiving incentive compensation in 2011 was 20 percent in the United States and 16 percent in Canada.

Standard No. 22 of the AFP Code of Ethical Principles and Standards, which addresses incentive compensation, states, "Members may accept performance-based compensation, such as bonuses, provided such bonuses are in accord with prevailing practices within the member's own organizations, and are not based on a percentage of contributions." The term "prevailing practices" is used to emphasize that fundraisers should not be the only person(s) on the organization's staff eligible for incentive compensation. AFP does not prescribe how or when incentive compensation can or should be provided, as this is clearly a management decision.

Organizations have other options to provide incentive compensation to fundraising professionals (see Exhibit 6.1).

In addition, the guidelines that accompany the AFP Code state that AFP members are prohibited from accepting percentage-based compensation, finder's fees, and commissions and that they are not to pay a third-party vendor in this manner.[9] Consequently, fundraising vendors working for a nonprofit (i.e., technology, Internet, and software companies; direct-mail and telemarketing firms; and fundraising consultants, to name a few) are prohibited from charging fees that are based on a percentage of funds raised or compensating their staff in this manner.

EXHIBIT 6.1   **COMPENSATION TABLES**

The following are common ways of providing incentive compensation that are acceptable under the AFP Code of Ethical Principles and Standards.

Percentage of Salary or Fee

One method uses a percentage of a fundraiser's salary to determine the bonus if goals are met or exceeded. For example, 5 percent of a $64,000 salary would be a $3,200 bonus (.05 × 64,000 = 3,200) if goals are met or exceeded.

(Continued)

EXHIBIT 6.1   *(CONTINUED)*

Nonfinancial indicators to be taken into consideration include the following:

- Number of new donors acquired
- Number of gifts upgraded
- Number of new expectancies
- Number of asks made
- Number of moves made

Examples of Incentive Compensation

Incentives can be awarded in many ways, including:

- Development program elements predetermined annually
- Percentage of importance to organization
- Scale and rating system defined

Weight/Rate System

An organization can weight the various fundraising techniques it uses. For example:

Annual fund campaign	40 percent
Major gifts program	40 percent
Bequest program	10 percent
Special events	10 percent

Rating Scale

Using a rating scale, a fundraiser might achieve a maximum total of 400 possible points, using a rating scale that varies between one and four. In order to calculate the number of points, the weight/rate system calculations could be as follows:

Annual fund campaign	40 percent × 4 = 160
Major gifts program	40 percent × 3 = 120
Bequest program	10 percent × 2 = 20
Special events	10 percent × 4 = 40
Total points	340

A fundraiser with 200–300 points might receive a $5,000 bonus, whereas a fundraiser with 300–400 points might receive a $10,000 bonus. In this example, the fundraiser would receive a $10,000 bonus.

For example, if a telemarketing firm compensates its fundraising staff based on a percentage of dollars raised, it is in violation of the AFP Code of Ethical Principles and Standards (Standard No. 24). Similarly, if fundraisers conducting on-street or face-to-face solicitations are compensated based on a percentage of dollars raised, this arrangement is also a violation of Standard No. 21.

THE AFP CODE AND BUSINESS

In July 2007, AFP made a significant change to the code of ethics by adding six new standards.[10] These new standards were added to accommodate the association's new for-profit membership category, "Business Member," which will expand the prevalence of the AFP code of ethics into the business community. Business members will be required to sign the AFP code of ethics upon joining, and by doing so commit themselves and their companies to abide by the code.

ABOUT THE AUTHOR

Paulette V. Maehara, CFRE, CAE, served as the president and chief executive officer of the Association of Fundraising Professionals (AFP) for 13 years, retiring in March 2011. Prior to joining AFP, Ms. Maehara served as chief executive officer of the Epilepsy Foundation and before this she held executive positions with Project HOPE and the American Red Cross (both at its national headquarters and at the National Capital Chapter).

Ms. Maehara has been selected by *The NonProfit Times* as one of the Top 50 Most Influential People in Philanthropy for 10 years, 1999–2009, and most recently, Maehara was awarded the prestigious Hank Rosso Medal for Ethical Fundraising by the Center on Philanthropy, at the University of Indiana in Indianapolis.

Ms. Maehara is a Certified Fund Raising Executive (CFRE), a Certified Association Executive (CAE) and has been a member of AFP since 1987. She now resides in Bluffton, South Carolina, with her husband, Thomas Henderson.

NOTES

1. National Center for Charitable Statistics, *Nonprofit Almanac 2011* (Washington, DC: Urban Institute, 2011), www.urban.org/UploadedPDF/412434-NonprofitAlmanacBrief2011.pdf.
2. Imagine Canada website, www.imaginecanada.ca/node/32.
3. Association of Fundraising Professionals, AFP Compensation and Benefits Study 2012, www.afpnet.org/Audiences/ReportsResearchDetail.cfm?Item Number=11222.
4. Association of Fundraising Professionals, Code of Ethical Principles and Standards of Professional Practice, 1984.
   Standard No. 16. A member shall not accept compensation or enter into a contract that is based on a percentage of contributions; nor shall a member accept finder's fees or contingent fees.
   Standard No. 17. Members may accept performance-based compensation, such as bonuses, provided such bonuses are in accord with prevailing practices within a member's own organizations, and are not based on a percentage of contributions.
   Standard No. 18. Members shall not pay finder's fees, or commissions or percentage compensation based on contributions, and shall take care to discourage their organizations from making such payments.
5. Association of Fundraising Professionals (formerly National Society of Fund Raising Executives, NSFRE), "Percentage-Based Compensation," 1992, www.afpnet.org/Ethics/EthicsArticleDetail.cfm?itemnumber=734.
6. Association of Fundraising Professionals Ethics Committee, Fundraiser Compensation Practices Survey, June 2003.
7. The Giving Institute, Standards of Practice and Code of Ethics, http://givinginstitute.org/about/standards-and-practice/.
8. "FTC Charges AICPA Illegally Restricted Accountants' Fees and Advertising; Group Settles Charges Under Consent Agreement Announced Today," *FTC News*, March 28, 1989.

9. Association of Fundraising Professionals, AFP Code of Ethical Principles and Standards, 2008, www.afpnet.org/files/ContentDocuments/CodeOf EthicsLong.

10. Association of Fundraising Professionals, Code of Ethical Principles and Standards, revised 2007:

Standard No. 7. Members shall present and supply products and/or services honestly and without misrepresentation and will clearly identify the details of these products such as availability of the products and/or services, and other factors that may affect the suitability of the products and/or services for donors, clients or nonprofit organizations.

Standard No. 8. Members shall establish the nature and purpose of any contractual relationship at the outset and will be responsive and available to organizations and their employing organizations, before, during and after any sale of materials and/or services. Members will comply with all fair and reasonable obligations created by the contract.

Standard No. 9. Members shall refrain from knowingly infringing the intellectual property rights of other parties at all times. Members shall address and rectify any inadvertent infringement that may occur.

Standard No. 10. Members shall protect the confidentiality of all privileged information relating to the provider/client relationships.

Standard No. 11. Members shall refrain from any activity designed to disparage competitors untruthfully.

Standard No. 23. Members shall neither offer nor accept payments or special considerations for the purpose of influencing the selection of products or services.

Standard No. 25. Any member receiving funds on behalf of a donor or client must meet the legal requirements for the disbursement of those funds. Any interest or income earned on those funds should be fully disclosed.

CHAPTER 7

Using Donations as Intended

PAUL MARCUS, LLB, CFRE

Accountability breeds response-ability.

—STEPHEN R. COVEY

It is no surprise that a Donor Bill of Rights,[1] which has been adopted by many leading fundraising organizations, declares that a donor's first right is to be informed of the intended use of donations and the capacity of an organization to use a gift effectively.

Obtaining a charitable gift is inspiring, motivating, and exciting. Selfless acts by donors for the betterment of others change lives. But when the euphoria of both giving and receiving a gift subside, difficult ethical issues can arise regarding the stewardship or use of funds as well as accountability to donors.

Through stewardship, organizations take responsibility for gifts entrusted to them. Henry Rosso provides a meaningful description of stewardship as "the heart of philanthropy and fundraising as its arms."[2]

An excellent summary of the steps involved in a stewardship program is provided by Kay Sprinkel Grace:

1. Begin involving donors in the stewardship program with their first gift.

2. Alternate messages to your donors.

3. Allocate budget to stewardship activities.

4. Be sure the stewardship practice is appropriate to the amount of the gift and the budget and image of the organization.

5. Determine what kind of involvement your major gift and planned gift donors, some of whom may be very busy with other organizations and their own professions, want.

6. Coordinate stewardship and cultivation outreach, so that current donors have an opportunity to convey their enthusiasm and commitment to prospective donors.

7. Tie stewardship outreach to the organization's mission.

8. Focus on intangible, rather than tangible, benefits.

9. Maintain stewardship with long-time and generous donors, even when their giving flags.

10. Keep all previous large-gift donors informed and part of your database, even those who make what seems to be a "one-time-only gift," unless and until you hear they no longer want to hear from you.

11. Establish relationships between donors and program staff whenever possible.[3]

Shortly before he passed away, Tim Burchill,[4] executive director of the Hendrickson Institute for Ethical Leadership at Saint Mary's University of Minnesota, wrote a piece describing seven ethical "dilemmas" in fundraising. He noted that "good people make bad choices simply because they are unprepared to deal with the ethical complexities of their actions." One of the "dilemmas" he noted was proper stewardship.

This chapter explores the steps to consider both prior to and after a donation is made to meet our ethical obligations.

BEFORE THE GIFT

Like consulting a good map before leaving on a trip, planning for the acceptance of a gift can eliminate many difficulties in the future. The statement of the Association of Fund Raising Professionals on The

Accountable Nonprofit Organization notes that an organization should do "what it says it will do."[5] Institutions should therefore not accept gifts they cannot deliver on based on donor expectations.

Consider the case[6] of an organization that serves the homeless but is minimally operable. The organization's executive director and board seem unwilling to make the necessary changes to make the improvements, and clients could receive better service elsewhere. A donor calls wishing to give a substantial sum to the organization's counseling program.

This case raises a number of interesting ethical questions. Whose decision is it whether to accept the gift? To what extent is there a responsibility to share the organization's financial situation with the donor, and who delivers this message? Does it matter if the donor is one of the top 100 wealthiest people in the country? If indeed the organization's leadership is dedicated to making substantial improvements and this donation will help, is there a stronger argument that the gift should be accepted?

CASE STUDY — HELPING THE HOMELESS

The organization you work for serves the homeless and has a counseling program that is minimally operable. You know that clients of the program could receive better service elsewhere. The executive director and board are not willing to make the comprehensive changes required to improve the services. A donor calls, wishing to give a substantial sum to the counseling program.

A. What should you do?
  1. Accept the gift and thank the donor.
  2. Advise the donor that the gift can be put to more effective use elsewhere.
  3. Give the donor the name of another organization that can make more effective use of the money for this purpose.
  4. Resign your position.

Answer: 1. Accept the gift and thank the donor, or else resign your position.

(Continued)

Standard No. 1 of the AFP Code of Ethical Principles and Standards states that members shall not engage in activities that harm the member's organization, clients, or profession. Standard No. 2 states that members shall not engage in activities that conflict with their fiduciary, ethical, and legal obligations to their organizations and their clients and profession.

In this case, advising the donor that the gift could be used more effectively elsewhere or giving the donor the name of another organization would cause harm to your organization's fundraising efforts. Although as a fundraiser you have an obligation to support donors' rights and intent, the ultimate use of the money is a management decision and not your call. Since the donor's intent is to help the counseling program (perhaps, even, to improve it), accepting the gift would be consistent with the donor's intent.

As a fundraiser, you agree to support the mission of your organization. Resigning your position would be an extreme move, but if you feel you cannot agree with the mission and operation of the organization to the extent that you must advise donors to direct their gifts elsewhere, then it is evident that you should not be working for that organization.

B. Would it be a violation of the AFP Code to tell the CEO and board that you will accept the gift only if certain specified improvements are made to the counseling program?
   1. Yes
   2. No
   3. It depends
   4. Don't know

Answer: 1. Yes, for the same reasons cited above. The decision whether or not to accept the gift is a management decision and not your call.

It would *not* be a violation of the Code to discuss with the CEO improvements to the counseling program that you think should be made.

C. Would it be a violation of the Code to suggest that the donor offer the gift on the condition that it be used to make certain specified improvements to the counseling program?

1. Yes
2. No
3. It depends
4. Don't know

Answer: 3. It depends; this is a close call. If the donor clearly understands and supports the mission of the organization and desires to improve the counseling program, it would not be inappropriate to discuss with the donor how best to bring about the desired improvement, but this discussion should be done in conjunction with the management of the organization. If the donor does not have such specific intent, however, it is not the fundraiser's prerogative to suggest what that intent should be or how to achieve it.

When determining gift acceptance, each situation will differ, and the overall philosophy should be to encourage a "culture of giving." Proper planning, however, by engaging in donor consultation and adopting appropriate policies, will help the process go more smoothly.

Donor Consultation

It is essential to thoroughly discuss in advance with potential supporters what their intentions are and what they hope to achieve through their philanthropy. This is the best way to satisfy ethical obligations, including Standard No. 14 in the Association of Fundraising Professionals (AFP)'s Code of Ethical Principles and Standards: "Members shall take care to ensure that contributions are used in accordance with donors' intentions."[7]

Key to the discussion is how the donation relates to the mission and priorities of the organization. What will the gift help achieve, and when will the impact be felt? How will the donor be kept informed?

Other matters to discuss include the organization's gift-acceptance policy and changes in circumstances (as described subsequently), legal constraints (bearing in mind that organizations must comply with all applicable laws), and gift recognition.

Of course, where appropriate, everything should be confirmed in a gift agreement signed by all parties.

Gift-Acceptance Policy

It is advisable for organizations to have a documented gift-acceptance policy. Furthermore, it is important that the decision on whether or not to accept a gift be made by individuals separate from the fundraisers, who may feel pressure to maximize revenue. For example, where a university, hospital, or arts organization has a separately incorporated foundation, the acceptance decision should be made by the parent organization outside of the foundation. Integrated institutions should have separate gift-acceptance committees or individuals charged with this responsibility.

Laura Fredricks suggests that a gift-acceptance policy be thought of "as a set of directions that is going to keep your organization on the proper route to soliciting, accepting, and acknowledging gifts and managing and overseeing gift funds."[8] Gift-acceptance policies may be simply general statements of principle or more comprehensive, but they should include reference to the following:

- The right to accept or decline gifts.
- Consistency with the organization's mission, priorities, and principles (such as academic freedom) along with legal requirements.
- Types of acceptable gifts.
- Equitable treatment of donors.
- Charitable receipting and accountability.

Consistency with mission and priorities is very important. The source of a gift may be problematic. For example, an environmental organization will likely have strict policies on this matter. Moreover, while donors' creativity can shape outstanding gifts, prior to accepting a gift outside of the institutional priorities, proper internal authorization should be obtained.

Organizations should review and update their gift-acceptance policies on a regular basis.

Change in Circumstances

Despite the best of intentions, unanticipated changes can occur once a gift has been confirmed. Organizations cease to exist or merge, and even this can be covered in a donor agreement, through a provision providing for the reallocation of the gift to a different entity.

More commonly, a program or department may be eliminated, and the donor may have passed on. The type of clause to be included in a gift agreement might read as follows: "Should circumstances arise that would make it extremely difficult or impossible to comply with the stated purpose of the gift as described above, the organization will endeavor to consult with you or your heirs regarding an alternative purpose, following as closely as possible your original intent. The name of the program will continue to recognize you."[9]

AFTER THE GIFT

A relationship of trust has been created between the donor and the recipient institution once a gift has been made. There is an ethical obligation to properly steward a gift once received. Again, Standard No. 14 in AFP's Code of Ethical Principles and Standards is a good example of the accountability responsibilities of an organization and its fundraising professionals.

It is also in the self-interest of an organization to properly steward its gift, as accountability and demonstrating impact may lead in the long term to the next, perhaps larger donation. The challenge for some organizations is the constant need to find new sources of revenue, as well as the cost of properly administering gifts.

In the guidelines to Standard No. 14, examples of unethical practice are set out:

1. Deciding to change an endowed annual lecture series to biannual, and using the funds in the interim year for travel by department members to an annual meeting.
2. Accepting a contribution for a specific use (e.g., "pediatric genetic clinical research") and then subsequently eliminating that program

and using those funds for another program within the pediatric department without obtaining the consent of the donor.

3. Borrowing from restricted funds for purposes other than the restricted purposes.

4. Diverting into the general operating budget funds intended to cover administrative costs for the program covered by a restricted contribution.

5. Using contributed funds remaining as surplus after the restriction has been fulfilled or has expired without the written consent of the donor.[10]

Again, the right systems in place for gift follow-up and administration will help ensure the proper use of funds. Notwithstanding the best-laid plans, ethical issues, as discussed subsequently, can arise.

Best Practice in Gift Follow-Up

Gift agreement in hand, it is important that copies, where not confidential, be provided to those actually charged with implementing the donor's gift: the recipient program within the organization, the central filing system, and the donor relations or stewardship department if in place. An annual review and meeting if appropriate with relevant units will help ensure that gift intention is fulfilled and that records are maintained. If a separately incorporated foundation is involved, confirmation from the parent organization that gifts have been used as intended should be part of the due diligence.

Regular reporting back to the contributors should be scheduled. This can take many forms, including phone calls, customized stewardship reports, and an annual donor report for all supporters.

Special arrangements should be made for reporting on endowed donations. Donors should be offered a copy of the organization's investment policies, including asset mix and timing for the first disbursement. Like an annual bank statement, a yearly endowment report for supporters should feature the current capital, inflation protection, and income distribution.

Altering Conditions

As noted earlier, agreements should provide for changes in circumstances where possible. Any alterations to the conditions of a gift require donor consent. Nonetheless, in the course of raising funds, difficult issues can arise as shown in the following two cases.

CASE STUDY   HELPING THE NEEDY

You are director of an international emergency relief program. Within one month, three large-scale disasters occur: an earthquake in Mexico, a hurricane in the Pacific, and a flood in the United States. Because of the severity of the disasters and the thorough, constant media coverage, donations have been pouring in. Most gifts are designated to either the earthquake or the hurricane victims; however, many people in the United States have lost their homes in the flood and are in desperate need of help.

As time passes, you see that the relief needs of the hurricane and earthquake victims will be easily met by 60 percent of the relief money coming in, but more than 95 percent of the money is designated by the donors for the hurricane and earthquake, leaving you with insufficient funds to meet the needs in the United States.

A. Would it be a violation of the AFP Code to use some of the donations designated for the earthquake or hurricane victims to assist victims of the flood?
   1. Yes
   2. No
   3. It depends
   4. Don't know

   Answer: 1. Yes. This would be a violation of Standard No. 14: Members shall take care to use contributions in accordance with donors' intentions.

B. To comply with the Code, should you return the donations that were not needed in the areas for which they were designated?

(Continued)

1. Yes
2. No
3. It depends
4. Don't know

Answer: 3. It depends. A member could contact a donor, explain the circumstances, and request permission to use the funds for a different disaster (Standard No. 16: Members shall obtain explicit consent by donors before altering the conditions of financial transactions). If permission is not provided, donations should be returned in order to comply with the Code.

BUILDING ON PRINCIPLE

Bucky Passer is the vice president for advancement and alumni affairs of a small college. After many months of careful cultivation, he succeeds in obtaining a pledge from a famous alum for the largest gift in the college's history. The only catch is, the alum insists that the college put his name on a building that was named for a previous donor (now deceased) as a condition of that donor's gift. Bucky tries to persuade the new donor to change his mind, but the donor is insistent.

A. What should Bucky do?

Answer: Bucky has a responsibility to vigorously and ethically raise funds for his college while ensuring that the intent of all donors is honestly fulfilled. Presumably the naming of the building (in perpetuity) was a part of the donor gift agreement, and to make any changes would be a violation of Standards No. 14 and No. 16.

Bucky may wish to get advice from counsel if the gift agreement is complex or if one was not written. Assuming the board approves significant naming opportunities, he will need to take the matter to his board with the advice that the original donor's name remain on the building.

B. Suppose the new donor agrees to a proposal to name the building jointly for both donors. Would this arrangement pass muster under the "donor consent" standard of the AFP Code?

Answer: The proposal on its own would not pass the "donor consent" test. The guideline to Standard No. 16 notes that a member may meet with surviving family members or legal representatives to discuss potential alteration in the original conditions of a contribution. Again, the gift agreement must be reviewed to ensure the donor's intentions are met whether or not the family members or representatives agree to altering the gift.

C. Suppose the college president and the board of trustees vote to rename the building for the new donor. What should Bucky do?

Answer: For this scenario, we will assume that the president and board have the ultimate authority to accept or decline a gift (certainly a gift of this magnitude). If the board and president are in breach of the terms of the donor's gift agreement and/or not complying with approved donor recognition and naming policies, Bucky should resign from the college. He will not be able to adhere to the AFP Code nor to practice his profession with integrity, honesty, and truthfulness at this institution. Should Bucky also be a whistleblower, or will that conflict with his fiduciary responsibility to the college?

Consider the aforementioned case of an international emergency relief program. Within one month, three large-scale disasters occur: an earthquake in Mexico, a hurricane in the Pacific, and a flood in the United States. Because of the severity of the disasters and the constant media attention, donations have been pouring in. Most of the funds have been designated to earthquake and hurricane relief and the needs will be met, but flood relief is falling short.

The matter is further complicated because charitable receipts have been issued and gifts have been received from tens of thousands of donors who have responded in a heartfelt way. Diverting donations designated to the earthquake and hurricane victims to assist victims of the flood would be unethical. In this case, obtaining permission from the donors to use the funds for a different disaster is required. Otherwise, donations must be returned. Where possible, dealing with the contingency of need being met—either in agreements, pledge forms, or at a minimum in publicity for large-scale operations—can help avoid the challenge in the future.

In the second case, a famous and wealthy alumnus offers the largest gift in a college's history. The only catch is, the alumnus insists that the college put his name on a building that was named for a previous donor (now deceased), as a condition of the gift.

Charities often find themselves in a situation where they previously "undersold" a recognition opportunity, or have already dedicated the best opportunities, while needs continue to grow. The temptation is even greater when the original donor is deceased.

In this case, renaming or even jointly naming the building would be unethical. The only recourse here is to meet with surviving family members or representatives to discuss a possible alteration in the original conditions of the gift. The ethical onus is even greater when a donor has passed away. If consent cannot be obtained, the new gift would graciously have to be refused.

CONCLUSION

Perhaps the most difficult dilemma an organization and its fundraisers face is taking the time and resources to properly accept and steward a gift. Donors can be impatient and "know what they want." Solicitors want to close gifts and "move on" to the next prospect. Boards have a responsibility to maximize revenue.

Yet organizations work hard to obtain donations; they should work equally hard to steward these contributions.

There is a Dutch proverb that states "a handful of patience is worth more than a bushel of brains." Accounting for the use of funds entrusted to an organization is the ethical thing to do. It is also the smart approach for organizations dedicated to building meaningful, long-term relationships with their supporters.

ABOUT THE AUTHOR

Paul Marcus, LLB, CFRE, has held leadership positions in the not-for-profit sector for the past 18 years. A lawyer by training, he is currently the first president and CEO of the York University Foundation, raising funds in support of Canada's third-largest university. In five years the York team has more than doubled revenue and expanded the donor base by 70 percent. Formerly, Marcus was senior vice president of the Mount Sinai Hospital Foundation of Toronto, where the team raised $150 million in phase one of the Best Medicine Campaign (at the time, the largest campaign in Canadian hospital history).

In 2006, Mr. Marcus received the Outstanding Fundraising Professional Award from the Association of Fundraising Professionals (AFP), Greater Toronto Chapter.

In 2007, Paul Marcus was chosen by AFP International to receive the prestigious Community Counselling Service Award for Outstanding Fundraising Professional, only the second Canadian recipient. A frequent speaker and volunteer, Mr. Marcus serves on AFP International's Ethics Committee. He is a member of the Young Presidents' Organization and a Certified Fundraising Executive. He is married to his wife, Pearl, and they have two daughters, Jaclyn and Michelle.

NOTES

1. A Donor Bill of Rights has been adopted by The Giving Institute (formerly the American Association of Fund Raising Counsel), Association for Healthcare Philanthropy (AHP), Council for Advancement and Support of Education (CASE), and Association of Fundraising Professionals (AFP), and has been endorsed by numerous organizations.
2. Henry A. Rosso, "Lessons from a Master's Lifetime Experience," *Rosso on Fund Raising* (San Francisco: Jossey-Bass, 1996), 145.
3. Kay Sprinkel Grace, *Beyond Fund Raising* (New York: John Wiley & Sons, 1997), 169–175.

4. I had the honor of serving briefly with Tim Burchill on the AFP International Ethics Committee.
5. The Accountable Nonprofit Organization was endorsed by AFP's board in 1995 and was developed for nonprofit readers by participants of Accountability and Nonprofit Organizations, a think tank program held in 1995 at the Mandel Center for Nonprofit Organizations.
6. This case and the two others cited in this chapter were developed by AFP and revised by its ethics committee in 2006–2007.
7. AFP Code of Ethical Principles and Standards, www.afpnet.org/files/Content Documents/CodeOfEthicsLong.pdf.
8. Laura Fredericks, *Developing Major Gifts, Turning Small Donors into Big Contributors* (Gaithersburg, MD: Aspen Publishers, Inc., 2001), 140.
9. From the York University Foundation.
10. AFP Code of Ethical Principles and Standards, www.afpnet.org/files/Content Documents/CodeOfEthicsLong.pdf.

CHAPTER 8

Ethical Considerations of Making the Ask

JERRY ROHRBACH, CFRE, CHFC

WHAT IS AT THE HEART OF SOLICITING GIFTS?

The meaning of philanthropy is rooted in the Greek word for "brotherly love." It is an act of giving of our time, money, or other personal resources for the benefit of an individual or an organization. Most often it is an unselfish act based on the altruistic motive of trying to do one's part in addressing the needs one sees in the world. Philanthropy is also big business today, raising hundreds of billions of dollars annually for hundreds of thousands of charitable causes—all solicited by millions of individuals, ads, articles, newsletters, magazines, television and radio stations, billboards, letters, and of course the Internet. Considering the amount of money and the scope of activity involved in asking for and receiving charitable support, one must wonder at the relative lack of controversy or misuse of funds in the charitable sector. Oh yes, we have all heard of some high-profile scandals, but by and large the public retains a very high regard for the philanthropic enterprise and its primary purpose to address charitable needs all over the world.

Charitable giving can thrive only in a context of the highest ethical standard. Prospective donors will hold charitable organizations and solicitors to the highest standard of integrity, honesty, openness, and efficiency. It only stands to reason that if a foundation, corporation, or individual is going to extend charitable support, such donors must firmly believe that an organization will use their contributions forthrightly and efficiently, as represented in the solicitation. Establishing and cultivating a personal connection with prospective donors is the most effective way to solicit and receive substantial gifts. Therefore, it is absolutely crucial to demonstrate that we say what we mean and mean what we say, and do it in a way that effectively pictures the cause we represent.

In an effort to maintain and promote that high ethical standard, many professional associations have developed and adopted well-defined codes of ethics for fundraising. Some of the broad-based leaders in this effort have been the Association of Fund Raising Professionals (AFP), the Independent Sector, the Council for Advancement and Support of Education (CASE), and the Partnership for Philanthropic Planning (formerly the National Committee on Planned Giving). Geographically dispersed governments such as those of the United States, Canada, Mexico, China, Australia, New Zealand, the Ukraine, Hungary, the UK, and the EU have expressed interest in fundraising ethics.

How Are You Approaching Donor Prospects for Gifts?

When an individual or organization approaches a prospective donor, whether it be face to face or via a written, visual, or audio medium, there are some guiding ethical principles that must always be present. It is appropriate to quote the Five Universal Principles for fundraisers that have been developed by the AFP and adopted by many international associations as well.[1]

Five important principles for acting as a fundraiser:

1. **Honesty.** Fundraisers shall at all times act honestly and truthfully so that the public trust is protected and donors and beneficiaries are not misled.
2. **Respect.** Fundraisers shall at all times act with respect for the dignity of their profession and their organization and with respect for the dignity of donors and beneficiaries.

3. **Integrity.** Fundraisers will act openly and with regard to their responsibility for public trust. They shall disclose all actual or potential conflicts of interest and avoid any appearance of personal or professional misconduct.
4. **Empathy.** Fundraisers will work in a way that promotes their purpose and encourage others to use the same professional standards and engagement. They shall value individual privacy, freedom of choice, and diversity in all forms.
5. **Transparency.** Fundraisers stimulate clear reports about the work they do, the way donations are managed and disbursed, and costs and expenses, in an accurate and comprehensible manner.

Honesty, integrity, transparency, and treating our donor prospects with dignity will naturally be the overriding themes in ethical fundraising. Without these, we cannot hope to retain the respect and support of our donors. Honesty engenders telling the truth about what we are soliciting a gift for. Donors have the right to know exactly how their gifts will be used.

Many of us will remember for some years to come the announcement of the American Red Cross stating that it was going to use approximately half of the hundreds of millions in charitable funds raised in response to the attack on the World Trade Center in 2001 for building up blood supplies across the country, for improving their telecommunications, and to prepare for future terrorists attacks. However, the money, everybody thought, was supposed to be used for the families of the victims and not for other Red Cross programs. The American Red Cross suffered intense public ridicule throughout all the national media over this and had to quickly change its policy on the use of these funds to offset a public relations disaster that could seriously jeopardize its ability to raise funds in the future.

Integrity engenders a high level of reliability about what is being communicated to a prospective donor. Exaggerations of the truth, hyperbole, half-truths, and misrepresentations will eventually be seen for what they are and may undermine the fundraising effort. Respect for your donor prospects will engender a dignified and open approach that will avoid arm-twisting, hard sells, and high-pressure tactics. There are instances when a fundraiser is simply exercising undue influence on a donor because of a closely developed relationship. For example, a fundraiser influences a donor to give an entire estate to a charity, essentially disinheriting the donor's children. This is not only unethical, but it also can lead to legal consequences.

In addition, think of the situation in which a solicitation claims that donations will "save the lives of countless children," when in fact the charity is using the gifts to pay down debt. In another example, a solicitor asks a donor for a major gift "to support its work to fight the spread of AIDS in Africa" when in fact 80 percent of the money will be used for the charity's operating needs in its American operations. Sometimes it is easy for a charity to get muddled about these issues, even with the best of intentions, but it is crucial to be as straightforward and honest about how a donor's gift will be used in reality.

Fundraising solicitors come in many forms. A solicitor could be an executive director of a charity, a paid fundraiser who is employed by the charity, a paid independent solicitor on contract for the charity, a board member or other volunteer, or even a friend. It may not always seem obvious to prospective donors just who it is that is soliciting them; still, they have the right to know. It is appropriate and proper to make sure that the prospective donor knows whether or not the solicitor is an employee, a volunteer, or a hired solicitor. If hired solicitors are used by an organization, then complete disclosure on how they are being compensated is the ethical thing to do. A cardinal principle in professional fundraising is that the fundraiser is not to personally gain from a donor's gift. Fundraisers are to be paid a salary or flat fee for doing their job, but they are not to be earning commissions or bonuses as a percentage of philanthropic funds they raise. For a detailed discussion on solicitor compensation issues see Chapter 5.

Volunteer fundraisers are also not to put themselves into a position where they are going to personally gain from a donor's gift. In a healthy philanthropic environment, the intention of the donors is solely to benefit the charitable cause they are interested in, and their philanthropic gifts must be preserved for that intention alone.

Examples of unethical behavior might include an employee fundraiser who receives a personal bequest from a donor who has a long relationship with the employee; a financial advisor, who is also a board member, being paid a finder's fee for bringing in a new major gift from a client; paying a telemarketing company 60 percent of each dollar it raises in new donations to the organization; and a fundraiser accepting a personal gift of more than token value from a donor with whom the fundraiser has become friendly as a result of employment with a charity. Charities would do well to develop internal policies regarding conflicts of interest and the acceptance of personal gifts to mitigate against these practices. Additional comments about these policies appear later in this chapter.

CASE STUDY   MOVEABLE ASSETS

You have built an excellent reputation as development officer for a fine arts organization in a small city. You've been able to enlist the support of many new donors and have cultivated numerous major gifts. You've been offered a higher-paying job at the city hospital.

A. Suppose you have been cultivating a wealthy philanthropist, Mrs. X, who has no real interest in the arts. Mrs. X has numerous health concerns. She is likely to respond favorably to a request for support of the hospital primarily because she has high personal regard for you. Would it be a violation of the AFP Code of Ethical Principles and Standards to ask Mrs. X to make the gift to the hospital instead?
   1. Yes
   2. No
   3. It depends
   4. Don't know

Answer: 1. Yes. It would be a violation of the Code. Standard No. 18 states, "Members shall adhere to the principle that all donor and prospect information created by, or on behalf of, an organization or a client is the property of that organization or

(Continued)

client and shall not be transferred or utilized except on behalf of that organization or client."

In accordance with this standard, the prospect information you have gathered about Mrs. X belongs to your old organization and should not be utilized on behalf of any other organization.

If your personal relationship with Mrs. X predated your employment with the arts organization, then it would not be a violation to begin new discussions with her once you have moved to your new organization, but bear in mind that Standard No. 4 forbids exploiting any relationship with a donor, prospect, volunteer, or employee to the benefit of the member or the member's organization. AFP recommends in this situation that you declare your previous relationship with the donor to your CEO or supervisor.

B. Suppose you have worked hard to write original text for planned-giving brochures that have been successful for the arts group. Would it be a violation of the Code to copy from them when you create the brochures for the hospital?
   1. Yes
   2. No
   3. It depends
   4. Don't know

Answer: 3. It depends, on what and how much you "copy." Standard No. 18 states, "Members shall adhere to the principle that all donor and prospect information created by, or on behalf of, an organization or client is the property of that organization or client and shall not be transferred or utilized except on behalf of that organization or client."

It would be a clear violation of the Code to copy text, slogans, taglines, or special terms you created for the old organization. The general tone, approach, and technical terms of a planned giving brochure are more difficult to define and measure, and therefore it may be more difficult to discern whether similar examples of such matters have been copied. The safest course is to steer clear of text and designs you have used before, or to seek approval from your prior organization. (Sometimes, there are agreements as to who owns the text.) In many cases, they probably would not be effective for the new organization.

C. You know that the hospital and the arts group solicit the same type of donors, although for entirely different purposes. Would it be a violation of the Code to make a list of donors to the arts organization from memory to add to the prospect list for the hospital?
1. Yes
2. No
3. It depends
4. Don't know

Answer: 1. Yes. In accordance with Standard No. 18, all donor and prospect information you have gathered for your old organization must be used only for that organization. That principle applies whether you keep the list of donors in your head, in a notebook, or in a computer file.

In our high-tech society, there are many ways to solicit a prospective donor for a contribution. These range from the nonpersonal to the very personal. Mass mailings of brochures, newsletters and nonpersonalized letters, audiovisual presentations, Internet sites, and blast emails are on one side of the spectrum. On the other hand, personalized letters, telephone calls, and face-to-face solicitations can become very personal.

A central consideration in all solicitations is to respect the preferences of your donors when it comes to their wishes as to how they prefer to be approached. This is not only ethical, but also quite practical if fundraisers intend to stay on the good side of their donors and donor prospects. When someone states the wish not to be solicited by phone, the fundraiser must respect that and appropriately code the donor's record. If an individual wishes to be removed from a mailing list, then it is ethical and practical to honor that wish. This may seem counterintuitive to some. To be successful in raising charitable support, the institution must be actively making the ask repeatedly via a variety of strategic means. Competition for the charitable dollar is intense. Some organizations are just too low key when they approach their prospective donors, and thus are not as effective as they could be. Other organizations may cross the line and become overly aggressive. Striking a balance is the key to success. It begins with one's views on how to treat donors and prospective donors. Being "donor-centric" in the solicitation approach is well known to yield the best results. Donor-centricity is accomplished by simply putting oneself (as the solicitor) in the prospective donor's shoes. What is it that your donors want to hear and learn of your mission and services? What are the passionate, heartstring issues that are really making a difference? What would you like to read about or hear about that would compel you to give? As a prospective donor to a charitable work you care about, how would *you* want to be treated and approached for a gift? An excellent example of a donor-centric approach is found in World Vision's (an international relief mission) tenets that undergird its fundraising efforts.

- Communicating clearly
- Being accurate, complete, current, and relevant in all communication
- Conveying realistic expectations of how a donation will be used
- Honoring supporters' contact preferences and restrictions
- Ensuring all donors' promises are fulfilled
- Seeking opportunities to educate donors on issues of injustice

Because of the increasing use of the Internet, email, and online giving as approaches to fundraising, this chapter pays particular attention to the use of these media in making the ask. Charitable organizations are getting increasingly progressive in how they are using cyberspace to get their solicitations out to their constituents. Again, AFP has done much to give charities and donors guidance on this topic from an ethical point of view found in its creation of the Principles of the E-Donor Bill of Rights, which are as follows:

- To be clearly and immediately informed of the organization's name, identity, nonprofit or for-profit status, mission, and purpose when first accessing the organization's website.

- To have easy and clear access to alternative contact information other than through the website or email.
- To be assured that all third-party logos, trademarks, trustmarks, and other identifying, sponsoring or endorsing symbols displayed on the website are accurate, justified, up-to-date, and clearly explained.
- To be informed of whether or not a contribution entitles the donor to a tax deduction, and of all limits on such deduction based on applicable laws.
- To be assured that all online transactions and contributions occur through a safe, private, and secure system that protects the donor's personal information.
- To be clearly informed if a contribution goes directly to the intended charity, or is held by or transferred through a third party.
- To have easy and clear access to an organization's privacy policy posted on its website and to be clearly and unambiguously informed about what information an organization is gathering about the donor and how that information will be used.
- To be clearly informed of opportunities to opt out of data lists that are sold, shared, rented, or transferred to other organizations.
- To not receive unsolicited communications or solicitations unless the donor has "opted in" to receive such materials.

Moving from the nonpersonal ask to the more personal ask adds some additional challenges. As solicitations become increasingly personal, not only is the organization's integrity crucial, but the solicitor's own personal integrity and credibility are also on the line. Personal solicitors must be reliable, trustworthy, genuine, and believable. When seeking major gifts or significant planned gifts, a gift from a donor should be viewed in the context of a relationship rather than just a transaction. When developing a close relationship with a donor—bonding the donor to the organization and key staff, including the principal fundraiser—the highest level of trust and ethical professionalism must be maintained. In the case where a major gift will involve a legal contract of some sort, including a gift pledge agreement, a named gift agreement, a gift annuity contract, or a charitable trust agreement supplied by the charity, it is essential to advise donors to seek their own independent legal counsel for guidance in regard to these legal agreements. In these gift arrangements, it is not enough just to rely on the trust bond that has been built between the solicitor and the donor.

What happens after the gift is made is just as important as what happens before. Too often fundraisers spend all the energy and effort cultivating and securing the gift; too little time and effort are invested to ensure that good stewardship of the gift is underway and that an ongoing fostering of the donor relationship will be adequately maintained. It stands to reason that most major donors do not appreciate being ignored or given too little information too late on how their gift is making an impact. An angry major donor can be a source of great angst to a charity's leadership and can possibly create a bad public relations situation that no one wants.

What Solicitation Laws and Regulations Does a Charity Need to Comply With?

It seems obvious that it is unethical to break the law or to not simply comply with it. However, it may not seem obvious that at times, there is a difference between what is ethical and what is lawful. For example, it may not be unlawful for a fundraiser to serve as the power of attorney for a key donor or as an executor of the donor's estate, but it may be unethical and a potential conflict of interest. Following the law to the best of one's ability is of course the best course of action. The reality is that governmental regulation of charitable fundraising, in both the United States and Canada, will likely increase in the future. This requires the charity and the fundraisers to be as informed as they possibly can in regard to the federal and state or provincial regulations that apply to their solicitation activities. Being ignorant of the law is never a good excuse for breaking the law. Consulting with qualified legal counsel is essential to be sure legal compliance and procedures are in place.

U.S. federal laws typically deal with how a charity is to acknowledge and receipt a donor's gift for tax deduction purposes. It is amazing how uninformed some charities can be about some of the complexities of these laws. For example, it is illegal to receipt a donor for the full value of a "gift" that is actually in part a payment for a ticket to some event, and in part a charitable gift. It is illegal for a charity to hire an appraiser on behalf of the donor for a gift of fine art or some other collectible. It is illegal for a charity to send a receipt for a stated value for a gift of tangible personal property. It is illegal to receipt a donor for a gift dated for December 31 when the gift was actually received (and postmarked) on January 31. There are similar examples of an eagerness to please a donor or just plain lack of knowledge leading to illegal activities.

Canadian federal law requires charities to be registered if they are to avoid federal income taxation. U.S. federal laws also require specific donor disclosure documents for charitable gift annuities, charitable remainder trusts, and pooled income funds. In the United States, the federal government requires all qualified charities to file Form 990 with the Internal Revenue Service. This form, which is public information, is supposed to reveal the charity's fundraising income and expenses. Increasingly, these annual forms are now being posted on the Internet by various charity watch organizations, and more and more savvy donors are reviewing them. Accuracy and truthfulness in filing these forms is not only legal and ethical, it is the practical thing to do to assure donors that the organization is being run efficiently.

CASE STUDY   NOT-SO-GOOD FORM

You are a development officer in a three-person develop-ment office. One day, while reviewing your organization's government-required federal revenue agency reporting form (such as the Form 990 in the United States or the T-3010 in Canada), you discover a sizable difference between the total amount of donations reported on the form and the amount published in the institution's campaign publicity. When you ask the chief financial officer about the discrepancy, the CFO

(Continued)

replies, "Don't worry, the form is only an informational return. The revenue agency does not audit it."

A. To be consistent with the AFP Code of Ethical Principles and Standards, what should you do?
   1. Inform the chief development officer about the discrepancy.
   2. Tell the CFO that the form must be filled out correctly.
   3. Inform the CEO that the form must be filled out correctly.
   4. Ignore the matter because the form is not your responsibility.
   5. Other

Answer: You have a responsibility to either (1) inform the chief development officer about the discrepancy or (2) tell the CFO that the form must be filled out correctly. This reasoning is based on Standard No. 5, which reads, "Members shall comply with all applicable local, state, provincial, and federal civil and criminal laws."

Standard No. 20 also reads, "Members shall, when stating fundraising results, use accurate and consistent accounting methods that conform to the appropriate guidelines adopted by the appropriate regulatory body for the type of organization involved."

If you see a discrepancy in the reporting of financial information, it is your responsibility to use channels within the organization to bring the organization into compliance with the federal laws, which are paramount to any ethical considerations.

B. Suppose the form is prepared each year by the organization's accounting firm. Under the AFP Code, would this arrangement absolve you from any duty in connection with the form?
   1. Yes
   2. No
   3. It depends
   4. Don't know

Answer: 2. No, this would not absolve you of your obligation regardless of who prepares the form. The same standards apply as in part A of this case.

C. Suppose you bring the discrepancy to the attention of the CEO, and the CEO says, "Don't worry about it, I will take full responsibility." To be consistent with the AFP Code, what should you do?
  1. Inform the board chair that the discrepancy violates the AFP Code.
  2. Keep quiet but make a record of the CEO's answer.
  3. Not worry about it; the practice does not violate the AFP Code.
  4. Ignore the matter because the practice is not your responsibility.
  5. Other

Answer: You could do a few things in response to this situation. You could inform the CEO that it is a violation of the law to sign something that is knowingly incorrect, or you could explore alternative routes within the organization, such as informing the board chair that the discrepancy violates the AFP Code. You should begin by discussing the situation with your immediate supervisor. If there is no response inside the organization, you can take your case to federal officials or go public, in which case you may be protected by the whistleblower protections in your resident country. In the United States, Sarbanes–Oxley may be applicable. However, you may also decide that you do not want to be a part of an organization that does not take accounting of its information seriously.

Currently in the United States, many states require most charities and fundraisers to register with the state. Registration always requires disclosure of the charity's financials for public access. In Canada, currently four provinces have provincial regulations regarding the solicitation of charitable funds. In time other states and provinces will be added to this list. States and provinces have similarities and differences in their fundraising regulations, and it is essential for charities and fundraisers to understand and know how to comply with these laws.

Noncompliance and questionable ethics can sometimes lead to expensive litigation and public humiliation for a charity. There is nothing like a state attorney general bringing your charity to court for unscrupulous fiduciary actions with charitable funds. Suppose that income from a charity's restricted endowment is being used to fund a summer home for the charity's president. Another charity may be caught using a major restricted gift for a purpose other than what the donor had specifically designated, such as using the money toward the construction of a building instead of for scholarships as the donor intended. Think about what happens when it comes to the surface that a donor's major gift intended for the general support of the charity's mission is being used to fund a winter "retreat" for the board of directors, which is conducted on a cruise ship in the Caribbean. Fundraisers, the ones who are most often making the ask, need to be sure they understand the laws themselves and then ensure that the charity is in compliance.

WHAT POLICIES CREATE THE BEST ENVIRONMENT FOR MAKING THE ASK?

There are three types of internal policies that charities should formulate and adopt as part of their operations to make clear to all concerned, especially to anyone representing the charity and soliciting charitable gifts, all of the procedures and issues related to receiving, using, and acknowledging those gifts. The first policy has to do with conflicts of interest. Potential conflicts of interest can relate to almost any employee or board member of a charity. Fundraisers can fall into this trap. They may be employed by a charity while doing moonlighting consulting work with another charity in the same community where the same donors may be supporting both organizations.

If a charity intends to encourage an environment and internal culture of accountability and transparency, a policy dealing with potential conflicts of interest would be advisable; this will help preempt even the perception that conflicts of interest might exist. All fundraisers, whether paid or volunteer, should be aware of their organization's policy and be required to report any perceived, potential, or actual conflict. In addition, prospective donors who wish to personally gain from a business relationship with a charity should be alerted that their charitable donation may appear as a potential conflict of interest. For the sake of preserving a charity's integrity, situations such as these should be avoided.

Second, a policy regarding the acceptance of personal gifts should be drawn up by all charities. Many times employees of charities are put into potentially compromising situations when they are in a position to receive personal gifts. This may be due to a business relationship or, in the case of fundraisers, because of the relationships they have built with donors. In fact, fundraisers often become very close to their donors, perhaps too close in some instances. Think of the donor who offers a beach house to the fundraiser for a week at no charge, or the donor who offers two free tickets to the Super Bowl to the executive director. Then there is the classic situation where a donor names the fundraiser as a beneficiary in his or her will. What is the fundraiser to do? How can these situations be mitigated? A clear policy prohibiting these gifts will do much to alleviate any perception of impropriety and give the employee a means to decline such gifts when offered.

Third, gift-acceptance policies have become increasingly popular among charities as a way to lay out a whole range of issues related to the solicitation of funds; donor acknowledgment procedures and recognition; endowment gift policies; naming gift levels; and the handling of various types of gifts, including securities, real estate, personal property, and various planned gifts. A little research on the Internet will provide a healthy collection of gift-acceptance policies used by a range of charities as models of what is involved. One of the benefits of such a policy is that a fundraiser will know how to handle any number of situations where the parameters of a major or planned gift are being proposed. For example, how will the charity handle planned gifts for naming opportunities? How much does a donor need to give for a named endowment? How many years can a gift pledge be spread for a naming opportunity? What gift agreements need to be signed for various endowments or naming opportunities? What age and gift size limits, if any, does the charity put on gift annuity agreements? Will the charity serve as trustee of charitable remainder trusts? What instructions need to be given to a donor who wishes to give shares from a mutual fund? Will the charity accept a gift of an automobile or real estate, and how is this handled?

CASE STUDY	INTERNET PROFITS AND NONPROFITS

As the director of development of a two-person fundraising operation, you want to use the Internet to streamline your operations. You contact several Internet fundraising firms and get the following proposals:

A. One firm offers to process donations for a stepped fee: $1 for donations of $10 or less, $2 for donations of $11 to $25, $5 for donations of $26 to $100, and $10 for donations of more than $100. Under the AFP Code, is this arrangement acceptable?

1. Yes
2. No
3. It depends
4. Don't know

Answer: 1. Yes. Such fees are standard practice and the position paper AFP Internet Transaction Guidelines[2] states that a donor-initiated transaction involving the transmission of a donation by a website operator to a charity does not fall within the purview of the AFP Code.

B. Another firm offers to process your donations for free in exchange for receiving your prospect list for use in soliciting for other organizations. Would this arrangement be acceptable under the AFP Code?

1. Yes
2. No
3. It depends
4. Don't know

Answer: 2. No. Standards No. 17, No. 18, and No. 19 apply here. This information is confidential, and donors must have the opportunity to have their names removed from lists exchanged with other organizations.

C. Another firm offers to conduct an Internet auction to raise money for your nonprofit organization. The company charges a standard auctioneer's fee of 10 percent of the funds raised, just as it does in its non-Internet auctions. Would this arrangement be acceptable under the AFP Code?
1. Yes
2. No
3. It depends
4. Don't know

Answer: 1. Yes. Under U.S. and Canadian tax law, the purchase of an auction item does not qualify for a tax deduction unless the amount paid exceeds the fair market value. At that point, the fee must be reasonable, and it must be based on the value of the services rendered and not the percentage of contributions. It is important to consult the tax laws in your country to determine whether this situation violates the AFP Code.

When a fundraiser is getting ready to solicit a major gift it is comforting to know exactly what the charity's expectations are in regard to the gift and that everyone related to the gift is on the same page. For example, it would be unwise to accept a gift of one amount for a naming opportunity from one donor and then a lesser gift from another donor for a similar naming opportunity. It could be a very unfortunate and embarrassing situation if a board member tells a donor that a gift of real estate would be wonderful, when after a more detailed review, the charity would be accepting a potential liability that has more problems than it is worth. Should a charity put a donor's name on a building in exchange for a verbal promise of a large planned gift? This may work with one donor, but not necessarily with another. Some might say that it depends on the size of the gift. It is important not to send donors mixed signals or for it to appear that the organization is not able to handle a more complex gift.

Another important issue to be covered in a gift-acceptance policy is the issue of donor confidentiality and privacy. The confidential maintenance and sharing of private information about donors is crucial to preserve the integrity of a charity. Access and use of this information needs to be monitored and controlled through well-documented policy and procedures. Nonpublic information gathered on a charity's donors is the property of the charity for which it is collected. Fundraisers who change employment with one charity and move to another cannot ethically share the previous charity's donor information with the new employer. For a more detailed discussion on this topic see Chapter 3 (on privacy).

A well-thought-out gift-acceptance policy customized to your organization can assure that consistency, competency, and professionalism will be exercised and preserved by all involved in the philanthropic process.

To inspire a donor to make a significant gift for a cause that is compelling and to do it in an ethical, genuine, and professional manner is indeed a rewarding experience for all involved. As fundraisers, if we will strive for the highest standards in the best practices of the philanthropic endeavor, we will continue to play an important role in making things better in this world. As a final thought, I'd like to conclude with a quotation from one of the great philanthropists of recent history, John D. Rockefeller Jr.:

> Some people have a less keen sense of their duty and responsibility than others. With them a little urging may be helpful. But with most people, a convincing presentation of the facts and the need is far more effective. When a solicitor comes to you and lays on your heart the responsibility that rests so heavily on his; when his earnestness gives convincing evidence of how seriously interested he is; when he makes it clear that he knows you are no less anxious to do your duty in the matter than he is, that you are just as conscientious, that he feels sure all you need is to realize the importance of the enterprise and the urgency of the need in order to lead you to do your full share in meeting it—he has made you his friend and has brought you to think of giving not as a duty but as a privilege.

ABOUT THE AUTHOR

Jerry Rohrbach, CFRE, ChFC, has more than 35 years' experience as a professional fundraiser and developed a specialty in securing planned and major gifts. He spent nearly 19 years with Temple University, Philadelphia as a director in major gifts and planned giving. He is currently serving as director of Planned Giving for the Eastern Pennsylvania and State of Delaware Division of the Salvation Army. In addition to his Certified Fund Raising Executive (CFRE) certification, Mr. Rohrbach earned the Chartered Financial Consultant designation (ChFC) in 2000. He is a popular speaker at professional conferences, workshops, and round tables on a variety of topics and is a co-founder of Planned Giving Day in Philadelphia. He is an emeritus board member of the Association of Fund Raising Professionals, Greater Philadelphia Chapter, having served as president and chairman of the board. In 1998, he was elected as Fund Raising Professional of the Year. He also served on the National Ethics Committee of AFP. He earned his bachelor's degree from Philadelphia Biblical University and his master's from Wheaton College in Illinois.

NOTES

1. International Statement of Ethical Principles in Fundraising, www.afpnet .org/Ethics/IntlArticleDetail.cfm?ItemNumber=3681.
2. AFP Internet Transaction Guidelines, www.afpnet.org/ResourceCenter/ ArticleDetail.cfm?ItemNumber=3287.

Honesty and Full Disclosure

SAMUEL N. GOUGH JR., CFRE

Recognizing potential problems is the beginning of the process of seeking solutions to ethical issues. It is common for questionable actions and decisions to be made because of failure to foresee the problem in the first place.

Ethical decision making involves a process of appraising and contemplating decisions and actions in light of prevailing conditions; questioning the appropriateness of behavior and the resulting good or harm to other people. This process calls for asking the right questions and for evaluating the available choices.

Questions about ethical fundraising frequently focus on donor privacy, bonus structures, executive compensation, personal relationships between donors and staff members, and fundraising costs. These queries usually reveal issues of honesty and full disclosure. This chapter offers guidance on ethical issues requiring honesty and full disclosure.

In 2004, the Independent Sector, a nonprofit, nonpartisan coalition of nonprofit organizations, foundations, and corporate philanthropy programs approved a Statement of Values and Code of Ethics.[1] In part the statement states, "Any code of ethics is built on a foundation of widely shared values."

The values of the Independent Sector include:

- Commitment to the public good
- Accountability to the public

- Commitment beyond the law
- Respect for the worth and dignity of individuals
- Inclusiveness and social justice
- Respect for pluralism and diversity
- Transparency, integrity, and honesty
- Responsible stewardship of resources
- Commitment to excellence and to maintaining the public trust

Ethical issues are different from legal issues that are determined by law or moral issues that are guided by character or conduct. For example, it is illegal to deliberately provide misleading information about an organization or to evade government laws and regulations.

Ethical behavior is less well defined. Ethical considerations start with clarifying what should be done and how ensuing actions affect others. Determining what is important and what is worthwhile helps to identify the need for ethical decisions.

To reach an ethical conclusion, questions may arise about the appropriateness of behavior and the good or the harm that might result. Thus, ethics becomes a process of appraisal and contemplation of actions and conditions. This process calls for asking the appropriate questions and evaluating the choices available.

In 1988, the Council for Advancement and Support of Education (CASE) convened a two-day "Ethics Seminar for Senior Professionals" for institutional advancement officers. Dr. James A. Donahue, then Associate Professor of Ethics in the Department of Theology at Georgetown University, served as facilitator.

Donahue presented five "C"s as "Some Criteria for Fund Raising Ethics."[2]

1. **Consistency.** The trust that constituents develop in institutions and individuals resulting from a pattern of regular and predictable behavior.
2. **Coherence.** The guiding principles and standards that reflect unity and harmony, which provide a common point of reference.
3. **Continuity.** A person's past or an organization's history, which provide the ethical backdrop for assessing present and future actions.
4. **Communication.** Direct and candid conversations with constituents and colleagues, which prevent misunderstandings and

create an environment where ideas and decisions can be shared, analyzed, challenged, and sharpened.

5. **Convictions.** The basic beliefs contained in the organization's mission statement.

During the course of the seminar, Donahue added a sixth "C"— creativity. **Creativity** is a way to develop opportunities, to explore imaginative and inventive options, and to educate constituents.

While in attendance, I asked that a seventh "C" be considered:

> **Consequences.** The effect that an action has on people and conditions (Consequences may be positive or negative; but either way they are a factor when decisions involving ethics are made.)

An illustration of four of the "C"s may be found in the following story.

An organization's fundraising committee set a major gift campaign goal of $250,000 to be raised between January 1 and December 31. With one week to go before Christmas, $235,000 had been raised in gifts and pledges.

The chair of the committee, an influential and goal-oriented person, suggested that the development officer call a press conference at the beginning of the new calendar year to announce that the campaign had been successful in reaching its goal. He reasoned that at the rate the gifts and pledges had been received during the last three weeks and in view of the supposition that year-end giving was expected to take the campaign "over the top," it would be safe to assume that $15,000 would be received in the next two weeks. He implied that if the press conference were not called, he might withdraw his $25,000 pledge and his future support of the organization.

The two immediate courses of action presented to the development officer were:

1. To call the press conference with the hope that the goal would be met by January 2.
2. Not to call the press conference and risk losing the support of the fundraising committee chair.

CHAPTER 9 HONESTY AND FULL DISCLOSURE

However, there were other choices available to the development officer.

He could tell the chair that if he called the press conference, the truth about the current status of the campaign at that time would have to be told, whether they had reached the goal or not. If no press conference was called, it might be possible to close the campaign without a lot of fanfare, but with an acknowledgment that X% of the goal had been reached and that the remainder of the goal was expected by Y date.

Another option would be to ask the chair if he would increase his pledge or his fundraising efforts to whatever amount was needed to make the campaign a success on the first day of the new year. To back up that statement, the chair might have to pledge as much as another $15,000.

The last alternative allows for use of Donahue's "C"s: (1) open communications, (2) putting forth professional and organizational convictions, (3) showing creativity, and (4) presenting the consequences of future actions.

When considering whether an action is ethical, the adage "tell the truth, the whole truth, and nothing but the truth" might be the response. This might imply that the solution to all potential ethical dilemmas is to be truthful (honesty) and to reveal everything (full disclosure). However, is honesty an absolute or is it relative to specific circumstances? Furthermore, what is meant by full disclosure?

Honesty and full disclosure are separate and distinct. Honesty is often linked to integrity. "Integrity is telling myself the truth. And honesty is telling the truth to other people," states Dr. Spencer Johnson, noted author of books on self-development. His books include *Who Moved My Cheese?* and *The One-Minute Manager.* Full disclosure means revealing all the relevant facts.

HONESTY

In *Cultivating Diversity in Fundraising,* Janice Gow Pettey refers to a Navajo observation. "The good man is honest and tells the truth to the people, and has a lot of money and livestock. And he's helping some people, poor people—so he's a good man."[3]

A factor that must be taken into consideration when discussing honesty is individual values. Values are often determined by religion or spirituality or the lack thereof. It should be recognized that people have a wide range of core values that guide their decisions and actions.

It should not be assumed that people who profess to be religious or spiritual are any more or less honest than the nonreligious. Honesty is not the exclusive province of people with religious beliefs. What is relevant is the definition of honesty and how people apply those definitions in their personal and professional lives. For example:

A church had a ban on accepting contributions from individuals involved in producing or selling alcoholic beverages. One of the members of the church was the CEO of a company that distributes liquor to stores in another city. For years this man has been a generous anonymous contributor to his church. The pastor of the church has known for years of this member's generosity, and although he has never revealed the donor's identity or the source of the donor's wealth, he has gratefully accepted his gifts.

Has the pastor been honest? Should he have denied the donor the right to do what the donor feels is the right thing to do based on his beliefs? Should the pastor let his congregants know the source of these gifts without revealing the identity of the donor?

There are numerous stories about the honesty of Abraham Lincoln, sixteenth president of the United States, and about his religious beliefs or spirituality. He never joined a church, but after the death of his four-year-old son, Edward, in 1850 he regularly attended Presbyterian churches.

A partial explanation of his views on religion is revealed in a passage that he wrote in 1846[4]:

> That I am not a member of any Christian Church, is true; but I have never denied the truth of the Scriptures; and I have never spoken with intentional disrespect of religion in general, or of any denomination of Christians in particular. . . . I do not think I could, myself, be brought to support a man for office whom I knew to be an open enemy of, and scoffer at, religion. Leaving the higher matter of eternal consequences between him and his Maker, I still do not think any man has the right thus to insult the feelings, and injure the morals, of the community in which he may live.

Whether his honesty resulted from his belief in a supreme being or from reading Thomas Paine, a recognized "free thinker," has been debated. In any case, his reputation for honesty remains unchallenged.

Neither honesty nor integrity should be abandoned for personal gain or to achieve an advantage in any situation. An unintended error or a difference of opinion does not jeopardize either honesty or integrity. However, willful deceit or the twisting of facts does not meet the standards for either. There is an African proverb that states, "One falsehood spoils a thousand truths."

When a potential donor asks for information about an organization to which he or she is considering making a gift, most often that person learns about the successes that have been realized—the people or causes helped, the plans for the future, and the donors who support the organization. That is honest information, but is it the full truth? What about the programs that have not worked, the plans made in the past that have failed, and the budget shortfalls? A Yiddish proverb asserts, "A half truth is a whole lie."

It has become more and more evident, especially in recent times, that a cover-up (usually a lie) is worse than the offense about which the lie was concocted. This has been true not only in the political and for-profit arenas, but in the nonprofit sector as well. This undermines the trust that the public has in the nonprofit sector.

There is little question that honesty is expected by an organization's constituents. When a lie is discovered, the ability to persuade as well as credibility may be lost. Mark Twain admonished, "When in doubt, tell the truth."

Occasionally the truth can be harmful to another person or expose that person to risk. Public acknowledgment of gifts not only thanks and expresses gratitude to the giver, it also may stimulate others to follow the example of the donor. However, a donor's relatives might take exception to the fact that a gift is made to an organization rather than to them. A donor may not want his or her generosity to an organization to be publicized for fear of being identified as a potential target of crime. In such cases, it may be in the donor's best interest to maintain anonymity.

Consider the example of a couple, major donors, whose generosity was publicly acknowledged by a representative of the organization in front of the donors and the other guests present. The donor's wife's face turned ashen. When asked what was bothering her, she said that she wished that the announcement had not been made. She felt that many people did not know that they had that much money to give and as a consequence, she became fearful for their safety. This was a case of good intentions on the part of the staff member yielding an unfavorable result. It was an honest mistake.

Is omitting the names of donors dishonest? Islam is one of the fastest growing religions in this country. However, some Muslims are reluctant to donate or to have it known that they are giving to Islamic causes. The reason might be to reduce public scrutiny or their desire not to draw attention from government agents. Therefore, unless required by law, is it acceptable to not publish donor lists?

The Association of Fundraising Professionals (AFP) Code of Ethical Principles and Standards states[5]:

> Members of AFP are motivated by an inner drive to improve the quality of life through the causes they serve. They serve the ideal of philanthropy; are committed to the preservation and enhancement of volunteerism; and hold stewardship of these concepts as the overriding principle of their professional life. They recognize their responsibility to ensure that needed resources are vigorously and ethically sought and that the intent of the donor is honestly fulfilled. To these ends, AFP members, both individual and business, embrace certain values that they strive to uphold in performing their responsibilities for generating philanthropic support. AFP business members strive to promote and protect the work and mission of their client organizations.

AFP members aspire to

> Practice their profession with integrity, honesty, truthfulness, and adherence to the absolute obligation to safeguard the public trust.

This portion of the Code sets a high bar for its members to reach. It equates integrity, honesty, and truthfulness with safeguarding the public trust, which is their responsibility. It extends to all of one's dealings with everyone with whom one comes in contact. Lowering the bar can have consequences, as shown in the following story.

A two-year, $50,000 grant was made to a youth literacy organization based on a proposal that was submitted to a major foundation. As a condition of the grant, the organization had to raise outright, unrestricted funds from individual contributors in an amount equal to one half of the grant.

As the grant funding came to a close, a final report was submitted to the foundation. It stated in part that individuals had contributed over $26,000 in gifts and pledges. The last of those pledges were to be fully paid within one month following the date that the report was submitted. The executive director of the organization signed that report believing that the organization had satisfied the conditions for funding. However, the development director had not informed the executive director that one-third of the unpaid pledges were made verbally with no written commitments from the individuals; thus, if the people who made them did not honor them, they were uncollectible.

First, it is questionable as to whether the crediting of pledges toward the required matching amount met the requirement that the funds had to be outright. Second, there was no guarantee that remaining unpaid pledges would be honored. The foundation rejected the report and requested that the grant funds be returned.

We are taught to repress our true feelings in order not to hurt others, which may mean honesty and truthfulness may suffer. We may say we feel fine when we do not. We may apologize when we do not mean it. We may even say thank you when we are not appreciative. These actions continue into our professional lives. Do they compromise our ability to be honest?

Marianne M. Jennings recounts a study, "Honesty and Survivor Management" by Frank Shipper, which points out that honesty is an important characteristic for workplace survival that is highly regarded by peers. However, being honest takes courage: "Some managers had survived the countless corporate downsizing over the past decade. These were managers who had not suffered a corporate loss of employment,

while many like them were left unemployed for spans of up to a year."
Shipper

> found two very important characteristics about these managers. First,
> this was a diverse group of people that included women and men
> of various ages, different races, and varying styles of management.
> Second, both the managers themselves and their employees used one
> common descriptive adjective: honest.

> They gave credit to their employees for ideas taken forward to senior
> executives and explained to them new rules, new strategies, and policy
> or procedural changes with candor. The business urban legends of
> politicking, networking, and climbing the ladder of succession on
> the backs of others were foreign to these managers. These managers
> understood not just being honest, but also the importance of the gospel
> principles of kindness and fairness. They were successful because of
> these qualities, not despite them. Their employment security resulted
> from a simple devotion to basic commandments of honesty.

Another reason to strive for honesty is to protect one's reputation,
which is among the most valued assets that a development professional
possesses. Reputation follows the development professional throughout
his or her career, and beyond.

A favorable reputation is built on a number of factors—accountability,
creativity, competence, fairness, professionalism, impartiality, and
diligence, to name a few. Honesty is paramount. In *All's Well that Ends
Well*, William Shakespeare said, "No legacy is so rich as honesty."[6]

In some cases, what might appear to have negative consequences
by being honest may have just the opposite effect. In the mid-1980s
researchers at Cleveland State University made a startling discovery.[7]

They conducted an experiment by creating two fictitious job candidates, David and John. The candidates had identical resumes and letters
of reference. The only difference was that John's letter included the
sentence "Sometimes, John can be difficult to get along with." They
showed the resumes to a number of personnel directors. Which candidate did the personnel directors overwhelmingly prefer? They preferred
difficult-to-get-along-with John. The researchers concluded that the

criticism of John made praise of John more believable. Exposing John's wart actually helped sell him. In this case, honesty was the best policy.

As I think back about the people who have mentored me, I realize that each of them was highly respected based on his or her reputation—a reputation that was highlighted by honesty. It is likely all of them at some point in their careers had their devotion to honesty tested.

Candor is often used as an alternative word for honesty. However, definitions of candor include frankness, bluntness, and outspokenness. Candor is no substitute for honesty. One can be frank, blunt, and outspoken without being honest.

A development officer at a shelter for homeless women tells a potential donor without reservation, "All gifts to the shelter provide direct assistance to the women who are served." If that was an honest statement, then none of the funds raised are applied to the costs of administration or fund raising. That is a frank, blunt, and outspoken statement, but is it an honest one?

FULL DISCLOSURE

Transparency is the hallmark of full disclosure. However, questions may arise concerning the process of providing the information to assure full disclosure. What does the public have the right to know? Is that information presented in ways the public will understand? Is the information provided without prejudice or bias? Does full disclosure help or hurt in building a relationship and establishing trust with constituents? Would the lack of information have an impact on current or future decisions or actions?

In answering those questions, consider:

- The effect, positive or negative, that full disclosure would have on helping the public to form opinions and to make decisions about the organization.
- The ability of the public to understand the context in which the information is provided.
- The consequences of either offering or not offering relevant information about the organization.

If there is a question about releasing information, remember that in most cases the information may come to light anyway; if it is discovered that information has been withheld, credibility and trustworthiness may be tarnished. Are the consequences worth the risks?

On the other hand, confidentiality is a significant factor that might argue against full disclosure. Who is the appropriate or authorized person to be providing the requested information? Avoid unauthorized disclosures.

A fundraiser has a responsibility to protect confidential information, particularly concerning prospects and donors and possibly financial and personnel matters. Regarding prospect and donor information, it is generally acceptable to have discussions with immediate staff colleagues in the organization, if there is a compelling need for such discussions. In going beyond these individuals, judgment must be employed.

One situation that might occur is a local news reporter calling the Manager of Donor Records to ask how much money a particular donor has given to the organization. Is this manager authorized to provide that information, and if so, would answering the question be a violation of donor confidentiality? What if the reporter happens to be on the organization's board? Does the response change?

Another common disclosure issue is the way in which fundraising costs are reported. For example, suppose a 14-year-old organization providing educational enrichment services to approximately 350 middle and high school suburban youth is at the end of the second year of a three-year capital campaign. The goal for the campaign is $10 million. In its campaign update report, a summary of the audited results is published for general distribution, as shown in Exhibit 9.1.

One of the organization's potential major donors asks how the $8 million was determined. What does "raised" mean and how many donors have contributed in what amounts? In answer to the question, it is explained that:

- Only written, signed pledges can be legally collected; should a person not honor a pledge, the organization would have to weigh the consequences of possible legal actions.

EXHIBIT 9.1   **SUMMARY OF AUDITED RESULTS**

Outright gifts and grants	$ 955,000
Pledges to be paid in full within five years	1,175,000
Bequests	1,500,000
Insurance policies owned by the organization (face value)	1,500,000
Irrevocable trusts	1,000,000
Revocable trusts	1,000,000
Real estate	500,000
Gifts-in-kind	500,000
Total	$ 8,130,000

- Bequests (i.e., gifts through wills) may be changed by the person making the bequest without the organization's knowledge.
- Insurance policies owned by the organization are counted at face value, but they may be cashed by the organization prior to maturity for less than the face value.
- The value of the gifts of real estate is determined through independent appraisals and the value of such gifts depends on their conformity with the organization's mission.
- Maintenance and insurance costs should be factored into the value of the gift.
- Gifts-in-kind are items of tangible personal property such as art, books, computer equipment, and automobiles. They are accepted by the organization if they conform to the mission of the organization. They are recorded at their fair market value. Gifts-in-kind valued in excess of $500 must be accompanied by a deed of gift, and a statement of the fair market value as determined by the donor. The value that a donor places on such gifts might be more than the actual value. (The IRS and the organization require an independent appraisal of gifts-in-kind valued at more than $5,000.)

And in answer to the second question:

- There were three outright leadership gifts, all from board members, in amounts of $50,000, $30,000, and $25,000. One-third of the total came from publicly traded securities.
- Two board members made gifts and written pledges of $100,000 each, with initial payments of $50,000 each in publicly traded stocks.
- One anonymous donor pledged, in writing, $500,000 to the campaign. The pledge is to be fully paid within five years.
- Two donors made challenge gifts of $50,000 each with the stipulation that their commitments be matched one-to-one by individuals who make gifts of $200 or more each before the campaign ends.
- Seven local and regional foundations made two-year grants that total $650,000.
- Corporate contributions over the past two years have equaled $400,000.
- Seventy-five thousand dollars has been received from personal, mail, and telephone solicitations and special events, along with smaller, outright gifts, grants, and pledges not solicited.
- Nine people notified the organization that they had placed the organization in their wills as outright beneficiaries. When their estates are settled, the organization might receive as much as $1,500,000.
- The parents of 23 of the youth being served either took out new, whole life insurance policies or converted existing, whole life policies with a total face value of $1,500,000. In each case, the organization is named as owner of the policies. (Four other parents told the head of the organization that they had designated the organization as contingent beneficiary of term life policies. These expectancies were not included in the report.) The age range of these parents is 32 to 49.
- The grandparents of five of the youth created charitable remainder unitrusts in amounts averaging $200,000 each. The organization

is named as a beneficiary and gifts will be received upon the death of the surviving spouse.

- The organization was notified by five elderly "friends" of the organization that they had revocable trusts that totaled $1 million.
- A local developer offered a tract of forest land, with three buildings on it, that is 60 miles from the organization. For tax purposes, the land is assessed at $500,000.
- A major computer manufacturer donated $500,000 in hardware, software, furniture, and peripherals.

The information described in these two lists demonstrates full disclosure. What effect has full disclosure had on helping this potential donor to make a positive or negative decision about a gift? Has the information provided the person with an understanding of how the total of $8 million was reached? Are there consequences of providing this information in this form?

Full disclosure should reveal all relevant facts and provide a person with the ability to make comparisons and judgments. Often, but not always, full disclosure is associated with accountability.

A discussion of full disclosure should mention "The American Competitiveness and Corporate Accountability Act of 2002," commonly known as the Sarbanes–Oxley Act, which was enacted in 2002. Although Sarbanes–Oxley is directed at for-profit entities, there are implications for the nonprofit sector as well.

In 2003, GuideStar.org published an article about Sarbanes–Oxley in collaboration with BoardSource and Independent Sector.[8] It began with the following statement:

> Passed in response to the corporate and accounting scandals of Enron, Arthur Andersen, and others of 2001 and 2002, the law's purpose is to rebuild public trust in America's corporate sector. The law requires that publicly traded companies adhere to significant new governance standards that increase board members' roles in overseeing financial transactions and auditing procedures.

According to the article, the seven primary provisions of Sarbanes–Oxley include:

1. Independent and competent audit committee
2. Responsibilities of auditors
3. Certified financial statements
4. Insider transactions and conflicts of interest
5. Disclosure
6. Whistleblower protection
7. Document destruction

The portion of Sarbanes–Oxley that addresses disclosure is worth noting. The article states that disclosure includes "information on internal control mechanisms, corrections to past financial statements, and material off-balance sheet transactions (adjustments). The Act also requires companies to disclose information on material changes in the operations or financial situation of the company on a rapid and current basis."

The article continues with recommendations regarding the implications for nonprofit organizations, such as releasing accurate financial information to constituents, the media, and public officials. By law, tax-exempt organizations must make their Forms 990 or 990-PF available to anyone who requests them. However, there are questions about accuracy and timeliness. Many nonprofit organizations endorse the IRS's preference for electronic filings as a remedy.

Full disclosure goes beyond financial matters. It expands to providing information about the crafting of policies and procedures, revealing involvements of board and staff members in outside activities that may pose potential conflicts of interest, and outlining the process for reaching management decisions. The appearance of impropriety can be as damaging as any actual infraction of ethical behavior. Full disclosure of all the facts often dispels that appearance. There is a parable about The Goat and the Goatherd that goes as follows:

A Goatherd had sought to bring back a stray goat to his flock. He whistled and sounded his horn in vain; the straggler paid no attention to the summons. At last the Goatherd threw a stone, and breaking its horn, begged the Goat not to tell his master. The Goat replied, "Why, you silly fellow, the horn will speak though I be silent."

Do not attempt to hide things that cannot be hid.

Before launching any fundraising effort, an organization should have clearly published policies and procedures for the acceptances of gifts, grants, and pledges. These policies and procedures should address strategic development issues and should be available for board and staff members to share with potential donors, when needed.

The key points to be covered include:

- Fund types
  - Operating funds
  - Endowment funds
  - Quasi-endowed funds (donor designated)
- Matching gift contributions
  - Procedures for processing
  - Gift receipts
  - Authorized signers
- Revenues that are not contributions
  - Procedures for processing
    - Sales of items
    - Special fundraising events
    - Raffles
    - Auctions
    - Fees for services
    - Loans
- Grants and contracts
  - Submitting the proposal
  - Follow-up to notification of acceptance from the funding agencies
  - Disbursements for grants and contracts
  - Fees
- Revenues—monetary methods of giving
  - Payment by check

- Methods of payment for donations other than cash or check (credit cards, wire transfers, and payroll deductions)
- Stocks and bonds—transfers, sending a stock/bond certificate with a stock/bond power form, and transferring the stock/bond to an account at a brokerage firm
- Revenues—nonmonetary methods of giving
  - Gifts-in-kind
  - Bequests
  - Insurance
  - Trusts and annuities
  - Tax forms
  - Required documentation
  - Tax issues
- Real estate—policies for acceptance of real property, organization-related property, investment property, and other property
- Endowed funds procedures
  - Endowment memorandum of understanding
  - Outright gifts
  - Planned gifts
- Gift opportunities
  - Unrestricted endowment funds
  - Restricted endowment funds
- Methods of giving
  - Gifts of cash, checks, and securities
  - Planned gifts
  - Gifts of real estate
  - Gifts of tangible personal property
  - Gifts of intangible property
  - Tax benefits to donors
- Gift or grant processing
  - Acceptance
  - Transmitted
  - Processing
  - Acknowledgment
  - Recognition

Written guidelines for board and staff members regarding their activities as well as procedural matters should be maintained.

A major university receives a bequest that includes valuable real estate (a vacation home) located several hundred miles from its campus. The president of the university makes a recommendation to the board of trustees that the property be sold to the highest bidder and that the proceeds from the sale—less expenses, such as real estate broker's, assessor's, and maintenance fees and taxes—be deposited in the university's unrestricted endowment fund. The board accepts the president's recommendation during a regularly scheduled board meeting.

After all other business at that meeting was concluded, a board member offers to buy the property immediately, outright, as is, with a promissory note in an amount twice the value that the county used for tax purposes. She notes that the acceptance of her proposal would save the university the broker's, assessor's, and maintenance fees.

What factors should the other board members take into consideration when making a decision about this offer? If it is decided that this sale should be made, how should full disclosure be handled?

CASE STUDY   FINDING HELP WITH BIG DONORS

Prudence Goodall, CFRE, is vice president for development of a major community charitable institution. She is approached by Tom Dollar, an active financial planner who is well connected in the community. Tom tells her he has a client who is ready to make a major gift ($100,000) for tax purposes and is willing to make the gift to Prudence's institution. Tom offers to reveal the name of the client to Prudence if she will ensure that the investments from the gift are made through Tom's firm.

A. Would it be a violation of the AFP Code of Ethical Principles and Standards for Prudence to agree with this deal?

Answer: Generally, this scenario offends the aspiration section of the Code. Any member engaging in this *quid pro quo* behavior of agreeing to reward the source of a prospective major donor with future business is clearly not acting with integrity, honesty, and truthfulness.

While the case does not fit into the narrow definition of "finder's fees," the same logic applies. The Guidelines under Standard No. 24 identify the three principles underlying the standard: (1) philanthropic giving is a voluntary action for the public benefit, (2) the seeking or acceptance of philanthropic contributions should not provide personal gain to anyone, (3) donors and potential donors must be protected from pressure or coercion.

Paying Tom Dollar would amount to paying a fee for generating a gift. Agreeing to ensure that the funds were invested in Tom Dollar's firm is an indirect form of personal inurement to Tom.

B. Suppose that Tom offered to reveal the identity of his client if, in return, Prudence would list Tom as a benefactor donor (gifts of $5,000 or more) on the institution's donor wall when the client makes the $100,000 gift. Would it be a violation of the Code for Prudence to agree to the deal on these terms?

Answer: The analysis under section A applies to this scenario also, as it is another form of *quid pro quo*. By identifying a name of a prospective donor who ultimately gives a gift, Tom would be providing information, and this would be a violation of Standard No. 24, if the equivalent "value" of his information were treated as a gift-in-kind. Further, any recognition he would receive could be seen as a form of personal inurement.

C. Suppose Tom offered to actually secure the donation if Prudence would give him 10 free tickets (face value: $10,000) to the institution's forthcoming charity gala. Would it be a violation of the Code for Prudence to agree to the deal on these terms?

Answer: Yes, whether Tom is compensated in cash, in future business dealings, in recognition, or in gala tickets, he is still expecting and receiving a perceived or real payment for finding the donor.

In another case, the full-time chief financial officer at a hospital contracts to provide accounting services in his free time to a group of grassroots organizations that advocate for the rights of immigrants. The hospital has no policies that address the outside employment of its employees.

Is the chief financial officer obligated to let the hospital know of this arrangement or of any other outside employment that he has, even if the other employment is unrelated to accounting or financial matters; if so, why? If not, what effect might not disclosing this information have on the hospital?

It should be noted that another reason for considering the appropriateness of honesty and full disclosure is the potential impact on the rights of donors, privacy, appearance of impropriety, and conflict of interest. These are subjects that are discussed in other chapters of this book. "To Accept or Not to Accept," one of the sample cases for ethics education provided by AFP, portrays how full disclosure might address a potential conflict of interest. Another case for ethics education, "Like Mother Like Son," illustrates the overlap of the appearance of impropriety and conflict of interest with honesty and full disclosure.[9]

Conclusion

Even the motives of prospective donors need to be examined to protect nonprofit organizations as well as the individuals charged with making decisions about what constitutes a charitable gift. The attorney for an estate, representing the deceased, offered to give a large university an apartment building only a few blocks from the university's campus. It was the attorney's contention that the university could convert the three-story, 15-unit building into a dormitory. The only condition of accepting this gift would be that the university could not sell the building within three years of the time that it took ownership.

Arrangements were made for two people from the university to see the building. During that visit it was noted that the interior of the building was in poor condition, and several code violations were apparent. Also, in talking with a few of the residents, it became evident that they were paying unreasonably high rents because they had few other choices of accommodations in the immediate area.

Such a gift would most likely result in a sizeable charitable deduction to the estate and reduce the taxes that the estate might have to pay. A stipulation of the gift was that the university could not sell the property for three years upon acceptance of the property.

The two university officers agreed that there were ethical, moral, and legal reasons why this gift could not be accepted. There seemed to be no clear charitable intent.

The lawyer was thanked for thinking of the university and told that the university declined to accept the gift.

Written board-approved policies, procedures, and actions often prevent any misunderstandings that might arise between the public and a nonprofit organization regarding honesty and full disclosure. It is the responsibility of the organization's leadership to ensure honesty and full disclosure. It is not a responsibility that should be taken lightly. Honesty and full disclosure take into consideration all of the ramifications of these aspects of ethical behavior.

If honesty is not possible, the alternative to truthfulness is to lie. The costs of lying include loss of credibility and reputation because most often, the lie will be discovered. In cases where telling the truth could be harmful, full disclosure might not be prudent.

A colleague once expressed a rule to use when considering whether a proposed decision or action meets the highest ethical standards. Ask if you would want your mother to read about it in the newspaper the next day. While there are no easy answers when questions arise about honesty and full disclosure, this approach might lead one to an ethical outcome.

About the Author

Samuel N. Gough, Jr., CFRE, is a co-founding partner and principal of The AFRAM Group, a fundraising, consulting firm headquartered in Washington, D.C. Having spent over 22 years in institutional advancement directing staff and managing resources at his alma mater, Howard University, he has been a full-time consultant for a wide range of nonprofit organizations over 17 years in the areas of nonprofit organizational management, development and advancement, and communications.

Mr. Gough was one of the initiators of the development program at Howard University, and he directed the Department of Development as the University successfully concluded its One Hundred Million-Dollar campaign. This was the largest and most successful campaign of any of the Historically Black Colleges and Universities and most of the majority educational institutions at that time.

Mr. Gough has written and often spoken on advancement-related subjects. He was a contributing author to *Cultivating Diversity in Fundraising*, by Janice Gow Pettey, which won the 2003 Council for Advancement and Support of Education (CASE) award for best research. He was also a contributing author to *Diversity in the Fundraising Profession*. His chapter in this publication entitled "Five Reasons for Nonprofit Organizations to Be Inclusive" was selected for reprint in *Reappraising Timeless Topics*.

Mr. Gough holds a bachelors degree in psychology from Howard University. He currently chairs the board of directors of the National Center on Black Philanthropy. He chairs the Publishing Advisory Committee and has served on the Ethics Committee, the Diversity Summit Task Force, and the International Community Ambassadors of AFP.

He is married to the former Betty A. Rhone and they have one son, Sean Nathan.

NOTES

1. "Statement of Values and Code of Ethics for Charitable and Philanthropic Organizations," *Independent Sector, A Vital Voice for Us All* (Independent Sector, February 3, 2004).

2. Barbara Marion, "New Directions for Philanthropic Fundraising,"*Decision-Making in Ethics: Putting Values Into Practice*, No. 6 (San Francisco: Jossey-Bass, Winter 1994), 59–60.

3. Janice Gow Pettey, *Cultivating Diversity in Fundraising* (New York: John Wiley & Sons, 2002), 87.

4. Abraham Lincoln, *Handbill Replying to Charges of Infidelity* (July 31, 1846).

5. The Association of Fundraising Professionals Code of Ethical Principles and Standards, www.afpnet.org/files/ContentDocuments/CodeOfEthicsLong.pdf.

6. William Shakespeare, *All's Well that Ends Well*, Act 3, Scene 5.

7. "Admitting Flaws," Afterhours Inspirational Stories, www.inspirationalstories .com/7/709.html.

8. "The Sarbanes–Oxley Act and Implications for Nonprofit Organizations," GuideStar, www.guidestar.org/rxa/news/articles/2003/sarbanes-oxley-act-and-implications-for-nonprofit-organizations.aspx.

9. Ibid.

CHAPTER 10

Choosing a Leadership Role: A Vision for Action

BARBARA A. LEVY, ACFRE

Without doubt the climate of ethical improprieties in the 2012 nonprofit sector can be attributed to grave omissions on the part of fundraising professionals and the boards they serve. It is evident that colleagues and peers are not bringing ethical ideals and practice into the realm of dialog and awareness. While challenging, the accusation is made with the observation that the majority of development professionals accept and sign their organization's code of ethics and then file it away for safekeeping. This chapter proposes ideas and techniques that will help development professionals and board members better understand ethical issues and take positive action in support of ethical practice. Many ideas are included that will illustrate options available to those who are willing to step forward in a leadership role.

The inconvenient truth (to borrow a phrase from former vice president Al Gore) is that the finger cannot be pointed in one direction. In fact, there are many responsible for the paucity of exemplary action, the lack of trust, and the resulting hesitancy on the part of savvy donors and volunteers to commit time, energy, and funds to support philanthropic causes. But there is hope.

There are actions to be taken by all that will help repair the fabric of this, the most philanthropic nation in the world. Philanthropy is rooted in intrinsic, individual, and personal values. One might argue that with so many different individuals representing a myriad of differing values, it would be difficult to agree on just a few. How is it possible to select the common values a board believes should be embraced by the organization it serves? Of course people and their values are different. What a despairingly dull world this would be if individuals brought only the same thoughts and ideas to the table. Yet, the more the topic of values is explored, the more likely it will be that we discover that the values people hold are more similar than different. For example, who does not value honesty, integrity, and trust? Who did not relate to the deepest, most personal value of family and home when this country was so viciously assaulted on 9/11? These were the values that inspired the unprecedented outpouring of contributions from this nation, from people who desperately wanted to make a difference.

Values drive every action, but they are taken for granted. Although people are very vocal about what others should do, scant attention has been given to voicing the values held most dear. With rare exceptions, people do not speak publicly of values such as honesty and integrity. These are assumed. When someone asks a question, the assumption is that the answer will be an honest one.

The charge now becomes imperative. The task before us is to take responsibility, to construct a leadership role in the promulgation, and support the promotion of ethical work. The price to be paid, if no one will take the reins, is greater chaos, escalation in unethical practice, and the ultimate destruction of the third sector.

As with many worthy efforts, an examination of one's own beliefs and values is important. Before you even begin to consider a leadership role, a look within will help you to identify your own understanding and biases regarding ethical practice. The inventory of ethical practice begins with the acknowledgment of personal values. Awareness of these values creates opportunities to initiate dialog with others about values and their relationships to ethical action. Having reviewed the personal inventory, one does not have to venture far to recognize the external improprieties that undermine ethical practice. Whether the issue is lack of confidentiality, abuse of trust, manipulation of information, or misrepresentation of intent, examples can be found daily in the news.

Ethical practice must be enhanced and promoted. When individuals choose to take a leadership role, the potential impact can be enormous. But such impact does not happen without a plan. An outline of one such plan includes the following three steps:

1. Initiate dialog about the most serious ethical concerns.
   a. With colleagues
   b. With board members
   c. With donors
2. Plan for the dissemination and promulgation of relevant information concerning ethical practice.
   a. List techniques for introduction.
   b. Identify and prioritize the audiences.
   c. Select techniques for dissemination.
   d. Develop a timeline.
   e. Establish ongoing practices.
   f. Teach steps to ethical decision making.
   g. Mentor more leaders.
3. Take it public.
   a. Implement plans for dissemination.
   b. Stir up the media with creative ideas to engage interest.
   c. Publicize the ethical focus of a board or an organization.
   d. Engage constituents in a dialog.
   e. Promote greater understanding of issues.

This chapter began with the observation that most fundraising professionals sign a code of ethics and file it away with other documents. Many professionals believe that ethical practice is their responsibility; however, the involvement of others is not only critical but necessary. In fact, ethical practice, much like the laws affecting fundraising practice, are typically considered to be solely the responsibility of development staff. The fundraiser must know and practice by these guidelines, but that in itself is not enough. The responsibility includes bringing discussion of these guidelines to the table. This is a surefire way to ensure that program staff and board members acquire a working knowledge and understanding of them. When one chooses to take a leadership role, initiating the dialog is the first step.

The proposed steps to engage others in ethics dialog inevitably lead to using illustrative examples. The following example demonstrates why it is imperative that all staff members of an organization have a working knowledge of ethical practice. Consider the following scenario:

A program staff member has developed a strong relationship with a major donor. The donor has become very interested in a current project and is concerned that limited funding may impede the progress of the project. Believing that he has a great idea, the donor approaches the staff member with the idea that his investment advisor has offered, for a fee, to find a client who would make a substantial gift to the project.

Now, consider the impact of this suggestion to a staff member who has no understanding of finder's fees and the highly unethical practice such an arrangement represents. The staff member, excited by a potential major gift, implements the suggestion of the donor's new funding idea and makes the contact with the investment advisor. Now, how does the development officer deal with this very complex and ill-advised action?

The pitfalls of this example illustrate the complex problems that exist when program staff is enthusiastic about but uneducated in fundraising protocol. A person receiving a finder's fee for bringing a gift to the organization is receiving personal inurement for a philanthropic transaction, a violation of IRS regulations. Once the transaction has been completed, it is extremely difficult to go back to the donor and the broker to tell them that they have violated the law. The resulting communication challenge can become extremely unpleasant. Worse yet, if the transaction and payment is consummated before the development office knows anything about it, little can be done to correct it.

This is a perfect illustration of why it is critical for all staff members to have basic knowledge and training in ethical practices. If the development director had provided such information to program staff, they would know that anything related to development must go through the development office. Even without further training, a staff member having that limited knowledge will be able to prevent problems. Taking it to the next step, providing staff a basic knowledge of ethical practice can assure the development office that entrusting program staff with donor relationships is an excellent way to strengthen donor loyalty.

Consider another example: On January 15, the support staff person answers a call. She recognizes the name of an important donor to the agency and makes a special effort to let this person know that she recognizes who is on the phone. The donor is pleased with the recognition and says, "I just wanted to let you know that I am putting a December 31 check in the mail for my contribution. Because I wrote it on December 31, I want to be certain that it is credited to the year in which it was written." The switchboard operator, eager to be helpful says, "Of course. Don't worry about a thing. I'll make certain that the development office knows this is for last year."

How easy it is to forget about our frontline staff! Our support staff member is the first person with whom a caller will connect. Of course, if you have one of those systems in which a caller has to punch the right buttons to get the development office, it may be your assistant who answers. The latter situation is less likely to cause a problem as hopefully, your development staff is better informed about fundraising policy and law. But, for the sake of illustration, let us consider the more removed support staff person who answers the phone. This person is doing a great job by recognizing the name of a donor and extending a special greeting. Furthermore, the individual believes that he or she is doing a great job by answering the donor's important question. However, he or she has not been trained enough to know that unless the date of cancellation on the envelope is December 31, by an IRS ruling, the check will count in the current fiscal year. Referring to the suggested steps to begin our process, step one recommends initiating dialog.

STEP 1: INITIATING DIALOG

The most practical exploration of ideas through dialog involves your organization's stakeholders, the people most likely to have a stake in ethical practice. Test various statements and ideas to create stimulating and challenging dialog. Examine the concentric circles of stakeholders

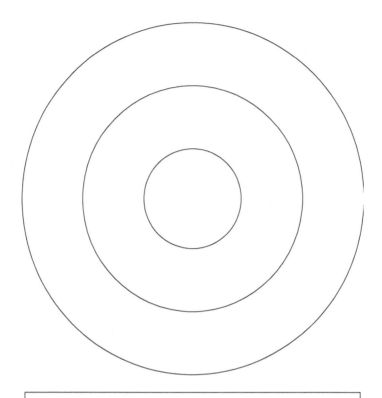

Inner Circle = Staff and board
Middle Circle = Constituents being served, neighborhood residents, families of constituents, current and past donors
Outer Circle = Community, state, out-of-state relatives

EXHIBIT 10.1   **CONCENTRIC CIRCLE OF RELATIONSHIPS**

and begin with those closest to the center (see Exhibit 10.1). Reviewing the circles and recognizing that staff and board are at the very center (heart) of an organization provides a guideline for understanding who your stakeholders are and how much they are likely to care about your organization. The further you go from the center, the less commitment and caring you are likely to find.

A different suggestion for fundraisers is to begin by asking staff colleagues to fill out the Ethics Quick Quiz (see Exhibit 10.2). This Quick

Quiz illustrates several common ethical issues. One could also choose to develop a different version of this tool. For example, select some of the standards illustrated by any code of ethical practice. This might include the standards published for most professions such as accountants, lawyers, estate planners, fundraisers, and gift planning specialists. The questionnaire is designed to be taken by anyone, staff or board member. It highlights various standards and will guide the content of the dialog.

EXHIBIT 10.2   **ETHICS QUICK QUIZ**

This questionnaire is designed to highlight a person's understanding of ethical issues. It is recommended that each person take the quiz and then score himself or herself using the accompanying sheet of answers.

1. T_F_ It is acceptable to hire a fundraising practitioner and compensate that individual with a percentage of the money raised.
2. T_F_ By hiring someone who is local, an organization gains access to the people that individual has successfully solicited in the past.
3. T_F_ A check dated December 31 is credited in that calendar year.
4. T_F_ Conflict of Interest Policies are guidelines to which board members may turn for recommendations. These policies do not have a legal impact on an organization.
5. T_F_ Development professionals may not give legal advice in the area of planned giving.
6. T_F_ Bonuses may not be ethically accepted by development professionals.
7. T_F_ Development professionals may share a donor's personal file with another donor interested in making the same kind of gift.
8. T_F_ Development professionals must declare conflicts of interest just as board members must.
9. T_F_ Once a donor gives a contribution designated for use in a particular program, the organization may use it to fill whatever need exists.
10. T_F_ Fundraising professionals may pay finder's fees for bringing new gifts to the organization when the gift identified is larger than the fee.

(Continued)

11. T_F_ Fundraising professionals may rely on other staff in the organization to track all legislation affecting the development process.
12. T_F_ Board members may rely on the chief financial officer to ensure that donations are used as intended by the donor.
13. T_F_ The CEO or executive director is held accountable for all unethical fund development practices in a nonprofit organization.
14. T_F_ Fundraising professionals are held accountable for activities that may conflict with their fiduciary, ethical, and legal obligations to their organizations and clients.
15. T_F_ A board member proposes a new prospect who has worked with the development officer in his former position at another organization. It is not ethical for the development officer to be the first contact to that prospect.

QUICK QUIZ ANSWERS

1. F – It is unethical to compensate any development staff based on a percentage of funds raised.
2. F – It is unethical for a development professional to bring donor information or contacts from one organization to another.
3. F – The envelope containing the check must be postmarked by December 31 to be credited in that year.
4. F – A board or staff member with a conflict of interest can inflict serious legal damage on an organization by ignoring that conflict.
5. T – Only attorneys may dispense legal advice.
6. F – When bonuses are available to all staff at the same level as the development professional, they are acceptable as long as they are not based on a percentage of funds raised.
7. F – A donor file is highly confidential and is not to be shared with anyone not on staff.
8. T – It is as important for staff members to declare conflicts of interest as it is for board members.
9. F – An organization that accepts a designated gift may use it only for the designated purpose.
10. F – It is highly unethical for a fundraising professional to pay a finder's fee.

11. F – Fundraising professionals are responsible for being aware of and complying with any law affecting the practice of raising money.
12. F – Board members must rely on the development professional to ensure that dollars raised are used as intended by the donor.
13. T – The CEO is responsible for all staff and board activity within his or her organization.
14. T – All fundraising professionals are responsible to ensure that all fundraising activity complies with ethical and legal standards.
15. T – A fundraiser who has a relationship with a prospect from a former position of employment may not ethically be the first contact with that prospect. It would appear that the fundraiser has brought this prospect from the previous organization.

The purpose of this exercise is not to point out who has wrong answers but to initiate discussion and establish understanding of ethical practices. When everyone has had an opportunity to complete the exercise, questions may be raised by the group (or the leader), and discussion can include all participants. From that point forward, the leader will be able to determine what participants know and what more they need to know.

The Quick Quiz can facilitate the development of your staff ethics education plan. Colleagues are not going to welcome a long dissertation on ethical practice. However, they will be grateful to have a basic knowledge of good practice, one that will help them keep relationships with donors strong, positive, and ethical. Some of the most important information to share concerns issues of confidentiality, the use of designated funds, the knowledge of when a gift must be postmarked to qualify as a year-end gift, and the issue of finder's fees. The conversation generated beyond these few issues serves to enhance the relationship between organization staff and the development department. Such discussion also opens the door to asking questions of development staff at any time.

The next step is to initiate dialog with board members. The discussion is likely to be a little more challenging because most board members believe they are ethical people and therefore do not need coaching or mentoring. Use of the Ethics Quick Quiz provides participants a method to quickly assess the level of their understanding of ethical practice. By keeping the results confidential, participants will be able to safely engage in learning and comprehending the vital importance of ethical standards and practice.

The importance of establishing a basis for values held by the group is essential. When people know that they will not be judged by others and that people sitting at the discussion table have similar values such as honesty, integrity, openness to new ideas, and so forth, conversation can be much more productive. People who believe that they cannot ask what they consider "dumb" questions are not likely to participate in the process. No one promised that dialog about ethical issues would be easy. There are times when there is no right or wrong answer, and there are times when it is very difficult for people to understand the reasoning behind a pronouncement of "unethical." Explaining the thought process behind this pronouncement illustrates the need for the leadership role to be dedicated to learning how to communicate. Messages must be delivered in ways that will not be challenging to the participant, and questions must be answered diplomatically, with a commitment to patience and understanding.

An alternative process to initiating dialog involves board members who meet with a small group of like-minded colleagues to share what they know, think, or worry about with regard to ethical practice. They might have an example of a code in hand or not. Such dialog can generate an interest in deeper exploration of issues, standards, and practices. It is in this familiar and safe setting where most people are likely to understand the connection to values. When people experience the "aha!" moment during their dialog about ethical issues, they often become energized and enthusiastic about the dissemination of information regarding ethical practices. When board members take on such a leadership role, they establish an uncontested, highly visible endorsement of ethical practice in the public eye. The people who have taken part in the initial small groups can then form new groups and begin the process again. Through repetition, endorsement from leadership, and ongoing dialog, the concepts of ethical practice begin to have more meaning to volunteers. From the staff perspective, there can be no greater testament to good teaching than when a mentor can step aside and observe the mentee perform.

Initiating a conversation with donors requires different strategies. In Appendix C of this book there is a copy of the *Statement of Values and Standards for Excellence of the Tucson Symphony Orchestra* (TSO). This document was developed and approved by the board of trustees as a guideline for their ethical practice.

The purpose of this document was to cement the ethical practice of this nonprofit organization, to articulate all components for both internal and external audiences. It begins with an introduction that focuses on the need to earn public trust in every possible way. The watchword *transparency* was enhanced by openness and responsiveness to public concerns. The statement of values includes both personal and organizational values. The Standards for Excellence and Guiding Principles include the following areas:

- Mission
- Governance
- Responsible stewardship
- Financial and legal
- Human resources
- Openness and disclosure
- Program evaluation
- Fundraising

The members of the board are proud of their work and its outcome. Using this document has become an effective tool for engaging donors in a conversation about ethical practice. Further, it clearly states the TSO values and practices.

Still another approach would be to include a statement of values in a newsletter. This will require some explanation about the importance of values. This section might begin with an opening statement about the exercise completed by the board regarding the values members find most important to their role with the organization. This too provides a good launching pad for dialog. Collaboration will help in creating additional methods to bring the topic to the discussion table. Spreading the word represents progress. It takes time, creativity, and commitment.

Whether the conversation is with colleagues, board members, or donors, one of the first questions to be considered when facing an ethical dilemma is whether the issue is one of ethical, legal, or moral implications. An example of such a dilemma is the case in which a magazine that regularly features naked or scantily clothed women offers to make a large contribution to a charity serving abused women. The catch is that the donor requests public recognition for this large contribution. The charity must determine whether or not to accept the gift. This issue is considered by many to be a moral issue, but is it illegal or unethical? Not necessarily. It is fairly predictable that 50 percent of any group will vote for the charity to accept the gift and the remainder of the group to reject it. The issue however is not an ethical one unless by accepting the gift, the organization or some of its constituents are harmed. If the resulting harm is clear, it is an ethical violation. If it is not clear, the issue becomes gray in nature, and the close relationship between ethical and moral impropriety comes into play.

The point in this illustration is the need to discuss and determine each issue and to be certain that if it becomes labeled an "ethical dilemma," it really is. There are some circumstances in which an issue is questionable in all three areas—ethical, legal, and moral. The previous case of the donor and the support staff is one of those. The legal component is the IRS requirement that in order to count a donation in the previous year it must bear a December 31 postmark. The ethical issue involves telling the donor that if the organization counts the donation in the previous year, the organization is not complying with applicable laws. And the moral issue is that a donor may be asking the organization to do something that she or he knows is wrong. The latter statement could most likely not be proven, but it does illustrate a breach in all three areas.

The Association of Fundraising Professionals (AFP) Case of the Dear Friend can be found in the case study entitled "The Dear Friend." This case provides an example that is well worth discussion in either a staff or board setting. The case lays out the circumstances of a staff member named John Dear. John has developed a strong relationship with a donor. When the donor unexpectedly passes away, she leaves a significant portion of her estate to this staff member and a smaller portion to the college. This case illustrates an example of an action that many would consider to be out of John's control. If he has developed a good relationship with a donor during that person's lifetime, and if that donor wishes to recognize his or her regard for John, then it is sometimes difficult for an observer to understand what could be unethical about accepting the gift stipulated in the will. It is a classic example of an act that is legal but unethical. In most ethics codes it is considered unethical to receive gifts of any significant dollar value. It also refers to the *appearance* of impropriety as an ethical issue. It could appear to the public that John is receiving personal inurement from his relationship with the deceased donor. If the public believes that it is illegal, it might just as well be illegal because perception is 99 percent of reality!

CASE STUDY   THE DEAR FRIEND

John Dear, the chief development officer for a large agricultural college, has a reputation in education circles for prowess in cultivating major gift prospects. Minnie Bucks is a wealthy farm widow and long-time personal friend of John's. Over the years she has made several large donations to the college. One day Minnie dies unexpectedly. A codicil in her will leaves a small portion of her wealth to the college and a much larger portion to John. The college president and the chair of the board call John in and tell him that to accept a bequest from a donor he has befriended would violate the AFP Code of Ethical Principles and Standards and, if word got out, would harm the college's reputation for propriety. They ask John to "do the right thing" and quietly turn over his bequest from Minnie to the college.

A. What should John do?
   1. Keep the money
   2. Turn over the money to the college

(Continued)

3. Make a gift of his own to the college equal to the amount of the bequest
4. Return the money to Minnie's estate
5. Other

Answer: 5. Other. If John has not yet received the bequest, he should refuse the funds and direct the executor and/or the courts to distribute the funds as they see fit. If he has already received the funds, the correct answer is 4. The primary AFP Standard in play here is Standard No. 4, which prohibits exploiting relationships for personal gain. However, an equally important issue is the appearance of impropriety, which brings Standard No. 1 into the discussion. This is an important and classic example of an act that is legal but unethical.

B. Suppose that for several years Minnie had been confined to a nursing home, where John visited her frequently, but she received few other visitors. Suppose, further, that the bequests to John and the college were made in a codicil drafted by Minnie's attorney the week before she died. Would John be violating the AFP Code if he accepted the bequest?
   1. Yes
   2. No
   3. It depends
   4. Don't know

Answer: 1. Yes, for the same reasoning as in the previous question.

C. Suppose John rather than the attorney had drafted the codicil, but it was properly signed by Minnie and witnessed by the nursing home administrator. Would John be violating the AFP Code if he accepted the bequest under these circumstances?
   1. Yes
   2. No
   3. It depends
   4. Don't know

Answer: 1. Yes; Standards Nos. 1, 2, 4, and 6 all apply. Fundraisers should never give legal advice or draft legal documents.

STEP 2: DISSEMINATION AND PROMULGATION

Planning for the promulgation and dissemination of information requires matching the message to the appropriate audience. To make the process even more complex, the generations represented by multiple audiences (such as those identified in the Concentric Circles) will value different pieces of the message and will want to hear it delivered in different ways. The constituents or stakeholders of an organization do not represent just one generation, but many. In their book *When Generations Collide*, Lynne Lancaster and David Stillman articulate the difference in how each generation lives, works, and relates. In Chapter 2, Lancaster and Stillman describe the four generational segments: Traditionalists (1900–1945), Baby Boomers (1946–1964), Generation Xers (1965–1980), and Millennials (1981–1999). Speaking of the generations' identities, they state, "The events and conditions each of us experiences during our formative years determine who we are and how we see the world. As a result of these events and conditions, each generation has adopted its own 'generational personality.' Icons can be people, places, or things that become reference points for a generation. These icons and conditions play out in the lives of each of the generations; they shape the attitudes, values, and work styles that the generations bring with them when they come to work every day."[1] All who venture across the tightrope of understanding the communication of ethical values to a broad generational audience would be well served to review the specific preferences of each generational audience *before* attempting to deliver the message!

The concept of rewards as related to ethical practice proposes that different generations will feel good about or rewarded for the work involved to understand and spread the word about ethical practice. The following illustrations of what has meaning for each generation suggest that enticing the buy-in or participation of each generation will require some thought about why this is worth the effort.

The following list highlights brief descriptions of the differences in perceived rewards among the generations:

- Traditionalists: "The satisfaction of a job well done."
- Baby Boomers: "Money, title, recognition, the corner office."
- Generation Xers: "Freedom is the ultimate reward."
- Millennials: "Work that has meaning for me."[2]

The upshot of this example? It is well worth the time to research how each generation wants to receive communication and recognition. In other words, you need to know the style of communication that will capture their attention. Preparing a presentation to a group of college students regarding ethical practice will demand some consideration of the language and examples that will capture their attention. Once you have captured their interest, it will be possible to better communicate the importance of such things as values and ethical standards.

Remember the time when a thank-you note was simply not acceptable unless it was handwritten? Today, one needs to consider the generational characteristics of the recipient. It may be hard to believe that different generations would view the handwritten note from differing perspectives. But just acknowledging that there is a difference suggests yet another opportunity to gather a different group for dialog. This time include a few cross-generational representatives. Test the waters with this group and find out which generation prefers which method of communication. The results may surprise you. When organizations acknowledge that there are differences among the generations, when they indicate that they are interested in knowing their opinions and preferences, the respondents may ratchet up their impression of the organization. After all, who is not impressed when asked their opinion?

It is especially impressive when that preference is employed. Teaching or promoting ethical practice will fall on deaf ears if it is perceived as preaching. In order to engage a different generation, it is helpful to understand what is important to them. When you can engage a group inclusive of different generations you have found one of the keys to success. Further, you are much more likely to have your message understood.

One final comparison provided by Lancaster and Stillman includes the following responses regarding a clash point around training:

- Traditionalists: "I learned it the hard way; you can, too!"
- Baby Boomers: "Train 'em too much and they'll leave."
- Generation Xers: "The more they learn, the more they stay."
- Millennials: "Continuous learning is a way of life."[3]

Dialog with constituents and donors takes on differing formats and requires agreement on desired outcomes. The message is "Look ahead, be certain you know what your desired outcome looks like!" One would consider initiating such dialog only after fully fleshing out the message to be delivered with staff and board. Once there is agreement within the organization about the key messages to be delivered, the messages will provide fuel for the dialog.

TEACHING STEPS TO ETHICAL DECISION MAKING

Not every audience will want to go through this process, but it is invaluable for those who will be dealing with the consideration of ethical dilemmas. It is an educational practice for those who want to better understand what ethical decision making involves. The steps are found in Exhibit 10.3. This process was developed in 1988 by four very experienced professionals in the field:

- Professor James Donahue, Georgetown University
- Michael Josephson, the Josephson Institute for the Advancement of Ethics

- Barbara H. Marion, CFRE, Consultant and Faculty, University of San Francisco
- Professor Michael O'Neill, University of San Francisco

This team of professionals developed a series of five questions to ask when trying to assess the more ethical path. They additionally included Michael Josephson's Ethical Principles Checklist. The remaining three tools include Five Criteria to Apply to the Decision, Three Intuitive Tests to Reference, and Four Impediments to Ethical Behavior.

EXHIBIT 10.3   **FIVE QUESTIONS TO ASK WHEN TRYING TO DETERMINE THE MORE ETHICAL PATH**

1. What are the critical facts of the situation?

   Take time to view the problem from all sides. Write down the critical facts. Review them. Have someone else review the facts for or with you. What else do you need to know? How serious is this issue?

2. What are the key, perhaps competing, values and ethics at stake?

   Is this an issue of honesty, of respect, of justice, of accountability, of fairness, or all of these? Rank the values and ethics in priority order by impact and importance. Rarely do all merit the same weight.

3. Who are the players and stakeholders in the decision?

   Does it involve donors, clients, staff, the community, volunteers, oneself, or even philanthropy? Again, rank these in priority order by the weight of their merit in the dilemma and the relative negative impact on each stakeholder.

4. What are the driving forces in the situation?

   Where is the pressure originating? Are the sources of the pressure reliable? May the pressure be without merit? Upon whom is the pressure being put? Given the available options, what course of action will send the pressure in what direction? Are these directions that would be more able to sustain the pressure without negative consequences? Are there directions in which the damage would be intolerable?

5. What is the worst case scenario and the effects or impact on all the players who are stakeholders?

How serious is the issue? Who is the most vulnerable? Who is the most resilient? What are the long-term implications? Who is the more innocent, the more at fault? Are there stakeholders who merit more protection than others? Are there stakeholders who would be more damaged? How would justice, or lack of justice, affect each stakeholder?

Five Criteria to Apply to the Decision

1. Consistency	Is this decision consistent with previous actions for which the organization, or the person, have become known? Does the decision fit with the organization's history?
2. Coherence	Is this decision in line with the decisions of other segments of the organization? Do the different parts of the organization reflect a unified decision-making process?
3. Communication	Has the discussion that led to the decision been open and candid? Have all the right people been involved in the decision?
4. Conviction	Is the decision consistent with the mission and purposes of the organization?
5. Creativity	Does the decision take sufficient account of new ideas and discoveries that might lead to new advances and reward for the organization? for society?

Three Intuitive Tests to Reference

1. Golden Rule	Are you treating others as you would want to be treated?
2. Publicity	Would you be comfortable if your decision appeared on the front page of tomorrow's newspaper? Or mentioned on the nightly TV news?
3. Kid on Your Shoulder	Would you be comfortable if your children were observing you? Are you living the example you preach?

(Continued)

EXHIBIT 10.3   *(CONTINUED)*

Four Impediments to Ethical Behavior

1. Self-Indulgence	Desire for money or power.
2. Self-Protection	Cover up of wrongdoing or error, shifting of blame.
3. Self-Deception	"Everybody does it" or "I/we have no choice."
4. Self-Righteousness	"I don't have a problem with it so it must be okay."

Source: The process described in this exhibit was informally developed by Barbara H. Marion, CFRE; Professor James Donahue, Georgetown University; Michael Josephson, The Josephson Institute for the Advancement of Ethics; and Professor Michael O'Neill, University of San Francisco.

The most effective way to make use of these tools is to test them with a real or hypothetical case. The steps provide informed guidance, good practice, and information that will produce constructive dialog. Try applying these tools to the Case of John Dear. Development staff should initiate the first dialog and training exercises and then assess the value of taking this exercise to a broader audience. Engaging others in dialog about ethical practice can be as simple as posing an ethical dilemma for consideration or as difficult as teaching accounting practices to a board member not inclined to understanding numbers. When it is made interesting with the use of human experience, an audience is more inclined to practice and eventually to understand the critical importance of this practice.

THE PLAN FOR DISSEMINATION

Development of the plan for dissemination includes a decision regarding timeline, prioritized audiences, and techniques and tools for introduction. It will require time and attention to detail. At this point, a committee with expertise in several different areas is helpful. The "dream team" for your committee might include specialists in generational messaging and in development of printed and technical materials along with someone knowledgeable in how to budget the components of the project. Be certain to add to this team representatives of the media who will know how to engage and involve their colleagues.

In the event that Choosing a Leadership Role sounds like an involved and complicated task, please be assured that even getting as far as Step 1 is more than most organizations are even thinking about today. A worthwhile goal demands a worthwhile vision. Remember that the vision of spreading the understanding of ethical practice is compelling and inspiring. The suggestions for Step 2 are multifaceted and not requirements.

To summarize, the techniques for introduction include the Ethics Quick Quiz, The Statement of Values and Standards for Excellence developed by the Board of Trustees of the Tucson Symphony Orchestra, and the review of a sample case "The Dear Friend," which illustrates unethical practice. The audiences identified so far include staff, board, and donors. Additional audiences might include students and other constituents. For example, in a professional symphony orchestra the musicians may not be included in discussions about the statement of values and standards of ethical practice. However, it is not unrealistic for an enthusiastic donor to enter into a conversation with a favorite musician. It is also possible that this donor might propose a plan for generating a large gift. The plan was originally offered by the donor's financial advisor in which payment of a fee to the advisor would ensure the identification of a large gift to endow a solo recital in which this favorite musician would perform. It sounds like a good idea if you are not familiar with the unethical nature of paying finder's fees. The unethical part of this practice is that someone is receiving private inurement by facilitating a large donation. With this illustration, it is easy to understand why the more detailed discussion of ethical practice must take place with all the internal constituencies of an organization.

In the prioritization of audiences, Exhibit 10.1, Concentric Circles of Relationships, provides the order (inside to the outside) in which the audiences should be involved. As already suggested, the techniques for addressing each audience vary widely. The use of illustrative ethics sample cases can engage audiences through case review and discussion.

Reaching further out in the concentric circles requires different steps, inasmuch as there is unlikely to be direct face-to-face access to some of these audiences. In this case the use of short newsletter illustrations could be helpful. Commentary on current events could stimulate thinking. It is critical to emphasize the importance of the use of ethical guidelines. Articulating examples of ethics standards that are followed by your organization will not only draw the attention of the public but will educate them in the process. A brief article in a newsletter about how the organization treats confidential information provides an example as well as an opportunity to have people self identify as not wanting their names to be given to other organizations. An article about a designated gift received by the organization will not only give visibility to the donor and the program but let others know that if they were to consider a special designated gift, this is an organization that can ensure ethical stewardship of that gift.

The development of a timeline provides two benefits. One benefit of a timeline assures continuity to participants to keep the process moving forward. The second is to alleviate the guilt of not moving fast enough! This process cannot be completed overnight. If it is to be worth doing, it must be done well. Develop your plan with some realistic time frames. After all, in the development office, the development of relationships that will yield philanthropic results is a high priority. There is no suggestion that ethics education is your sole priority, but it certainly ranks up in the highest level. In order to achieve a level of understanding, confidence, and competence, it needs to be on your agenda every month, just like your top 25 prospects.

Remember, all the examples in this chapter are not just about talk; this chapter is about practice. As an organization becomes more knowledgeable and talks openly about ethics, people are much more likely to establish and maintain the highest standards in ethical practice for that organization.

Taking a leadership role in anything is work; there is no question about it. Is it worthwhile? There is no question about that either. One of the rewards of establishing best practices in ethics is that you will see new leadership rise to the surface. Those who become invigorated by their newly found understanding and realization of the importance of ethical practice are more likely to step up to the leadership plate. In many organizations, the same leadership has held the reins for a long time. Part of that phenomenon is due to the fact that people are willing to sit back and let those who want to lead do so. When you introduce a new and very important issue, you are likely to inspire some of those who have been sitting back to step up to the plate and take on the new role of promoting ethical practice. Remember that comment about "no greater testament to good teaching than when a mentor can step aside and observe the mentee perform?" When you go through the process by all means, gather those who most value the focus and help them become leaders in the process.

As the organization implements plans for dissemination, consider the tools employed along this journey. Take the opportunity to involve someone who enjoys writing and develop a series of articles about ethics. Use them in newsletters. Consider taking the concept to the local editorial board to request a series in the local paper. The topic is certainly timely, and no one appears to be writing about *solutions* to the ethics crisis in this country.

Recruit a media specialist to brainstorm ideas for engaging the media. One chapter of the Association of Fundraising Professionals (AFP) made the decision that all members would include a copy of the Donor Bill of Rights with their thank-you letters. It happened that one of the editors at the local paper received two such thank-you letters in response to contributions. He was so impressed with the information that he called the AFP member and suggested an article in the paper.

With the notion that it is always good to "catch someone doing something right," it could prove very rewarding for a print publication to focus on a board that has adopted a focus on ethical practice and share that accomplishment with the community. Interviews on electronic media programs could also prove instructive. One cautionary note for any of the public media ideas: be absolutely certain that the person being interviewed is someone who knows and understands these issues well and who delivers the agreed-on key messages!

Fundraising professionals enjoy the challenge of solving examples of ethical dilemmas and, more importantly, of learning how to avoid them. When all is said and done, it is one thing to work out an example of a dilemma, and quite another to be involved in a real one! With all the focus on the dilemma, there has been little dialog on the art of embracing ethical practice as a part of an individual's core being. When a person chooses to immerse him- or herself in ethical practice, it implies far more than simply knowing how to solve ethical dilemmas. During one presentation, a panel participant challenged the group to define the difference between ethical and moral. This philosophical issue had the participants completely stumped. The result, this moderator went home to the dictionary to attempt to offer a cogent answer. The definitions highlight the philosophical question. An ethic, according to *Webster's New World Dictionary: Third College Edition*, is "1. a system of moral standards or values; 2. a particular moral standard or value."[4] The word *ethics* is defined as "1. the study of standards of conduct and moral judgment; moral philosophy; 2. a treatise on this study; 3. the system or code of morals of a particular person, religion, group, profession, etc."[5]

The word *moral* is defined as "1. relating to dealing with, or capable of making the distinction between right and wrong in conduct; 2. relating to, serving to teach, or in accordance with, the principles of right and wrong in conduct."[6] The dictionary definitions illustrate the very tightly woven fabric of value, moral, and ethic. One might wonder then if there can be a policy that is moral but unethical. In resolving dilemmas, one must determine whether an issue is ethical or moral. When determining the answer to that question, it will be important to provide the rationale for that decision. It could prove very difficult to find an issue that is immoral yet still considered ethical. When choosing a leadership role in this arena, one would do well to initiate dialog on these two important words. It offers still another point of entry into the process of the dialog.

Public Affairs and Public Policy

Public affairs and public policy encompass the entire realm of operations for this orchestra. The resulting document is one the board is proud to share with donors and other constituents. The process of developing this document was educational. More importantly it involved many who had not given these concepts more than a passing thought. It was an extremely valuable process and one that is highly recommended for any nonprofit organization.

Public trust cannot be taken for granted until an organization does something "wrong." It is worth repeating that the public only need *perceive* that something is wrong to inflict real damage. If that is how the public sees it, rest assured that the organization in question will spend many years trying to recover the public trust it believed it had enjoyed. When an organization has its blinders on and is looking only within, it is open to some extremely challenging problems in the arena of public awareness. A board president or CEO has the opportunity to take a preventive step such as the one suggested rather than be surprised when the public's misunderstanding of nonprofit standards becomes an unpleasant challenge.

Think about the messages you hear and listen to every day. Who is sending the message? Normally, a business or company recruits a "spokesperson." And normally, that person is someone who is recognized by the audiences to whom he or she is delivering a message. Think about those ads for sportswear and the person who comes to mind is probably a Hollywood star, a notable politician, or a sports figure who has instant recognition. Why not consider a notable person in your community to deliver some key messages related to ethical practice? When ethical practice is presented as something that everyone should be thinking about, your message gains significant credibility. Your spokesperson becomes a figurehead for your message, and your organization enjoys visibility and acceptance. This plan requires some strategic planning. The development of the key messages was hopefully completed in an earlier step. However, the strategic choice of the right spokesperson or spokespersons will require some critical thinking and planning. The plan will need to include several points:

- Who will offer the impeccable standards you are seeking in your spokesperson?

- How many messages do you want to deliver to how many audiences?
- What is/are the right vehicle(s) to deliver your messages?
- What do you want your audience to remember?
- What do you want the spokesperson to do?
- Should the message include a call to action?

Selecting a spokesperson is not necessarily easy. However, the right spokesperson can be extremely effective. A board or committee working on this project will enjoy the challenges and the discussions they will have in making the necessary decisions will further develop their own understanding of ethical standards issues.

The rewards of leaderships are many and diverse. One of the most significant has to do with self. Peter Senge, author of *The Fifth Discipline*, suggests that there are Core Disciplines required for the building of the Learning Organization. These disciplines are easily adapted to the leadership process proposed in this chapter. The disciplines include: personal mastery, mental models, shared vision, and team learning. Senge says of personal mastery, "When personal mastery becomes a discipline—an activity we integrate into our lives—it embodies two underlying movements. The first is continually clarifying what is important to us. We often spend too much time coping with problems along our path that we forget why we are on that path in the first place. The result is that we only have a dim, or even inaccurate, view of what's really important to us."[7] Does this sound familiar? Throughout this chapter the reader has been advised to become more familiar with the principle of ethics.

Another recommendation is to know the preferences of your audiences. The Senge model clearly articulates the process. There remains one caution when choosing this leadership role. Do not be discouraged by the many choices of action. This passion to instill ethical standards and practice is a step-by-step procedure, and no one has ever avoided the process of putting one foot in front of the other! It simply is not realistic to believe that change can be effected overnight. If it could, this country would have far greater understanding and appreciation for ethical practice. Just as steps have been outlined, recommendations for timeline planning made to accomplish over a period of years, the reader is encouraged to embrace the role of process in this vision. If one piece becomes a stumbling block, enlist support and help from a colleague. If a tactic explored does not appear to be effective, try another approach. Leadership is about flexibility. Remember that Edison had to fail eight times before he succeeded with the electric bulb. Be assured that successes are worth the challenge. Striving toward ethical practice is well worth the journey. Involving and inspiring more people to speak on behalf of ethical practice is admirable and an important contribution to the leadership team. It will take a nation of leaders to spread the understanding and practice of ethical standards that reflect the values held dear by so many: integrity, honesty, and accountability. When people understand the principles and standards, they will embrace a more ethical stance for those organizations they serve.

About the Author

Barbara A. Levy, ACFRE, began her fundraising career in 1973. She is a nationally recognized speaker and consultant on organizational and board development, strategic planning, and fundraising. She is among the few senior professionals to qualify for and earn the Advanced Certified Fundraising Executive (ACFRE) credential issued by the Association of Fundraising Professionals. In 1998, she received international recognition when presented with the Outstanding Fundraising Executive Award at the International Conference of the Association of Fundraising Professionals. She is a published author of works including *The NSFRE Fund-Raising Dictionary*. The second edition is now available online as the *AFP Fundraising Dictionary*. She also coauthored *Successful Special Events: Planning, Hosting, Evaluating*. Among her many volunteer activities is her current service on the AFP International Ethics Committee.

NOTES

1. Lynne C. Lancaster and David Stillman, *When Generations Collide* (New York: Collins Business, 2005), 14.
2. Ibid., 77.
3. Ibid., 278.
4. Victoria Neufeldt, Editor in Chief, David B. Guralnik, Editor in Chief Emeritus, *Webster's New World Dictionary of American English* (New York: Simon & Schuster, 1994), 466.
5. Ibid.
6. Ibid., 882.
7. Peter M. Senge, *The Fifth Discipline: The Art and Practice of the Learning Organization* (New York: Currency Doubleday, 1990), 141.

CHAPTER 11

The Context and Development of International Codes and Standards

ANDREW WATT, FInstF

Traditional boundaries, imposed by treaty and by limitations of culture, distance, and communication techniques, have blurred. Individuals can access news as it breaks, respond to an appeal instantly, and give online. The only limiting factor on the speed of one's reaction is oneself. When things go wrong, the impact is every bit as fast, if not faster. Under these circumstances, it is hardly surprising that individuals (and the societies in which they live) feel the need to establish controls that will enable best practice and limit the impact and consequences of bad practice.

It can be assumed that this can be accomplished in many ways and at many different levels. This is done at a supranational level through organizations such as the United Nations, or specialist bodies such as the Worldwide Alliance for Citizen Participation (CIVICUS), Worldwide Initiatives for Grantmaker Support (WINGS), or the International Center for Not-for-Profit Law (ICNL); at a national level through legislation and regulation, through self-regulation by professional associations such as the Association of Fundraising Professionals (AFP), Association of Healthcare Professionals (AHP), or Council for the Advancement and Support of Education (CASE); and at an individual level through voluntary participation in and support of all of these processes.

For many, philanthropy is an essential part of existence. It is at the heart of one's own moral, ethical, or religious values. It influences the way in which one views the world and interacts with fellow citizens as well as the way in which one individual joins together with others to influence governments to support the wellbeing of others. Governments, international corporations, and organizations operate within the same structures as individuals, developed and defined by the same values over the course of time. The importance of civil society—the partnership between government and citizens for the common good—and the impact on it of globalization is difficult to underestimate.

CIVIL SOCIETY AND GLOBALIZATION: TWO KEY INFLUENCES ON THE DEVELOPMENT OF REGULATORY AND SELF-REGULATORY STRUCTURES

The world has become far smaller during the course of the past 50 years. Commerce, trade, politics, culture, and technology are increasingly interconnected with interdependent links across the globe. Communications ensure the transfer of knowledge and ideas at the click of a button; commercial processes merge seamlessly around the globe; yet, defining the concept of globalization is extraordinarily hard. Like all concepts, it is intangible; no one individual, corporation, or government can be held responsible and still the consequences of globalization are tangible and manifested around the world. David Rothkopf, Department of Commerce advisor to former U.S. president Bill Clinton, described globalization as:

> The word we came up with to describe the changing relationships between governments and big business. But what is going on today is a much broader, more profound phenomenon. It is about things that

impact some of the deepest, most ingrained aspects of society...it is about the emergence of totally new social, political and business models.[1]

It can be assumed that consumers appreciate the convenience and cost benefits of globalization, while at the same time recognizing the need to monitor and control the impact of it. We fear for the future of our children and our societies and agree on the need to regulate the consequences of our society's actions.

While globalization is not a new concept, the scale of its impact has increased exponentially, even over the past 50 years. When Columbus left the old world in 1492, he established trade routes across the newly discovered world that allowed certain countries to establish global, not continental, spheres of influence. Spain, Portugal, and England grew wealthy through the exploitation of the resources of their new colonies. At one step, the world shrank.

The Industrial Revolution of the nineteenth century was the time of the establishment of multinational companies, introducing a global supply chain that, supported by falling transportation costs and increasing efficiency of transportation and communication, allowed companies to manufacture and sell in a global market. A European cotton manufacturer, following the American Civil War, could control the growth of raw product in India and Egypt, oversee the processing of raw materials in Italy, finish and pack in the UK and sell to the United States, Africa, and back to India. At each stage in the process, conditions of work and workers' welfare could be controlled as effectively as if they had been concentrated in one of the great manufacturing centers of Europe.

The nineteenth century, under the pressure of such rapid change, also was the time of the rise of great social issues, addressed through political campaigns and the political process. Over a period of 100 years, the abolition of slavery, the regulation of child labor, political emancipation, the emancipation of women, the state of public health, the development of education, and improvements in social welfare ensured a profound change in views on the responsibilities of society to its members as well as a new understanding of how to address them through collective action. This understanding of the responsibility of society to act collectively, in addition to an awareness of individual responsibility, supported the growth of political activism and a central, societal response to social issues.

The growth of philanthropy over this period was directly linked to the development of new industrial wealth on a global scale and to the need to address the social issues that ensued from such wealth. Individuals such as Andrew Carnegie and families such as the Rothschilds recognized that the impact of their actions would be felt globally; therefore, they had the responsibility to think on a universal scale. The government also operated on a worldwide scale inconceivable during an earlier era. Decisions taken centrally at a strategic level had to be supported by a vast array of minute detail underpinning the colonial administration of the nineteenth century empires. Political and social values were considered to be universal and applicable to all.

By the present day, global awareness has become absolute. On the one hand, corporations such as Microsoft now span the world. On the other, change is increasingly driven by individuals who, through technology, can share and market new concepts to a globally competitive market. Society has moved from an industrial age through an age based on the sharing of information via technology; we have now arrived at a point where the tools at one's disposal have become a commodity and change, innovation, and development come from the talents of individuals in an environment where speed of reaction and innovation ensure success. Small changes in today's volatile society can have a disproportionate and immediate impact on a global scale. It can be presumed that society is aware of that, while looking for ways to counter this inherent instability.

CIVIL SOCIETY

Many individuals live in an increasingly secular society; yet, the value structures that underpin these lives derive from religious beliefs and philosophical constructs held and developed over several millennia. Media coverage of politics and religious activity is increasingly couched in extreme terms, questioning whether values expressed through these vehicles are wholly appropriate for use in the twenty-first century. One can recognize the rapid impact that extremism of all sorts can have in creating rippling effects around the world; still, our need for structured values does not disappear. Indeed, as it becomes harder to apply familiar structures to the daily lives of individuals, it becomes more important to take the values that societies hold and know have been tested by time and ensure that they are incorporated into structures that are seen as appropriate by the world. Standards must be applied and principles recognized by those who operate in a global environment.

The growing importance of civil society and the partnership between government, commerce, the nonprofit sector, and the public has had a profound influence on the development of nonprofit structures over the past 50 years. The boundaries of civil society are blurred; but, collectively, civil society partnerships build social capital based on trust and shared values, influencing the political process and creating a more cohesive society.

The principles of civil society are not restricted by national boundaries. Recognition of the need for commonly agreed positions in the nonprofit world has led to the establishment of organizations such as CIVICUS, WINGS, and the ICNL.

CIVICUS is an international alliance of members at a local, national, and international level that forms a global network of state, private sector, and civil society organizations. It acts as a forum to engage citizens and ordinary people in the debate on issues with a global impact, among them the governance of nonprofit organizations and activities. The work of CIVICUS has been influential in the development of regulatory principles for nonprofits in a global environment. Both WINGS and the ICNL have also been active in this sphere—WINGS in the development of good governance for foundations worldwide and the ICNL in feeding into the process of development of regulation at a national and supranational level. WINGS is a global network of membership organizations and support organizations serving grant makers, established in January 2000, providing a forum for learning, collaboration, and the promotion of philanthropy worldwide. The ICNL aims to establish a legal framework for a strong and effective civil society, providing technical assistance to over 90 countries in areas such as regulatory frameworks, governance, and accountability.

MOVING TOWARDS REGULATION OF NONPROFITS IN A GLOBAL SOCIETY

As little as 10 years ago, ignorance of nonprofit (broadly, organizations funded in part or wholly by philanthropic contributions) operations was rife, and it could be said that it was nonprofits that were to blame. Nonprofits used statutory reporting vehicles to hide the reality of running a successful nongovernmental organization (NGO). It was thought that the public could not understand that running an NGO, like running any organization, required strategic investment over the long term and that levels of necessary investment would vary depending on the nature of the organization and the activities that it needed to fund. When politicians, the press, or the public focused negatively on what the nonprofit sector was doing, the sector hid and waited for the storm to subside. Press coverage of accounting anomalies at the National Kidney Foundation in Singapore has caused an ongoing investigation of the organization's finances with high-profile coverage in the press. This, in turn, has led to a review of charity regulation in Singapore, but it took some time for other charities to take this as an opportunity to highlight their own best practice.

In 2003, by contrast, a scandal involving the misappropriation of funds by a supplier of fundraising services to Breast Cancer Care Scotland demonstrated the power of positive action. Negative coverage of the case proved to be highly damaging to the public perception of charities in Scotland, causing an immediate downturn in voluntary contributions to charity. A coalition of Scottish charities and support groups came together to form "Giving Scotland." The coalition worked with foundations, regulators, and the media to demonstrate to the public that the sector subscribed to strong ethical practices (the Codes of the Institute of Fundraising) that had been developed with the support of government. The campaign promoted awareness of the need for a wholesale review of regulation of charities in Scotland and was responsible, in part, for generating the momentum leading to the Charities and Trustee Investment Act (Scotland) 2005.

This scenario will sound familiar. No one organization is likely to be prepared to be the one to start the process of public education for fear that other organizations might exploit the opportunity. Who would argue for sustained investment at 30 percent when comparable organizations are producing literature that promotes the concept that "all of your gift goes to the cause"? Who would argue that heat, light, and fuel at headquarters are necessary to ensure that objectives are met elsewhere? Few in the nonprofit sector have been prepared to stand and take that risk.

Typically, it takes a succession of scandals and the threat of direct regulation to affect a sea change in attitude within the not-for-profit sector, allowing organizations to begin to collaborate and discuss the tools that are necessary to improve transparency and accountability. The concepts behind those tools are not complex; they include:

- Standardized reporting and accounting:
  - Clearly agreed-on definitions of fundraising activities
  - Templates for board reports
- Sector benchmarking to provide internal comparative analysis
- Web platforms for presenting statutory reports
- A credible structure to underpin self-regulation, such as the Donor Bill of Rights

CROSS-BORDER REGULATION

During the past 10 years the huge increase in cross-border giving and international aid has caused more and more money to be raised in a wide range of countries, going to support causes around the world. Donors and regulators together share a need to see principles of transparency and accountability applied to these processes; and inevitably, regulatory and self-regulatory structures put in place ensure that those principles are applied. This regulation has to be imposed at a national level; however, the breadth of this activity increasingly requires cross-border regulation, and at the very least, cross-border dialog. Nonprofit organizations, regulators, and practitioners recognize the benefit of internationally established standards of good practice to ensure that funds are raised and applied in an ethical manner.

A considerable influence on this process evolves from increasing concern that nonprofit organizations could be used as a cover for the channeling of terrorist funds. At the same time, it is generally accepted that a healthy nonprofit sector is vital, not only to the community but also in the development of any comprehensive antiterrorism strategy. The nonprofit sector has been responsible for addressing issues of the abuse of human rights, of the environment, of socioeconomic deprivation, of freedom of speech, and of freedom of association.

Well-established structures for the regulation of nonprofit activity already exist in the United States, Canada, and the United Kingdom. It is not a coincidence that it is in these environments that effective self-regulation of fundraising activity has been firmly established as well. In each of these environments there exists a regulatory structure for nonprofits that encompasses fundraising activity, an established reporting structure for nonprofits (although this has some significant differences between North America and the UK) and access to training and professional development opportunities in the field of fundraising.

The underlying purpose of such regulation is twofold; it should provide an environment in which nonprofit organizations can flourish and it should provide an administrative framework in which they can conduct their affairs and report on their activities. An enabling environment, simply defined, will provide nonprofits with operating rules that are fair, transparent, and nonpolitical.

Responsibility for the regulation of nonprofits in the United States and Canada sits, in the main, with the relevant revenue agencies. This is not surprising when it is considered that the most recent major regulatory provision for foundations in the United States was the 1969 Tax Act. The impact of the Act has been considerable over the intervening years in terms of increased revenue and of increased numbers of foundations; the price that has been paid for the generated revenue was to ensure that far greater demands are made on foundations in terms of accountability for these revenues and of regulatory oversight. However, the current role of the Internal Revenue Service (IRS) is not to ensure a favorable or enabling environment for nonprofits; rather, it is to register nonprofits and to ensure that nonprofits fulfill the statutory requirements imposed on them by the Act.

In the United Kingdom, the role of regulator of charities sits with the Charity Commission for England and Wales and the Office of the Scottish Charity Regulator. The role of these bodies is somewhat broader than that of the IRS or the Canada Revenue Agency (CRA). An important part of their role is to register charities and to review their financial returns. These returns must include a narrative report from the board of the organization, setting out the achievements of the charity for that year and interpreting the accompanying accounts. The role of the regulator is to act when a charity fails to perform its statutory reporting obligation or fulfill its charitable purpose. The regulator has an additional role, however, that requires it to support and mentor the charity as it performs those obligations; in effect, the regulator is both watchdog and friend. This role can be conflicting at times, but when, as is usually the case, it is successful, it fulfills an enabling role that U.S. and Canadian regulators do not. It is interesting to compare the data held by GuideStar for the United States with that held for the English charitable sector by GuideStar UK. There is a greater depth of information and a greater ability to interrogate that information on the UK site than on the U.S. site, directly reflecting the difference in quality of the information gathered as part of the regulators' statutory function.

Areas of the world with a developing nonprofit structure also seek to provide a regulatory framework for charities. In some cases this has been developed alongside existing regulatory processes. In others, a dedicated charity regulator has developed a similar role to that of the Charity Commission for England and Wales.

In the Philippines, nonprofits (to qualify for beneficial status) must register as cooperatives or as nonstock corporations. Their purposes must be recognized as consistent with definitions provided in the Civil Code. In both cases, registration is with existing entities, the Cooperatives

Development Authority, or the Securities and Exchange Commission. Specific provisions are made in the Civil Code to cover both trusts and donations.

In Singapore, a Commissioner of Charities has been established within the Ministry of Community Development, Youth and Sports. The role of the commissioner is broadly similar to that of the Charity Commission for England and Wales. It encompasses an enabling role for the sector, providing resources, and signposting designed to create a favorable operating environment for nonprofits.

However, the underlying purpose of regulation remains the same: to ensure that nonprofit status and benefits are conferred on those organizations that fulfill legitimate nonprofit activity for the benefit of the community, nationally, or internationally; to ensure that the activities of those organizations are legitimate; and to ensure that those organizations are fully and transparently accountable to the society that they exist to serve.

ACCOUNTABILITY

Another driver towards transparency has been the increasing focus on the development of international accounting standards for nonprofits. Many bodies have played a role in this process. The United Nations (UN) Nonprofit Handbook project, approved by the UN Statistical Commission and developed by the Johns Hopkins Center for Civil Society Studies, led by Dr. Lester Salamon, has been influential in the drive towards the introduction of consistent definitions of nonprofit activity. As part of the project, countries are introducing requirements to define operating expenditures and sources of revenue in their statutory annual returns and as part of the system of national accounts. So far, 26 countries have committed to implementing a version of the Handbook as part of their reporting requirement, from Latin America, Asia, Africa, Europe, North America, and the Middle East.

On a national basis, regulators and the nonprofit sector have been driving the process towards improved statutory reporting vehicles. Part of this process has been to standardize definitions of nonprofit activity, particularly as it relates to the solicitation of funds. At the same time, sector-led benchmarking initiatives in certain countries have allowed practitioners to isolate fundraising activity more effectively as part of the accounting process, enabling them to feed into the process of defining fundraising activity with greater authority.

At an organizational level, this process can be seen as achieving a far higher standard of reporting of nonprofit activity, of use not simply in relation to the regulator but also in public communications. The website of GuideStar UK (www.guidestar.org.uk) provides a clear example of how the relationship between the statutory reporting requirement and the need for public communications can be managed to the benefit of the charity. GuideStar populates its site with the information supplied to the Charity Commission by registered charities. Each charity has the ability to post comment in relation to each section of the site, amplifying the basic information return and linking each line of the accounts to the purposes of the charity. This process improves transparency, allows the charity to communicate effectively and interactively at an appropriate level with any interested enquirer, and allows the charity to demonstrate that it follows best practice across the full range of its activities.

SELF-REGULATION

Self-regulation can only successfully exist within the enabling regulatory framework set out above. A successful regulatory framework should provide freedom to individual organizations to go about their business with autonomy. If that autonomy is to work, however, organizations and the sector in which they exist need to be able to demonstrate beyond doubt that they follow and enforce ethical practice.

Over the years, many of the best discussions between members of the public, legislators, and the press have related to the existence of structures for self-regulation within the sector: the Donor Bill of Rights, the Fundraising Promise of the Fundraising Standards Board (FRSB) (formerly named the Institute of Fundraising's Donor's Charter), and the International Statement of Ethical Principles in Fundraising. Most commentators are unaware of such self-regulatory structures. Many do not realize that charity decisions are not made in a vacuum, that there is a commonly agreed upon list of standards that charities follow. Donors and members of the public need to know that their rights and perspectives are taken into account every step of the philanthropic process; in knowing this, confidence increases.

Accountability and ethical issues are arising all the time in countries around the world. Major nonprofit scandals and controversies have affected sectors in countries as diverse as Brazil, Mexico, England, Ireland, Egypt, the United Arab Emirates, the United States, and Spain.

One international initiative designed to address these issues is the drive to develop the International Statement of Ethical Principles in Fundraising.

The 3rd International Fundraising Summit took place on July 14, 2005, in London. The principal topic under consideration was the International Statement of Ethical Principles in Fundraising. The development of this project was initially proposed by AFP as the purpose of the 1st International Fundraising Summit in Toronto, Canada, in 2003.

More than 30 countries participated in the development of this statement. The final draft encapsulates their common principles. It has no legal authority but its moral authority will be as strong as the number of organizations that support and implement it.

It was agreed that the statement should address macro-level principles but that local codes should address details and specificity relevant to their region and culture.

Five key principles are identified by the document:

1. Honesty
2. Respect
3. Integrity
4. Empathy
5. Transparency

One issue that has sparked considerable comment is percentage-based compensation (PBC). In principle, participants at the 3rd Summit were in agreement that the statement should set out appropriate practice in order that bad practice should be eliminated or redressed. Two positions emerged. The first was that the statement should absolutely prohibit PBC, the second that a universal statement was obliged to support fundraisers in the cultural and national context in which they worked.

It was pointed out that practices vary from country to country, and that in some, PBC had been, or is thought to be, the only ethical means of compensation for fundraisers. This is changing, but gradually, and the universal statement should support countries in the process of change rather than dictate it. Therefore, the statement should be resolute as to the ideal but should help to set out the route map necessary to achieve it.

Participants at the 3rd Summit agreed to charge a drafting committee to produce a further revision for consideration in October 2006. The Statement was ratified at the 4th International Summit, in Noordwijk, in October 2006.

There are, in addition, other international initiatives for the regulation of not-for-profits. The European Commission (EC), in particular, has proposed a "Framework for a Code of Conduct for Non-Profit Organizations to Promote Transparency and Accountability Best Practices." The code focuses on fundraising ethics as a key element for regulation.

The International Statement establishes common ethical principles but, as currently drafted, allows for national subsidiarity. Each National Association needs to work within the boundaries of what is considered to be ethical within its own culture, while demonstrating common ground with its peers around the world.

Many fundraisers, wherever they are based, do not accept percentage-based compensation; others are paid by a variety of means, some of which include an element of percentage-based compensation. This will not change immediately, however the International Statement is drafted. All fundraisers, whether they are members of informal networks, or members of formal associations, are subject to the laws and codes that prevail in their own countries.

The purpose of the Statement is to establish what constitutes best practice and at the same time to provide a framework that is flexible enough to allow all countries to use the statement in conjunction with their own national codes.

Interest in fundraising ethics is being expressed by governments as geographically dispersed as the United States, Canada, Mexico, China, Australia, New Zealand, the Ukraine, Hungary, the UK, and the EU.

Endorsement of the International Code could provide an important tool for the promotion of fundraising ethics; it could also help to demonstrate that self-regulatory initiatives are both more effective and more flexible in regulating fundraising activity than direct regulation by governments.

FUNDRAISING ASSOCIATIONS AND THEIR DIFFERING APPROACHES TO SELF-REGULATION

There are many fundraising associations around the world. Of these, some have a formal constitution supported by a code of conduct or ethical code. The majority of those organizations publish a code of conduct that is binding on members, both individual and organizational. These codes address certain principles, common to all associations and demand that their members:

- Conduct themselves at all times with complete integrity, honesty, and trustfulness.
- Respect the dignity of their profession and ensure that their actions enhance the reputation of themselves and their fundraising association.
- Act according to the highest standards and visions of their organization, profession, and conscience.
- Advocate within their organizations adherence to all applicable laws and regulations.
- Avoid even the appearance of any criminal offense or professional misconduct.
- Bring credit to the fundraising profession by their public demeanor.
- Encourage colleagues to embrace and practice their Code of Conduct.

The simplest approach to codes of conduct or ethics is exemplified by the Dutch and French codes below. Both address the principles set out above. Members are asked to abide by the terms of the code and clear sanctions are established should they be deemed to be in breach of any aspect of it. It is felt that the principles are clearly expressed and sufficiently general to be applied to all circumstances in which fundraisers might find themselves.

DUTCH CODE OF CONDUCT FOR FUNDRAISERS

Following is the Dutch Code of Conduct for Fundraisers.

Article 1 Professional Conduct

a. The behavior of the members of the Dutch Fundraisers Association (NGF) will be respectful towards natural and legal bodies they approach for their fundraising activities.
b. Members will do everything to follow their profession with honesty, integrity and dignity, in order to preserve the image of the profession and the public trust in it.
c. Members will perform their activities in accordance with the law, the operative legislation and good customs.
d. Members will do everything to prevent that their conduct might lead to damaging the image of other members, their organisations or fundraising in general.
e. Members will not raise funds for personal benefit.
f. Members will follow this code of conduct consequently and stimulate others to do so as well.

Article 2 Trust

a. Members will not mislead natural or legal bodies while performing their fundraising activities.
b. Members will be prepared to give all the information which one can reasonably assume to be relevant in the framework of fundraising, regardless the fact that this information might have a negative impact on it.

Article 3 Professional Competence

a. Members will continuously dedicate themselves to improve their professional skills.
b. Members will dedicate themselves to make their knowledge and skills available to others with whom they work together, so that each one can perform his/her tasks as good as possible.
c. Members will be prepared to share their experiences with other members and stimulate each other to achieve a continuous improvement of their professional skills.
d. Members will enhance their fundraising activities to be in concordance with those of other members.

Article 4 Carefulness

a. Without the explicit previous approval of the concerning source, members will not disclose any confidential information they obtained from employers, customers, donors, fellow-members or any other source, in the course of their professional duties.
b. Members will respect the privacy, the freedom of choice and the interests of any person who comes in touch with their organisation, especially in the framework of their fundraising activities.
c. Members will take into account that the act of giving, also when this happens in accordance with a written agreement, in the first instance and on principle should happen on the basis of one's own free will.

Article 5 Conflict of Interest

a. Members will not promote any conflicting or contradicting interests without the explicit approval of both parties.

FRENCH CODE OF PROFESSIONAL ETHICS

The goal of the Association de Fundraisers, previously the "Union pour la Générosité," is to enhance philanthropy for humanitarian and social foundations and associations as well as for nonprofit organizations working for the common good.

With this in mind, the Association de Fundraisers, much like its counterparts in other countries, has adopted a code of professional ethics, which serves as a reminder of the principles that the members of the Association refer to and which defines the rules they strive to respect and have respected in their professional endeavors. The members of the Association promote the causes they serve, not only through their high degree of professionalism which they demonstrate in fundraising activities and in setting up associations, but also for personal reasons in favor of the causes which they serve.

In their quest for the support of, the sympathy towards and the participation of the public in the associations they work for, the members of the Association personally share all or part of the values that motivate these associations.

The members of the Association are committed to constantly improving their professional knowledge and expertise in order to efficiently contribute to the development of resources, actions and programs led by the organizations they promote.

Beyond their legal and professional engagements, they also feel morally responsible for the means used and the truthfulness of the messages as well as the strict management and proper use of collected funds.

They ensure that donors and members are fully and clearly informed about the destination of collected funds, that personal information in the database is not used against their wishes and that the intent, the expectations and the wishes of the donors are taken into account and respected. They also guarantee the respect of the beneficiaries' dignity in the association's communications and especially in the fundraising process.

In performing their jobs with a high degree of integrity, honesty, and good faith, the Association's members strive to preserve the public's confidence in the organizations and continually seek to enhance appeals for generosity.

In particular, the members of the Association:

• Promote the values of generosity and altruism.
• Are committed, while developing the necessary professional specialization, especially in the areas of fundraising and management, to the preservation and advancement of volunteer action and objectivity in association circles.

- Ensure that all documents soliciting generosity accurately describe the organization's identity and mission, and clearly explain how the funds will be used.
- Explicitly provide donors with the possibility of correcting or withdrawing personal information.
- Guarantee that the donations are used in accordance with the association's missions, the motivation behind the appeal and the donor's wishes.
- Encourage the institutions they work for to adopt strict book-keeping and management procedures, develop internal control mechanisms and be up to the task of satisfactorily passing external audits.
- Manage the sums with which they are entrusted to the sole benefit of the organizations for which they work.
- Advise the organizations to undertake only those fundraising projects that can be achieved according to their professional experience and a rational analysis of existing data.
- Are paid either a salary, a previously agreed upon wage or by the hour, and not by commission or percentage linked to the amounts they collect, whether they work for associations, fundraising agencies or fundraising consulting companies.
- Bring to the attention of their employers, clients and donors any potential links that may lead to a conflict of interest.
- Neither seek nor accept any gratuity as "facilitators."
- Preserve the confidential nature of the documents and files with which they are entrusted by the organizations they work for.
- Ennoble, through their conduct, the overall profession, thereby contributing to its advancement and recognition.

Within this framework, the members of the Association de Fundraisers are aware of their role in the emergence of a tertiary sector. The nonprofit sector brings together on one hand associations, foundations, societies and cooperatives, and on the other it strives to create a fairer, more just and human society, one based on the principles of solidarity. This code of professional ethics must not cause them to lose sight of the humanitarian, social cultural or environmental goals they pursue daily in the exercise of their professions.

However, a more complex fundraising environment demands a more comprehensive approach.

INTERNATIONAL CODES OF PROFESSIONAL ETHICS

In the United States, AFP's Code of Ethical Principles and Standards and the Donor Bill of Rights not only set out the principles of ethical practice, but also, through the detailed use of case studies, illustrate the scenarios in which the principles apply. The Donor Bill of Rights establishes the best practice that a donor can expect of a fundraiser.

These principles are rigorously enforced by AFP through a clearly defined disciplinary process.

In the United Kingdom, AFPs' sister organization, the Institute of Fundraising, has taken a different approach. A Code of Conduct sets out the principles of ethical practice for an individual fundraiser and incorporates the key principles already discussed. Members of the Institute also agree to abide by a set of Codes of Fundraising Practice, relating to specific areas of fundraising, for instance, direct marketing or public collections. These codes set out the law and are therefore mandatory, what is considered mandatory for the Institute's members, as well as general best practice for fundraisers in these specific areas.

As part of a government sponsored initiative, the Institute has also been instrumental in establishing (in 2006) an independent body, the Fundraising Standards Board (FRSB). The FRSB acts as a fundraising watchdog for the public. So far, over four hundred of the United Kingdom's largest charities have endorsed the "Fundraising Promise" (broadly equivalent to the Donor Bill of Rights) and have agreed that they and their staff should be held accountable by the FRSB to the Promise and to the Codes of Fundraising Practice of the Institute of Fundraising. The FRSB enforces standards rigorously. It also has a remit to act as an arbitrator on behalf of a donor to resolve situations that a member organization has been unable to address satisfactorily. It has the power to publish the records of disciplinary proceedings as a sanction against delinquent organizations.

The Fundraising Institute of Australia, Ltd. (FIA) is currently developing another approach to this area. FIA has undergone a consultation process to produce the Principles and Standards of Fundraising Practice. Included in the principles are:

- Code of Ethics
- Code of Professional Practice
- Acceptance and Refusal of Donations
- The Fundraisers Promise to Donors
- FIA Complaints Process

The Standards of Fundraising Practice equate to the Institute of Fundraising's Codes of Fundraising Practice and refer to specific areas of fundraising technique or practice.

In the United Kingdom and Australia, in particular, government has played an integral part in the development of self-regulatory processes and structures. These structures are seen as robust by regulators and as playing a pivotal role in the relationship between citizens and this aspect of civil society.

The role of the nonprofit sector in resource development is viewed by governments as an integral function of nonprofit organizations. Indeed, engagement in the process of fundraising within the community is seen as a hallmark of good citizenship in all countries with a vibrant nonprofit sector.

About the Author

Andrew Watt, FInstF, is president and CEO of the Association of Fundraising Professionals (AFP), the professional association of individuals responsible for generating philanthropic support for nonprofit organizations.

AFP is the largest community of fundraising professionals in the world and has 30,000 members in more than 200 chapters.

Mr. Watt joined AFP in 2006 and was promoted to president and CEO in March, 2011.

From 1993–2005, Mr. Watt was employed by the Institute of Fundraising in the United Kingdom, ultimately as deputy chief executive. In 2006, he was made an Honorary Fellow of the Institute of Fundraising in recognition of his extraordinary service to the profession.

Mr. Watt has been a strong proponent of the value of the nonprofit community and fundraising throughout his career. Viewing nonprofits as a critical interface between the public and government, he has long emphasized the importance of forging strong consensus-based coalitions both within the philanthropic community and between the public and private sectors that demonstrate the value and impact of charities and their work.

Mr. Watt has served as both a volunteer and board member of many nonprofit organizations. He is a graduate of the University of Edinburgh and is married with two children.

NOTE

1. David Rothkopf, quoted in Thomas Friedman, *The World Is Flat: A Brief History of the Twenty-First Century* (New York: Farrar, Strauss & Giroux, 2005), 45–47.

12

Turning a Profit in the Nonprofit World: The Ethical Responsibilities of Businesses in the Fundraising Sector

OWEN WATKINS

Businesses and the people in them feel the pressure to succeed every single day. Success is defined through the bottom line, and pressure can come from shareholders, from the competition, from management, from co-workers and from the board. Whether a business is a one-man shop or a large corporation, its raison d'être is to turn a profit for its owners. Milton Friedman held that corporations have an obligation to make as much money as possible while conforming to the basic rules the society, both those embodied in law and those embodied in ethical custom[1] and nothing more. The question at issue is if a business has nonprofit organizations as its clientele should it aspire to do much better and hold itself to a higher standard? Does the ethical custom of the nonprofit world occupy an elevated position, comparatively?

At its core, the consideration of ethics compels us to weigh up what we believe to be good and what we believe to be bad and comport ourselves accordingly. But we immediately run into problems as good and bad are clearly subjective views, so whose subjective view is right? The English courts have attempted to resolve this question when deciding whether someone has acted as a reasonable person with the concept of *the Man on the Clapham Omnibus.*[2] This imaginary person is assumed to be reasonably educated and reasonably intelligent—Average Joe—and against whom the actions of a defendant in certain types of case can be measured. He should prove equally useful in considering ethics.

We're primarily interested in the practicalities of business ethics. A number of writers have been critical of the field, and the way in which it is approached " . . . most of what we read under the name business ethics is either sentimental common sense or a set of excuses for being unpleasant."[3] However, we are approaching business ethics in the nonprofit world not as an academic exercise, but from a practical perspective. Therefore, for the purpose of this chapter, let's co-opt the Man on the Clapham Omnibus, and see what he has to say about the ethical responsibilities of businesses in the fundraising sector. But for the sake of brevity, let's simply call him Joe. For the sake of simplicity, we will have Joe consider businesses as organizations providing goods or services to the nonprofit sector, be they one-man shops, consultancies, or larger corporations. The terms *business* and *vendor* shall be used interchangeably.

It is presumably accurate to say that Joe would expect *any* business that operates in the nonprofit world to behave *at least* as well, from an ethical standpoint, as a business in the commercial world. But would he be of the opinion that a different, higher ethical standard should apply? In seeking to work with nonprofit clients, would Joe feel that that a business in the sector was buying into the social mission of its clients, and think there should be considerations other than simply the making and maximizing of profit?

Businesses that become Association of Fundraising Professionals (AFP) business members may choose to do so for a variety of reasons: because they support the aims of the sector; because they believe it will give them a competitive advantage; because they believe that it will give them access to an expanding client base, and so on. Support for the sector can be manifested in a number of different ways. This can be through pro bono or at-cost services and expertise, through making charitable donations, through supporting events, providing scholarships, preferential rates, and so on. But in becoming members, they are also explicitly undertaking that they will strive to *promote and protect the work of their client organizations*. In fact, they are stating that they aspire to put philanthropic mission ahead of personal gain.[4] In doing so, they are making the active choice to establish distinct aims for the business beyond, and even above, that of generating profit.

Joe would be quite right to think that by signing up to such a code, a business would be definitively nailing its colors to the mast, and stating its commitment both to the sector and its clients. It would not be enough for such a business to follow the obligation outlined by Friedman; its duties would go beyond the financial. Joe would understandably view any such business that gained financially, or otherwise, at the expense of its clients as having explicitly broken the AFP code. Placing corporate gain over the objectives of the client would definitively run contrary to its letter and spirit. We can be confident that Joe would see the subsequent sanction for profiting at the expense of the client as entirely reasonable. However, what if a business was working in the sector, but not a member?

The sector is atypical in that nonprofits are in business, in existence, to serve a range of third party beneficiaries—their missions. To return to first principles, they achieve this by raising funds, and then applying these funds to the advancement of their missions, whatever they may be. The purpose of the donations that have been secured, from whatever source, is explicitly to support the mission of the nonprofit. Therefore, any expenditure on goods or services should be designed to facilitate or promote the pursuit of mission, or raise more funds.

Nonprofits have less freedom than businesses when it comes to spending money. It is self-evident that the money available to a nonprofit is finite, but often it has a variety of restrictions attached to its use, and it is usually easier for a nonprofit to raise funds for specific projects than for unrestricted usage. The funds available for activities such as resource mobilization are generally the least restricted of those at the disposal of the nonprofit, and are also by definition the most useful to the nonprofit due to the flexibility with which they can be used.

In addition, donors have two very reasonable expectations regarding the gifts that have been made. First, that their gifts will be used of the purposes for which they were donated—this is respecting donor intent.[5] This is also captured in the AFP code of Ethical Principles and Standards.

STANDARD NO. 14

Standard No. 14 states first that members shall take care to ensure contributions are used in accordance with donors' intentions.[6]

Second, that their donations should be used as efficiently as possible in support of those purposes. It is at this point that a light must be shone on the ethical obligations of a business operating in the nonprofit sector.

Where a business has nonprofit clients, whether it is a member of the AFP or not (and especially if it is a member) it should have an understanding of how precious each of the dollars spent with vendors is. The combination of limited funds, restricted funds, and the intent of donors when making gifts confers an additional responsibility on both the nonprofit and the vendor. When working in the sector a business should respect the need for the nonprofit to achieve value on behalf not just of its mission, but also its donors.

A vendor with nonprofit clients should be cognizant of the fact that nonprofits, when they are buying goods and services, are using funds that have been generated in support of the charitable aims of the organization. If that is not clear to the vendor, then the nonprofit should take responsibility for ensuring that the nuances of working in the nonprofit sector are fully understood by vendors, and that those vendors consequently have a clear grasp of the expectations of a nonprofit client.

It has been seen that donors can reasonably have the expectation that the nonprofit will deploy those funds as effectively as possible. Equally, nonprofits can have the expectation that informed businesses working in the sector are working in good faith, and will to some degree be supportive of the aims and objectives of their clients—be that explicit through AFP membership, or implicit in recognizing the source of the funds through which goods and services are purchased.

Joe might contend that the best way in which a business can behave ethically in relation to its nonprofit clients is to be as effective and efficient as possible in doing the work for which it is being paid. The responsibility as ever is on the client to carry out appropriate due diligence in terms of satisfying itself as to the credibility of a vendor and awarding contracts. The vendor's responsibility is to present itself in an accurate and honest way, and to ensure that the products or services presented to the client are suitable for the client's needs. Standard No. 7 of the Code of Ethical Principles and Standards speaks to precisely this point regarding business members.

STANDARD NO. 7

Standard No. 7 states members shall present and supply products and/or services honestly and without misrepresentation and will clearly identify the details of those products, such as availability of the products and/or services and other factors that may affect the suitability of the products and/or services for donors, clients, or nonprofit organizations.[7]

Once again, for AFP members the standard, and expectations, of the nonprofit sector of its vendors is clear. The expectation is that the business will take due consideration of the aims of the nonprofit, both overall in terms of its mission, and specifically with regard to the goods and/or services being offered and procured. It is this approach that is intended to sensitize businesses in the nonprofit world to the sometimes atypical requirements of nonprofits and the various conditions under which they operate. Where business does not have an understanding of these conditions, it must be the nonprofits' responsibility to be the educator rather than become a passive injured victim.

This is equally true when we ask Joe to consider the matter of public trust in nonprofits. Nonprofits in general are privileged to enjoy higher public trust than other sectors, but trust in organizations can be fragile and easily damaged—especially in the face of actual or perceived malpractice by a nonprofit or its agents. Such occurrences result in the erosion of public trust, but the impact of the reduction in trust is not limited to the nonprofit directly involved; it generates a reversed halo effect where nonprofits in general become less trusted, and a reduction in trust translates in time into a reduction in donations. The part that trust plays in relationships, and the importance of those relationships, is understood in the commercial, political, and nonprofit sectors alike. Leonard Berry wrote in 1995 that "the inherent nature of services, coupled with abundant mistrust in America positions trust as perhaps the single most powerful relationship marketing tool available to a company."[8]

Prime Minister Tony Blair, in 2002, stated that "It is crucially important that public trust and confidence in the charitable and not-for-profit sector should be maintained and if possible increased."[9]

In the same vein, but on a more individual level, Ken Burnett wrote of the need to protect the special bond between a charity and its supporters and to ensure that "the overriding consideration is to care for and develop that special bond and not to do anything that might jeopardize it."[10]

Fundraising for a nonprofit is built upon the trust that donors have for that nonprofit, and as we have seen, those donors have the expectation that money will be spent for the purposes for which it was given. This is entirely understood by fundraising professionals, and is of such central importance to nonprofits that it is at the head of the list of aspirations of AFP members, both business and non.

AFP members both individual and business aspire to:

- Practice their profession with integrity, honesty, truthfulness and adherence to the absolute obligation to safeguard the public trust.[11]

These are strong and direct words that set a clear standard for the ethical behavior expected of an AFP member. In stating that public trust in nonprofits is of paramount importance, secondary to no other consideration, it leaves no scope for misunderstanding or compromise. Business members that have signed up to the code can be expected to have read and understood its stipulations, and to behave accordingly.

Given that enjoying public trust is fundamental to the success and ongoing prosperity of nonprofits, we can be assured that Joe would expect that a business would do nothing that could jeopardize the health of its nonprofit clients. The parallel can be drawn here with his attitude to a business' role in charity expenditure. The responsibility to ensure that a business is fully appraised of the needs and expectations of the nonprofit in relation to public trust would rest with the nonprofit. However, once conscious of these needs—of the importance of public trust and of the requirement to protect it at all costs—a nonprofit could have the very clear expectation that this consideration should supersede that of profit for the business.

Therefore, Joe has shown us that, in assessing its conduct on the ethical scale, a business should take into account three main factors:

1. Considerations of the profit generated on an activity with a nonprofit.
2. Considerations of the suitability of the goods and or services offered to the nonprofit.
3. Considerations of the impact of its actions on public trust in both the nonprofit, and the sector.

In doing so, and in communicating effectively with its clients about their needs and expectations, it can be confident of staying towards the good end of Joe's ethical range.

Ethics can be a challenge because most of its focus rests in the space between the easy absolutes of good and bad, and requires thought. Despite the difficulty, we can be confident that the Man on the Clapham Omnibus would hold that businesses in the nonprofit sector should aspire to a higher standard, should not profit at the expense of their clients, should buy-in to the mission of their nonprofit clients and in doing so protect public trust. Nonprofits have considerations above and beyond those of organizations operating in the commercial sector and as such, and as the client, are entitled to demand compliance with these elevated aspirations. The nonprofit sector is an atypical one, with atypical requirements, and where the actions of a business compromise the ability of a nonprofit to serve its mission, those actions should be found to be unethical.

ABOUT THE AUTHOR

Owen Watkins accidentally became a fundraiser in 2000, and since then has worked for both nonprofits and the agencies that serve them. He has successfully managed a number of fundraising agencies in both the UK and the United States, and today he's responsible for advancing the management and cultivation of UNICEF's Pledge donors (monthly givers) from recruitment (through DRTV, F2F, and Telemarketing) to long-term stewardship and retention. This role involves support for approximately 50 markets, with a file of regular donors running into the millions.

As a volunteer, Mr. Watkins has also served in a variety of roles with the Association of Fundraising Professionals, including on the AFP ethics committee. While in the UK, he had a number of different roles with the Public Fundraising Regulatory Association, and was involved in its establishment in 2000. He has had an active interest in ethics, specifically business ethics, throughout his career and has taken every opportunity to involve himself in this field, including support for the development of UNICEF's Ethical Fundraising Policy.

Before life in the nonprofit sector, Mr. Watkins was a buyer and negotiator for a global mining corporation, working in such varied countries as Angola, Belgium, Russia, and the UK. Continuing with the international theme, he is a regular speaker at fundraising conventions internationally, and in 2012 added Argentina to the diverse range of countries in which he has presented.

NOTES

1. R. E. Frederick, *A Companion to Business Ethics* (Malden, MA: Blackwell, 2002), 88.
2. Room, R. ed., *Brewer's Dictionary of Phrase and Fable*, (1996), 761.
3. C. Jones, R. Ten Bos, and M. Parker, *For Business Ethics: A Critical Approach* (New York: Routledge, 2005), 1.

4. AFP Code of Ethical Principle and Standards (2007), 4.
5. AFP Donor Bill of Rights, Right IV.
6. AFP Code of Ethical Principles and Standards (2007), 20.
7. Ibid., 12.
8. L. Berry, "Relationship Marketing of Services Growing Interest, Emerging Perspectives," *Journal of the Academy of Marketing Science* 23: 242.
9. Strategy Unit, HM Government Cabinet Office, *Private Action, Public Benefit: A Review of Charities and the Wider Not-for-Profit Sector* (2002), 6.
10. K. Burnett, *Relationship Fundraising* (London: White Lion Press, 1992), 48.
11. AFP Code of Ethical Principles and Standards (2007), 4.

CHAPTER **13**

Ethical Decision Making

JANICE GOW PETTEY

Never let your sense of morals prevent you from doing what is right.

—ISAAC ASIMOV

All bad precedents begin as justifiable measures.

—JULIUS CAESAR

Decision making is part of our daily routine. What to have for dinner tonight? Which route to work will take the least time? Oil and vinegar, or ranch dressing on that salad? Pay with credit card or debit card? Many decisions are relatively easy to make, but what about those more complicated decisions? A woman you know well asks whether a particular outfit is flattering. Perhaps your answer is "no," but you know she just bought this outfit and is very pleased with it. Tell her what you think, or tell her what you think she wants to hear?

Your eight-year-old child sees a homeless person sitting on the sidewalk holding a sign asking for help. Your child asks you why no one is helping this person, and can she sit down and talk to him? Or perhaps, invite him home for dinner. What do you say?

A long-time donor offers you her box seats for the All-Star game. She says it's just a little thank you for all your good work. Do you say "thank you" and take the tickets? What if you accept the tickets and then find you are unable to attend, and a friend offers to buy them from you?

Some decisions involve a choice between an obvious right and an equally obvious wrong. There are other decisions that do not appear to have a right and a wrong. In fact, they may appear to be two rights. These are what Rushworth Kidder, founder of the Institute for Global Ethics and author of *How Good People Make Tough Choices* and *Moral Courage*, refers to as "tough choices" which, according to Kidder, are those that "pit one right value against another." He refers to these as "genuine dilemmas" precisely because each side is firmly rooted in one of our basic, core values. . . . They are:

- Truth versus loyalty.
- Individual versus community.
- Short-term versus long-term.
- Justice versus mercy.[1]

How then do we strive to make ethical decisions? Are there guides to help us navigate a decision-making path, without a road map? Or, as Yogi Berra has reputedly said, "When you come to a fork in the road, take it."

This chapter presents three frameworks for ethical decision making, and at the end of the chapter, we review codes and standards as guides to making ethical decisions.

FRAMEWORKS FOR ETHICAL DECISION MAKING

In *Ethics for Fundraisers*, author Albert Anderson offers a set of principles as a guide to ethical fundraising. Anderson's principles "serve as exploratory probes for discovering which one will most likely discover the right thing to do."[2] His three ethical domains are respect, beneficence, and trust.

1. "Respect the essential worth and well-being of each person."[3] In Chapter 2, "Rights of Donors," Jim Greenfield maintains that the

rights of donors begin with organizational respect for the donors and their generosity. Gene Scanlan, in Chapter 3, illustrates how privacy of information relates to respect.

2. A core component of the nonprofit sector is to practice good works. As the Roman poet Virgil observed, "The noblest motive is the public good."

3. Developing and maintaining trust can also be described as building enduring, trustworthy relationships using the following five principles:
   a. Truth telling
   b. Promise keeping
   c. Accountability
   d. Fairness
   e. Fidelity of purpose

Anderson's model of ethical decision making next involves three questions that follow a reflective consideration of the principles of respect, beneficence, and trust.

1. What seem(s) to be the ethical issue(s)—that is, what does one judge to be right or wrong in this situation?
2. What action(s) would seem to make the situation right—that is, what ought we do?
3. What ethical principle(s) and ultimate governing framework would justify the action(s)?

Marilyn Fischer, in *Ethical Decision Making in Fund Raising*, provides another approach to ethical decision making. Fischer presents a hierarchy of three basic value commitments for fundraisers:

1. Organizational mission.
2. Relationships.
3. Sense of personal integrity.[4]

Fischer has developed an ethical decision-making chart using the key values of organization mission, relationships, and personal integrity in a matrix that requires describing alternatives. Fischer's process acknowledges conflicting responsibilities, and she writes "there is no single formula which, if applied correctly, will yield an 'ethically correct' decision. Instead, ethical decision-making is a matter of interweaving ultimate concerns with the facts and considerations of a particular situation."[5]

Fischer stresses the importance of fostering diversity as a component of respect and ethical behavior. "The opportunities that exist for us to increase the numbers of donors among diverse constituencies are at the same time challenging and necessary. First, we must understand each other better, and be prepared to learn from others, including those from other cultures that have practiced philanthropy longer than the United States has been a nation."[6]

A third ethical decision making process is described in Barbara Marion's article "Decision Making in Ethics," published in *Ethics in Fundraising: Putting Values into Practice*. Marion refers to Michael Josephson, founder of the Joseph and Edna Josephson Institute of Ethics' 10 core ethical values:

1. Honesty
2. Integrity
3. Promise keeping
4. Fidelity and loyalty
5. Fairness
6. Caring for others
7. Respect for others
8. Responsible citizenship
9. Pursuit of excellence
10. Accountability[7]

An eleventh value, safeguarding the public trust, was later added for nonprofit organizations.[8]

Marion further offers us a road map designed as a set of questions to assist us in finding the best ethical route. They are:

- **Clarify the problem.** Identify the driving forces and maintain objectivity.

- **Identify the key, competing values at stake.** Identify and rank the values at stake. Which of the organization's values are at stake?
- **Identify the players and stakeholders.** Who should have a role in the decision-making process? Consider the most vulnerable stakeholders.
- **Identify the most plausible alternatives.** Be sure to include the "less popular" alternatives.
- **Imagine the potential outcomes.** Discuss both short-term and long-term outcomes as well as best-case, worst-case scenarios.
- **Evaluate the potential outcomes.** Consider the positive and negative potential for each outcome.
- **Decide on a course of action.** Act thoughtfully and deliberately.
- **Test the decision.** See Chapter 10 on leadership, where Barbara Levy presents the five "C"s of testing as developed by Jim Donahue (1988): consistency, coherence, communication, conviction, and creativity.
- **Share the decision with someone else.** See Chapter 10 on leadership for the importance of communication in ethical decision making.
- **Implement the decision.** Marion encourages us to minimize the negative impacts on various stakeholders, demonstrating respect for their rights and privacy.
- **Evaluate the results or consequences.** Reviewing results and intended or unintended consequences provides additional learning opportunities in ethical decision making.
- **Modify policies and procedures.** Regularly review policies and procedures for consistency with organization's ethical values.[9]

CODES, CREEDS, AND STANDARDS

Organization codes, creeds, and standards provide structure to the collective commitment to uphold values. Along with mission, vision, and

values statements, a code or a set of ethical standards commit an organization to a process accepted by all stakeholders. The Association of
Fundraising Professionals (AFP), the Council for Advancement and Support of Education (CASE), the Association of Professional Researchers
for Advancement (APRA), the Association for Healthcare Philanthropy
(AHP), and the Partnership for Philanthropic Planning (formerly the
National Committee on Planned Giving) all have codes of ethics or
standards. Additionally, there are numerous country-specific international codes for ethical fundraising. Andrew Watt provides an excellent
overview of ethical fundraising from an international perspective in
Chapter 11 of this book.

AFP's Code of Ethical Principles and Standards was amended and
expanded to apply to for-profit businesses involved with or supporting
fundraising in October 2007.

The changes, which include the addition of seven new standards
and the alteration of one standard, now allow for-profit businesses
to join AFP as members and actively promote ethical and efficient
fundraising.

The changes do not alter or lower the standards that AFP applies
to all its members, who are required to sign the association's code of
ethics annually.

The new standards relate to how business members interact with
charities and their responsibilities to their clients. The new standards
include:

Standard 7: Members shall present and supply products and/or
services honestly and without misrepresentation and will clearly
identify the details of those products, such as availability of the
products and/or services, and other factors that may affect the
suitability of the products and/or services for donors, clients, or
nonprofit organizations.

Standard 8: Members shall establish the nature and purpose of any
contractual relationship at the outset and will be responsive
and available to organizations and their employing organizations
before, during, and after any sale of materials and/or services.

Members shall comply with all fair and reasonable obligations created by the contract.

Standard 9: Members shall refrain from knowingly infringing the intellectual property rights of other parties at all times. Members shall address and rectify any inadvertent infringement that may occur.

Standard 10: Members shall protect the confidentiality of all privileged information relating to the provider/client relationships.

Standard 11: Members shall refrain from any activity designed to disparage competitors untruthfully.

Standard 23: Members shall neither offer nor accept payments or special considerations for the purpose of influencing the selection of products or services.

Standard 25: Any member receiving funds on behalf of a donor or client must meet the legal requirements for the disbursement of those funds. Any interest or income earned on the funds should be fully disclosed.

In addition, language has been added to Standard 21 so it now reads:

Members shall not accept compensation or enter into a contract that is based on a percentage of contributions; nor shall members accept finder's fees or contingent fees. Business members must refrain from receiving compensation from third parties derived from products or services for a client without disclosing that third-party compensation to the client (for example, volume rebates from vendors to business members).

Charitable sectors in the United States and Canada both account for more than seven percent of each country's gross domestic product and employ millions of individuals. The recent changes to AFP's Code will increase the prevalence of the Code of Ethics in the business community as nonprofit organizations and their vendors raise billions of dollars annually.

The Independent Sector (IS) provides comprehensive guidance on ethical practices for voluntary and philanthropic institutions and their leaders in *Obedience to the Unenforceable: Ethics and the Nation's Voluntary and Philanthropic Community* (revised 2002). The title of the report is taken from the words of John Fletcher Mouton, who observed, "Obedience to the unenforceable is the extent to which the individuals composing the nation can be trusted to obey self-imposed law."

IS recognizes three levels of ethical behavior. The first level is about obeying laws. The second is composed of those behaviors where one knows the right action but is tempted to take a different course. The third level of ethical behavior involves conflicting options where there may appear to be two "rights." From these three levels of ethical behavior come essential values and ethical behaviors shared by all organizations in the independent sector, including:

- Commitment beyond self.
- Obedience of the laws.
- Commitment beyond the law.
- Commitment to the public good.
- Respect for the worth and dignity of all individuals.
- Tolerance, diversity, and social justice.
- Accountability to the public.
- Openness and honesty.
- Responsible stewardship of resources.

The Independent Sector believes it is essential that, at a minimum, all organizations in the sector

- Adopt an organizational creed of ethical practices.
- Conduct an ethics audit or self-evaluation every year.
- Subscribe to and abide by a set of codes or standards.
- Involve all of their constituencies in the process.
- Infuse the process and the documents into the culture of the total organization.[10]

We must be reminded, however, that the usefulness of principles, standards, and codes cannot replace individual ethical principles. "When Aristotle talks about responsibility he makes a distinction between our professional, social, or cultural role, and our moral obligation. It is quite possible to play the role of fundraiser, grantmaker, or nonprofit volunteer well, and yet fail to think and act in an ethically responsible way."[11]

ABOUT THE AUTHOR

Janice Gow Pettey, EdD, CFRE, is the editor of *Ethical Fundraising: A Guide for Nonprofit Boards and Fundraisers.* She is the vice president of Resource Development at The Asia Foundation and is chair emeritus of AFP's International Ethics Committee. Dr. Pettey is an adjunct professor at the University of San Francisco. She resides in San Francisco.

NOTES

1. Rushworth M. Kidder, *How Good People Make Tough Choices* (New York: William Morrow and Company, 1995), 18.
2. Albert Anderson, *Ethics for Fundraisers* (Bloomington and Indianapolis: Indiana University Press, 1996), 73.
3. Ibid., 74.
4. Marilyn Fischer, *Ethical Decision Making in Fund Raising* (New York: John Wiley & Sons, 2000), 21.
5. Ibid., 26.
6. Janice Gow Pettey, *Cultivating Diversity in Fundraising* (New York: John Wiley & Sons, 2002), xxvi.
7. Barbara Marion, "Decision Making in Ethics," in *Ethics in Fundraising: Putting Values into Practice. New Directions for Philanthropic Fundraising* (San Francisco: Jossey-Bass, 1994), 56.
8. Note: The Josephson Institute has modified these 11 values and now refers to "The Six Pillars of Character." They are trustworthiness, respect, responsibility, fairness, caring, and citizenship.
9. Marion, 57–59.
10. Independent Sector, *Obedience to the Unenforceable: Ethics and the Nation's Voluntary and Philanthropic Community* (Washington, DC: Independent Sector, revised 2002).
11. Anderson, 99.

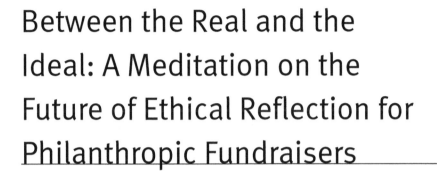

CHAPTER 14

Between the Real and the Ideal: A Meditation on the Future of Ethical Reflection for Philanthropic Fundraisers

PAUL C. PRIBBENOW, PHD

What we have loved, others will love, and we will teach them how.

—WILLIAM WORDSWORTH, *The Prelude*

When I was asked to reflect on the future of ethics for philanthropic fundraisers, my first thought was how daunting an assignment this seemed. Surely in our fast-paced, increasingly complex twenty-first century professional lives, fundraisers have only begun to scratch the surface of the ethical challenges and opportunities that will accompany new technology, increasing pressure to raise more and more philanthropic dollars, diverse and new strategies to do our work, and heightened public scrutiny of our efforts.

But then I was reminded of a lesson I learned well from my friend and colleague, Robert Payton—former college president, corporate foundation president, director of the Center on Philanthropy, and professor to all of us who study and care about philanthropic studies. The lesson always began with Bob reaching into his wallet and presenting "the card" for you to see.

Bob's card had three lists on it:

1. The seven deadly sins: pride, lust, gluttony, sloth, envy, covetousness, and anger.
2. The cardinal and theological virtues: prudence, justice, fortitude, and temperance, along with faith, hope, and love.
3. Gandhi's "seven deadly blunders," which include (among others) wealth without work, knowledge without character, and politics without pride.

The lists illustrate a couple of ideas that are crucial to ethical reflection. First, the classic virtues and vices remind us that there is great wonder in human experience. As fundraisers, we are guilty time and time again of having a limited perspective on our moral lives. We tend to focus only on the current ethical dilemma, forgetting that ethics also is about the values and commitments that make our work possible. Too often, we lack the imagination needed to see beyond the techniques of our work, beyond the dollars we raise, beyond the structures of our organizations. We easily lose sight of the wonder of the philanthropic covenant, the process of promise making and promise keeping that is at the core of a vital, healthy human relationship. Bob's lists are full of ethical promise and intrigue. We could use some promise and intrigue in our fundraising.

Second, the lists also challenge us to think about the common history we share as human beings. Bob's lists are primarily from Western sources. Your lists may come from different experiences. The point is that the values and commitments reflected in our lists remind us that an essential part of the human experience is our striving to find what is common in what we feel, what we value, what we care about, and what we seek to make real and genuine in our world. Contemporary Americans spend much more time worrying about differences and individual rights and personal opinion than they do about the common good, the body politic, and public conversation.

Think about how often you or I or our colleagues engage each other in genuine conversation about the common values that ground our work. We have codes of ethics, we have certification processes, we have research and curriculum and education, but do we have genuine conversations with the public we hope to serve and with the other participants in the philanthropic process? Those conversations are important—and too often overlooked—parts of our ethical reflection.

Bob Payton keeps that card of lists in his wallet and shares it with his friends and colleagues and students because he knows that we are not in this alone and that we do not need to reinvent the wheel when it comes to ethical reflection, but that we do need to know our history and be willing to talk about it![1]

That, then, is how I understand what is important about the future of ethical reflection for fundraisers. The poet William Wordsworth tells us that "What we have loved, others will love, and we will teach them how." I find this story about the "lists" particularly instructive because the fact is, that no matter the specific ethical challenges and opportunities we may face in our professional work, we have what we love—these rich and remarkable resources at our disposal—to help each other learn how to reflect ethically. Our challenge is to recognize and make those resources available for our colleagues and ourselves.

I am not naïve about the complexity of the ethical issues we will face as fundraisers in the future. Surely this volume offers all of us a healthy dose of reality about the sorts of ethical challenges and opportunities we will face in the years ahead. But if we focus only on the dilemmas we may face as we pursue our professional work, we may miss the many sources of guidance and inspiration that come from the ages.

This is particularly important because of the tension we all know in our work as fundraisers (and by extension this applies to all professions) between our ideals and the reality of daily experience. The question that professions in the American context have faced time and again in their evolution is the tension between the social compact for professions—the ideal aspirations of professional work—and the economic and expertise side of professions—the reality of life in the trenches. As professionals, our ethical reflection and decision making must explore and address both the ideal and the real.[2]

I think this tension between real and ideal is important on many levels, but in particular because it has genuine implications for our ethics and our moral decisions. Simply put, a focus on bold ideals often leaves us with vacuous principles untethered to the reality of our daily work, whereas a focus on the cold technique and "dull" work of fundraising leads to a set of transactional rules and guidelines, devoid of a sense of context, often interpreted simply as an easy application of the code to ethical dilemmas. We will never resolve this tension, but we must understand it and look for ways to develop a framework for the ethics of philanthropic fundraising that links the real and ideal in an integrated whole, allowing the tension, if you will, to define our character and our actions. That, it seems to me, is at the heart of the future of ethical reflection for our profession.

In this way, philanthropic fundraising is by no means unique among American professions; the tension between the social compact and technical expertise is at the heart of the professional adventure in our society, but fundraising may have an advantage because of its relative maturity (or lack thereof!) and the opportunity we all have to get it right!

What shall we do as a profession and as professionals to navigate the tension, to move toward an integrating framework for ethics in our profession? I want to suggest three linked themes that I believe may help us begin to define this framework and find the resources for our future ethical reflection.

PHILANTHROPY IS A PUBLIC PRACTICE

The first theme is the most important because it situates the work of philanthropic fundraising in relation to its highest and noblest cause: philanthropy is a public practice in a healthy democracy. Philanthropy is the "impulse to generosity" at the heart of the American character.[3] As with other professions, our work is first and foremost possible because it serves the public trust, public needs, and public goods. This understanding of philanthropy raises up issues of loyalties and priorities in our lives in a way that I find provocative and intriguing. It also points to the sorts of roles we must play not only in pursuit of our professional work, but in our need to be teachers and leaders in public discourse and in encouraging civic reflection.

This notion of philanthropy as a public practice also demands that we understand that philanthropy itself cannot be "ghettoized" in a sector. How we love each other (the literal meaning of philanthropy) takes many forms and demands ongoing refashioning. In this sense, I look to the metaphor of philanthropy as common, political work as the basis for sustaining an understanding of the public practice of philanthropy. The public practice of philanthropy will occur in various and evolving social arrangements, and our ethical reflection will need to be mindful of how those different structures and relationships continue to serve the public, common good.[4]

FUNDRAISING AS VOCATION

The second theme of our moral framework is the notion of philanthropic fundraising as a vocation or calling. If we serve a public good, then we are all public servants. A vocation, as Frederick Buechner reminds us, is that place where our deep gladness intersects with the world's deep need.[5] The ethical implications of this notion are significant because it points to our character (as a profession and as professionals) and the need to think as much about virtues and vices as we do about rules and consequences. Too much of professional ethics today is driven by responses to ethical dilemmas rather than deliberation about the sort of people we are, the character we exhibit and practice. Ethics is about much more than the problems we face; it also is about the riches of human life and experience. As professionals, we need to embrace moral reflection about the good we accomplish in our work and how that good is linked to the sorts of people we want to be.

This notion of profession as calling also brings up interesting issues about how our professional calling fits with the mission of the organizations we serve. There needs to be an ongoing dialog between personal calling and institutional values, looking for ways in which professional commitments and values are honored in organizational mission and practices. This, it seems to me, is the proper understanding of the work of stewardship.[6]

REFLECTIVE PRACTICE

The final theme then directs our attention to how ethics and ethical decision making must be reflective practice. If we have this larger framework for our work, we are pushed beyond the transactional and dilemma-oriented focus of a technical approach toward a genuine dialog between theory and practice, between character and rules, between social and historical context and the circumstances of our daily work, between the ideal and the real. It is helpful in this regard to recall another lesson from Bob Payton—the need for all of us to articulate our philanthropic autobiography, linking moral reflection to our own life experiences.

There are several important components to this understanding of ethics as reflective practice. First, ethical decision making must be conversational and dialogic. For example, University of Dayton professor Marilyn Fischer's decision-making framework for fundraising ethics demands that we consider public, organizational, professional, and personal perspectives on a given situation.[7] The work of Independent Sector also is helpful as organizations develop more deliberative processes for ethical decision making, becoming more reflective as practitioners within organizations.[8]

Second, we also must see how our work is educational and pedagogical. University of San Francisco professor Michael O'Neill is right to challenge us with the notion of fundraisers as moral teachers—teachers about values within our organizations, with donors, and in the wider public.[9]

Here, then, is a renewed challenge to all of us to refine a framework for thinking anew about ethics in our profession. We have the opportunity to model for the rest of society how a profession can integrate the ideal and real in its self-understanding and ethics and in that way point to our critical role in sustaining American democracy—any citizen's highest calling!

ABOUT THE AUTHOR

Paul Pribbenow, PhD, is the eleventh president of Augsburg College (MN), a private liberal arts college associated with the Evangelical Lutheran Church in America (ELCA).

Mr. Pribbenow also has served as president of Rockford College (Illinois); research fellow for the Center of Inquiry in the Liberal Arts at Wabash College (Indiana); dean for college advancement and secretary of the board of trustees at Wabash College; vice president of the School of the Art Institute of Chicago; and associate dean of the Divinity School of the University of Chicago.

Mr. Pribbenow holds a BA (1978) from Luther College (Iowa), and an MA (1979) and a PhD (1993) in social ethics from the University of Chicago.

Mr. Pribbenow is a member of the Association of Fundraising Professionals (AFP) National Ethics Standing Committee. He also serves on the boards of the Minnesota Private College Council, Minnesota Campus Compact, Pillsbury United Communities, and VocalEssence.

Mr. Pribbenow publishes a bimonthly email newsletter entitled *Notes for the Reflective Practitioner* and has edited two collections of essays entitled *Serving the Public Trust: Insights for Fund Raising Research and Practice*, Volumes 1 and 2 (Jossey-Bass, 2000 and 2001). He currently is at work on a book manuscript entitled *Public Service: Philanthropic Fundraising as a Calling*.

NOTES

1. The preceding section is adapted from Paul Pribbenow, "Public Character: Philanthropic Fundraising and the Claims of Accountability" in E. Tempel, S. Cobb, and W. Ilchman, eds., *The Professionalization of Fundraising: Implications*

for Education, Practice, and Accountability (San Francisco: Jossey-Bass, 1997). R. Fogal and D. Burlingame, eds., *New Directions for Philanthropic Fundraising* 15 (Spring 1997): 111–126.

2. See Paul Pribbenow, "Love and Work: Rethinking Our Models of Professions," in P. Pribbenow, ed., *Serving the Public Trust: Insights into Fundraising Research and Practice, Volume 1* (San Francisco, Jossey-Bass, 2001). D. Burlingame, T. Seiler, and E. Tempel, eds., *New Directions for Philanthropic Fundraising* 26 (Winter 1999): 29–50.

3. See Claire Gaudiani, *The Greater Good: How Philanthropy Drives the American Economy and Can Save Capitalism* (New York: Times Books, Henry Holt and Company, 2003) for a thorough review of how generosity intersects with democracy and capitalism in the North American context.

4. I argue for this understanding of philanthropy as public practice and the implications for ethical reflection in Paul Pribbenow, "Are You a Force for Good?" in *Advancing Philanthropy*, (Spring 1998): 4–8.

5. Frederick Buechner, *The Hungering Dark* (New York: HarperCollins, 1969), 31–32.

6. See Paul Pribbenow, "Stewardship and Public Life: To Whom Much Is Given Shall Much Be Expected," in *Advancing Philanthropy* (Fall/Winter 1998): 28–35.

7. Marilyn Fischer, *Ethical Decision Making in Fund Raising* (New York: John Wiley & Sons, 2000).

8. Independent Sector, *Statement of Values and Code of Ethics for Nonprofit and Philanthropic Organizations* (Washington, DC: Independent Sector, 2004).

9. Michael O'Neill, "Fundraising as an Ethical Act," *Advancing Philanthropy* 1 (1994): 30–35.

CHAPTER 15

Assessing Ethical Fundraising: The Creation and Use of the AFP Ethics Assessment Inventory

ROBERT SHOEMAKE

E thical fundraising is at the heart of the Association of Fundraising Professionals (AFP). As its mission states: "AFP, an association of professionals throughout the world, advances philanthropy by enabling people and organizations to practice *ethical and effective fundraising*" (emphasis added).[1] Each AFP member must annually affirm his or her obedience to the AFP Code of Professional Principles and Standards. In spite of this emphasis, individual fundraisers and their organizations may wonder just how ethical they are and how their ethical performance compares to AFP colleagues. By using the AFP Ethics Assessment Inventory (EAI), they can now find out. This essay describes how the EAI came to be, how it works, how it is used by individual fundraisers, fundraising organizations, and the AFP, and what has been learned since it was launched in September 2011.

BACKGROUND

Conceptual work on what became the AFP Ethics Assessment Inventory began in 2008 when the Center for Ethical Business Cultures (CEBC) at the University of St. Thomas–Minnesota responded to a Request for a Proposal (RFP) from the Association of Fundraising Professionals to design a new generation of ethics training for use by AFP's membership. One element of that training design was to be a research-based assessment tool that could be administered online. As a result of financial constraints caused by the Great Recession, the project needed to be developed in phases, with the assessment tool becoming phase one. Its development became one of three strategic priorities to be accomplished during 2012, AFP's fiftieth anniversary year. Oversight for the project was provided by the AFP Ethics Committee and by Rhonda Starr, AFP's vice president for education and training.

BUILDING THE AFP ETHICS ASSESSMENT INVENTORY

Creating the EAI required a two-step process: a *qualitative phase*, with research to identify the elements that should be included in the tool, and a *quantitative phase*, using an iterative process to build a validated survey instrument.

Qualitative Phase

The qualitative phase began by gathering data using the key informant research methodology. Information about the subject in question, in this case, ethical fundraising, is gathered from informants who are knowledgeable about the subject—AFP members. The issue was posed as follows: *Think of an AFP colleague whom you consider to be highly ethical. Describe the behaviors of that person which lead you to this conclusion.* This statement was distributed electronically to a random sample of 10,000 AFP members. Nine hundred fifty-five people responded, with a total of 2,528 individual responses.

To analyze these data, a research panel was formed. Its task was to develop the basic structure of the survey instrument by identifying

1. The characteristics of an ethical professional fundraiser.
2. Supporting statements that define each characteristic.

The panel of fundraising practitioners included Brendan Bannigan, CFRE; Audrey Kintzi, ACFRE; Michelle Rovang Burke, Roberto Soto Acosta, and Jeremy Wells, CFRE. It met at the University of St. Thomas in Minneapolis, Minnesota, July 12 to 13, 2010.

The panel used an iterative process of qualitative data clustering to review and analyze the 2,528 responses to the initial questionnaire. This process required the panel members, alone and together, to examine each of the more than 2,500 responses four times. First, the panelists identified the broad characteristics found in these responses. Working alone, each panelist examined all of the statements to identify those that were similar, clustering the statements into naturally occurring groups. Still working alone, they examined the responses a second time, sorting the statements into categories based upon the broad themes, which they discerned. These categories were based on each panelist's experiences and duties as a professional fundraiser and as a member of AFP. There were no restrictions on the number of categories identified during this first round of examination. After working individually, the panel worked as a group, looking at the categories each panelist had identified to select the main themes. The panel identified six broad themes as characteristics of ethical fundraising practice: Accountable, Adherent/Observant, Courageous, Integrity, Transparent, Trustworthy/Sincere.

Again working individually, each panelist reexamined the 2,528 responses, putting each response into one of these six categories. Finally, each panelist again reviewed the responses to select five to seven statements that, in their judgment, best illustrate each of the six categories.

At the conclusion of this qualitative phase, the 2,528 responses had been distilled into six characteristics of ethical fundraising practice and 29 statements illustrating these six characteristics.

From a research perspective, it is important to underscore that this entire process happened within the institutional and cultural boundaries of AFP. Nothing was imposed from the outside. All of the 955 people who provided the initial 2,528 individual responses and the members of the research panel that analyzed those data were shaped by AFP's values, ethical culture, and Code of Ethical Principles and Standards. The CEBC research team, led by its director of research, Dr. Douglas Jondle, designed the research protocol, observed the work of the research panel, and provided logistical support but the panel did all of its work independently.

Quantitative Phase

Like the qualitative phase, the quantitative phase was iterative. The CEBC research team converted the 29 illustrative statements into 44 survey items. These 44 items were sent to a pool of approximately 100 AFP members, including the members of the AFP Ethics Committee, to be reviewed for clarity and understandability. These edited items became the alpha version of the survey instrument.

Alpha Version: The alpha version was sent to a random sample of 10,000 AFP members. Two hundred fifty-seven responses were received. Factor analysis of the results from the alpha version eliminated 12 items.

Beta Version: The beta version, now containing 32 items, was sent to a random sample of 2,500 AFP members. Three hundred ninety responses were received. Factor analysis of the results from the beta version eliminated 18 items.

Gamma Version: The gamma version, now containing 14 items, was sent to a random sample of 5,000 AFP members. Three hundred sixty responses were received. Factor analysis confirmed the statistical validity of the instrument.

Research Panel Once Again: Though not part of the initial research design, the CEBC team decided to reconvene the research panel to review the final validated version of the survey tool. Four of the five panelists were able to participate. In addition to reviewing the validated instrument, the panelists examined the strategy for presenting the results to survey users. They returned to the 2,528 descriptive phrases used by the initial respondents for language to amplify and describe each of the six characteristics of ethical fundraising practice. This language is incorporated into the presentation of survey results.

Designing a Presentation Format: Though not a part of the initial proposal, it became clear to the research team that the way in which survey results were presented to users of the assessment tool would be critical to its long-term usefulness. In addition to testing the presentation strategy with the research panel, CEBC used two focus groups to confirm the presentation design, a group of senior AFP practitioners who attended the 2011 AFP Think Tank in Orlando, Florida, and a group of less tenured AFP practitioners who form the Education Committee of the Minnesota chapter of AFP.

Online Platform: The final step prior to launching the AFP Ethics Assessment Inventory was the development of the online platform for its administration that was done in collaboration with online survey vendor Qualtrics. In September 2011, the EAI was officially launched. By the time of its launch, more than 2,000 AFP members had participated in its creation.

CRITICAL DIMENSIONS OF ETHICAL FUNDRAISING

Beyond the assessment tool itself, perhaps the most important result of the research described above has been the identification of the six key dimensions or characteristics of ethical fundraising. Based on the more than 2,500 descriptions of ethical practice, these characteristics name the most important themes in ethical fundraising. The six characteristics are listed in alphabetical order together with the descriptive language identified by the research panel. In a separate essay in this volume, my colleague Paul Pribbenow, CFRE, who chaired the AFP Ethics

Committee during the period in which the EAI was created, reflects at length on each of these characteristics.

Accountable

As an AFP professional fundraiser with multiple accountabilities you accept responsibility for your actions. This includes making sure that funds are used effectively, efficiently, and for the purpose for which they are given. You take care to honor donor intent and represent the donor's best interest. You make decisions and recommendations for giving that are in your organization's best interest. You provide conscious oversight of the organization's financial records.

Adherent/Observant

As an AFP professional fundraiser it is your duty to act according to the highest standards of the profession and to adhere to and advocate for the AFP Code of Ethical Principles and Standards of Professional Practice. You accept responsibility to avoid the appearance of any unethical behavior. You must understand and follow all applicable laws that pertain to your profession. You must keep current with the best practices of the fundraising profession.

Courageous

As an AFP professional fundraiser you believe it is your responsibility to constantly adhere to the highest standards of performance and not compromise those standards under pressure. You are not afraid to identify something as unethical. You stand up for what is right, even when it is not popular. You are willing to tell a donor "no" when a gift is not consistent with the organization's mission. You believe that ethical behavior extends beyond the job and act accordingly in your private life.

Integrity

As an AFP professional fundraiser you convey authenticity and honesty in all personal and professional interactions. You are above reproach and do not stretch ethical boundaries. You are accountable for mistakes made and take appropriate measures to correct them.

Transparent

As an AFP professional fundraiser you make all your processes, procedures, and communications as clear and open as possible. You disclose all pertinent information and ensure it is reported accurately. You respect the wishes of donors, providing accurate answers to questions about your organization.

Trustworthy/Sincere

As an AFP professional fundraiser you exhibit conscientious and thoughtful leadership. You are sincere in your actions. You say what you are going to do and do what you say. Information, conversation, and decisions are maintained confidentially. You treat all people with courtesy and respect.

TAKING THE AFP ETHICS ASSESSMENT INVENTORY

Users of the EAI respond online to a 14-item survey questionnaire. Results are private, seen only by the user. They are presented electronically in a format that can be saved and printed by the user. To facilitate ongoing research, AFP and CEBC will collect the aggregate data from all users, but these data will be anonymous.

Based on their responses to the survey instrument, the EAI provides users with three snapshots of ethical performance:

1. The user's assessment of themselves.
2. The user's assessment of the organization in which they work.
3. A comparison of the user and their organization.

The EAI and the Quest for Alignment

Behind the design of this survey instrument is an assumption that the best ethical decisions will be made when there is alignment between the individual moral compass of the fundraising professional, the principles and standards of the profession as a whole, and the values of the organization in which the fundraising professional work. The three panels provide a picture of alignment at this moment, based on the user's perceptions. It is important to note that there are usually gaps in at least some of these categories.

Mapping and Interpreting Users' Individual Results

The AFP Ethics Assessment Inventory provides a snapshot, based on each user's evaluation of their ethical performance at this moment in time. This assessment is not a test that users can pass or fail. Rather, it is intended to aid in the lifelong process of improving ethical performance as a fundraising practitioner. The inventory is designed to point out areas of strength and areas in which users might want to grow in their practice—based on each user's evaluation of their performance.

The benchmark for each score (the number 100 in Exhibit 15.1) represents the average score of fellow AFP practitioners who have completed this instrument. That is, the norm to which users are compared is derived from peers in AFP. A score above the mean suggests an area of strength as compared to colleagues in AFP; a score below the mean suggests an area in which there is an opportunity for growth as compared to AFP peers.

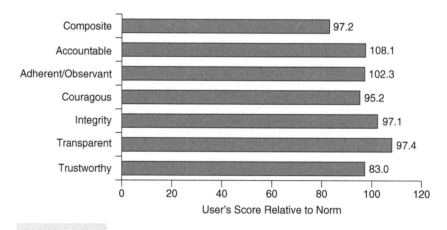

EXHIBIT 15.1   **USER'S INDIVIDUAL SCORE**

In Exhibit 15.1, this user's composite score is 97.2, slightly below the norm. In two categories, Accountable and Adherent/Observant, this user scores above the norm. In the other four categories, this user scores below the norm. The score in the category Trustworthy/Sincere is further from the norm than all of the other categories. This may be an area in which this user struggles and where he or she might want to concentrate in strengthening their professional practice. Because no one but the individual user sees these results, each person can choose what they do with the results.

Mapping and Interpreting Organizational Results

Exhibit 15.2 of the AFP Ethics Assessment Inventory provides a snap-shot, based on each user's evaluation, of their organization's ethical performance at this moment in time. The benchmark for each score (the number 100 in Exhibit 15.2) represents the average score of organizations that have been evaluated by fellow AFP practitioners. Each user's organization is compared to the norm for other organizations. It is important to underscore that these organizational scores are based on each user's perception in evaluating the organization in which they work.

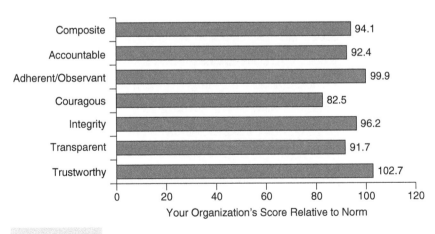

EXHIBIT **15.2**   **ORGANIZATIONAL SCORE**

The organization rated in Exhibit 15.2 has a composite score of 94.1, a bit below the organizational norm. This organization scores below the norm on every category except Trustworthy where it scores slightly above the norm. Based on this user's perception of their organization, the most challenging category is Courageous.

Comparing and Interpreting Individual and Organizational Results

Exhibit 15.3 compares the user's individual results with their organization's results. The benchmark for this panel (the number 100 in Exhibit 15.3) is the user's evaluation of them. This exhibit provides a snapshot of the alignment between the user's individual ethical performance and that of their organization at this moment in time. Recall that both the user's score and that of their organization are based on the user's perception.

In Exhibit 15.3, this user's organization scores 11.4 points below the user's overall score. The organization scores below the user in every dimension except Trustworthy. Exhibit 15.3 provides a snapshot of the alignment in ethical practice of the user and their organization. As noted above, this is important because of a belief that the best ethical decisions

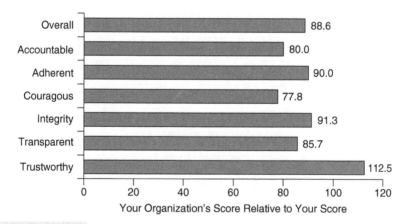

EXHIBIT 15.3   **COMPARING THE USER AND THEIR ORGANIZATION**

are made when an individual's moral compass, the ethical principles of their profession, and the values of the organization in which they work are all aligned. If there is a persistent ethical disconnect between an individual fundraiser and the organization in which they work, it may suggest that that individual does not fit in that organization.

In examining each of these three exhibits, an observer can see that there are gaps between the norm and the user's scores. We do not yet have a large enough data set to be able to draw substantive conclusions about these gaps. For example, what size gap might be considered normal and what size would indicate a significant issue. As the data set continues to grow, we will be able to do additional analysis and discover additional relationships between the data in order to answer these and other questions that may arise.

USING THE AFP ETHICS ASSESSMENT INVENTORY

Whether speaking of individuals, organizations, or AFP, change in ethical performance tends to be an evolutionary process as individuals, groups, and organizations learn, practice, and habituate new behaviors. For this reason, it cannot be emphasized enough that the EAI is intended as a developmental tool. It does *not* tell users or organizations whether or not they are ethical. Rather, at a given moment in time, it points to areas of strength and areas in which there are opportunities for growth in the practice of ethical fundraising. While the data can point the way, it is up to users to decide what actions they will take.

The EAI and Individual Fundraisers

The EAI was developed precisely because ethical practice is essential to fundraising as a profession and to AFP as an organization. By allowing AFP members to assess their individual ethical performance, it becomes a vehicle for strengthening the profession. Its usefulness to an individual fundraising practitioner depends in large measure on that person's ability to honestly evaluate their ethical performance. While almost everyone *wants* to perform at the highest ethical standard all the time, the reality is that no one does. Individuals who evaluate themselves based on their performance as they wish it to be rather than as it really is will get a skewed picture that will be less helpful to their personal development. Individuals who evaluate themselves as honestly as possible will get a picture that, while certainly less than perfect, will provide them with information they can use to improve their ethical performance.

The EAI and Fundraising Organizations

The EAI is designed for use not only with individuals but also with organizations. In the same way that it provides individuals with a snapshot of their ethical performance at a given moment in time, it provides organizations and their leaders with a snapshot of that organization's ethical performance. This picture can be used within organizations to assess the ethical culture of a given fundraising organization.

For example, a university with 50 gift officers in its development office is an organizational member of AFP. As a result of that membership, each one of those gift officers can use the EAI to assess their individual performance, including their individual perceptions of their organization. Working with AFP (this is necessary because the organizational picture is not automatically created), the EAI can also provide the organization as a whole with a snapshot of its ethical performance. As with individuals, this snapshot identifies strengths and opportunities for growth. It has the potential to give organizations and their leaders valuable insight into their organization's ethical culture. (Note: It is important to underscore that an organizational profile would be an aggregate of all of the individuals who complete the survey. It would *not* reveal information about any single individual.)

The EAI and AFP

The research on which the EAI is based and the EAI itself have the potential to assist AFP in its mission of advancing philanthropy through "ethical and effective fundraising" in at least three ways:

1. The six dimensions of ethical fundraising.
2. Data-driven training.

3. An ongoing research relationship with the Center for Ethical Business Cultures.

As was noted at the beginning of this essay, the EAI is intended as the first step in a new generation of ethics training within AFP. The six dimensions of ethical fundraising identified by this research provide AFP with a framework that can be used to structure the design of that training. Individual modules can be built that focus on specific dimensions of ethical performance; for example, courage or transparency. Entire courses, such as ethics for new AFP members, can be developed based on the six characteristics. When used in conjunction with the EAI, the effectiveness of these curricular materials can be tested and they can be modified in a process of continuous improvement, with a long-term goal of strengthening the ethical performance of its members, of AFP, and the fundraising profession.

As with individuals and organizations, the EAI provides AFP with rich data about the strengths and opportunities for growth in the ethical performance of fundraising professionals. These data can be used to develop training modules that target specific segments of AFP's global membership. Suppose, for example, that the data suggest that fundraisers in a certain sector of the industry have challenges with Transparency. A training module can be developed focusing on that particular industry sector. Or suppose that the data indicate that fundraisers who have been AFP members for two to five years are consistently having difficulty with adherence to the AFP Code of Ethical Principles and Standards. Training can be developed that specifically addresses those practitioners. Because the data allows the training to be more focused, it should also be more effective.

The Center for Ethical Business Cultures (CEBC) conducts research on the ways in which ethical organization cultures are created and sustained. The longitudinal data provided by the EAI will allow CEBC and AFP to track ways in which AFP's ethical performance changes over time. The EAI will also provide a way for AFP to assess the effectiveness of specific training as it is developed and used. Because AFP plays such a central role in professional fundraising, initiatives that improve the ethical performance of its members can only enhance the ethical performance of the profession as a whole.

WHAT WE ARE LEARNING

At the time this text was written, the EAI had been in use for just over a year. While the sample size of EAI users is still too small to draw large conclusions, certain things are becoming clear.

- The tool is working exactly as hoped for. As the number of users has continued to grow, the aggregate data have been very consistent. As software developers know, new software often comes with unintended glitches. To date, the EAI has been glitch-free. A reliable ethics assessment instrument will provide value for AFP and for all its users.
- Tenure in AFP makes a difference in who uses the EAI. Only 16 percent of fundraisers in their first year of AFP membership (28 percent of AFP members) use the EAI. In years 2 through 10, EAI use tracks AFP membership. Beginning in year 11, EAI use increases significantly. Those who have been AFP members for 11 through 15 years (10 percent of AFP members) represent 14 percent of EAI users. Those who have been in AFP longer than 16 years (10 percent of AFP members) comprise 19 percent of EAI users. Together these two groups represent 20 percent of AFP members but fully a third of EAI users.

These data are suggestive in at least three different directions:

1. With new AFP members, they may underscore a need to emphasize very early on the critical role that ethical performance plays in long-term success as a fundraiser. AFP may want to intensify its focus on the ethical dimensions of fundraising with those in their first year of AFP membership.
2. With fundraisers who have been part of AFP for more than a decade, it would seem that the longer they have been part

of AFP, the more they internalize AFP's emphasis on ethical fundraising. Consequently, they find it valuable to assess their ethical performance.

3. It may be that the more experience one has as a fundraiser and the more one has had to grapple with difficult ethical challenges without clear black-and-white answers, the more eager one is to understand one's own ethical performance as compared to one's peers. To tie these observations together, it would seem that the data may be pointing out both a need and an opportunity. New members need to learn how important ethics are to fundraising; experienced members are convinced of that importance and might become mentors to their more junior peers.

These are early observations from the AFP Ethics Assessment Inventory. More, and more significant, will surely come with continued use. This instrument has the potential to become a key part of AFP's toolbox, providing data to individual fundraisers, organizations and AFP as a whole that can assist each user and can enhance ethical fundraising.

FREQUENTLY ASKED QUESTIONS (FAQs)

Here is a list of frequently asked questions in relation to the AFP Ethical Assessment Inventory:

- **Who built this tool?** The AFP Ethical Assessment Inventory was developed by the Center for Ethical Business Cultures at the University of St. Thomas–Minnesota, a 35-year-old nonprofit that works with leaders to create ethical and profitable cultures.
- **What does the EAI measure?** The EAI assesses the ethical performance of AFP fundraising practitioners along six dimensions of ethical practice.
- **Is this a test that I can flunk?** No. The EAI is a developmental tool, designed to point out areas of strength and opportunities for growth in the ethical dimensions of your work as a fundraising professional.

- **Will my participation or involvement affect my AFP membership?** No. Use of the AFP Ethical Assessment Inventory is completely voluntary.
- **Will anyone besides me see the results?** No. Only you will see your personal data. AFP and CEBC will collect the aggregate data from all users for research purposes, but these data will be anonymous.
- **Can my score mean that I am unethical?** No. Your score compares you to your peers within AFP. It presents your results along a continuum that points out areas of strength and areas in which you can improve your ethical performance. The creators of this instrument assume that you can continually improve the ethical dimensions of your practice as a fundraiser over a lifetime.
- **How often should I use this tool? If the results are a "moment snapshot"—how often should I check back in to reassess?** Until the data suggest otherwise, the EAI should be used not more frequently than once every six months.
- **How is the AFP Ethical Assessment Inventory relevant to me as a professional fundraiser?** There is a saying in the total quality movement that you can't improve what you don't measure. The EAI measures your ethical performance so that you can continue to strengthen it. Given the critical importance ethical performance plays in successful fundraising, strengthening ethical performance seems highly relevant.
- **Why should I use the AFP Ethics Assessment Inventory?** You don't have to. Using the EAI is completely voluntary. You should use the EAI if:
  - You believe that your ethical performance is relevant to your success as a fundraiser.
  - You want a concrete picture of your ethical performance as a fundraiser.
  - You want to use the information provided by that picture to continue to improve your ethical performance.
- **Why did AFP develop the EAI?** Ethics is at the heart of AFP's mission: "AFP, an association of professionals throughout

the world, advances philanthropy by enabling people and organizations to practice *ethical and effective fundraising*." AFP created the EAI as a tool for its members to use to assess and strengthen their practice as ethical fundraising professionals.

- **How will I use the results to help me in my career?** Ethical performance as a fundraiser is not a guarantee of long-term success. However without it, you will certainly fail. You can use the results from the EAI to identify areas of your ethical performance, which can be enhanced, and areas of strength, you can continue to develop.

ABOUT THE AUTHOR

Robert C. Shoemake serves as the director of programs and membership at the Center for Ethical Business Cultures at the University of St. Thomas. The Center is a not-for-profit educational organization that assists business leaders in creating ethical and profitable business cultures at the enterprise, community and global levels. He is a member of the adjunct faculty at the University of St. Thomas, teaching business ethics in its Opus College of Business and theology in its College of Arts and Sciences.

Mr. Shoemake has worked in business, academia, and the nonprofit sector. He has served on numerous other nonprofit boards in the arts, civic engagement, and affordable housing.

Mr. Shoemake received a Master of Divinity from Emory University's Candler School of Theology and a Bachelor of Music Education in voice and choral conducting from the University of South Carolina. He has completed further graduate study at institutions in South Carolina and Minnesota.

NOTE

1. Association of Fundraising Professionals, www.afpnet.org/About/content.cfm?ItemNumber=4385 (accessed October 27, 2012).

CHAPTER 16

Regulation, Ethics, and Philanthropy

AUDREY KINTZI, CATHLENE WILLIAMS

E thics is fundamental to any profession, especially for those who engage in doing the public good through private action. Philanthropic fundraising is possible because of public trust in the work of nonprofits, and public trust can be reinforced by properly understood enforcement and standardization of polices. Laws and government regulation of nonprofits often come about in response to a lack of ethical conduct in the management of nonprofits, in particular in the aftermath of high-profile scandals.

The integration of ethics and regulation was the focus of the October 2011 AFP think tank "Regulation, Ethics and Philanthropy: A Sector-Wide Dialogue in the Interest of the Public Good." The think tank sought clarity on such questions as: How does ethical practice strengthen charities? Would external regulation improve or diminish the value-added work of nonprofits? How might nonprofits maintain their distinct identity—neither public nor private, with or without further regulation by the government? What are the major ethical challenges facing nonprofits? How can a strong ethical stance strengthen the sector so that external oversight is less necessary? How does one build an ethical organization?

Organized by AFP's Research Council, the two-day think tank attracted 29 participants, several of whom participated by phone conference because of the snowstorm that grounded many travelers. This was the sixth in a series of think tanks held every two to three years to bring together scholars and practitioners to discuss research priorities for the sector. Funding for the think tank was provided through the AFP Foundation for Philanthropy with a generous grant from the Edyth Bush Charitable Foundation, Inc.

Content Presentations

Audrey Kintzi, ACFRE, chair of the 2011 Think Tank, gave an overview of a webinar presented in October 2010 by Rushworth Kidder, PhD, president and founder of the Institute for Global Ethics. Dr. Kidder's theme was moral courage and ethical fundraising. He spoke about the concept of building ethical fitness and a culture of integrity by examining core shared values, making ethical decisions, and acting with moral courage.

Five core values related to ethics are respect, compassion, honesty, fairness, and responsibility, all of which are important to building trust between fundraisers and those with whom they work. Ethical issues arise not only when there is a clear right versus wrong, but also when two or more core values are in conflict (right versus right). Five tests might be used to guide ethical decision making: Is it legal? Does it conform to government regulations? Does it pass the "stink test?" Would you want your decision to appear on the front page of the newspaper? What would Mom (or Dad) think?

Kidder's third component of ethical fitness is moral courage, defined as "the willing endurance of significant danger for the sake of principle." If we do nothing to act on our ethical decisions, he said, it's no different than having no values or not making a decision. Using a diagram of intersecting circles depicting values, danger, and endurance, he noted that moral courage occurs at the intersection of these three elements. It involves "sticking your neck out" for a moral principle. As John Wayne would say, "Courage is being scared to death and saddling up anyway."

How should AFP help its members think about ethical issues before problems arise? Ms. Kintzi offered the example of the Southern Minnesota AFP Chapter, where every chapter meeting begins with discussion of an ethics case and the values inherent in ethical decision making. Ethics training can help to build a culture of integrity in our organizations.

Melanie Leslie, professor of law at Benjamin N. Cardozo School of Law, challenged participants to think about how to prevent and manage conflicts of interest in governance of nonprofit organizations. "We like to think that nonprofit boards make decisions that are in the best interest of the nonprofit, but sometimes transactions involve conflicts of interest that can open the nonprofit to scrutiny by legal authorities," she said.

As of tax year 2008 the IRS requires all conflict of interest transactions to be disclosed on the nonprofit's tax return. The IRS also requests that the nonprofit provide a statement on why each transaction was made. The IRS presumes a transaction is good for the nonprofit if:

1. It is approved by a majority of independent board members (or a committee of the board).
2. Those approving relied on appropriate data.
3. There is adequate documentation of the basis for the decision. Most states also have laws that require a transaction have advance approval by a majority of disinterested directors after full disclosure, and that the transaction is fair.

Legal guidelines provide a general framework for decisions by boards, but they can't completely eliminate bad decision making. Even if transactions involving a conflict of interest are within the law, they may make the nonprofit look bad to constituents, which can do more harm to the nonprofit than any other form of liability.

To avoid problems, Professor Leslie recommended that the safest course of action (the bullet-proof approach) is to avoid transactions in which board members might obtain a benefit, either directly or indirectly. She also recommended that every nonprofit have conflict of interest policies in place that require board members to disclose conflicts and that structure transactions to eliminate conflicts. Policies should be easy to understand and should be made clear to board members.

The second best approach is to develop sound procedures that work against bad groupthink, a situation in which board members self-identify with the board and it becomes difficult for them to dissent from a board decision. Sound procedures include:

1. Bring it to the full board (not a subcommittee).
2. Full disclosure of the conflict and the terms of the deal (with the interested director out of the room during the discussion/decision).
3. Ask if this deal is the best deal (Does the nonprofit need this quality of good or service? Is the price better than market price?).
4. Document that there is no better deal available on the market.

Michael DeLucia, trustee of the Agnes Lindsay Trust, and former director of charitable trusts for the New Hampshire Attorney General's Office, spoke about government regulations and charitable fundraising. "There is a great need for *both* effective government regulation *and* greater self-regulation in the nonprofit sector," he said, "and there is a need for more collaboration between government regulators and the sector."

Mr. DeLucia is a proponent of government education programs for nonprofits on what is meant by compliance and legal behavior. He cited examples of this, including collaboration by state attorneys general to simplify state regulations affecting nonprofits and to develop videos and webinars for nonprofits on state regulations, and the Governance Checklist on Part VI (Governance) of IRS Form 990, which asks questions that can help guide nonprofits toward developing good governance procedures.

There are four major trends that affect regulation of the charitable sector, he said:

1. The proliferation of charities. Thirty-two nonprofits are created/approved each hour in the United States, based on a 40-hour

workweek at the IRS. Is this a positive or a negative development? How does it impact fundraising, regulators, duplication of services, and quality of boards/fiduciary duties?

2. Increased scrutiny by regulators and the media. Entities including the IRS, state attorneys general, the U.S. Senate Finance Committee, and the U.S. House Committee on Government Oversight are all responsible for some aspect of nonprofit oversight.

3. The persistence of fraud and embezzlement. Authors in a recent publication estimated that the cost of fraud in the charitable sector is approximately $40 billion annually—a staggering percentage of the charitable giving that donors contribute annually to nonprofit organizations. The authors concluded that fraud may be easier to perpetrate in nonprofits because of factors such as

   i. An atmosphere of trust.
   ii. Weak internal controls.
   iii. Lack of financial expertise.
   iv. Reliance on voluntary boards, whose members may lack skill in scrutinizing financial statements or in providing the tough oversight that is needed. DeLucia suggested boards need to implement internal controls, work with their auditors to identify vulnerabilities in their organizations, and create an anonymous reporting (whistleblower) system for employees that ensures confidentiality.

4. The movement toward self-regulation. DeLucia cited Independent Sector's work in developing the 2005 report to Congress, *Strengthening Transparency, Governance and Accountability*. Another model for moving toward self-regulation is the collaboration in New Hampshire among the Attorney General's Office, the New Hampshire Center for Nonprofits, the New Hampshire Charitable Foundation, and Certified Public Accountants. Results of this collaboration include a guidebook for directors and officers and video presentations on fiduciary responsibilities of nonprofit board members. He also mentioned AFP's Code of Ethical Principles and Standards and AFP's ethics enforcement policies and process as good examples of self-regulation.

DISCUSSION SUMMARIES

Breakout discussions were held to discuss case studies related to the issues raised. Recorders for each breakout reported to the group on the *is* and the *ought* of each case study situation, and how fundraisers, individually and in common, might respond to the ethical, legal, and regulatory issues raised.

CASE STUDY	CASE STUDY 1: A PARTICULARLY CHALLENGING MONDAY

This case relates to two letters received by Bill, a new development officer with an arts organization.

1. An event planner, Jane, notifies him that she will be charging the nonprofit a finder's fee for a sponsorship she has secured for a dinner auction event to raise money for the nonprofit.
2. A donor to his previous nonprofit notifies him that she intends to change her will, removing a $100,000 bequest previously intended for his former employer and substituting the organization for which he now works.

In the case of the finder's fee, the group developed this list of points to ponder:

- This may not be an issue for someone who is coming to the nonprofit sector from the for-profit scene.
- If the contract has been signed, there may be no recourse, but Bill could hint that Jane will not be hired again!
- Does the sponsor know there's a finder's fee? Find out what the donor knows about this, and how he/she reacts.
- We don't really know how much the event planner is being paid, and if this is a small or large donation/payment. It could make a difference if we knew these facts.
- The board should be familiar with it, the CEO should have signed off, and is the CFO part of this transaction.
- There is a difference between the Code of Ethics and IRS regulations, and Bill should be aware of this. For AFP standards, it's a no-no. Never pay a finder's fee, no matter what.

- Where does the responsibility fall? There is a difference, even if subtle, between a large organization with many employees and clear lines of responsibility versus a small organization where employees have multiple responsibilities.

Possible actions to take in this situation are:

- Study the contract and make sure this finder's fee is in the contract.
- Evaluate whether this is an advertising fee or a donation. There should be disclosure on which this is, because of how the donor/sponsor will be handled, but no matter what, there is no finder's fee allowable.
- Be more alert and astute the next time there is a contract of any kind to be signed.
- It's legal if it's a contract, so there is no choice about paying her, but Bill should have a conversation with Jane about why there can be no finder's fee.
- Find out if the board knows about this, has sanctioned it, and finds it unobjectionable.
- Be prepared to present yourself as a professional the next time you interview, and be clear on what that means.
- Position this in the context of accountability, a major issue in fundraising, and this can protect Bill internally and externally.
- Talk with the president about this situation, just in case he/she negotiated it and innocently committed this infraction.

In the case of the previous donor who wants to change her will to benefit Bill's new organization, the group developed this list of points to ponder:

- If a donor personally gives us a gift, it must be of nominal value.
- Ideally, donors, CEOs, vendors understand the AFP code of ethics. Our standards should be made clear to the donor. This helps with the big issue of accountability.
- If the fundraiser didn't ask for the donor to transfer her gift to the fundraiser's current organization, then it really isn't

(Continued)

an infraction on the part of the fundraiser. It was the donor's choice as a result of hearing about this career move.

- However, the donor wouldn't know about the fundraiser's new organization if he/she hadn't worked for the previous organization. That puts a different perspective on the relationship.
- Bill needs to document how this relationship has evolved and that he didn't have undue influence.
- What if Bill left the previous organization because of problems he knew about, but feels duty-bound or by loyalty not to share these? How does that affect how he will speak to Mrs. McCarthy (the donor)?
- Fundraisers often make friends, intentionally or unintentionally, but they need to remember they are doing this for the cause, even though there is a personal relationship. This is a good reason to involve volunteers!

Possible actions to take in this situation are:

- Bill could counsel the donor to leave the gift where it is because he can vouch that it will be used well.
- Besides the ethics question, there is also the matter of Bill setting up expectations with his organization which aren't reasonable, so it's a danger for him personally/professionally.
- Get outside counsel who can talk with the donor about her intent, her circumstances, her loyalties.
- Offer to introduce Mrs. McCarthy to Bill's replacement, and encourage her to have all the facts before she makes the decision to change her gift.

The group developed a list of recommendations for think tank professionals and AFP action:

- AFP could have a service that backs up the employee/fundraiser and supports the decision (provided the decision is congruent with AFP's code of ethics).
- Be alert to trends in expectations of fundraising professionals (e.g., more pressure to work on commission, more demand for professionals to prove they are bringing in

results; but these demands don't take into consideration the time and effort it takes to raise funds).

- AFP needs to widely publicize that there are strict standards of behavior.
- Potential employers could/should sign the code. AFP then could develop a process by which the organization is held accountable.
- Encourage volunteerism, which ensures at least to some degree that the relationship is between the donor and the organization.
- Continue to educate fundraisers that they are facilitators, and they can never forget why they do fundraising. It's not about honor and glory for the fundraiser (which sometimes becomes the focus) but about the cause.
- AFP needs to remind us it's not about the money. It's about good causes that have a price tag.
- Advise professionals not to send mixed messages to organizations and donors because of how recognition is carried out.
- AFP can aid members on how to urge their leaders/boards to establish policies against which to measure such decisions as illustrated in this case study.

CASE STUDY

CASE STUDY 2: SERVING TWO MASTERS: HOW SHOULD A BOARD HANDLE AN UNUSUAL CONFLICT OF INTEREST?

This case is about a board member of Friends of Marine Animals (FOMA) who has been aggressively trying to convince the rest of the board to support his idea to focus solely on the plight of the manatees. Frustrated by the continued lack of response from the board, he has recently started a new organization—Save

(Continued)

Our Sea Cows (SOSC), and he asks the FOMA board to support it. The board is worried that his new organization is a competitor that will draw on their donors and volunteer base.

The group discussed the missing context in the case:

- Need more information about Arthur's intent, his history with FOMA, the size of gifts he has made to FOMA, whether he plans to continue to support FOMA (financially and as an advocate).
- Clearly some members of the board question Arthur's intent and fear zero-sum fundraising competition between FOMA and SOSC.
- Do they have any evidence that Arthur cannot be trusted to live up to his duties of care, obedience, and loyalty to FOMA?
- Is Arthur posing a legal or ethical threat to FOMA or is this just a personality conflict?
  - There is concern that Arthur might appropriate information from FOMA to use for SOSC benefit. We don't know whether FOMA has policies and procedures in place to guard against taking privileged information to SOSC.
  - We don't know whether FOMA has an ED or other leadership who could take the initiative to work with Arthur outside the board context to resolve the issue.
- It appears that the board chair has abdicated the leadership role in this case.
- If there is staff, we know very little about how effective their working relationship is with the board.

The group described the situation (what *is*):

- The law isn't helpful in this case.
  - While state and federal laws guard against appropriation of privileged information among for-profit entities, they are largely silent on the issue of what constitutes privileged information or improper exchanges of such among nonprofits.
  - Some state regulations govern nonprofit conflicts of interest and donor confidentiality. We don't know anything about FOMA's state.

- Part VI of the IRS 990 return lists governance practices and policies that could be helpful to FOMA. We don't know whether FOMA has adopted any of them.
- FOMA board members did not assume the responsibility of speaking up as issues arose—either in committee or as a full board.
- Passive resistance on the board's part probably fueled Arthur's determination that *he* would have to do something on his own.
  - If FOMA has policies, processes, and procedures in place to deal with proposals for new programming, changes to the mission, conflicts of interests, and/or privileged information, the board clearly needs to boost its understanding of and capacity to enforce them.
  - There is not necessarily a conflict when a person serves on two boards; it depends on the person's behavior. Arthur was with FOMA for a long time. He may have clear loyalties to FOMA that should be respected.
- Serving on the board of, or raising money for, another organization—even one with a similar mission—does not necessarily raise a conflict of interest.
- Grant makers and other donors are free to give to whomever they wish and often give to similar causes.
  - The key question isn't whether Arthur fundraises and advocates for SOSC. It's whether Arthur continues to honor his duties of care, loyalty, and obedience to FOMA.
  - Arthur's behavior may (advertently or inadvertently) confuse FOMA donors and prospective donors. There's a danger that some supporters will perceive a shift in FOMA's organizational direction unless efforts are made to publically reinforce its focus on its current mission and clarify its relationship with SOSC.
  - At the same time, FOMA does not want to do/say anything that creates more confusion, reflects negatively on Arthur or SOSC, or breeds ill will with prospective funders.
- FOMA will have to walk a delicate tightrope to keep its mission and focus clear in the minds of its supporters and prospective supporters.

(Continued)

The ideal state in this situation (the *ought*):

- The ideal is predicated on what you perceive to be the *is*. Are we truly on a course that identifies the issue?
- FOMA could have benefitted from established policies, processes, and procedures to deal with proposals for new programming and changes to mission.
- A FOMA committee could have dealt first with Arthur's proposal to help manatees to the exclusion of other animals—perhaps electing to test a pilot program focused on protecting the manatees to see how it would work from the perspectives of mission effectiveness, messaging, and fundraising.
- The FOMA board might consider making a deal that would make SOSC a subprogram of FOMA, or offer advertising/sponsorship for SOSC.
  - An "ounce of prevention is worth a pound of cure," especially when combined with a little personal attention. This situation might have been prevented.
- The FOMA ED/board chair could have taken Arthur aside early on to hear him out and work through a solution that would acknowledge and provide an outlet for Arthur's concern for the manatees while protecting the mission of FOMA.
  - Ideally, FOMA board members would understand what governance entails and their responsibilities as board members.
  - This case could have been a win-win situation. By taking advantage of Arthur's enthusiasm and being willing to accept new ideas, the board might have created a situation where both FOMA and SOSC benefited.

Findings, conclusions, and intriguing questions raised by the group were:

- Since there are no legal constraints about privacy of donor information, the nonprofit sector needs to have clear policies/procedures in place to protect donor information. We need the context of the law but ethical decision making is not a subsidiary of law.

- We need to be more intentional and active in creating guidelines for ourselves and our board members; more importantly, we need to create more opportunity for stimulating conversations around these issues.
- AFP has a huge opportunity to lend its expertise to the process of educating nonprofit executives and board members on these issues.
- As we include business members and vendors in AFP we must take more responsibility to engage/train and ensure that employees of these groups understand AFP ethical standards.
- Many people from the for-profit world want to give back to society by becoming involved in the nonprofit world. If they really want to make a difference, they can be a great asset to the nonprofit.
- AFP should consider how board members might fit into new membership models being considered.
  - Nonprofits have an obligation to let donors know what's going on with their organizations, including any shifts in mission, purpose, or organizational direction. The best way to clarify any confusion that arises is to focus on sharing and reinforcing your own mission and how it addresses vital community needs—not try to explain how yours differs from someone else's.
- Maintain a professional stance and minimize adversarial posturing.
  - Nonprofits need to have clear, consistently enforced policies, processes, and procedures in place to deal with ideas for new programming, proposed changes to the mission, conflicts of interests, and/or privileged information. Board member orientation, continued education, and disclosure are essential to strengthening board capacity and willingness to deal with issues that arise.
- Nonprofit leaders (executive and board) need special coaching in how to facilitate education and enforcement.
- All dilemmas are not necessarily conflicts; however, all conflicts do need to be disclosed.

(Continued)

- How many new nonprofits emerge because existing organizations refuse to consider programming ideas that might
expand or strengthen their missions? At what point does
the proliferation of nonprofits contribute to donor fatigue
and overall resource scarcity? Answers to these questions
may call for some serious thinking about how existing nonprofits can become more inclusive, creative and accepting
of new ideas.
- We lament board members taking information about our
organizations and donors elsewhere. Yet, we ask board
members to give us as much information as possible
about people they know and with whom they have worked
on behalf of other organizations. To what extent are we
practicing a double standard?

CASE STUDY

**CASE STUDY 3: THE FOR-PROFIT
CEO WHO WANTS TO DO
THE RIGHT THING**

In this case, a major national for-profit corporation asks a professional to help it create and maintain a new "Let's Give Now"
feature on its website, in which 10 percent of every purchase
made on the website would be given to a charitable cause.
Consumers would check a box allowing the corporation to
divide the contributions among a pool of 10 different charities,
selected by the CEO of the corporation.

The group discussed the known facts about this case:

- Major national for-profit corporation has a website and
wants to create "Let's Give Now" section of website.
- Offer 10 percent of every purchase to a total of 10 charitable
organizations.
- CEO has selected the charities and he or family members
serve on boards of these charities.
- Some charities are okay, but others raise questions.

- CEO was under investigation by SEC for possible insider trading; corporation has had severe financial difficulties recently.

And the missing context in the case:

- Who is the professional being approached by the CEO?
- For-profit third-party processor?
- Fundraising consultant?
- Representative of a nonprofit?
- What is the professional's existing relationship with the CEO?

Issues raised by this case include:

- No question — responsibility for due diligence.
- Are we dealing with ignorance of nonprofit best practices or deceptive intent?
- Is there charitable intent from CEO or donor?
- How do you judge character?

The reality of the situation is:

- Don't take things at CEO's word: Don't trust him.
- May not be anything left for each charity after administrative costs.
- Must contact 10 organizations and get approval to use brand, establish gift parameters.
- Not a good deal for everyone — only a good deal for CEO, who will probably be exasperated: "Why won't you take this money?"

The ideal in this situation would be:

- CEO wants to support but hasn't worked out all the specifics — there is genuine philanthropic intent and trust.
- Need formal criteria for which charities are selected to benefit.
- You can do your due diligence on the for-profit companies as well as the charities.
- Mutual and written agreement amongst all parties.
- Potential benefit to charities is worth the effort.
- Clear disclosure and audit trail for gifts.

(Continued)

The group developed the following findings/list of questions related to this case:

- Due diligence: Do fundraisers underestimate how much investigation they should do about organizations or donors they are associated with?
- Are there privacy issues?
- How many sources of information are you using?
- Moral character of donor: How do you assess the person's intent?
- Is there a true philanthropic connection or are they just using you to burnish their image? (Michael Milken example.)
- Are you potentially rushing to judgment?
- For-profit mind-set versus philanthropic mind-set: Is there a fundamental difference in the way we think?
- Should we be concerned about the number of former for-profit people entering the nonprofit workforce (particularly regarding compensation)?
- What is the competitive advantage of the Code and how do we consistently communicate that?
- Establishment of clear best practices: Do we have consistent rules that we can cite to be our escape hatch in situations like this?
- Checklists and processes are critical.
- CEO may not be conscious of impropriety—may just need to be educated on best practices.
- Use regulators and policies as your "bad cop."

Paul Pribbenow, PhD, CFRE, president of Augsburg College, led a discussion about potential next steps for individual fundraisers, for AFP, and for the fundraising profession in three broad areas: education and formation, management and leadership, and advocacy and public policy.

For philanthropic fundraising professionals who need resources to help them grow in their understanding and practice of ethical fundraising:

1. Continue the important ethics education work now under way in the creation of the Ethics Assessment Inventory Tool, and aggressively pursue and support the development of additional ethics education resources—including, but not limited to, curriculum, case studies, reference guides, and web-based materials—that help fundraisers develop more nuanced capacities to analyze ethical situations and make ethical decisions.
2. Develop in these ethics education resources the sort of teaching methods that help professionals move beyond ethics simply as compliance to codes and standards to a conversational, narrative approach that grounds ethical decision making in the complexities and wider contexts in which professional work is pursued.

For nonprofit executives and board members who need resources to help them understand the claims of ethical fundraising and its links to other legal and regulatory issues:

1. Forge a partnership with other like-minded organizations (e.g., Independent Sector, BoardSource, and Association of Governing Boards) to develop resources to promote best practices and educate nonprofit sector leaders about the claims of ethical fundraising on governance and organizational management.
2. Develop a campaign that helps AFP members (and other fundraising professionals) promote these resources in the organizations they serve, including accessible educational materials, templates for organizational policies and practices related to fundraising, and reference guides that help sector leaders recognize the links between ethics, the law and regulatory requirements.

For the wider public, that needs clear, concise, and targeted information about ethical fundraising and philanthropy:

1. Develop and launch a highly visible public image campaign that promotes ethical fundraising through the use of concrete and compelling illustrations.

2. Reinvigorate AFP's advocacy and public policy efforts with the intention of making AFP the go-to source at both federal and state/provincial levels for information and counsel on the claims of ethical fundraising for public policy and regulatory requirements.

CASE STUDIES

Case Study 1: A Particularly Challenging Monday

Bill is a new development officer with an arts organization. He arrives to the office on the Monday of his second week on the job, checks his email and regular mail, and quickly realizes that this is going to be a particularly challenging Monday.

First Correspondence—Special Event   Bill's organization has been working with Smith Event Planning on the implementation of a dinner auction event. It's the first of what they hope will be a successful annual signature event for the organization. Bill has received an email from Jane Smith telling him that she has found a major sponsor for the dinner auction, Tom's Furniture, who has agreed to a Gold Level sponsorship of $10,000. Jane goes on to tell him that she will be invoicing the charity for a 10 percent finder's fee ($1,000). Bill remembers that there are sometimes ethical considerations when it comes to finder's fees and isn't sure whether he should authorize the finder's fee or challenge this as being something that may compromise his position as an ethical fundraiser.

Should Bill's organization pay the finder's fee for this sponsorship?

Why or why not? What can Bill do to ensure that he isn't caught by surprise like this in the future when dealing with the event planner?

Second Correspondence—Bequest   While working for his previous organization, Bill developed a close relationship with a donor, Mrs. McCarthy. About a year ago, Mrs. McCarthy decided to make a $100,000 planned gift to Bill's previous organization. Today, Bill opens his mail to find a letter from Mrs. McCarthy, which states that she has learned that Bill had learned of his new appointment, and that she intends to change her will, removing a $100,000 bequest previously intended for Bill's former employer and substituting the charity where Bill now works.

What should Bill do? This would certainly be a great way to start a new job, bringing a $100,000 planned gift commitment to the organization after just one week in the role.

But are there ethical concerns?

What actions should Bill take or not take?

Case Study 2: Serving Two Masters. How Should a Board Handle an Unusual Conflict of Interest?

At least one member of the board of Friends of Marine Animals (FOMA) left every board meeting frustrated and disappointed. Arthur Phillips had been aggressively trying for months to convince the rest of the board to support his idea to focus solely on the plight of the manatees.

FOMA aspired to the broader mission of protecting the interests of all marine life by advocating clean water and marine environmental protection laws. Although the other FOMA board members liked manatees as much as anyone else, they thought that helping the manatees to the exclusion of other equally worthy animals was not in keeping with the organization's mission. Arthur was so loud and so persistent in his pleas, however, that none of the FOMA board members argued with him about the manatees. They just didn't say anything. Arthur talked, they listened or doodled, and then moved on to other business.

Disappointed by the continued lack of response, Arthur had recently started a new organization—Save Our Sea Cows (SOSC)—for the purpose of protecting the manatee. He recruited a board, drafted bylaws, and organized a convention to introduce the organization to the environmental and funder communities. At the May meeting of FOMA's board, Arthur spoke enthusiastically about SOSC. He asked the board for its support and requested advertising space in FOMA's magazine. The board chair said that the board would consider Arthur's request and let him know at next month's meeting. Moments later

Arthur was closing up his briefcase, on his way to an appointment with a large foundation that was also one of FOMA's largest funders.

The moment that the boardroom door shut behind Arthur, the noise level rose dramatically. "What does he think he's doing?" exclaimed Eleanor Marshall. "He can't start a competing organization and expect us to support him! In fact, if he's going to run Save Our Sea Cows, he shouldn't even be on our board. Whose interests will he have in mind?"

"He can do what he wants," observed Walter deMarco. "He wants to save the manatees and he's doing something about it." "Our mission is to clean up the marine environment to help the animals," said another board member. "We wouldn't have done a manatee campaign anyway."

"We certainly wouldn't have," complained Eleanor, "even though his sea cow platform has consumed our meetings for months." Eleanor glared at the board chair. "I don't want to hear another word about sea cows at a FOMA meeting, and I don't think we should support Arthur's new organization. It's hard enough to raise money in the vast sea of nonprofits that are already out there. We don't need another one vying for funds that could be ours."

"Maybe now that he has SOSC he'll leave us alone," suggested a board member. "I doubt it," Eleanor scowled. "Besides, as I said, it's inappropriate for him to sit on our board now. His new organization will be drawing on our same donors, our same volunteer base. He's the competition now."

"Don't feel so threatened," countered Walter. "Arthur's fond of manatees and he's willing to fight for them. He'll attract the hardcore manatee lovers, and we'll still appeal to people and funders interested in the big marine environment picture."

"Save Our Sea Cows is another animal lobby that takes away from our message that protecting the marine environment will help all the animals," another board member said. "Arthur's group will divert attention and quite possibly money from our cause. And our cause is helping his. All of his donor connections are through us. Program officers from our funders are going to get suspicious. He shouldn't have done this."

"But he did," interjected the board chair, who had long been silently watching the volley among the other board members. "He started a new group and we need to address it. Our conflict-of-interest policy doesn't mention this type of scenario. But we can't ignore him any longer."

Case Study 3: The For-Profit CEO Who Wants to Do the Right Thing

A major national for-profit corporation, with an established website for consumers to purchase its products online, is asking you to help it create and maintain a brand-new feature on its Internet website—"Let's Give Now." The corporation's CEO tells you in your first meeting that he "wants to do the right thing" and wants "to give back to the community" but that the laws governing charitable solicitation on the Internet are confusing. He wants to retain you to guide him, "within reason."

He offers you his vision for the website and states these basic facts: First, he wants to offer to give 10 percent of every purchase made on its website to a charitable cause. Consumers may simply check a box allowing the corporation to divide the contributions among a pool of 10 different charities. The 10 charities are named. The CEO tells you that the charities are credible and established, that he personally selected the charities—and that he or members of his family serve on the boards of those 10 charities. His children attend 2 of the prep schools that are on the list of 10. He personally vouches for all 10 and tells you there is no need for you to do any due diligence on these charities.

Before signing any agreement to proceed, you do a quick check on the 10 charities and discover that a number of them are indeed established and credible, but that others have run large deficits in recent years and that the compensation of several senior executives of these charities strikes you as excessive, especially in troubled economic times.

Out of curiosity, you also do a quick check on the corporation and its CEO, as well. The corporation has had severe financial difficulties in recent years and the CEO was under investigation by the SEC for possible insider trading. The SEC and the CEO signed a cease-and-desist order under which the CEO admitted no wrongdoing but did disgorge all the profits he made in selling company stock. "That is all water under the bridge," the CEO tells you. "Let's not dig up the past."

The CEO presented you with a draft description to persuade customers to select the charitable giving option ("Let's Give Now") for use on the Internet site. "You don't need to edit this, but let me know what you think." He also presented you with a contract, under which you assume full responsibility for implementing the project.

Questions

Do you need to obtain permission from the 10 charities? Or can you simply notify them once the funds have accumulated? The CEO believes no prior approval is needed. "Who would turn the funds down, once we collect them?" he asks you.

To keep things simple, the CEO wants to provide checks to each of the 10 charities at the end of each calendar year to keep administrative costs down. Is this appropriate?

Although the CEO wants you to design the program, he wants to have the corporation handle the funds generated, handle the financial accounting, and keep the funds in the corporation's bank accounts until distributed. "Let's not complicate this, okay?" he tells you. "You have my word that no profits will be diverted."

You discover that the corporation makes profits by selling the names and addresses and purchasing habits of its customers to other corporations and other websites. The CEO says this is a common business practice and should not complicate your work, since individuals are the customers of the corporation and not the charities. You mention a concern about privacy issues, but the CEO tells you "don't get technical."

The CEO wants a sentence included on the website (in bold letters) that states, "Your contribution is tax deductible." Is this a concern for you?

Your compensation for helping out will come in the form of a commission, to be taken from the charitable 10 percent portion of the sales—and you will not be paid until the end of the calendar year, like the charities themselves. All of the administrative expenses associated with the program will be taken out of the charities' 10 percent portion. The CEO says that these disclosures about administrative expenses can be fully disclosed in the corporation's annual audited financial statements and need not be made on the Internet website. "Let's keep it simple," he tells you.

Do you need to notify any state agency? The CEO says that he is not soliciting for these charities and that the charitable gift is incidental to the business operations. He tells you that state laws govern only the traditional types of solicitation—by phone or by letter, for example. "The Internet is free from all that bureaucratic regulation," he says. When you ask about accountability, he tells you that the entrepreneurial spirit is what made America what it is today. "Let's get this done. I don't want you to be part of the problem here."

ABOUT THE AUTHORS

Audrey Kintzi is the vice president, development at Saint Mary's University of Minnesota. Ms. Kintzi has been working in the development field for over 25 years.

A graduate of Mankato State University, Ms. Kintzi holds a bachelor's degree in Mass Communications—Public Relations and Theatre—Directing/Acting. In 1994, Ms. Kintzi obtained her master's degree in Continuing Studies—Business and Speech Communications, also from Mankato State University.

In 1991, she obtained the designation of CFRE (Certified Fundraising Executive). In October of 2004 she obtained her ACFRE (Advanced Certified Fundraising Executive). This advanced fundraising credential has been conferred on fewer than 100 people internationally. In February of 2001, Ms. Kintzi was awarded the Paid-Staff Excellence Award for Disaster Fundraising by the American National Red Cross. In November 2004 Ms. Kintzi received the Outstanding Fundraising Professional from the Association of Fundraising Professionals—Minnesota Chapter.

Cathlene Williams is a published writer/researcher and educator with more than 30 years' experience in the nonprofit world. In 2009 she established the consulting firm Cathlene Williams LLC, specializing in curriculum development, project management, and business writing/editing. Ms. Williams formerly was vice president for education and research for the Association of Fundraising Professionals (AFP). Ms. Williams has served in numerous volunteer positions, including the editorial board for the international journal *Nonprofit and Voluntary Sector Marketing*, and the ASAE Research Committee and Environmental Scan Task Force. She was co-editor of *New Directions in Philanthropic Fundraising*, and she represented the AFP on the National Advisory Committee for Project Streamline, an initiative of grantmaker and grantseeker organizations to improve the application, monitoring, and reporting requirements of grantmakers. She also served on the American Society of Association Executives (ASAE) Certified Association Executive (CAE) Exam Committee, the CAE Commission, and is currently chair of the board of the Child Development Center of the Annandale (VA) Christian Community for Action (ACCA). She holds a master's degree from the University of Northern Iowa, and a PhD in public policy from George Washington University.

CHAPTER 17

Leadership, Governance, and Giving

ROBERT FOGAL

"We put imagination to work," said David Odahowski, president of the Edyth Bush Charitable Foundation, welcoming participants to the Orlando area for the research think tank Leadership, Governance and Giving. Organized by AFP's Research Council and co-sponsored by the Philanthropy & Nonprofit Leadership Center at Rollins College, the two-day think tank attracted 37 participants from a variety of organizations in the United States and Canada. This was the fifth in a series of think tanks held every two to three years to bring together scholars and practitioners to discuss research priorities for the sector.

The purpose of the 2008 think tank was to highlight and respond to key issues presented by fundraisers' ultimate leadership challenge: guiding those to whom they report—board members and senior executive staff—so they, in turn, provide the organizational leadership at the highest levels required for successful fundraising.

CONTENT PRESENTATIONS

Dr. Elizabeth Boris opened the proceedings with an overview of the nonprofit sector. Research on the sector began fairly recently, she said, and there is still much we don't know about how the sector serves society's needs. What we do know is that the context of the sector impacts who we are and what we do.

Environmental Trends

- National economic status.
  - Financial meltdown/subprime mortgage crisis.
  - Federal and state budget deficits.
  - Growing income inequality.
  - Health care crisis.
  - Status of U.S. democracy: trust, engagement.
- Changing demographics: aging, diversity.
- Global warming/environmental degradation.
- Globalization.

Political Trends

- Intense partisanship.
- Financial crisis and the war dominate political agenda and resources.
- Limited discretionary dollars for other programs.
- Search for revenues leads to the nonprofit sector.
- Malfeasance in the nonprofit sector leads to stronger government oversight.

In this context, we can identify key trends in the nonprofit sector:

- Fast-growing part of the U.S. economy.
- More transparent than ever before.
- Increasingly visible via electronic media.
- Heightened congressional interest.
- Declining government grants and direct support.
- Growing fee-for-service revenues leading to fears of blurring boundaries with business sector.

These sector trends are heightening the interest of government policy makers. Congressional hearings on nonprofits seem to threaten the sector's charitable status. There are demands for:

- Enhanced accountability and disclosure.
- Governance standards.
- Documented efficiency (reasonable costs).
- Effectiveness metrics.
- Evidence of diverse beneficiaries.

Responses in the sector to this mélange of trends and influences are both reactive and proactive:

- Burnout/turnover/financial stress/shutdown.
- Entrepreneurial activities.
- Innovative communications, fundraising, program delivery, volunteering—through the Internet.
- Mergers, partnerships, infrastructure creation.
- Advocacy, policy development, lobbying and political activities.

The historic character of the nonprofit sector continues to anchor its existence:

- Values base: trust, integrity, commitment.
- Mission: promote and enhance common good.
- Governance: oversight for public purposes.
- Finances: donations, volunteer labor, government grants, contracts, fees for services, events, member dues.
- Accountability: transparency, performance.

And the sector continues to fulfill critical roles in our country:

- Social, cultural, religious, economic:
  - Service providers.
  - Values guardians.
  - Employers.
  - Advocates.
- Individual and community engagement.
- Civic and political participation.

The scope of the sector is an important factor in the public recognition of its role:

- 1.9 million nonprofits in mid-2008 (National Center for Charitable Statistics).
- 1.5 million registered with the IRS (Nonprofit 501(c)(3) and other organizations).
- 0.4 million religious congregations.
- 1 million registered charitable 501(c)(3) nonprofits (including public charities and private foundations).

The sector impacts all areas of United States' society, and its growth assures this will continue to be the case. See Exhibit 17.1.

The diversity of the nonprofit sector can be one of its strengths:

- Diverse types: hospitals, shelters, museums, rights advocates, research institutes, and more.
- Varied sizes: financial giants like Harvard University and small-budget agencies like PTAs.
- Different structures: federated, membership, and so on.
- Varied organization: staffing, revenue generation.
- Innovative: new program and outreach models.

EXHIBIT 17.1   **SECTOR GROWTH OVER TEN YEARS, 1996–2006**

Change, 1996–2006	Subsector Total Percentage
Arts, cultures, and humanities	72.1
Education	81.6
Environment and animal related	119.8
Health	28.0
Human services	56.8
International and foreign affairs	103.4
Other	79.6

Source: The Urban Institute, National Center for Charitable Statistics, Core Files (1996–2006).

The sector's economic impact is clearly documentable:

- Contributed $666.1 billion (5 percent) to GDP.
- Paid $489.4 billion in wages and salaries.
- Employed an estimated 12.9 million (9.7 percent) of U.S. employment.
- Spent $840.5 billion and gave away another $74.7 billion for total outlays of $915.2 billion.
- 38 percent of nonprofits that report to the IRS held assets of about $3.4 trillion.

The reality, however, is that a very small proportion of nonprofit organizations and institutions account for the vast majority of its economic impact. See Exhibit 17.2.

Private contributions continue to be a defining quality of public charities:

- Private contributions were estimated at $306 billion in 2007 — about a 1 percent real increase over 2006 (*Giving USA*).

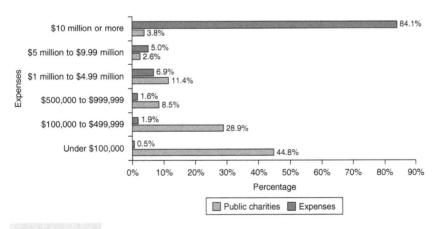

EXHIBIT 17.2   **DISTRIBUTION OF THE TOTAL EXPENSES OF U.S. 501(c)(3) PUBLIC CHARITIES BY EXPENSES, 2006**

Source: The Urban Institute, National Center for Charitable Statistics, Core Files (1996–2006).

- Individual contributions were $229 billion, representing about 2 percent of personal income and about 75 percent of all private contributions.
- Tax itemizers account for about 80 percent of individual contributions in dollar terms.

In spite of all the nonprofit sector contributes to American society, Boris pointed out that we need new tools to measure performance.

With regard to fundraising effectiveness, giving has been at about 2 percent of GDP for the past 40 years. What would it take to move that percentage upward? Research suggests a greater focus on retaining past givers might yield benefits.

Studies on overhead and fundraising costs of nonprofits show underinvestment in the infrastructure of nonprofits. Cost ratios are not an effective way to evaluate what nonprofits are doing for those they serve. "Research suggests that a focus on efficiency, least amount spent, results in below optimal investment in organizational effectiveness," Boris stated. "The sector needs to make a better case for the legitimate costs involved in administration and fundraising. We undermine the sector when we claim we have no overhead costs."

Another powerful component of the nonprofit sector is the contribution made by volunteers:

- 26.7 percent of the population volunteered in 2006, or 61.2 million volunteers.
- 6.5 percent of the population volunteers each day, or over 15 million volunteers per day.
- 12.9 billion hours were volunteered, equivalent to 7.6 million full time employees earning $215.6 billion.

However, Boris noted that nonprofits don't do an optimal job of managing volunteers. "Leadership by nonprofit board members and staff is critical," she said, "as well as greater collaboration and coordination among organizations that serve the public good." She also recommended that the sector focus efforts on improving transparency and accountability, and that nonprofits take advantage of their ability to be advocates in the public policy process.

What We Know and What We Need

Dr. Rita Bornstein organized her presentation around two clusters of observations:

1. What we know about leadership in the nonprofit sector.
2. What we need.

We know that leadership is more professional and respected than once thought, as reflected in:

- The proliferation of nonprofit centers, courses, degree programs.
- Many more professionals being certified or degreed.
- Higher compensation, inducements, and incentive pay.
- More career mobility.
- Greater respect, status, and voice (for example, leadership on community and government boards and commissions).
- The focus on ethics, standards of practice, and accountability.

We also know that leadership is more complex, as witnessed by:

- State and federal laws, regulations, and reports.
- Public scrutiny and mistrust.
- Proliferation of nonprofits and competition (worldwide).
- The pressure for coordination and cooperation.
- Demands for program expansion.
- An escalation of goals for fundraising campaigns.
- Pressure for improved performance.
- Technology's benefits and costs.

Finally, we know that leadership is being impacted by a shifting (i.e., boom to bust) job market:

- Boomers are retiring if they can afford to.
- Professional mobility is impeded by economics.
- Turnover means a loss to the organization of relationships and personal knowledge.

- A lack of turnover (i.e., opportunities for career advancement) may lead to resentment and burnout for individuals.
- The likelihood of an inadequate pipeline of diverse, trained, and experienced professional.

Bornstein argued that we need systematic recruitment, training, evaluation, and mentoring in nonprofit organizations for staff and volunteers alike. Homegrown talent is preferable to recruiting outsiders who tend to have a high failure rate. Organizations will benefit by providing in-house opportunities for cross-training, lateral shifting, career mapping, promotion, rewards, and recognition.

She stressed that leadership no longer takes place in a hierarchical system in most organizations. Instead, there is a more holistic, team-based approach to leadership. Governance should be achieved through shared leadership between the CEO and the board, and the development team should reflect a distribution of expertise among professional fundraisers, the CEO, and the board.

Three styles of leadership were identified:

1. Integral leadership sees the organization as a coherent whole and aims to weave mission, program, and fundraising/giving together.
2. Integrative leadership is comfortable considering two opposing ideas at once, not seeing them in terms of either–or but forging an innovative third way, incorporating elements of each and improving both.
3. Conceptual age leadership depends highly on the intuitive and creative right brain and less on the analytical logic of the left brain.

Engaging the Board

Dr. David Renz addressed the range of challenges involved with engaging the board. Of particular importance is the need for boards to understand and apply to themselves three standards of accountability: legal, political, and organizational.

Legal accountability centers on fiduciary responsibilities.

- Core fiduciary duties:
  - Duty of care.
  - Duty of loyalty.
  - Duty of obedience.
- Recent new federal layers:
  - Sarbanes–Oxley Act (commonly referred to as SOX).
  - Pension Protection Act of 2006.
  - And the IRS is thinking...

The Internal Revenue Service believes that governing boards should be composed of persons who are informed and active in overseeing a charity's operations and finances. If a governing board tolerates a climate of secrecy or neglect, charitable assets are more likely to be used to advance an impermissible private interest. Successful governing boards include individuals not only knowledgeable and passionate about the organization's programs, but also those with expertise in critical areas involving accounting, finance, compensation, and ethics.

The IRS suggests that boards are accountable for certain good governance practices:

- Mission statement.
- Code of ethics.
- Due diligence.
- Transparency.
- Fundraising policy.
- Financial audits.
- Compensation practices.
- Document retention policy.

The political layer of accountability may be not be legally mandated but we know we had better pay attention:

- How are the organization and board perceived in the community and by their constituents?
- Are they viewed as credible? Effective? Accountable?

The Sarbanes–Oxley Act has put pressure on nonprofits that is largely political in nature, but no less real:

- Legally binding.
  - Whistleblower policy and protection.
  - Document retention and destruction.
- Political guidance.
  - Independent audits and audit committees.
  - Quality of financial statements.
  - Insider transactions and conflicts of interest.
  - Full disclosure of status and changes.

These all flow into and support organizational accountabilities:

- Building and sustaining effective boards.
- Attracting essential resources.
- Efficiency and stewardship.
- Making the difference the organizations exists to make—achieve organizational effectiveness.

The kinds of tasks that are included in a board's organizational accountability are:

- Selecting the chief executive.
- Supporting and assessing the chief executive.
- Ensuring adequate financial resources.
- Developing systems of accountability (financial and other resources, performance outcomes).

Too often, boards don't do enough to develop their own capacity as leaders in policy and governance. Renz emphasized that assessing and developing board effectiveness requires:

- A systematic approach to building board capacity.
- Refining board design to meet future needs.
- Implementing thoughtful recruitment and selection.
- Preparing members to serve.

- Developing systems to support monitoring (benchmarks, dashboards).
- Setting actual goals for the board and measuring the board's achievements.

Renz posed three simple questions that, if answered well, remove a lot of clutter from discussions about board effectiveness:

1. What enhances board member engagement?
2. What hinders or diminishes board member engagement?
3. How are these factors affecting your fundraising?

Citing research by the Urban Institute, Renz stated that many nonprofit boards are not involved in fundraising and community outreach. When we recruit board members, we should be honest about what we need and clear about our expectations.

Building Public Confidence

Dr. Adrian Sargeant cited Brookings Institute data on the low level of public trust in the nonprofit sector. "Only 16 percent of Americans have a great deal of confidence in nonprofits," he said, "and 70 percent say we waste money." Sargeant provided two examples from the UK of efforts to build public confidence in the nonprofit sector.

Among the many issues that may impact public perceptions of nonprofits, Sargeant emphasized the following absurdities:

- Roughly 40 percent of U.S. nonprofits report public contributions claim zero costs of fundraising—that "100 percent of your gift goes to those who need it."
- Administration and fundraising costs together total only 4 to 5 percent.

Sargeant explored in detail two examples from the United Kingdom for building public confidence in the nonprofit sector:

- The CharityFacts website (www.charityfacts.org) provides information on fundraising and philanthropy for members of the media, researchers, and the general public.

- The Impact Coalition (www.impactcoalition.org.uk) is a group of charities that promote better public understanding of how charities work and the benefits they bring to society by improving accountability, clarity, and transparency (ImpACT). The group has agreed to speak with one voice on a specific set of messages:
  - Charities are effective and do a good job,
  - To raise more money, charities have to spend money,
  - Charities use donations carefully and wisely,
  - Charities are highly regulated and adhere to a range of strict standards,
  - Charities work together,
  - Charities need the public's donations because they really do make a difference.

The matter of public confidence in nonprofits is critical to stemming the declining number of donors. Donor retention is the single largest challenge facing fundraising. See Exhibit 17.3.

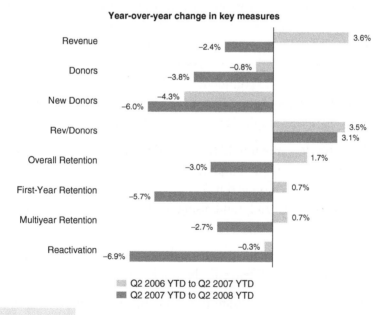

Year-over-year change in key measures

Measure	Q2 2006 YTD to Q2 2007 YTD	Q2 2007 YTD to Q2 2008 YTD
Revenue	3.6%	−2.4%
Donors	−0.8%	−3.8%
New Donors	−4.3%	−6.0%
Rev/Donors	3.5%	3.1%
Overall Retention	1.7%	−3.0%
First-Year Retention	0.7%	−5.7%
Multiyear Retention	0.7%	−2.7%
Reactivation	−0.3%	−6.9%

- Q2 2006 YTD to Q2 2007 YTD
- Q2 2007 YTD to Q2 2008 YTD

EXHIBIT 17.3 **OVERALL INDEX MEDIANS**

Source: Target Analytics, a Blackbaud Company.

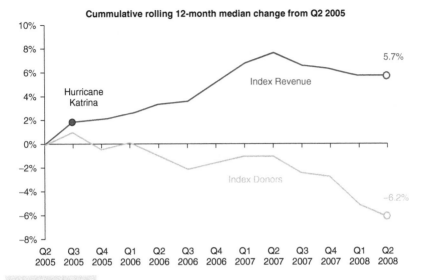

Cummulative rolling 12-month median change from Q2 2005

EXHIBIT 17.4   **THREE-YEAR OVERALL INDEX REVENUE AND DONOR TRENDS**

Source: Target Analytics, a Blackbaud Company.

It is clear that the donor pool is steadily decreasing. See Exhibit 17.4.

In addition to the declining pool of donors for current gifts, Sargeant reported that participation in bequest giving is unchanged in a century of our best efforts and online giving still accounts for only 2 percent of giving in spite of the tremendous growth of e-commerce.

Sargeant asks, "Wouldn't it be good if every fundraiser knew . . . "

- One or two models of giving behavior?
- The underpinning psychology of giving? Philanthropic psychology?
- What drives bequest giving?
- How people make decisions about the future—and what language is most effective?
- What drives public trust in the sector—and in organizations—and why does this matter?
- The three things that drive donor loyalty—and why this matters?
- The characteristics of successful nonprofit websites—and the links between these characteristics and facts of performance?

He also suggested we set standards for the knowledge and skills needed for effective fundraising, and incorporate what we have learned from research into educational programming for fundraisers, CEOs, and board members.

Demographics and Their Impact on Organizational Vitality

Gary LaBranche, CAE, president and CEO of the Association for Corporate Growth, summarized various studies of nonprofit (c)(6) professional organizations, highlighting membership demographics and their impact on organizational vitality. One study documented that:

- Association members earn, on average, $10,000 more per year than nonmembers, even if they have the same education levels and job types.
- Association members are 19 percent more likely to say they are "very satisfied" with their jobs than are nonmembers.
- Successful, happy people gravitate toward associations—they desire to associate with others like themselves.
- The conclusion employers can reach from this research is that it is in their best interest to encourage high-value employees to involve themselves in associations and the positive environments they provide.

Another study on professional membership organizations presented findings pertinent to AFP's own well being:

- Association volunteers are highly engaged in a variety of volunteer activities and volunteer more time than the national average.
- Association volunteers are driven by values and career growth.
- The best way to recruit volunteers is by directly asking them to participate.
- Younger volunteers are slightly less engaged in volunteering, but they believe more strongly in volunteering.
- Age, career status, and family status all affect an individual's capacity and motivation to volunteer for associations.

- Association members seek connections between their careers and volunteerism.

LaBranche pointed out implications of the studies on membership organizations, particularly as related to building boards and engaging volunteers:

- The *why* remains—research indicates desire for association.
- The *how* is different—more fluid, personal, and customized.
- The *when, where, and what* is different—it is highly accessible, experiential, and "my" way.

DISCUSSION SUMMARIES

Mark Brewer, president and CEO of the Community Foundation of Central Florida, designed and facilitated breakout discussions on the issues raised by plenary speakers and how the sector can respond. Facilitators for these sessions were Janice Gow Pettey, CFRE, principal of J.G. Pettey & Associates; Thomas Jeavons, PhD, executive director of ARNOVA; and Karla Williams, ACFRE, principal of The Williams Group. As the think tank facilitator, Mark Brewer provided a synopsis of the breakouts and posed a number of questions that came out of the discussions. The facilitators then led a final discussion of what participants think is good about leadership, governance, and giving in the nonprofit sector, what needs to be changed, and the priorities for change.

Leadership

Leadership in nonprofit organizations is defined by both role and function. Board members and CEOs are expected to lead because of their institutional positions. Others in an organization may lead because of their knowledge or specialized expertise. Leadership may involve vertical as well as horizontal relationships, with influence flowing down, up, and sideways. The content of leadership may be strategic or operational.

In all circumstances, successful leadership is the result of people and ideas coming together around an organization's mission and shared vision. The effectiveness of leadership in all its manifestations directly affects an organization's success in obtaining philanthropic support.

Leadership and Public Trust

- How can you instill or regain a high level of public trust in the nonprofit sector? In nonprofit sector leadership? In fundraising?
- Will definitive metrics help to achieve renewed confidence in what nonprofits deliver as public benefit?

Leadership in New Times

- How do you lead in tough times, having only the experiences of good times?
- How do you support leaders of the next generation to lead for their times, not yours?
- What will a new leadership style look like that is less driven by task and function and more open to relationship building? What are the required competencies?
- How do you overcome differences in communication styles and content among generational groups (the Greatest Generation, Baby Boomers, Gen Xers, and Millennials), especially with regard to the role and purpose of organizational leadership?

Leadership at Different Levels

- What are the distinctive leadership challenges for different organizational actors: boards, CEOs, and individual development professionals?
- How will the fundraising professional champion philanthropy from the middle with the board, staff, the community, and donors?

Nonprofit Leadership as a Business Model

- To what extent can the nonprofit sector become more business-like without losing its mission-centered culture?
- How can nonprofits increase salaries and strengthen infrastructure without compromising the primary commitment to mission?

- What will you do in hard times when you have to choose between client services and employee remuneration?

Leadership Influences Fundraising

- Why do some organizations welcome development staff in strategic discussions and decision making, while others banish them from top-level participation?

Governance

Boards of directors play a decisive role in building and sustaining philanthropic support. While this includes many of the actions involved with major-gifts fundraising, the scope of a successful board is much broader. The most successful boards demonstrate a capacity for all the following:

- Knowing and telling the organizational story, which provides the narrative for its values.
- Educating board members about the organization as well as their own roles and responsibilities.
- Creating a collective identity and sense of well-being within the board itself.
- Analyzing issues and problems in all their complexity.
- Developing strong constituency relations.
- Shaping a strategic approach for the organization's future.

These dimensions of board life have an enormous impact on an organization's operational competence. A board that gives attention to its performance in all these areas is practicing governance at the highest level. Rules and regulations that pertain to the organization's corporate life will be implemented with a vision and purpose that establish a sound organizational future.

Designing Governance

- What structures and processes make it possible for a board to work more effectively and efficiently?

- Do you fully understand the CEO's and board's roles? How do these roles affect the board's work?
- How do you develop succession planning for boards as well as executive staff?
- How do you build organizational cultures that honor the commitments (and the work) of volunteers, staff, and donors, without allowing the exploitation of any for the sake of the mission?

Developing and Evaluating Governance

- How do you ensure the board creates and sustains mutual accountability among its members for governance and advocacy?
- How can you collectively educate your board about their fiduciary responsibilities?
- How can you help produce better board chairs?
- What do you know about optimal complementary mixes of skills/knowledge/types of people on boards?
- What circumstances and conditions make it possible to improve governance and giving on a sustained basis?

Giving

Fundraising professionals who aspire to philanthropic leadership and governance usually strive to achieve transformational giving. Their work is driven by the vision of the organization that engages donors through meaning and satisfaction, adding a sense of value to their lives as well as to the donee organization. This approach contrasts with the organization where fundraising is motivated by a utilitarian or transactional philosophy, often expressed as, "We need more money. Let's hire a fundraiser."

Integrating fundraising into an organization's leadership and governance requires that fundraising professionals be well grounded in the principles and techniques of philanthropic fundraising. They also may need certain organizational development skills, such as change management and coaching.

Cultures of Giving

- To what extent is the language of mission overcome by the language of organizational need in fundraising practice?
- How do you practice accountability to those who give? How does accountability contribute to a culture of philanthropy?
- How does good governance strengthen giving?
- What successful approaches to building diversity in giving and fundraising can you build upon?

Competencies for Philanthropic Fundraising

- To ensure that fundraising becomes a true profession, what will constitute a more systematized education program involving staged assessments of competency?
- What need is there for a common syllabus to teach fundraising?
- How could licensing and accreditation further the fundraising profession?
- What knowledge and competencies will best equip fundraising professionals to contribute to an organization's philosophy of governance and leadership?

ABOUT THE AUTHOR

Robert E. Fogal coaches senior nonprofit executives, volunteer leaders, and fundraisers. He has held chief development officer positions in higher education, health care, human services, long-term care, and religious institutions. He also served as director of The Fund Raising School at the Center on Philanthropy at Indiana University. Mr. Fogal has been an active leader in the Association of Fundraising Professionals locally and nationally.

CHAPTER 18

Both Sides Now: The Ethics of Grantmaking and Grantseeking

BRUCE SIEVERS, PhD

Nonprofit activity rests on a foundation of public trust—a trust that the primary incentives in the nonprofit sector are neither profit nor power but rather voluntary action directed toward the public good. For this reason, ethics is central to the work of the nonprofit sector in a way in which it is not for the for-profit or governmental sectors.

While this may seem a rather idealistic way of describing the complex mixture of activities that define the nonprofit world, the assumption of trust is firmly anchored in fundamental justifications for the sector. For example, legal analysts emphasize the importance of the nondistribution constraint as providing a curb on self-interested activity on the part of those who operate nonprofits. Economists discuss the creation of public goods as the goal of nonprofit enterprise (sometimes hindered by the problem of unethical free-riders). And policy experts emphasize the public trust associated with the tax benefits received by nonprofit organizations. Clearly, the public perceives the work of the sector as relying on its trust.

This trust implies an assumption of ethical behavior. This is actually true for all professional fields. It is precisely because professionals exercise power and authority without the normal restraints of strong governmental regulation, market forces, or political control (and we desire them to remain free of such forces, as much as possible) that professions are assumed to operate according to ethical principles. This is why we are so shocked when we learn of the violations of trust by journalists such as Stephen Glass and Jayson Blair, the AMA's paid endorsement of medical products, and the Enron and WorldCom accountants who were complicit in financial frauds. We defer to professionals' expertise and feel betrayed when then they act dishonestly or deceptively.

But there is a further elevation of trust expectations for practitioners in the nonprofit sector because, in addition to working as professionals (in education, health care, environmental protection, or whatever field in which they may be engaged), they are the beneficiaries of donated funds and volunteer effort. Moreover, the public benefit of nonprofit organizations provides going beyond performing reliable services to clients; they seek to provide public goods that enhance the entire society rather than provide primarily personal benefit to nonprofit professionals and volunteers.

The high level of trust that undergirds the nonprofit sector has particular implications for the relationship between those who provide philanthropic support and those who receive it. Grantors, in providing crucial resources for the nonprofit sector, occupy a privileged position of power that tends to insulate them from criticism and oversight, posing a constant danger of philanthropic hubris. Grantees, in their unending quest for life-sustaining organizational support, may be tempted to push boundaries in fundraising techniques and the management of information. In the absence of stronger external regulatory mechanisms (which I discourage, as noted subsequently), it is important for both sides of the philanthropic exchange relationship to strengthen their internal stance on ethical standards and practices. In this chapter, I will discuss four levels on which to consider these ethical relationships.

THE TRUST RELATIONSHIP

The most basic level on which ethical issues arise between grantmakers and grantseekers is that of interpersonal relationships—how people are treated in the daily give and take of the grantmaking process. Three aspects of this behavior deserve special attention:

1. Simple courtesy and politeness.
2. Honesty.
3. Responsible handling of information.

All three are elements of building a respectful and trusting relationship.

Unfortunately, a large body of anecdotal evidence, along with the few studies that have been undertaken of grantor–grantee relationships, suggest vast room for improvement on both sides of the exchange. However, the first category, *courtesy and politeness*, applies especially to foundations. Any conversation with a group of nonprofit executives concerning experiences in dealing with foundations will quickly elicit a "Can you top this?" list of stories of insensitive, impolite, or arrogant treatment by foundations during the grants process. The inappropriate behaviors range from unwelcoming attitudes in initial telephone contacts, unanswered mail, and missed appointments to lecturing prospective grantees, losing proposals, and sending neophyte interns to represent the foundation in important meetings with applicants; such experiences occur all too frequently to be dismissed as aberrations. Improvement of these simple aspects of "customer service" would contribute greatly to building trust and respect for foundations in the nonprofit world.[1]

Honesty is a universal ethical principle that should apply on both sides of the equation. Honesty is required on the part of the foundation in announcing criteria for selection, applying those criteria in reviewing proposals, providing straightforward feedback to both those who are awarded and denied grants, and portraying an accurate picture to the public of the goals and decision-making process of the foundation. On the applicant side, honesty is essential in the description of the organization and program, presentation of financial information, status of staffing and board membership (including anticipated changes), and prospects for future revenue sources. There is a temptation on both sides to manipulate the process by avoiding difficult truths or presenting only the most positive information, whereas, in this interaction, as with most human relationships, the development of trust depends upon the honest exchange of information.

The third prerequisite to the creation of a trust relationship is the *responsible handling of information.* A substantial component of the interaction between funders and fundraisers consists of the transfer of sensitive information, and managing such information has many ethical consequences. For example, how much information is it appropriate and necessary for a nonprofit organization to reveal to the foundation? Is there a trade-off between transparency and confidentiality? What are the limits to the information that is appropriate for a foundation program officer to pass on to other foundations or to his or her own board? Given the importance of personal and organizational reputation in grantmaking, what principles should guide discussion among grantmakers of common applicants? Although such questions have no universal answers, they are useful means of encouraging reflection on principled action by grantmakers and nonprofit practitioners.

THE GRANTS PROCESS

Beyond the interpersonal aspects of the grantmaker–grantseeker relationship lie questions relating to the operational aspects of a grants program. These have to do with the mechanics of foundations' applications processes, requirements imposed upon grantees, and ways in which foundations exercise power in setting the agendas for the fields in which they operate.

The Paper Chase

Although the grants application process is usually viewed as a purely administrative matter, it has important ethical dimensions as well.

The central ethical issue arises from the relationship (or lack thereof) between the requirements imposed by foundations and the actual use of the information. Nonprofit organizations spend huge amounts of time and financial resources developing and submitting proposals to foundations. Yet a significant portion of this effort is wasted because the information is unneeded for decision making, is required to be submitted in a different form from other proposals to foundations, or is handled carelessly. It is an all-too-common experience for applicants to wait for months for a response (which may never come), receive a rejection letter that displays a complete ignorance of what the application was requesting, spend $10,000 in time submitting a grant for $5,000, meet with a foundation representative who has not read the proposal, or submit grant reports that are never reviewed.

It is true that foundation staffers are typically overwhelmed with proposals and lack the time to respond to all phone calls and inquiries. But foundations could do much better in simplifying application procedures, increasing staff to improve responsiveness to the field, and periodically querying applicants (both successful and rejected) to assess the usefulness and fairness of their grant processes.

Strategic Philanthropy

There have been many discussions in recent years of the pros and cons of "strategic philanthropy"—the effort to apply philanthropic resources strategically in the chosen fields of foundations' activity. Although there are many practical issues at stake in this debate, I want to focus here on an underlying ethical question having to do with the exercise of power through the control of resources. In the contemporary enthusiasm for becoming more strategic, foundations are typically narrowing their focus, becoming more proactive, and seeking quantitative results from grantmaking. This has the consequence, often unintended, of becoming more directive and less responsive to the interests and concerns of the nonprofit community.

The power and influence that flow from money, combined with the near absence of a negative feedback loop in philanthropy, result in potential manipulation of and control over nonprofit organizations. The question, "Who can and should define the purposes and success criteria for nonprofit work?" is lost amidst the anxious search for funding. From the foundation side, the often uncritical importation of the business model and its associated conceptual framework—including an emphasis on "bang for the buck," measurable outcomes, performance milestones, bottom lines, forced collaboration, and scaling up—can lead to a diminished sense of vision in the nonprofit sector. More than just a matter of donor choice, I suggest that this is an epistemological failing of the field. In the context of other professional fields, Donald Schon has called this kind of restricted social perception a form of "selective inattentiveness" to important features of social life.[2]

Agenda Setting Foundations make funding choices based on a wide spectrum of reasons; therefore, it is appropriately a matter of discretion on the part of donors and foundation boards to determine which, among the enormous array of potential targets of social concern and interest, they choose as the preferred objects of their support. This freedom of donor discretion is an essential aspect of the way modern philanthropy works, and it offers many advantages in stimulating creative, nonbureaucratic, pluralistic solutions to social problems. Social problems and interests are, in effect, limitless, and funds are finite; it is inevitable, then, that choices are made according to the particular interests and concerns of the donors and their representatives.

At the same time, systematic thinking is rarely applied to the selection of the most fundamental areas of interest when foundations are first established. Indeed, donor preferences are often influenced by personal histories of donors or current trends in social thinking that are not subjected to rigorous critical analysis. The result is that in any given period, foundation funding can flow in quite arbitrary ways. This is ironic in light of the fact that a great deal of attention is often paid to the strategy of grantmaking *after* the most basic choices have been made.

Even after foundations are established, shifts in priorities and guidelines can occur with the advent of a new CEO or a change in the constellation of board members. Such changes in foundation priorities can create unpredictable patterns of funding drawn to popular topics of the day, such as elementary education or particular diseases, while fundamentally important but less fashionable arenas of social concern can be easily ignored.

ACCOUNTABILITY

"Nonprofit accountability" has achieved buzzword status in recent years. This is a topic that has not so much to do with the relationship between grantmakers and grantseekers, but between *both* and the *public at large*. The combination of freedom and trust enjoyed by nonprofit organizations implies an ethical obligation to society. Absent the mechanisms that assist popular control over other elites—the market in the for-profit arena and elections in government—nonprofits, and especially foundations, are quite free to set their own rules of behavior.[3] The problem arises when public trust is violated—whether through carelessness, self-dealing, or outright malfeasance. When abuses occur, as they inevitably will in such an unmonitored operating system, the question becomes: What should be done?

Such questions of accountability have been raised as long as charitable organizations have existed. The establishment of philanthropic funds as far back as ancient Greece prompted the creation of legal vehicles to ensure their proper and honest administration. The Elizabethan Statute of Charitable Uses of 1601 contained provisions to guarantee the appropriate application of charitable donations to the causes intended by donors. Congressional oversight of American philanthropy began simultaneously with the creation of the first large general-purpose foundations a century ago. The reason for this concern is simple: The allocation of funds for important social concerns outside the control of the state or other authority leaves open the clear possibility of abuse.[4]

When such abuse occurs, the immediate social reaction is typically a call for stronger governmental oversight. Although it is in the interest of both philanthropy and the nonprofit field as a whole to demonstrate that public trust is merited,[5] I want to suggest that the general trend toward greater government regulation over the nonprofit sector is potentially detrimental in the long term. This poses something of a paradox: Moves toward greater accountability and oversight would seem to increase ethical behavior and therefore public confidence in the work of the sector. Yet I am arguing they do not. Why?

Onora O'Neill succinctly analyzes this problem in her Reith Lectures, *A Question of Trust*. She argues that ever-expanding government regulatory mechanisms produce an "audit culture" that actually undermines public trust.[6] In the United States, for example, there appears to be no evidence that the passage in 2002 of the Sarbanes–Oxley legislation imposing greater accountability on corporate boards has actually increased public trust in the corporate sector, although it has perhaps provided a measure of reassurance that the bad guys are more under control. There is an ironic twist to such efforts to increase government oversight in that they actually can crowd out efforts to strengthen ethical standards within a field.

The clear implication of this argument is that the nonprofit community must take the lead in setting standards for its *own* ethical behavior and in initiating discussions, educational activities, and training sessions to implement them. To be meaningful, these standards should include such sensitive issues as conflicts of interest, compensation and benefits, transparency, and governance.[7] There have been efforts in this direction in the past. Most such efforts, however, have been quite timid in their aspirations and weak in their consequences. They have done little to establish meaningful standards of behavior for the field. The newly convened Council on Foundations task force entitled "Building Strong and Ethical Foundations: Doing It Right," the latest effort aimed at establishing ethically grounded procedures and standards for the operation of foundations, shows some promise for taking a next step.

By encouraging such self-regulation, however, I do not mean to endorse *all* forms of uniform assessment of nonprofit operations. While it is commendable and necessary for the field to seek to establish norms of acceptable behavior in *governance* and the *practice* of grantmaking, I want to suggest the attempt to impose rigorous performance standards on the *outcomes* of nonprofit activity is misguided. In fact, the field risks shooting itself in the foot by promising such outcome accountability, for two reasons:

1. The sheer number and complexity of variables in the realms of social action make it extremely difficult to arrive at meaningful comparisons of performance. In other words, the vast range of variables involved in social action, the role of the single variable of foundation funding, long-time horizons, absence of a uniform feedback mechanism like the market, and lack of conditions for controlled experimentation cumulatively frustrate attempts to arrive at precise numerical calculations of results.

2. Beyond the practical problems of measurement, there is a deeper philosophical question having to do with employing appropriate frameworks to define social intention. Thinkers from many philosophical traditions have addressed this issue, sharing a common critique of the distortions that can result from imposing a categorical framework grounded in one framework of reference on another.[8] This observation serves as a caveat about the effect of money or power on defining social reality in conformity with the belief system of the power holder. Those who solicit philanthropic support for their work in the complex arenas of nonprofit activity are the vulnerable to such external pressures. A simple example is the distorting effects of the exaggerated emphasis on standardized test scores in evaluating educational activity, which, as we frequently hear from teachers, typically results in teaching to the test, skewing the educational curriculum in the direction of the tests.

Another example is the growing popularity of ratings systems for nonprofits, such as that of Charity Navigator (CN). CN uses financial ratios, such as the ratio of program to administrative expense, to rank charities, including creating Top Ten and Slam Dunk lists. Despite producing impressive looking charts and numbers, the ratings are virtually meaningless in terms of assessing the quality and value of the nonprofit organizations that are ranked. By encouraging a simplistic "bang for the buck" evaluation of nonprofit organizations, such efforts are not only misleading but are positively counterproductive in conveying to the public a distorted message about the nature and purpose of nonprofit work. Even greater distortions can occur in cross-cultural contexts.

PUBLIC GOODS

The most general level to consider the relationship of philanthropy to ethics is the overall role of private wealth and private initiative in a democratic society. The focus here is neither on questions of philanthropic practice nor operations but rather on the overarching ethical implications of the nonprofit enterprise, that is, the complex responsibility of private sector institutions seeking to address fundamental public problems. This topic might best be described as the dangers inherent in privatization and the public sphere. I will not seek to treat such a large and complex question exhaustively here, but rather to sketch an outline of an argument.

Philanthropy has been an integral part of the evolution of civil society from its earliest origins, both as a moral force for the improvement of humankind and as a financial resource enabling nonprofit organizations to remain independent of the market and the state. In this role, philanthropy has supplied a base of support for private action, separate from and, since the seventeenth century, defended against the state. In the United States, the confrontation between the defense of the prerogatives of private power and the authority of the state occurred early in the nation's history in the struggles between the Federalists and the Jeffersonians. The pivotal *Dartmouth College* case in 1819 provided the clearest early formulation of the rights of private wealth to pursue social purposes through, in Mark McGarvie's description, "the [U.S. Supreme] Court's perception of distinct realms of public and private action, and the role of the courts in the protection of private action from public interference."[9]

The subsequent development of the nonprofit sector in the United States embraced and further refined the interplay between public and private domains of action. At stake have always been two fundamental concerns:

1. The protection of the ability of private associational life to operate freely without state intrusion.
2. The role of private means in achieving public ends.

The first has been well explored elsewhere and falls outside the primary focus of this chapter. The second lies at the heart of philanthropy's role in society.

The core of the second concern is this: In the commercial sector, *private* means are used to create *private* goods. In the governmental sector, *public* means are used to achieve *public* goods. In the nonprofit sector, *private* means are used to create *public* goods. The result, for the nonprofit sector, is a delicate balancing act between adhering to the dictates of private inspiration and intention on the one hand, and assuming the responsibility to achieve public benefits on the other.

This balancing act is difficult to maintain because of two fundamental challenges to the creation of public goods in the liberal democratic state: (1) the problem of collective action[10] and (2) value pluralism.[11] Individually, these two problems create difficulties for achieving common aims in liberal democracies; together they create a formidable obstacle to the successful application of private resources in a way that can be beneficial for society as a whole.

The two problems converge in the practice of private philanthropy. In a system of free, unfettered private decision making for the allocation of philanthropic resources, there is a presumption of something akin to an invisible hand that rationalizes the entire system for the overall benefit of society.[12] But the incentive of mission achievement works in the nonprofit world much like the incentive of profit in a for-profit enterprise—that is, the cumulative effect of maximizing individual missions generally fails to take into account the collective impact on society. This becomes the philanthropic version of the problem of collective action.

Individual donors and, by extension, foundation boards prominently illustrate the effects of value pluralism. Indeed, one of the deepest held principles of private philanthropy is that giving interests should reflect the fundamental convictions of the donors, whether brilliant, inspired, controversial, or just wacky. We cherish the ability of individuals to choose their idiosyncratic paths of inquiry and interest. The question for social policy arises when these involvements become more than just individual expressions of personal pastimes or social engagements, but are exercises in social power in the form of the advancement of particular public agendas by philanthropic actors. In this situation, society is not only accommodating the coexistence of different and potentially conflicting value orientations of its citizens—an essential characteristic of liberal democracy—but is also facilitating the use of major private resources directed by small groups of people to advance particular causes or value positions without a broader social response mechanism.

These characteristics of private philanthropy, combined with an expanding donor base, result in an ever-increasing fragmentation of organized giving. Absent counterforces within or outside the field that might encourage consideration of the larger collective consequences of individual funding decisions, philanthropy becomes a simple magnifier of individually determined interests and goals. One might consider this an unproblematic situation—the philanthropic equivalent to the marketplace of ideas, in which the best programs, like the best ideas, float to the top. But the world of private philanthropy, with its financial power and growing social influence is not simply a free, transparent, democratic marketplace that expresses private preferences and beliefs and subjects them to critical feedback.[13] To the contrary, it is a powerful source of social change and agenda setting, operating with minimal external input that steers major resources on important public purposes.[14]

While this system has many virtues, it can also have unintended negative consequences in several dimensions of social life. It can adversely affect social equity, as Stanford's Rob Reich has shown in his study of local philanthropic support flowing into public schools. As he points out, private funding can exacerbate the already unequal status of rich and poor school districts, aggravating an existing lack of fairness in the distribution of social services.[15] There are many other areas, such as health care, private education, and particular geographic areas where similar questions of equity arise.

Second, it can distort the public decision-making process through the influence of private wealth in the public arena. The concern voiced early on by the Walsh Commission in its report charging that "the concentration of wealth in the large foundations, such as the Carnegie and the Rockefeller, was being used by industrial magnates to gain control of the universities and, thereby, the social and educational side of American life,"[16] has remained an ongoing critique by those who object to the "private government" aspect of foundation activity. Michael Walzer succinctly summarizes this position in his observation that, "American philanthropy, as currently organized is radically dependent upon... 'the princely gift.' Indeed, philanthropy has probably never been organized in any other way ... But the price we pay for 'the princely gift' is the power of princes."[17]

Finally, beyond policy influence, philanthropy can transport the deficiencies of the market into the social realm. These deficiencies include both the problem of achieving collective goods through market mechanisms, as described previously,[18] and promoting the concept of the market as the preferred vehicle for social decision making. The collective goods problem arises in the unfettered pursuit by multiple independent actors of their individually defined social aims. Championing a preferred social decision-making model can subtly (and not so subtly) shape public perceptions of the relations between the public and private sectors and options available for social agenda setting.[19]

What might be done about these unintended and generally unexamined influences of philanthropy? I am certainly not arguing for stringent limitations on foundations, or even for substantially increased governmental regulatory control, which carries with it threats of politicization and bureaucratization. Even Michael Walzer maintains that a good egalitarian society would include a freely operating philanthropic sector because of the important contribution philanthropy can make to pluralism and civic-mindedness.[20] Philanthropy is an essential contributor to the liberal democratic state, and remedies to its shortcomings should be sought from within rather than outside the field.

While it would take another chapter to explore this issue adequately, I will suggest four possible areas in which philanthropy might pursue paths toward strengthening the public sphere, rather than following its current tendency to reinforce the trends towards privatization. I believe this could be accomplished without inflicting damage on the system of philanthropy itself. First, the field needs to increase its awareness of the problems described here associated with privatization, such as exacerbating inequality, fragmentation, and the problem of collective goods. Second, there should be greater encouragement in donor education activities of analysis of social implications of fundamental agenda setting—that is, critical assessment of the basic goals of the foundation rather than just effectiveness in grantmaking. Third, philanthropy could play a much stronger role in championing the importance of a healthy public sphere in contemporary society.[21] Finally, philanthropy could do more to improve the *means* through which the public comprehends and addresses the vast array of private influences on decisions on social policy, such as supporting vehicles to strengthen the processes of responsible media and deliberative democracy.

These latter topics open issues for another discussion. Nevertheless, the ethical implications of the use of important private resources to accomplish vital public purposes are profound, and foundations have the opportunity to take leadership in both examining those implications and addressing them in practice.

ABOUT THE AUTHOR

Bruce Sievers is a visiting scholar and lecturer at Stanford University and adjunct professor at the Institute for Nonprofit Organization Management at the University of San Francisco. He is a senior fellow emeritus with Rockefeller Philanthropy Advisors. Mr. Sievers holds a PhD in political science from Stanford University and studied at the Freie Universitaet Berlin as a Fulbright Scholar. He was the founding executive director of the California Council for the Humanities and the Walter and Elise Haas Fund. His book, *Civil Society, Philanthropy and the Fate of the Commons* was published in 2010. Other recent publications include: "Philanthropy's Blindspots," "What Civil Society Needs," and "Philanthropy's Role in Liberal Democracy."

NOTES

1. Beyond observing basic norms of courtesy and politeness, many additional aspects of foundation behavior with potential ethical implications remain matters of subjective judgment, such as the style of office space, reasonableness of compensation and benefits, and travel policy. Beyond adhering to minimal legal requirements, these practices for the most part lie outside the realm of regulation by government or even peer organizations, and they simply revert to the personal judgment of a foundation's board and staff members. A 1991 report produced by Independent Sector, *Obedience to the Unenforceable*, captured the essential character of these behaviors.
2. See Donald Schon's general discussion of epistemological issues in professional life in *The Reflective Practitioner: How Professionals Think in Action* (New York: Basic Books, 1983).
3. Charles Lindblom provides an insightful analysis of this process of social control in *The Market System: What It Is, How It Works, and What to Make of It* (New Haven: Yale University Press, 2001).
4. A contemporary manifestation of this long-standing attention to nonprofit accountability is to be seen in the multiple initiatives by both state and national governments seeking to assert greater oversight of the nonprofit sector. One example is the current (at the beginning of 2005) examination by the U.S. Senate Committee on Finance of legislative approaches designed to place more specific financial and operational requirements on nonprofit organizations. Another example is California's Nonprofit Integrity Act of 2004, signed into law by Governor Schwarzenegger, that imposes new requirements on governance and fundraising by California nonprofits. The stated purpose of such legislation is to ensure greater transparency, public accountability, and socially beneficial application of resources.
5. Following several recent well-publicized missteps and scandals involving the Red Cross, United Way, and a number of private foundations, a recent Brookings poll found that only 15 percent of the respondents said they had "a great deal of confidence" in charities. Plummeting public confidence in nonprofits has been accompanied by state and national legislative initiatives to exert more stringent control over the sector.

6. Onora O'Neill, *A Question of Trust* (Cambridge, UK: Cambridge University Press, 2002).

7. Often, the most effective way to promote ethical practices is for the field to take the lead through individual nonprofits or foundations modeling best practices. An example is the growing agreement among foundations that the traditional practice of accepting free tickets to arts and other events should be discouraged. Over a decade ago a few foundations on the west coast decided not to accept such "freebies" on the grounds that it could be seen as clouding the grantor–grantee relationship and that it in fact deprived the ticket-donating organizations of needed income (reasoning that if was deemed important for foundation trustees or staff to attend the events, the foundations should pay for their tickets). While not an ethical issue of large significance, the traditional practice added to the image of foundations as comfortably ensconced centers of power. Beginning from this small base, the practice of paying for tickets has spread widely through the field.

8. For example, Gilbert Ryle's concept of "category mistake" and distinction between "thin" and "thick" descriptions, A. N. Whitehead's "fallacy of misplaced concreteness," and Donald Schon's "selective inattentiveness."

9. Mark D. McGarvie, "The *Dartmouth College* Case and the Legal Design of Civil Society" in Lawrence Friedman and Mark McGarvie, eds., *Charity, Philanthropy, and Civility in American History* (Cambridge, UK: Cambridge University Press, 2003), 100.

10. Todd Sandler has stated the problem of collective action most succinctly in his phrase: "individual rationality is not sufficient for collective rationality" (Todd Sandler, *Collective Action: Theory and Applications*, University of Michigan Press, 1992, p. 3). This sums up the sense of a large body of work relating to the "tragedy of the commons," the prisoner's dilemma, free-riding, externalities, the use of common pool resources, and other aspects of the disjuncture between the pursuit of individual interests and the interest of collectivities. The problem is structural, as illustrated by the prisoner's dilemma; even when there is agreement on a common definition of "interest," the forces of individual self-interest can work to defeat the achievement of optimal interests for the group. Garret Hardin, Mancur Olsen, and many others have demonstrated that the absence of a supervening regulatory power can lead to the destruction of the commons.

11. The problem of value pluralism in a liberal democracy poses a further challenge to the task of achieving common ends. Here, as most notably described by Isaiah Berlin, not only is there the practical problem of reconciling individual interests with a common one, there is no (nor can there be, according to Berlin) common definition of "good." Values are individually defined and are often incompatible, so any attempt to forge a common definition of the good society (or a broad sense of the common good within society) is doomed to

failure. This general problem of pluralistic values has remained an unresolved dilemma for liberal democratic theory.

12. This of course presumes that one views the goal of private philanthropy as benefiting society (in accordance with the public benefit provisions written into federal tax law and state regulatory legislation) and not just as an extension of the prerogatives of personal wealth.

13. The number of foundations in the United States has now grown to approximately 70,000 (a threefold expansion since the early 1990s), and the nonprofit sector has grown significantly faster during the past decade than have the for-profit sector or the governmental sectors.

14. An early example of philanthropic influence was the transformation of American medical education initiated by the Rockefeller Foundation. A more recent one is the much-discussed impact of conservative foundations on the American political agenda during the past two decades.

15. Rob Reich, "Philanthropy and Its Uneasy Relation to Equality," in William Damon and Susan Verducci, eds., *Beyond Good Intentions: Learning to Do Good, Not Harm, in Philanthropy* (Bloomington: Indiana University Press, 2006), 27–49.

16. Marion R. Fremont-Smith, "Foundations and Government" (New York: Russell Sage Foundation, 1965), 561.

17. Michael Walzer, "Socialism and the Gift Relationship," in *Dissent* (Fall 1982), 436.

18. It should be noted that this poses a kind of ironic second-order problem of collective goods, since, as Todd Sandler has pointed out, charities are themselves entities that generally pursue public goods and consequently face their own challenges in overcoming obstacles to the provision of public goods. See Sandler, 107–111.

19. Especially during the past two decades, there has been an increasing emphasis on (along with corresponding criticism of) the transfer of social services previously seen as public sector responsibilities to the market arena. See, for example, Peter W. Singer, *Corporate Warriors: The Rise of the Privatized Military Industry* (Ithaca, NY: Cornell University Press, 2003); Ed Skloot, "Evolution or Extinction: A Strategy for Nonprofits in the Marketplace" (www.surdna.org/speeches/eoe.html); Derek Bok, *Universities in the Marketplace: The Commercialization of Higher Education* (Princeton, NJ: Princeton University Press, 2003); Lester Salamon, *Holding the Center: America's Nonprofit Sector at a Crossroads* (New York: Nathan Cummings Foundation, 1997).

20. Walzer, "Socialism and the Gift Relationship."

21. For a clear statement of this need, see Mark Rosenman's commentary, "Grant Makers Must Focus on Government's Role" in *The Chronicle of Philanthropy* (February 17, 2005): 35.

CHAPTER 19

Ethical Relationships between Grantees and Funders

CARLEEN K. RHODES, CFRE

I have considered professional ethics in the past primarily from the viewpoint of the fundseeker and nonprofit executive—that is, until 2003 when I was hired to lead the staff of the Saint Paul Foundation. Now I have the opportunity and the obligation to consider my organization's behavior and ethics and that of its staff, board members, and volunteers as both a fundseeker—since we are a community foundation that raises money—and as a grantmaker.

But I can assure those of you from nonprofits, I clearly recall the tango you regularly dance as a supplicant seeking funds. And for those of you from foundations, I have gained great respect for the tough decisions you need to make allocating limited resources.

Hopefully, with somewhat of a view from both sides of the table, I would like to pose some challenges to us all that will require openness and honesty; they may be uncomfortable and difficult, but they are important if we are going to affect the kinds of change society needs of us.

So what are some of the ethical issues that affect the relationship between fundseekers and funders, and what opportunities can we pursue or attitudes can we adopt to strengthen the relationships? I offer four observations:

1. Ethics is a bottom-line issue.
2. We need to actively practice our ethical principles.
3. Funders and grantees need to see themselves at the same table—not on other sides of it.
4. While most of us have accepted the challenge of striving to be personally and institutionally ethical and accountable, we have a much larger ethical obligation across the sector and society that requires time and attention.

FIRST: ETHICS NEEDS TO BE VIEWED AS A BOTTOM-LINE ISSUE FOR NONPROFITS AND FOUNDATIONS ALIKE

Aspiring to ethical principles is not just the right thing to do, it is a business necessity—and in many ways, we are expected to act like businesses. A customer needs to trust a company when buying a product. Similarly, clients, students, donors, and nonprofits need to trust us as a foundation and community leader, or our bottom line will be affected.

For the 27 years of my career as a development professional and then a nonprofit CEO, I thought our focus on "ethics" was important but somewhat redundant. Weren't we all involved in mission-oriented causes? Why else would anyone work or serve a nonprofit organization if he or she did not have a lofty calling to do good? I happen to believe professionals can be very passionate about mission.

Are there not more critical issues than ethics that should command our attention—issues more connected to our social missions—poverty, hunger, the education of our children, the care of our elderly, the condition of our environment? These sometimes seem more important than does lofty thinking.

It seems self-congratulatory for us to create our statements of principles and applaud ourselves for our high standards. It seems like waving the flag and sharing recipes for apple pie. There are people with equally lofty integrity and dedication to serving their constituents in the private and government sectors. We do not have the exclusive claim on aspiring to and being capable of the highest integrity.

Scandals in all sectors—public, private, and nonprofit—have caused all of us to recognize that our reputations are tremendously vulnerable when a few can misbehave, painting us all as greedy cheats and lacking in principles and integrity. And it teaches the Pollyannas among us, including me, that while one might like to assume good intent, not everyone will deliver.

In the nonprofit world, the United Way scandal, telemarketing scams, and other shocks have made us pay attention. We rallied and joined in the public criticism and declared what behaviors are not acceptable and, more importantly, what behaviors are acceptable. Foundations have had their share of misbehavior and have drawn attention as well. The Council on Foundations and its members have responded, denounced certain behaviors, and created principles and standards of behavior.

Much of the discussion of corporate accountability in the academic and business literature focuses on formal structures for ethical accounting, auditing, and reporting. Accountability means openness and a commitment to disclosure: corporations fulfill their responsibility for accountability by keeping records of nonfinancial measures that matter to the community (e.g., environmental performance, hiring practices, etc.) and making those records public.

Can we be more clear and honest with each other in our relationships? Funders usually have clear guidelines and use them as their lens for granting or denying requests. Can we take more time to explain our rationale for both the grants and the denials? Can we stay engaged after the decision moment? Often we are on to the next stack of applications and do not have the luxury of time to offer such clarity. But if we do not, we leave nonprofits in the position of assuming they understand why a decision was made, but maybe drawing the wrong conclusion.

At the Saint Paul Foundation, I am very impressed with how we interact with our grant applicants. Sometimes, when it is clear to us that a program has not been well developed, we offer capacity grants and counsel as an alternative. We do not rest on letters to communicate grant or denial decisions; we precede them with phone calls. We have conducted an independent evaluation of our grants program and know that while we do a really effective job with many applicants, the process is still mysterious to others, often those who are least sophisticated. We need to do more to help strengthen the communication process and assure our stakeholders that we have understood their requests and listened to their concerns.

We recently conducted meetings with 25 representatives of African immigrant communities so that we could gain their insights on how we could support them more effectively. Of course, they had varying views, but the open forum informed us all.

We also need to do more work to be clear about why our guidelines are focused as they are. We need to have regular conversations with staff and board members so that we have up-to-date shared interpretations of our focus areas. We need to be able to explain, for example, why we do not provide operating support. We need to have clear criteria and be able to communicate what might fit and what will not.

For nonprofit leaders, can we be more honest in our disclosures? Admit to funders what challenges we anticipate in a project as well as the outcomes we hope to achieve? We should talk to foundation staff ahead of time to test ideas and fit with foundation guidelines. Foundation staff would much rather review proposals based on such understanding. We can ask for explanations and rationale for decisions so we can learn for the future. And we need to understand that sometimes there will not be a fit. Just as fundseekers should not stray from their programmatic focus and manipulate a project to fit a foundation's guidelines, funders should not stray from their guidelines when reviewing grant requests.

That should be part of the ethical pact: to understand each other's goal and priorities. Do we think of foundations as prospects for cultivation where we want to learn what they want to achieve, not sell them on our projects?

Literally, our right to function in our society as we function today is being challenged. Our bottom line as a sector is truly in jeopardy if we are not successful at demonstrating that our standards and expectations are extremely high and transparent to our partners and to those who would judge us.

SECOND: WE NEED TO ACTIVELY PRACTICE OUR ETHICAL PRINCIPLES

Early in my career as a fundraising consultant—I think about 1980—I had a client that helped children with serious behavior problems. They coined a phrase to guide the efforts of their social workers' interactions with these kids. It was "Catch 'em being good." In their therapy at Washburn Child Guidance Center, the children got lots of attention for good behavior and, to the degree possible, their bad behavior was ignored.

What has been most important in our collective work to define ethical behavior, accountability, transparency, and so forth, is that we have made it much more clear what good behavior looks like. It is not just that we have defined what is wrong; we have made it clear for those who want to behave well what that looks like.

A favorite quote of mine comes from Bob Payton taken from Rushworth Kidder's book *How Good People Make Tough Choices*. "Ethics is the science of morals; and morals are the practice of ethics. It is possible to act morally with no ethical understanding and possible to claim to be ethical, while acting immorally. Morals is about a certain kind of behavior; ethics is thinking about that behavior."[1]

We need to combine intellectual aspirations about ethics with models for behaving ethically. Paul Pribbenow calls that the focus on the ideal and the real. It is like any form of knowledge or skill. When we try it out in a real-life situation, we discover its utility. In the process, we make the goal live.

Rushworth Kidder, in a chapter on foundation codes of ethics in *Improving and Strengthening Grant-Making Organizations*, provided an excellent example of an ethical dilemma—a foundation board struggling with the decision to fund an organization they had funded for a long time after they discovered some financial improprieties. Was their loyalty to the constituents served by the organization so they should continue funding? Or should they reveal the impropriety and decline to make another grant—a decision that might result in the organization closing down? As Kidder puts it, "The choice lies not between right and wrong but right and right."

I suggest the following process for practicing our commitment to our ethics for both grantees and funders.

Declare What Is Expected and Set the Bar High

Even well-run organizations may function on unstated principles. Leaving implementation open to interpretation may be very subjective and unstated norms can become deeply ingrained.

At our foundation, we recently completed a code of business conduct. We are living in an age of transparency, and it is the responsibility of every staff member at the foundation to ensure that we are following that code and to report any breaches in it. The most heated discussion of the various sections of our code was at the board level—defining how to implement the commitment to avoiding conflicts of interest. The question centered around not whether we should avoid conflicts but how far we could possibly go to avoid the conflict. Could board members stay in the room if a grant application was being considered from an organization on whose board they served? Could they speak at all and answer questions?

While the decision was to made to allow board members to stay and to be available to answer questions if asked, the board chair chose to leave the room during all votes for grants for organizations to which she was connected, just to make sure there was no appearance of conflict. As the person presiding, the board chair decided she needed to stretch to even a higher standard of performance. The thorough conversation in the previous year served us well at future board meetings.

But there is an ethical dilemma in this as well. Board members are recruited because of their engagement in and knowledge of the community. While their silence during deliberations creates equity in the grant review process for organizations without an advocate in the room, we actually lose the benefit of their community expertise and their volunteer perspective. We depend more heavily, as a result, on the professional staff assessment of requests. They, too, are not immune to having good experiences and impressions—or bad ones—that shape their views of community organizations.

Educate Board and Staff about What Is Expected

We know that developing the code of business conduct or signing the principles of grantmaking is not the end of the matter but rather the beginning. We are committed, as many professionals and board members are, to reviewing them frequently and keeping those high standards fresh in our minds. We need to regularly reeducate our staffs and boards to assure ongoing shared understanding.

Create a Safe Environment for Honesty and Revelation

Creating a safe environment is especially important to the partnership between grantees and funders. That is why conversations about real issues need to occur alongside formal presentations of requests. Foundations need to create a space for organizations to be honest—both in the application and reporting processes. We need to reinforce that we're in the business of investing in innovation and that we know this involves risk. We need to communicate that it is acceptable if a specific project happened to fail. What was learned from it? How might the organization grow from that experience?

Expect Appropriate Behavior

The Minnesota Council on Foundations was the first regional grant-makers association in the country to develop ethical guidelines in their principles for grantmakers. Their leadership in establishing a code of conduct for grantmakers—eight years before anyone else in the country—has proven useful to funders of all sizes in Minnesota. The principles serve as an educational tool for foundation boards and corporate giving committees. Most foundations want to excel and meet the standards. Some, like family foundations, want to meet all the criteria, but cannot easily address the diversity requirement through board service. They have found other creative ways to engage members of the broader community in their work. One result of publishing the standards and recognizing this particular challenge was the creation of a toolkit for creating an inclusive organization that the council shares with others across the country.

Developing ways to institutionalize our commitment to ethics is needed, regularly using our statements of ethical principles in our performance management, and decision making is key.

THIRD: WE'RE AT THE SAME TABLE

We need to get past the power imbalance that many perceive exists between funders and fundseekers and recognize that we are all in this together. We need to perceive ourselves as partners and stakeholders.

When I was seeking funds, whether from an individual, corporation, foundation, or government entity, I thought it was *my* job to build the credibility and trust. Many funders met me more than halfway, and many made it difficult to relate. As Bruce Sievers has said, sometimes it seemed that they wanted to make my life difficult by asking for information in formats that didn't exist and leading me on when they might never make a grant. I perceived they had all the power and I needed to perform to get a share of it.

As a funder, I have a much different perspective of the dynamic. Any foundation, unless it is an operating foundation only running its own programs, can accomplish its goals only through investment in the nonprofit sector. It is our obligation to fund good ideas and programs. As an alternative view to our perceived position of power, we are actually dependent upon others to have any impact at all.

Because we do get to decide where to partner, however, we have a decided advantage in many conversations. To address the perceived power imbalance, funders and fundseekers need to view each other as customers and take time to develop relationships, trust, and a sense of shared goals.

Some funders need an attitude adjustment; they need to set aside their egos. They need to do more homework and feel bold enough to be honest and share difficult information.

Ultimately, we are interdependent if we seek to have impact so we need to find common interests.

FOURTH: WHILE MOST OF US HAVE ACCEPTED THE CHALLENGE OF STRIVING TO BE PERSONALLY AND INSTITUTIONALLY ETHICAL AND ACCOUNTABLE, WE HAVE A MUCH LARGER ETHICAL OBLIGATION ACROSS THE SECTOR AND SOCIETY THAT REQUIRES TIME AND ATTENTION

It is important to lift our discussion of ethics to the institutional level. I have considered conversations about ethics to be about how we relate to people—participants in our programs, individual donors, staff members, and community members. I saw it as relational, connecting to people, being honest, building trust.

While it still comes down to those one-on-one interactions, I think we are talking about taking the challenge to a much higher level—to challenge ourselves to practice institutional ethics. How do we create and lead institutions that are ethical—doing what is right in our communities?

How do institutions work together to focus resources on the most critical issues? Do the strong fundraising organizations just keep getting stronger? Do they take into account the shifting demographics of our country and pressing social issues? Are large institutions—nonprofits and foundations—becoming versions of gated communities? Is "big" the issue?

It is a much more complicated topic with more potential for significant impact if we can begin to address this broader social need.

As disasters impact our communities, many questions are being asked about how institutions have or have not responded. The ethics and intentions of institutional response or nonresponse have been openly challenged. It is great that new nonprofits are being established to meet emerging issues. It is the pillar of our democracy that any group of individuals can see a need and organize to address that need. Maybe it will be a new nonprofit that will establish an umbrella organization to focus our collective efforts on areas of greatest need.

ONE FINAL POINT

We all have read or are familiar with the premises of Thomas L. Friedman's book, *The World Is Flat*. How does our conversation about ethics need to change in a flattening world? How will it matter in the future? When a blogger can bring down Dan Rather and CBS News, we are all vulnerable to the person or entity who picks up on our questionable behavior. But more importantly, how can we use that power of easy access to information to blast our stand on what is ethical to all who could possibly care?

Our future success, our ability to do our work, depends on how we are perceived by those outside our sector—government leaders, corporate leaders, the media, and citizens. We are under tough scrutiny, not because we cannot deliver good services (Enron probably delivered good services to many customers) but because our integrity and privileged status are being challenged. We can stand up and advocate for what we believe to be right.

ABOUT THE AUTHOR

Carleen Rhodes is the president and CEO of the Minnesota Community Foundation. Ms. Rhodes joined the team in 2003 with decades of experience in nonprofit management and fundraising. She has spearheaded efforts to create new tools for philanthropy including the statewide giving portal GiveMN (that has raised more than $50 million for 6,000 nonprofits in just over two years), and a competition website to engage citizens in solving problems, Minnesota Idea Open. She is actively engaged in a number of community endeavors related to economic development, ending homelessness, education, and advancing philanthropy. Previously, she was president of the Minnesota Children's Museum and a partner in the national fundraising consulting firm Bentz Whaley Flessner.

NOTE

1. Rushworth M. Kidder, *How Good People Make Tough Choices* (New York: William Morrow, 1995), 17.

CHAPTER 20

Regulation in the Nonprofit Sector*: Symbolic Politics and the Social Construction of Accountability

ROBERT D. HERMAN

In this chapter I intend to do two things:

1. I present a perspective on understanding the current surge of activity regarding enhancing the U.S. national government's regulation of the U.S. nonprofit sector, focusing principally on charitable organizations (though I believe the perspective is also relevant to regulation of grantmaking foundations, with certain modifications).

2. I argue that an enhanced emphasis, among sector-serving professional associations, university programs in philanthropy and nonprofit management, and especially within charities themselves

---

*Prepared for presentation at the Association of Fundraising Professionals 2005 Think Tank on Fundraising, "Promoting Ethics as Guiding Force in Philanthropic Fundraising," Washington, DC, September 7–8, 2005. My thanks to Max Stephenson and Scott Helm for their helpful comments on this draft.

on the moral (or ethical) foundation of charity could be a more far-reaching and effective response to current problems of accountability.

I am not intending to argue for or against increased regulation of charities. I believe some increased regulation is likely and that it is futile and unwise to argue against any change (though I certainly have views about specific details). I also believe certain (minimum) standards of behavior by charities are desirable (though reasonable people are likely to disagree about the specific details of those standards). Thus, in the first section, rather than focusing on details of hearings held by the Senate Finance Committee or the report issued by the Panel on the Nonprofit Sector, I will present ideas that I believe help us to understand, at least to some extent, the institutional pressures for enhanced regulation and the sector response to date.

PERSPECTIVES ON REGULATION

All law is regulation or intended regulation, I suppose one could argue. In general usage, regulation is regarded as law directed at proscribing and prescribing actions and practices in certain industries (e.g., telecommunications, securities, or pharmaceuticals) or in certain broad categories of institutions (e.g., employment law, pension law, or environmental law) where, typically, governmental agencies are created and charged with implementing the regulations. One long-familiar form of governmental regulation is price regulation. This is an area of substantial controversy and a fair amount of research performed by economists and others. Sometimes price regulation occurs in what have been called "natural monopolies," though the concept of natural monopoly is sometimes criticized as unrealistic as a political accomplishment.[1] A recent, thorough, and nonpolemical review of the economics literature on price regulation, in situations when uncontrolled competition is considered undesirable—usually because technological realities make provision by one or a few firms optimal—is provided by Armstrong and Sappington.[2]

Of greater relevance to regulation of charities is what is called non-price regulation. Typical examples are health and safety (Occupational Safety and Health Administration), equal employment opportunity (Equal Employment Opportunity Commission), and environmental pollution prevention and clean-up (Environmental Protection Agency). In contrast to price regulation, which some economists and historians have argued has been favored by the regulated industry (regulatory capture can be a pleasant situation for both the regulators and the regulated); non–price regulation typically applies across all or at least a wide range of industries. Accordingly, the actions of a regulatory agency affect firms with more diverse interests, and the regulatory agency's actions are potentially of interest to a broader section of the public. Research and theory about non–price regulation, then, would seem to be the more relevant area in which to search for results or insights that might be useful as we think about the enhanced regulation of charities and its likely effects.

U.S. charitable organizations are currently subject to a wide variety of government regulations, including regulations mandated by local governments (usually relating to fundraising solicitations), state governments, and the national government. Irvin (2005) considers the basis for state regulation and annual reporting and also provides some evidence suggesting that six states without registration and annual financial reporting by charities operating in those states have no more charity fraud (according to attorneys general) and no pattern of difference in charitable contributions from the U.S. average. Irvin proposes partial deregulation in all states and a move to more consistent, nationwide forms and reports.[3]

A 2005 special issue of the *Nonprofit Quarterly* is entirely devoted to articles concerning regulation and accountability. In that issue, Bowman and Bies[4] consider some of the issues relating to self-regulation in the nonprofit sector, including self-regulation via hierarchical (or corporate) association monitoring, accreditation, and codes of conduct. Their review suggests that neither association monitoring nor codes of conduct are strong ways of ensuring that charities meet the relevant standards. Accreditation, which is fairly common in education and health care but not in other areas of charitable activity, certainly has not totally prevented undesirable behavior, which often seems to be a stronger form of self-regulation.

The interest in enhanced national regulation of charities is intended to improve the accountability of charities (at least this is the charitable interpretation), though McCambridge's[5] argument that regulation and accountability are not the same thing is convincing. Whatever the motives of individual legislators (I am certainly in no position to have any knowledge of such, and speculation about individual motives seems pointless anyway), what in the political system makes for increased interest in enhanced regulation of charities? The short answer is that charity regulation is an excellent issue for symbolic politics.

Symbolic Politics

The corporate governance scandals that occurred in the opening years of this century involving big business (e.g., Enron, WorldCom) were, in rather different ways, preceded by some well-publicized scandals in charitable organizations (e.g., United Way of America, Covenant House) as well as more recent well-publicized public relations difficulties for some charities (the Red Cross and the Nature Conservancy). No doubt many politicians regard the Sarbanes–Oxley Act (SOX) as a great success, both instrumentally (believing that it has helped prevent corporate fraud and restored investor trust) and symbolically (believing that the public overwhelmingly approves and supports that legislation). While only two provisions of SOX apply to nonprofit corporations (those relating to whistleblower protection and document destruction), the political moment seems right for continuing legislation that can be presented as improving governance and accountability in charities.

Matten[6] has analyzed German businesses response to the German government's enactment of a waste management act. He maintains that the 1996 German "Closed Substance Cycle and Waste Management Act" mostly expressed rhetorical hopes about eliminating waste with many details left unspecified. Matten writes that the "act has quite a substantial symbolic content in that it prescribes a certain regulatory intent . . . without at the same time transforming this intent into concrete and enforceable legal requirements."[7] He observes that the act did have the effect of encouraging many industries in Germany to voluntarily develop and implement take-back schemes and promote other self-regulatory product responsibilities (perhaps to avoid more stringent legal requirements).

Of course, all political proposals today have symbolic aspects (even the names of acts are now carefully crafted to send a message), but the balance between substance and symbol in legislation varies. It is too early to assess the extent of substance and symbol in legislative proposals for enhanced charity regulation. Nonetheless, the response from at least some parts of the nonprofit sector indicate that various umbrella groups are seriously promoting greater self-regulation as well as trying to shape the outcomes of legislation.

Social Construction of Accountability

If regulation is intended to improve accountability, but if regulation is not identical to accountability, then what is accountability? Accountability can be and has been defined in differing ways. For example, some definitions emphasize a bureaucratic and legal basis, whereby accountability involves reporting to higher authority and the nature of the reporting is bound by rules and procedures. Other definitions focus more on the variety of expectations of various constituencies and of giving an account to these stakeholders, though such accounts may not be legally prescribed (see Kearns, 1994, for more thorough review of definitions and a presentation of a more encompassing framework).[8] More recently, Ebrahim[9] has observed that charity accountability has often been described as a matter of three relationships: upward to donors or patrons, downward to clients, and internal to the mission.

The amorphousness of the accountability concept permits many meanings; thus, it can be related to other concepts in many possible ways. For example, the Independent Sector's Panel on the Nonprofit Sector report (2005) was titled "Strengthening Transparency: Governance Accountability of Charitable Organizations." Are the three distinct but related concepts; does doing the first in the sequence well lead to do the second well, then the third?

Accountability, at a minimum, includes meeting reporting requirements (for charities this means in most states, for example, filing annual reports with the state attorney general, filing the IRS Form 990 as well as other forms), usually with some degree of financial review by an independent body. Increasingly it means providing reports on program outcomes or even program evaluations. More elaborate and detailed enumerations are possible. Whatever the specific items, accountability seems to be considered as an outcome of activities performed by an organization. In short, accountability is generally conceived within a "machine metaphor" of organization.[10] In this view, an organization is like a machine, designed to achieve certain goals, whereby the processes and activities can be fit together and managed so that what is intended is what happens (the notion of organizations as "managed systems" [Elmore, 1978][11] expresses the same conception). Thus, being accountable is a matter of doing the right thing. Achieving accountability is something an organization can build into its systems, manage, and control.

This way of thinking about accountability is reflected in the notion of accountability as a set of tools. In 1999, a Canadian Panel on Accountability and Governance in the Voluntary Sector issued a report describing ways of improving accountability and governance among Canada's charities, in which the authors of the report write that accountability is not a single tool but many different tools. This, of course, makes a great deal of sense. Since accountability involves reporting to (even managing?) stakeholders above, below, and within, a variety of processes must be designed and tools used. (The notion of managing stakeholders can be a troubling one. Can accountability be circumvented or diminished if an organization succeeds in substantially shaping a stakeholder group's criteria for assessment and then provides information consistent with those criteria?) The perspective I'm advancing here is not an alternative, but a supplement to the common managed-system view of accountability.

In addition to seeing accountability as something organizations can try to design into their managed system, I believe we must recognize that accountability is often a socially constructed outcome. By socially constructed I mean that accountability (what it is conceptually as well as how well an organization achieves it) is also a matter of what interested actors judge it to be. Social constructionism considers that reality, some parts of reality at any rate, are *created* by people's beliefs, knowledge, and actions. Reality does not just exist "out there," independently of people (for a more thorough exposition of social constructionism as applied to charitable effectiveness, see Herman and Renz, 2004).[12] Thus, accountability is not just something that can be achieved by using the right tools; it is not something that can be controlled.

A fascinating case study and analysis of the social construction of accountability is given in a recent paper by Stephenson and Chaves (2005). The Nature Conservancy (TNC) is one of the largest and, according to commonly used criteria, most successful nonprofit organizations in the United States, yet a series of investigative reports published in the *Washington Post* in the spring of 2003 brought on an "accountability crisis" there. Stephenson and Chaves (2005)[13] show how the meta-narrative frame used by the reporters puts the "facts" into the framework of a familiar story. Of the many "charges" brought against TNC, most (or so it seems to me) are achieved through rhetoric and embellishment. However, one could see the TNC case not as an accountability crisis but as an argument about what TNC had become and the values it seemed to promote. Nonetheless, the series of events became regarded as reflecting difficulties of accountability. As a result, TNC undertook a variety of activities to improve their tools of accountability (see the TNC website at http://nature.org/aboutus/ for more information on TNC's accountability and governance processes).

The Nature Conservancy case is unusual in that it seems to have been largely media initiated (the troubles experienced by the American Red Cross with how they handled donations following the 9/11 attacks also had a significant media component). Probably, most of the time, the social construction of accountability is unremarkable and unnoticed, as stakeholders for any specific charity may share the same conception of accountability and the same judgment of how well the charity is achieving accountability. However, stakeholders, particularly powerful ones, may have occasion to believe something is amiss and frame that as a problem in accountability. Being judged as accountable may depend more on the extent to which stakeholders are satisfied than on whether various accountability tools are used.

ETHICS AND A CULTURE OF INTEGRITY

As noted at the outset, I am not arguing against enhanced charity regulation (or enhanced regulation of grantmaking foundations). However, some simple changes in regulation that have already been made (e.g., the change in valuation for automobile donations) and more vigorous enforcement of current regulations (as in the revocation of tax exemption for four credit counseling agencies) show that some true abuses (at least that's how I think of them) can be ameliorated with current law and regulation.

No doubt attempts to ferret out the businesses disguised as charities and to prevent shady dealings perpetrated by some charities seeking the easy way necessitate adjustments to law and regulation. I would hope that most charities (i.e., the core group, those staff, volunteers, senior managers, and board leaders committed to the mission of the organization) want to go well beyond achieving the legal minimum in relation to good governance and appropriate accountability processes. Creating and maintaining a culture of integrity[14] is obviously not something that can be done quickly or by fiat. I have no simple solutions to propose how organizations' ethical cultures are achieved; I am sure it is an achievement that can be described as "top-down and center-out." The top leaders (the board and top management) are clearly crucial in establishing and supporting a culture of integrity, but so too are those at the center (the core group) of the organization's day-to-day operations.

I believe achieving a culture of integrity includes a top-down and center-out commitment to *managing toward the morality of the mission*.[15] What is distinctive, I believe, about charitable organizations is their moral imperative, that of responding to the unmet (or undermet) needs of some portion of the living and future community (see Ostrander and Schervish 1990[16] for a thorough development of the idea that philanthropic exchange is based on moral claims as distinguished from commercial and political exchange). The idea that businesses maximize profit (and should, according to many) has been the basis for management in such organizations. Managers ask how any particular objective or process contributes to the bottom line, and (though difficult) a single metric (the dollar) is used for measuring those contributions. A profit maximization function provides the basis for making decisions. Charitable organizations lack a maximization function; the best substitute, I believe, is evaluating objectives, processes and so forth in relation to how they contribute to achieving the mission and to the extent to which they are consistent with the moral basis of the mission.

This view has long been advocated (in different terms) by some (most?) in the fundraising profession. Fogal[17] follows Henry Rosso, a well-known fundraiser and founding director of The Fund Raising School (a program of the Indiana University Center on Philanthropy), in distinguishing three stages of charitable fundraising development. In the initial stage (typically occurring when charities are starting up), the emphasis of the fundraising program is on selling what the organization is about. In the second stage, the emphasis becomes one of developing relationships with donors and of soliciting. In the final stage, the charity is part of building "a human community that achieves a common good. Donors are regarded and thoughtful participants in the organization's life and work."[18] How many charities have achieved this stage? Probably not many, but it surely seems like the ethical ideal to strive for.

Sector-serving organizations, such as the Association of Fundraising Professionals (as well as all the others), and university programs in philanthropy and nonprofit management have obligations in regard to promoting and modeling a culture of integrity. Professional and other sector-serving organizations can create (and several have created) a code of ethical conduct, including enforcement procedures. They can also promote publications and sessions that draw attention to issues of ethics and to the idea of managing toward the morality of the mission. University programs in philanthropy and nonprofit management can and should (as noted in the Nonprofit Academic Centers Council curricular guidelines) include consideration of ethics codes and the values undergirding the institutions of philanthropy.

Such actions by professional associations and university programs have some promise of helping charity leaders pay attention to and improve ethical values and practice in their organizations. Of course, the reach and impact of professional associations and university programs are limited. A commitment to high ethical conduct cannot be imposed by professional associations or academic courses. Such commitment must come from those who are attracted to participate (in whatever or however many ways, as employee, volunteer, or donor) in the charitable sector. Fortunately, the charitable sector has attracted those with a passion about certain moral claims. Maintaining the distinctiveness of nonprofit charities seems to me fundamental to continuing to do so.

ABOUT THE AUTHOR

Robert D. Herman is professor emeritus at the Department of Public Affairs, Henry W. Bloch School of Management, University of Missouri–Kansas City. His research interests focus on nonprofit governance, nonprofit executive leadership and nonprofit organizational effectiveness. He is the author of more than 30 peer-reviewed articles and author or editor of three books. He received the Association for Research on Nonprofit Organizations and Voluntary Action (ARNOVA) 2010 Award for Distinguished Achievement and Leadership in Nonprofit and Voluntary Action Research.

NOTES

1. T. J. DiLorenzo, "The Myth of Natural Monopoly." *The Review of Austrian Economics* 9(2) (1996): 43–58.
2. M. Armstrong and D. Sappington, "Recent Developments in the Theory of Regulation" in M. Armstrong and R. H. Porter, eds., *Handbook of Industrial Organization*, Volume 3 (Amsterdam: North-Holland, 2005).

3. R. A. Irvin, "State Regulation of Nonprofit Organizations: Accountability Regardless of Outcome," *Nonprofit and Voluntary Sector Quarterly* 34, no. 2 (2005): 161–178.

4. W. Bowman and A. Bies, "Can the Charitable Sector Regulate Itself?" Special issue. *The Nonprofit Quarterly* 12 (2005): 39–43.

5. R. McCambridge, "Is Accountability the Same as Regulation? Not Exactly," Special issue. *The Nonprofit Quarterly* 12 (2005), 3–5.

6. D. Matten, "Symbolic Politics in Environment Regulation: Corporate Strategic Responses," *Business Strategy and the Environment* 12(4) (2003): 215–226.

7. R. D. Herman, "Conclusion: The Future of Nonprofit Management," in R. D. Herman (ed.), *The Jossey-Bass Handbook of Nonprofit Leadership and Management*, 2nd ed. (San Francisco: Jossey-Bass, 2004).

8. K. P. Kearns, "The Strategic Management of Accountability in Nonprofit Organizations: An Analytical Framework," *Public Administration Review* 54, no. 2 (1994): 185–192.

9. A. Ebrahim, "Accountability Myopia: Losing Sight of Organizational Learning," *Nonprofit and Voluntary Sector Quarterly* 34(1) (2005): 56–87.

10. G. Morgan, *Images of Organization* (Beverly Hills, CA: Sage, 1986).

11. R. F. Elmore, "Organizational Models of Social Program Implementation," *Public Policy* 26(2) (1978): 185–228.

12. R. D. Herman and D. O. Renz, "Doing Things Right: Effectiveness in Local Nonprofit Organizations, A Panel Study," *Public Administration Review* 64(4) (2004): 694–704.

13. M. Stephenson and E. Chaves, "The Nature Conservancy, the Press and the Social Construction of Accountability." Paper presented at the conference Boards and Beyond: Understanding the Changing Realities of Nonprofit Organization Governance, Kansas City, MO, 2005.

14. T. H. Jeavons, "Ethical Nonprofit Management." In R. D. Herman, ed., *The Jossey-Bass Handbook of Nonprofit Leadership and Management*, 2nd ed. (San Francisco: Jossey-Bass, 2004).

15. Herman, "Conclusion."

16. S. A. Ostrander and P. G. Schervish, "Giving and Getting: Philanthropy as a Social Relation," in J. Van til, ed., *Critical Issues in American Philanthropy: Strengthening Theory and Practice* (San Francisco: Jossey-Bass, 1990).

17. R. E. Fogal, "Developing and Managing the Fundraising Program," In R. D. Herman, ed., *The Jossey-Bass Handbook of Nonprofit Leadership and Management*, 2nd ed. (San Francisco: Jossey-Bass, 2004).

18. Ibid., 421.

CHAPTER 21

Restoring Public Confidence in the Nonprofit Sector

WILLIAM A. SCHAMBRA

S urveys of public attitudes toward the nonprofit sector have not been sources of cheerful news lately. As Brookings scholar Paul Light noted recently, "public confidence in charitable organizations was shaken in the weeks and months following the terrorist attacks on New York City and Washington, DC, and has yet to rebound."[1] If this is a function of isolated acts of corruption, then we can draft more stringent guidelines for ethical behavior, pledge to do better in the future, and wait for time to heal all wounds. But I suspect that the crisis in public trust is a product of a deeper problem facing the sector, which it desperately needs to understand.

Here is the root of the problem: The nonprofit sector has begun to run afoul of one of the most powerful and enduring American prejudices—a profound distrust of large institutions. No matter where found—in government, the economy, or the culture—large institutions sooner or later come to be seen as remote, bureaucratic, inflexible, unresponsive, and undemocratic. And this happens in only the loosest correlation with episodes of actual abuse or corruption.

This distrustful sentiment was present at the founding of the nation. The framers of the Constitution barely achieved its ratification because its opponents could not conceive that a large, distant national government could become anything other than an oppressive tyranny. Entire political movements, from Jacksonian Democracy to modern-day conservative Republicanism, have been built upon distrust of big government. At the end of the nineteenth century, the rise of "big business"—the large, vertically integrated corporations—prompted powerful, populist efforts to cut them down to size. In the 1950s, "big unionism" seemed to many to be choking and stifling free enterprise. Big institutions, always and everywhere, have triggered big reactions from the American public.

But the nonprofit sector seemed to be largely immune from this reaction. Even as big government, big corporations, big unions, and the big professions—law, medicine, education, and so forth—were on the rise and earning their share of public distrust, the nonprofit sector largely managed to avoid it. That is because "bigness" did not seem to come to the sector in the same way or to the same degree that it came to others. It rather appeared to remain essentially the realm of smallness, immediacy, and intimate community. Its local civic institutions—neighborhoods, churches, and ethnic and voluntary associations—were run not by distant, arrogant bureaucrats, but by friends and neighbors. No arcane professional expertise was required to be part of civil society; it was enough to bring amateur personal idealism, compassion, and small gifts of time and energy. There was no radical division between the organization's "expert" and the subordinate "client." In a system of mutual self-help, a provider in 2008 was likely to be tomorrow's receiver.

Historians debate how long this state of affairs lasted. It is certainly there in the pages of Alan Ehrenhalt's *The Lost City*, an account of the vigorous urban and suburban community life in 1950s Chicago neighborhoods. Still, in an important sense, how long or to what degree this was an accurate description of American social life is beside the point. The critical fact is that this *view* of the nonprofit sector as nonbureaucratic, small, local, voluntary, and rooted in friendship and neighborliness remained deeply implanted in the popular imagination until very recently. Indeed, it is still a potent, popular image or myth about the sector.

PUBLIC CONFIDENCE

The failure of the sector to live up to this image or myth at moments of high public visibility contributes significantly to the erosion of public confidence in it. When citizens rallied eagerly to support the Red Cross after September 11, for instance, they expected their gifts to go immediately to the victims, as though neighbors were supporting neighbors. They were disillusioned to find that some funds were going instead to finance management overhead and rebuild reserve funds. When they responded generously to pleas for funding to reopen a shuttered Statue of Liberty, they were not amused to discover that all the while the Statue of Liberty Foundation was in fact sitting on a respectable endowment, reserved for educational programs.

Neither of these incidents, nor many others we could all cite, involved practices that were unethical or corrupt. They would not have run afoul of codes of ethical conduct, no matter how rigorous. Along with generous salaries for executives, sizeable and well-compensated staffs, or international site visits for board members, these practices are simply standard operating procedures for large, complex nonprofits. And yet the public is perplexed and disappointed whenever events conspire to make such practices visible. That is because they contravene the public's still-powerful conviction that the essence of the nonprofit realm is smallness, neighborliness, and charity.

Unhappily, a great deal is happening within the sector that may only make the public confidence problem worse. Nonprofits are entering the marketplace with business ventures of their own, often lured or shoved by their foundation supporters. But in some cases they end up adopting the worst characteristics of bottom-line big business, putting "profits before people." We have only begun, for instance, to feel the public and congressional backlash against nonprofit hospitals, whose market-dictated fee structures produce the appearance of actually overcharging those whom they were intended to serve in the spirit of charity.

As everyone knows, the largest nonprofits have also come to rely heavily on government funding. Consequently, as they seek to comply with a stifling web of regulations, nonprofits begin to take on the trappings of distant and unpopular government bureaucracies. They also come to have—not to put too fine a point on it—a vested interest in sustained and increasing levels of government taxing and spending. The leadership of the nonprofit sector now sees its fate as inextricably linked to that of big government, and that leadership has become ever more openly committed to fighting on its behalf. As Independent Sector president Diana Aviv put it in her inaugural address, "We should be fighting for substantial and sustainable support from the federal government and the states . . . whether that includes rolling back the massive tax cuts of recent years or increasing public revenues in some other way."[2] Whatever the substantive merits of such proposals, wedding one's own credibility to that of big government at least doubles the g-force dragging against efforts to buoy public confidence in the sector.

To some degree reflecting these developments, the nonprofit sector is rapidly professionalizing itself. That might seem to be an unalloyed good. But as ever more nonprofit positions are filled by trained experts, who are graduated in ever-larger numbers from the swelling list of centers for nonprofit management education, the once close link between the everyday citizen and the nonprofit organization is weakened even further. In large nonprofits, volunteers have long since ceased performing the critical service functions. Even the interaction with the community is put in the hands of professionals. Fundraising is often done by experts, not by enthusiastic volunteer staff or board members. Even volunteering itself is being professionalized. We hear more and more about "volunteer management," as though volunteers were a somewhat balky resource requiring expert processing before they can be useful, rather than the heart and soul of the sector.

Now, many nonprofit experts argue that the best way to restore public confidence in the face of these developments is *not* to reexamine our own behavior, but rather to attack the unrealistic, foolish, mythical expectations that lead the public to judge that behavior so harshly. It's time to tell the American people that, in Lester Salamon's words, this is "no longer your father's nonprofit sector." As he argues, "America's charities have moved well beyond the quaint, Norman Rockwell stereotype of selfless volunteers ministering to the needy and supported largely by charitable gifts," though regrettably, "popular images remain rooted in this older image." We need to get beyond the "ritualistic celebration of charitable giving and volunteerism," in an effort to bring "popular perceptions into better alignment with the realities that now exist."[3]

But what would that confidence-restoring "realistic" message sound like? "Yes, we're big, complex, professionally managed organizations, not at all like quaint neighborhood barn-raisings and more like big corporations and big government. Get used to it." Would such a lecture, however soothingly delivered by sophisticated professionals to the amusingly naïve general public rebuild public trust in the sector? That is doubtful. Not only is this approach patronizing, it also asks the public to understand and embrace a bewilderingly vague and complicated statement of purpose. The public must now accept that the sector is no longer what they thought it was. Instead, it is becoming like the other sectors, but it still does *something* that is different from and better than what they do. As for the "something," to quote Buffalo Springfield, "what it is ain't exactly clear."[4]

And that, finally, is the real problem facing the sector as we try to restore the confidence of the American people in what we do. It's hard even to explain, much less defend, to the public the "something" we do, because we can no longer explain it to ourselves. We seem to have lost our bearings, our fundamental sense of direction or purpose, the ability to say what it is we do that is essential, unique, and indispensable to the Republic.

Perhaps instead it would be useful to revisit the assumption that we must throw away our old, sturdy, well-defined self-understanding for a new, ill-defined one. Other sectors of American society, after all, have found ways to cope with the animus against bigness by moving away from remote, complex, professionalized, centralized organization, toward decentralized, immediate, relationship-based, informal "networks." Big corporations come to be challenged by small, nimble start-ups; big government is challenged by decentralist Republicans and "reinventing government" Democrats; big medicine is challenged by traditional, home-based self-help approaches; big media is challenged by blogging and the Internet; big education is challenged by charter schools and home schooling. After observing the fate of the American automotive industry in the 1970s, most sectors have learned that condescending lectures about "we're big—we don't have to care" are no substitute for serious efforts to adapt to the American aversion to organizational size.

FAITH-BASED INSTITUTIONS IN THE NONPROFIT SECTOR

Certainly, at least one part of the nonprofit sector, namely, the faith-based institution, is learning to recapture smallness and immediacy in the face of largeness and complexity. For much of the twentieth century, large mainline denominations sought to adapt themselves to the secular, professional world by softening their convictions, lowering creedal demands on parishioners, and assuming the managerial techniques of large modern organizations. They also watched their pews empty.

However, we are in the midst of a renewal of "spirituality in America,"[5] as a *Newsweek* cover story put it. Its most visible feature is, perhaps, the rise of the mega-churches with congregations that may fill auditoriums with 10,000 or 15,000 seats. While outside observers typically notice first this bigness, the sprawling, mall-like structure is swamped by teeming masses of worshippers on Sunday. The deeper meaning of the mega-church, they note, is to be found elsewhere. It's really in the church's small, intimate, spiritually intense groups, meeting throughout the week, designed to address the full range of human needs: spiritual sustenance, child care, job search, education, recovery from addiction, or just filling the lonely hours. As a recent article in *Mother Jones* put it, "[b]y taking on roles as various as those of the neighborhood welcome committee, the Rotary, the corner diner, the country club mixer, the support group—and, of course, family and school—mega-churches have become the tightly knit villages that many Americans think they grew up in."[6]

The faithful in these houses of worship often regard giving, perhaps to the extent of tithing, to be not a burdensome chore but an essential part of their relationship to God and his community. Furthermore, members are asked to do more than simply write generous checks to support professional clergy and providers of services. They are asked—no, they consider themselves mandated by their God—to become actively, immediately, personally engaged in charitable service to others. They must *become* the Good Samaritan. There is no existential wringing of the hands about this purpose. The newly vibrant churches are unlikely to be distracted from their central, spiritual, and charitable missions by ancillary profit-making enterprises, or by the pursuit of government grants for service delivery.

To the extent that some do so become distracted, their pews and enrollments lists, too, will soon empty, as the televangelists discovered in the wake of the Jim and Tammy Faye Bakker scandal in the mid-1980s. This clarity of purpose fuels enormous grassroots energy and draws citizens by the thousands into burgeoning small groups and ministries. For them, voluntarism, charity, neighborliness, and community are not quaint, risible, Norman Rockwell throwbacks to yesteryear. They are living, breathing, essential expressions, in pastor and author Rick Warren's now famous phrase, of the "purpose-driven life." And this is occurring across lines of race, income, educational status, and denomination in the very midst of a complex, sophisticated organizational milieu that, the experts tell us, had eradicated forever the essential preconditions for the "tightly knit villages" people "thought they had grown up in."

There's a deeper significance to the recent spiritual resurgence: Similar such moments throughout Anglo-American history have had profoundly transforming and energizing consequences for civil society, or what we know as the nonprofit sector. Those moments mobilized citizens behind new movements for social change and reform and created wholly new modes of organization to reach those purposes. As we were reminded by Adam Hochschild's recent book *Bury the Chains*, a history of the English origins of the antislavery movement in the late eighteenth century, a faith-based movement of Quakers and evangelical Anglicans swelled from 12 impassioned men meeting in a London printer's shop in 1787 to a vast and successful crusade to abolish what had once been considered an indispensable cornerstone of the economy of the West. Along the way, new methods of organizing, mobilizing, and institution building were invented: "Each of these tools, from the poster to the political book tour, from the consumer boycott to investigative reporting designed to stir people to action, is part of what we take for granted in a democracy," Hochschild writes. "Two and a half centuries ago, few people assumed this."[7]

This applies as well to all subsequent great movements of reform, from abolition to prohibition to the civil rights movement. Each of these were rooted in vital spiritual traditions, and each of them spun off new, unprecedented, sometimes wildly unorthodox organizational forms, which overturned expert expectations about the way citizens were likely to assemble and behave. In the early 1960s, the prominent theologian Harvey Cox scanned the staid, comfortable, undemanding, and increasingly empty mainline churches and could imagine nothing other than the coming of "the secular city," a civilization drained of religious belief. More recently, he was compelled to write *Fire from Heaven*,[8] explicitly rescinding the secular thesis. Now the story he told was about a completely unanticipated Pentecostal movement, which had swept the world and was beginning to have profound and largely beneficial effects everywhere on culture, politics, and society.

This spiritual resurgence, along with the often unanticipated organizational and institutional consequences it is likely to have, presents a deep challenge to the nonprofit sector and its effort to recapture public confidence. Many of the more significant nonprofits were, of course, born precisely in moments of religious upsurge in the past. That would seem to prepare them well to harness the energies of the recent resurgence. But as corporatization, bureaucratization, and professionalization have worked their changes over the years, the spiritual zeal of the founders has been replaced by the methodical techniques of the managers. Indeed, modern nonprofit managers are often embarrassed about or ill at ease with the original religious impulse at the root of their organizations. Writing in the secular 1960s about foundations, Warren Weaver noted that while it was once said that "religion is the mother of philanthropy," currently "religion is more accurately to be referred to as the unobtrusive great-grandmother of philanthropy."[9] A great-grandmother, incidentally, that many wish to keep locked in the attic.

Edging uneasily away from spiritual origins coincides, of course, with Salamon's suggestion that we grow up, stop spinning pleasant tales about the sector's voluntarism and charity, and embrace some other, newer, if scantily sketched, purpose. But the irony is that this advice comes at the precise moment when Americans are evidencing an ever-greater hunger for spiritual sustenance through connectedness, community, and charitable engagement, which was once the peculiar province of the nonprofit sector. And people have made it clear that if the secular nonprofit sector no longer wishes to meet that need, they can and will meet it elsewhere—that is, within the religious sphere, where indeed new modes of organization have arisen for just that purpose.

The nonprofit sector may be able to talk people out of expecting much from its agencies by way of voluntarism, charity, and community. But the notion that cultivating a new, more realistic image of the sector will restore its standing with the public overlooks one fact: Right next door stands a vibrant, charitable, voluntary faith community, which by its very existence gives the lie to sophisticated explanations about why such a sector can no longer exist. The unflattering comparison is unlikely to build confidence in the nonprofit sector. In the final analysis, just as with the automobile industry, people are more likely to take their business elsewhere, so to speak, where their needs are met rather than patronized or dismissed.

It's additionally ironic that the nonprofit sector should downplay its roots in voluntarism and private charity at the precise moment the now-legendary multitrillion-dollar intergenerational transfer of wealth may be underway. It promises to make available vast new private-sector resources to the foundation and nonprofit world. The impending retirement of baby boomers, as well, could make millions of volunteers with considerable professional skills and disposable income available to the sector. As has often been pointed out, most trends over the past century—everything from television to longer workweeks to women moving into the workplace—have *subtracted* time and energy from the civic sector. The new availability of boomers wondering what to do with 20 remaining years of good health may well be the first significant modern trend that actually *adds* human time and energy to civil society. But these potential resources are unlikely to be attracted by a sector that, with remarkably bad timing, dismisses its own past as a Norman Rockwell fantasy, in the name of reinventing itself as a profitable enterprise or as a quasi-governmental agency.

An Approach for the Future

Is there another approach? I would suggest that the sector might consider revisiting its own assumptions and behavior, before attempting to change public expectations of them. This is the central question: Might it not be possible for the nonprofit sector to refound itself upon, rather than rejecting, its once central values of voluntarism, charity, smallness, face-to-face relations, neighborliness, and community? If other sectors of society, which have become large, centralized, and professionalized earlier and more comprehensively than the nonprofit sector, have managed to spawn trends toward smallness, immediacy, and community, why can't the nonprofit sector, where such values were once its very reason for being? Rather than regarding its historical rootedness in faith as a source of embarrassment, why can't the nonprofit sector draw on it as a source of strength—a proud tradition that gives it an edge in the effort to meet growing public yearning for spiritual purpose or meaning?

I suspect that no part of the nonprofit sector has a greater stake in confronting these questions than its fundraising executives. The notion that public confidence in the sector could be significantly enhanced if only fundraisers pledged to be more honest, transparent, and ethical compels them to bear far too great a burden of expectation. To repeat: The primary public relations problem for the sector is not unethical behavior (though, of course, that never helps). It is rather that the sector's otherwise ethical standard procedures no longer accord with enduring public expectations, whenever events compel a comparison. Standing at the front door of nonprofit agencies, fundraisers are more likely than most to have a sense of the discrepancy between organizational reality and public expectation. I suspect they fully appreciate how flawed is the advice that support for the sector can be increased only by talking people out of expecting too much from it.

At the same time, of course, fundraisers play a key role in helping an agency develop and articulate its statement of purpose. They understand the power of the "myth" of a sector rooted in voluntarism, charity, and neighborliness, and how critical it will be for harnessing the spiritual and voluntary energies and the new financial resources that may either revitalize the sector, or, flowing elsewhere, render it obsolete.

Consequently, fundraising executives may be in the best position to pose to their own organizations the kinds of radical questions that now need to be addressed—radical in the true etymological sense that they go "to the root" of an organization's understanding of itself. That promises to be a difficult and demanding task. But in the final analysis, public support for and confidence in the sector cannot be restored by downgrading the sector's age-old vision of voluntarism and charity to accord with institutional reality. It can be restored only by serious efforts to upgrade institutions to accord with that still-potent and compelling vision.

ABOUT THE AUTHOR

William A. Schambra is the director of the Hudson Institute's Bradley Center for Philanthropy and Civic Renewal. Prior to joining the Hudson Institute in January of 2003, Mr. Schambra was director of programs at the Bradley Foundation in Milwaukee. Before joining Bradley in 1992, Mr. Schambra served as a senior advisor and chief speechwriter for Attorney General Edwin Meese III, Director of the Office of Personnel Management Constance Horner, and Secretary of Health and Human Services, Louis Sullivan. He was also director of Social Policy Programs for the American Enterprise Institute, and co-director of AEI's "A Decade of Study of the Constitution." Mr. Schambra was appointed by President Reagan to the National Historical Publications and Records Commission, and by President George W. Bush to the board of directors of the Corporation for National and Community Service. Mr. Schambra has written extensively on the Constitution, the theory and practice of civic revitalization, and civil society in *The Public Interest, Public Opinion*, the *Wall Street Journal*, the *Washington Times, Policy Review, Christian Science Monitor, Nonprofit Quarterly, Philanthropy and Crisis*, and is the editor of several volumes including *As Far as Republican Principles Will Admit: Collected Essays of Martin Diamond*.

NOTES

1. Stephanie Strom, "Public Confidence in Charities Stays Flat," *New York Times*, September 13, 2004, www.nytimes.com/2004/09/13/national/13giving.html?.ex=1191833729&ei=1&en=1b2773fccc4c13022.
2. Diana Aviv, "Purpose, Power, and Participation: Ideas for the Future of Our Sector," Opening Plenary Address, Independent Sector Annual Conference (San Francisco, November 2, 2003).
3. Lester M. Salamon, ed., *The State of Nonprofit America* (Washington, DC: Brookings Institution Press, 2002), 4–24.
4. Stephen Stills, *For What It's Worth*, produced by Charles Greene and Brian Stone (1967).
5. "Spirituality in America," *Newsweek*, August 29–September 5, 2005.
6. James M. Twitchell, "Jesus Christ's Superflock," *Mother Jones*, www.motherjones.com/news/feature/2005/03/megachurches.html.
7. Adam Hochschild, *Bury the Chains: Prophets and Rebels in the Fight to Free an Empire's Slaves* (New York: Houghton Mifflin, 2005), 6.
8. Harvey Cox, *Fire from Heaven: The Rise of Pentecostal Spirituality and the Reshaping of Religion in the 21st Century* (Cambridge, MA: Da Capo Press, 1995).
9. Warren Weaver, "Pre-Christian Philanthropy," *America's Voluntary Spirit*, ed. Brian O'Connell (New York: The Foundation Center, 1983).

Ethical Codes and Standards: Association of Fundraising Professionals (AFP) Code of Ethical Principles

The Association of Fundraising Professionals (AFP) exists to foster the development and growth of fundraising professionals and the profession, to promote high ethical standards in the fundraising profession and to preserve and enhance philanthropy and volunteerism.[1]

Members of AFP are motivated by an inner drive to improve the quality of life through the causes they serve. They serve the ideal of philanthropy; are committed to the preservation and enhancement of volunteerism; and hold stewardship of these concepts as the overriding principle of their professional life. They recognize their responsibility to ensure that needed resources are vigorously and ethically sought and that the intent of the donor is honestly fulfilled. To these ends, AFP members embrace certain values that they strive to uphold in performing their responsibilities for generating philanthropic support.

AFP members aspire to:

- Practice their profession with integrity, honesty, truthfulness and adherence to the absolute obligation to safeguard the public trust;
- Act according to the highest standards and visions of their organization, profession and conscience;
- Put philanthropic mission above personal gain;
- Inspire others through their own sense of dedication and high purpose;
- Improve their professional knowledge and skills, so that their performance will better serve others;
- Demonstrate concern for the interests and well being of individuals affected by their actions;
- Value the privacy, freedom of choice and interests of all those affected by their actions;
- Foster cultural diversity and pluralistic values, and treat all people with dignity and respect;
- Affirm, through personal giving, a commitment to philanthropy and its role in society;
- Adhere to the spirit as well as the letter of all applicable laws and regulations;
- Advocate within their organizations, adherence to all applicable laws and regulations;
- Avoid even the appearance of any criminal offense or professional misconduct;
- Bring credit to the fundraising profession by their public demeanor;
- Encourage colleagues to embrace and practice these ethical principles and standards of professional practice; and
- Be aware of the codes of ethics promulgated by other professional organizations that serve philanthropy.

Ethical Standards

Furthermore, while striving to act according to the above values, AFP members, both individual and business, agree to abide (and to ensure, to the best of their ability, that all members of their staff abide) by the AFP standards. Violation of the standards may subject the member to disciplinary sanctions, including expulsion, as provided in the AFP Ethics Enforcement Procedures.

Member Obligations

1. Members shall not engage in activities that harm the members' organizations, clients or profession.
2. Members shall not engage in activities that conflict with their fiduciary, ethical and legal obligations to their organizations, clients or profession.
3. Members shall effectively disclose all potential and actual conflicts of interest; such disclosure does not preclude or imply ethical impropriety.
4. Members shall not exploit any relationship with a donor, prospect, volunteer, client or employee for the benefit of the members or the members' organizations.
5. Members shall comply with all applicable local, state, provincial and federal civil and criminal laws.
6. Members recognize their individual boundaries of competence and are forthcoming and truthful about their professional experience and qualifications and will represent their achievements accurately and without exaggeration.
7. Members shall present and supply products and/or services honestly and without misrepresentation and will clearly identify the details of those products, such as availability of the products and/or services and other factors that may affect the suitability of the products and/or services for donors, clients or nonprofit organizations.
8. Members shall establish the nature and purpose of any contractual relationship at the outset and will be responsive and available to organizations and their employing organizations before, during and after any sale of materials and/or services. Members will comply with all fair and reasonable obligations created by the contract.
9. Members shall refrain from knowingly infringing the intellectual property rights of other parties at all times. Members shall address and rectify any inadvertent infringement that may occur.

10. Members shall protect the confidentiality of all privileged information relating to the provider/client relationships.
11. Members shall refrain from any activity designed to disparage competitors untruthfully.

Solicitation and Use of Philanthropic Funds

12. Members shall take care to ensure that all solicitation and communication materials are accurate and correctly reflect their organizations' mission and use of solicited funds.
13. Members shall take care to ensure that donors receive informed, accurate and ethical advice about the value and tax implications of contributions.
14. Members shall take care to ensure that contributions are used in accordance with donors' intentions.
15. Members shall take care to ensure proper stewardship of all revenue sources, including timely reports on the use and management of such funds.
16. Members shall obtain explicit consent by donors before altering the conditions of financial transactions.

Presentation of Information

17. Members shall not disclose privileged or confidential information to unauthorized parties.
18. Members shall adhere to the principle that all donor and prospect information created by, or on behalf of, an organization or a client is the property of that organization or client and shall not be transferred or utilized except on behalf of that organization or client.
19. Members shall give donors and clients the opportunity to have their names removed from lists that are sold to, rented to or exchanged with other organizations.
20. Members shall, when stating fundraising results, use accurate and consistent accounting methods that conform to the appropriate guidelines adopted by the American Institute of Certified Public Accountants (AICPA)* for the type of organization involved.

(*In countries outside of the United States, comparable authority should be utilized.)

Compensation and Contracts

21. Members shall not accept compensation or enter into a contract that is based on a percentage of contributions; nor shall members accept finder's fees or contingent fees. Business members must refrain from receiving compensation from third parties derived from products or services for a client without disclosing that third-party compensation to the client (for example, volume rebates from vendors to business members).

22. Members may accept performance-based compensation, such as bonuses, provided such bonuses are in accord with prevailing practices within the members' own organizations and are not based on a percentage of contributions.

23. Members shall neither offer nor accept payments or special considerations for the purpose of influencing the selection of products or services.

24. Members shall not pay finder's fees, commissions or percentage compensation based on contributions, and shall take care to discourage their organizations from making such payments.

25. Any member receiving funds on behalf of a donor or client must meet the legal requirements for the disbursement of those funds. Any interest or income earned on the funds should be fully disclosed.

ASSOCIATION FOR HEALTHCARE PHILANTHROPY (AHP) STATEMENT OF PROFESSIONAL STANDARDS AND CONDUCT

All members shall comply with the Association's Statement of Professional Standards and Conduct:

Association for Healthcare Philanthropy members represent to the public, by personal example and **conduct**, both their employer and their profession. They have, therefore, a duty to faithfully adhere to the highest **standards** and **conduct** in:

I

Their promotion of the merits of their institutions and of excellence in health care generally, providing community leadership in cooperation with health, educational, cultural, and other organizations;

II

Their words and actions, embodying respect for truth, honesty, fairness, free inquiry, and the opinions of others, treating all with equality and dignity;

III

Their respect for all individuals without regard to race, color, sex, creed, ethnic or national identity, handicap, or age;

IV

Their commitment to strive to increase **professional** and personal skills for improved service to their donors and institutions, to encourage and actively participate in career development for themselves and others whose roles include support for resource development functions, and to share freely their knowledge and experience with others as appropriate;

V

Their continuing effort and energy to pursue new ideas and modifications to improve conditions for, and benefits to, donors and their institution;

VI

Their avoidance of activities that might damage the reputation of any donor, their institution, any other resource development **professional** or the profession as a whole, or themselves, and to give full credit for the ideas, words, or images originated by others;

VII

Their respect for the rights of privacy of others and the confidentiality of information gained in the pursuit of their **professional** duties;

VIII

Their acceptance of a compensation method freely agreed upon and based on their institution's usual and customary compensation guidelines which have been established and approved for general institutional use while always remembering that:

a. any compensation agreement should fully reflect the **standards** of **professional conduct**; and,
b. antitrust laws in the United States prohibit limitation on compensation methods.

IX

Their respect for the law and **professional** ethics as a standard of personal **conduct**, with full adherence to the policies and procedures of their institution;

X

Their pledge to adhere to this **Statement** of **Professional Standards** and **Conduct**, and to encourage others to join them in observance of its guidelines.

ASSOCIATION OF PROFESSIONAL RESEARCHERS FOR ADVANCEMENT (APRA) STATEMENT OF ETHICS (REVISED AUGUST 2004)[2]

Association of Professional Researchers for Advancement (**APRA**) members shall support and further the individual's fundamental right to privacy and protect the confidential information of their institutions. **APRA** members are committed to the ethical collection and use of information. Members shall follow all applicable national, state, and local laws, as well as institutional policies, governing the collection, use, maintenance, and dissemination of information in the pursuit of the missions of their institutions.

Code of Ethics

Advancement researchers must balance an individual's right to privacy with the needs of their institutions to collect, analyze, record, maintain, use, and disseminate information. This balance is not always easy to maintain. To guide researchers, the following ethical principles apply:

I. Fundamental Principles

A. Confidentiality Confidential information about constituents (donors and non-donors), as well as confidential information of the institutions in oral form or on electronic, magnetic, or print media are protected in order to foster a trusting relationship between the constituent and the institution. This means that the information is not available for anyone except development professionals, and their agents, to see.

B. Accuracy Advancement researchers shall record all data accurately. Such information shall include attribution. Data analyses and their by-products should be without personal prejudices or biases.

C. Relevance Advancement researchers shall seek and record only information that is relevant to the cultivation, solicitation, and/or stewardship strategy with the prospect.

D. Self-Responsibility Advancement researchers often play a significant role in developing and monitoring advancement department policies on information storage and confidentiality. It is important that advancement researchers lead by example. First, advancement researchers should develop clear policies and procedures for the prospect research department on the collection, storage, and distribution of constituent information and analysis. Second, when possible, advancement researchers should advocate for the development and adoption of institution wide **ethics** guidelines and privacy policies which are at least as complete as the **APRA Statement of Ethics**.

E. Honesty Advancement researchers shall be truthful with regard to their identities and purpose, and the identity of their institutions during the course of their work.

F. Conflict of Interest Advancement researchers should be careful to avoid conflicts of interest. Prospect research consultants should have explicit policies which outline how they will deal with conflicts of interest between clients. Advancement researchers who are employed full-time for an institution and also perform consulting services should be certain that the consulting services do not represent a conflict of interest with their primary employer.

II. Standards of Practice

A. Collection

1. The collection of information should be done lawfully, respecting applicable laws and institutional policies.
2. Advancement researchers should be experts on the reliability of sources (print, electronic, and otherwise), as well as the sources utilized by third parties to gather information on their behalf.
3. Advancement researchers should not evade or avoid questions about their affiliations or purpose when requesting information in person, over the phone, electronically, or in writing. It is recommended that requests for public information be made on institutional stationery and that these requests clearly identify the requestor.
4. Advancement researchers should use the usual and customary methods of payment or reimbursement for products or services purchased on behalf of their institutions.
5. Advancement researchers who are employed full-time for an institution and also perform consulting services should develop clear understandings with their primary employers about the use of the employers financial and human resources.

B. Recording and Maintenance

1. Advancement researchers shall present information in an objective and factual manner, note attribution, and clearly identify information which is conjecture or analysis. Where there is conflicting information, advancement researchers should objectively present the multiple versions and state any reason for preferring one version over another.

2. Advancement researchers should develop security measures to protect the constituent information to which they have access from access by unauthorized persons. When possible, these measures should include locking offices and/or file cabinets and secure and frequently change passwords to electronic databases. Advancement researchers should also advocate institution-wide policies which promote the careful handling of constituent information so that constituent privacy is protected. The use of constituent databases over a wireless Internet connection is not recommended.

3. Where advancement researchers are also responsible for donor giving records and their maintenance, they should develop security measures to provide very limited access to the giving records of anonymous donors. Access to these records should be limited to only those staff who need the information to successfully cultivate, solicit, or steward said donor.

4. Where there is no existing case law which outlines clearly the rights of a donor in accessing advancement files (paper and/or electronic), advancement researchers should work with their institutions legal counsel to develop an institution specific policy regarding this access. This policy should be put in writing, approved by the President/CEO, and distributed to any advancement professionals who might field a request for such access.

5. When electronic or paper documents pertaining to constituents must be disposed, they should be disposed in a fashion which lessens the danger of a privacy breach. Shredding of paper documents is recommended.

C. Use and Distribution

1. Researchers shall adhere to all applicable laws, as well as to institutional policies, regarding the use and distribution of confidential constituent information. Careful consideration should be given to the use of electronic mail and faxes for the delivery of constituent information.

2. Constituent information is the property of the institution for which it was collected and shall not be given to persons other than those who are involved with the cultivation or solicitation effort or those who need that information in the performance of their duties for that institution.

3. Constituent information for one institution shall not be taken to another institution

4. Research documents containing constituent information that is to be used outside research offices shall be clearly marked *confidential.*

5. Vendors, consultants, and other external entities shall understand and agree to comply with the institution's confidentiality policies before gaining access to institutional data.

6. Advancement researchers, with the assistance of institutional counsel and the advancement chief officer, should develop policies which address the sharing of directory information on their constituents with other institutions. Constituent requests to withhold directory information should be respected in all cases.

AMERICAN SOCIETY OF ASSOCIATION EXECUTIVES (ASAE) STANDARDS OF CONDUCT

- Maintain exemplary standards of professional conduct
- Actively model and encourage the integration of ethics into all aspects of management of the association(s) which employ(s) me

- Pursue the objectives of the association(s) that employ(s) me in ways that are ethical
- Recognize and discharge my responsibility and that of the association(s) that employ(s) me to uphold all laws and regulations in implementing the policies and conducting the activities of the association(s)
- Strive to continually advance my knowledge and achieve higher levels of excellence in association management
- Maintain the confidentiality of all privileged information, except when so doing becomes an ethical or legal breach of conduct
- Serve all members fairly, holding foremost the interests of the association that employs me and its industry or profession; faithfully executing my duties and never using my position for undue personal gain; and promptly and completely disclosing to appropriate parties all potential and actual conflicts of interest
- Actively encourage all people qualified or eligible to be a part of the association(s) which employ(s) me to participate in the activities and leadership of the association as appropriate
- Communicate all association internal and external information to the elected leadership(s) and membership of the association(s), which employ(s) me in a truthful and accurate manner to facilitate timely execution of their fiduciary responsibilities
- Actively advance, support, and promote association membership and the profession of association management through word and deed

COUNCIL FOR ADVANCEMENT AND SUPPORT OF EDUCATION (CASE) STATEMENT OF ETHICS

Institutional advancement professionals, by virtue of their responsibilities within the academic community, represent their colleges, universities, and schools to the larger society. They have, therefore, a special duty to exemplify the best qualities of their institutions and to observe the highest standards of personal and professional conduct.

In so doing, they promote the merits of their institutions, and of education generally, without disparaging other colleges and schools.

Their words and actions embody respect for truth, fairness, free inquiry, and the opinions of others.

They respect all individuals without regard to race, color, sex, sexual orientation, marital status, creed, ethnic or national identity, handicap, or age.

They uphold the professional reputation of other advancement officers and give credit for ideas, words, or images originated by others.

They safeguard privacy rights and confidential information.

They do not grant or accept favors for personal gain, nor do they solicit or accept favors for their institutions where a higher public interest would be violated.

They avoid actual or apparent conflicts of interest and, if in doubt, seek guidance from appropriate authorities.

They follow the letter and spirit of laws and regulations affecting institutional advancement.

They observe these standards and others that apply to their professions and actively encourage colleagues to join them in supporting the highest standards of conduct.

The CASE Board of Trustees adopted this Statement of Ethics to guide and reinforce our professional conduct in all areas of institutional advancement. The statement is also intended to stimulate awareness and discussion of ethical issues that may arise in our professional activities. The Board adopted the final text in Toronto on July 11, 1982, after a year of deliberation by national and district leaders and by countless volunteers throughout the membership.

EPHILANTHROPY CODE OF ETHICAL ONLINE PHILANTHROPIC PRACTICES[3]

The ePhilanthropy Foundation (acquired by Network for Good in 2008) exists to foster the effective and safe use of the Internet for philanthropic purposes. In its effort to promote high ethical standards in online fundraising and to build trust among contributors in making online transactions and contributions with the charity of their choice, this code is being offered as a guide to all who share this goal. Contributors are encouraged to be aware of non-Internet related fundraising practices that fall outside the scope of this Code.

Ethical Online Practices and Practitioners will . . .

Section A: Philanthropic Experience

1. Clearly and specifically display and describe the organization's identity on the organization's website;
2. Employ practices on the website that exhibit integrity, honesty, and truthfulness and seek to safeguard the public trust.

Section B: Privacy and Security

1. Seek to inspire trust in every online transaction;
2. Prominently display the opportunity for supporters to have their names removed from lists that are sold to, rented to, or exchanged with other organizations;
3. Conduct online transactions through a system that employs high-level security technology to protect the donor's personal information for both internal and external authorized use;
4. Provide either an "opt-in" and "opt-out" mechanism to prevent unsolicited communications or solicitations by organizations that obtain email addresses directly from the donor. Should lists be rented or exchanged, only those verified as having been obtained through donors or prospects "opting in" will be used by a charity;
5. Protect the interests and privacy of individuals interacting with their website;
6. Provide a clear, prominent and easily accessible privacy policy on its website telling visitors, at a minimum, what information is being collected, how it is being collected, how it can be updated or removed, how this information will be used and who has access to the data.

Section C: Disclosures

1. Disclose the identity of the organization or provider processing an online transaction;
2. Guarantee that the name, logo and likeness of all parties to an online transaction belong to the party and will not be used without express permission;
3. Maintain all appropriate governmental and regulatory designations or certifications;
4. Provide both online and offline contact information.

Section D: Complaints

1. Provide protection to hold the donor harmless of any problem arising from a transaction conducted through the organization's website;
2. Promptly respond to all customer complaints and to employ best efforts to fairly resolve all legitimate complaints in a timely fashion.

Section E: Transactions

1. Ensure contributions are used to support the activities of the organization to which they were donated;
2. Ensure that legal control of contributions or proceeds from online transactions are transferred directly to the charity or expedited in the fastest possible way;
3. Companies providing online services to charities will provide clear and full communication with the charity on all aspects of donor transactions, including the accurate and timely transmission of data related to online transactions;
4. Stay informed regarding the best methods to ensure the ethical, secure, and private nature of online ePhilanthropy (Network for Good) transactions;
5. Adhere to the spirit as well as the letter of all applicable laws and regulations, including, but not limited to, charity solicitation and tax laws;

6. Ensure that all services, recognition and other transactions promised on a website, in consideration of gift or transaction, will be fulfilled on a timely basis;

7. Disclose to the donor the nature of the relationship between the organization processing the gift or transaction and the charity intended to benefit from the gift.

GIVING USA FOUNDATION STANDARDS OF PRACTICE AND CODE OF ETHICS: PROFESSIONAL CODE OF ETHICS

Member Firms believe it is in the best interest of the client that:

- Initial meetings with prospective clients should not be construed as services for which payment is expected.

- No payments of special consideration should be made to an officer, director, trustee, employee, or advisor of a not-for-profit organization as compensation for influencing the selection of fundraising counsel.

- Fees should be mutually agreed upon in advance of services.

- A flat, fixed fee is charged based on the level and extent of professional services provided. Fees are not based on the amount of charitable income raised or expected to be raised.

- Contracts providing for a contingent fee, a commission, or a fee based on percentage of funds raised are prohibited. Such contracts are harmful to the relationship between the donor and the institution and detrimental to the financial health of the client organization.

- Fundraising expenditures are within the authority and control of the not-for-profit organization.

- Solicitation of gifts is undertaken by Board members, staff, and other volunteers.

- Subsequent to analysis or study, a Member Firm should engage a client only when the best interest of the client is served.

- Members Firms should not profit directly or indirectly from materials provided by others, but billed to the Member Firm, without disclosure to the client.
- Member Firms do not engage in methods that are misleading to the public or harmful to their clients; do not make exaggerated claims of past achievement; and do not guarantee results of promise to helps clients achieve goals.
- Any potential conflict of interest should be disclosed by the firm to clients and prospective clients.
- Member Firms will not acquire or maintain custody of funds and/or gifts directed to client organization.

INDEPENDENT SECTOR: OBEDIENCE TO THE UNENFORCEABLE[4]

Americans are concerned about the ethical behavior of their leaders and leadership institutions. In recent years repeated violations, and growing media attention to them, have made us even more aware of how important standards of ethical behavior are to preserving our integrity as a society and how vital it is for us to be able to trust one another.

The concern about lapses in ethical conduct touches every part of society. But the public expects the highest values and ethics to be practiced habitually in the institutions of the charitable, nonprofit sector. Because these institutions, fundamentally, are dedicated to enhancing basic human values, expectations of them are particularly high. Those who presume to serve the public good assume a public trust.

The Statement's Preparation and Premises

In 1989, the Board of Directors of Independent Sector asked a broadly representative group of 30 persons to define as clearly as possible what this sector and all of its organizations should stand for. They came from a broad spectrum and included foundation, corporate giving, and nonprofit leadership; legal scholars; journalists; consumer and social advocates; representatives of higher education and the religious community;

government regulators of the sector; and ethicists. Their purpose was to ensure continued public confidence and address issues raised by the well-publicized misbehavior of some voluntary and philanthropic institutions.

In 2002, the Independent Sector Board of Directors asked the IS staff to revise and update the report in light of similar concerns about public trust and sector accountability.

This report seeks to provide guidance on what voluntary and philanthropic organizations should stand for and act upon in relation to ethics and values. Its purpose is not to set definitive standards, because these already exist among the policies of some individual organizations and in codes issued by several national groups.

During the 18 months the Committee on Values and Ethics deliberated in 1989 and 1990, and in the subsequent deliberation by the IS Board of Directors in 2002, this statement evolved into what should be the general ethical concerns and behaviors of the independent sector, a richly diverse community of voluntary and philanthropic organizations held together by our commitment to community service. The statement examines our unique tradition of voluntary association, the freedoms and obligations associated with it, some basic values and behaviors for all of us to consider, and ways to express these values. Higher levels of specification will need to be worked out by each organization.

This statement also draws upon the experiences of the Committee members. In their time together they learned that the process of recognizing how values affect our decisions creates its own value. By collectively having to think through the dimensions and impact of ethical behavior, Committee members shared, built, tore down, and then built again as they began to understand and appreciate the complexity of the task. As individuals and as a group, they became much more conscious of why and how we act in an ethical manner. The Committee came to a keen appreciation for the great benefits that accrue to an organization from undertaking a process by which ethical matters are discussed and deliberated.

Engaging in this process is more important than any single code or standard. The process also needs to be dynamic, addressing the ongoing societal changes that affect the ethical dimensions of decisions made in the independent sector. For example, several decades ago diversity by race, gender, disability, and sexual orientation among the trustees and staff of a nonprofit organization may not have seemed an expression of ethical behavior. Today, it is necessarily an ethical decision. Years ago, protection of privacy for individuals in the health system might have been only a secondary consideration; today, it is a constant ethical dilemma.

Defining, examining, and instilling ethical behavior is a vital process for all of us in the independent sector. Whether one's interest is AIDS or ozone, the character of our organizations ultimately will have an ethical component. We may stop and examine them or act instinctively. We earn the public's trust through our work in solving problems, and through our ethical behaviors. The Committee believes, as does author and social commentator Sissela Bok, that "trust is a social good to be protected just as much as the air we breathe or the water we drink." In addition to understanding the importance of the process, the Committee came to understand the complexity of ethical practice. Most often it does not involve the black-and-white evidence of law. It is the gray domain of ethical choices that creates tensions and dilemmas for those entrusted with the leadership as well as the day-to-day operations of voluntary and philanthropic institutions.

Obeying the law is the first and most obvious of our ethical obligations. It is "obedience to the unenforceable," however—as England's Lord Justice of Appeal John Fletcher Moulton said more than 65 years ago—that best measures the ethical behavior of individuals and of nations. The true test of greatness, he explained, "is the extent to which the individuals composing the nation can be trusted to obey self-imposed law." In the independent sector, public trust stems from our willingness to go beyond the law or even the spirit of the law. We act ethically because we have determined that it is the right thing to do.

To Whom Is This Statement Addressed?

The ethical behavior of an institution is the ultimate responsibility of its trustees. The responsibility is shared, however, with staff leaders and other staff and volunteers of the institution. Their roles in establishing and maintaining ethical standards within their organizations are distinct. The commitment is a shared one because it is critical that ethical considerations permeate every level within an organization.

Furthermore, the process of establishing ethical standards and their practice must take place among all those who benefit from the freedom accorded to the voluntary and philanthropic sector. Thus, this statement is addressed to both grantseekers and grantmakers. It applies to the largest and the smallest of our organizations—to family trusts, foundations, funds administered by banks and law firms, religious congregations, individual philanthropists, and corporate giving programs—from the neighborhood to international levels. Over 1.2 million charitable, advocacy, and philanthropic organizations and religious congregations exist in the United States, and if the local affiliates of these organizations and religious congregations are included, the number far exceeds 2 million. Therefore, we are speaking to all who are part of the nation's independent sector.

Our Traditions

Americans have always been committed to and dependent upon what we perceive and describe as "organized neighborliness." We were a society of neighbors long before we had formal communities. We addressed our dependence through what James Luther Adams described as the "exercise of the freedom of association." We created new institutions— churches, unions, granges, fire companies—and they became our networks for mutual activity. This "social capital" continues today as an essential part of our democratic structure, always offering opportunities for a commitment beyond the self and participation in the process of creating common good. The sector is as diverse as its component neighborhood improvement societies, churches and citizens who support them, overseas relief organizations, private schools and colleges, corporate foundations and public service programs, fraternal benevolence societies, conservation and preservation groups, local service organizations, community foundations, civil rights organizations, arts organizations, and millions of others. Whether one's interest is wildflowers or civil rights, arthritis or clean air, oriental art or literacy, the dying or the newborn, organizations are at work. If no charitable effort suits one's passions, it is possible in America to start one that does. This freedom of association for our voluntary and philanthropic organizations is protected in law and in the public's mind. While the independent sector has historically enjoyed widespread confidence and support, that public trust cannot be taken for granted.

Public Expectations

Almost all independent sector organizations depend to some degree upon donations, which is money people are not obligated to give. They do so voluntarily in the faith that trustees, staff, and other volunteer stewards will spend the money in the most judicious way to achieve the results for which the contribution was solicited. This is very much an act of faith because people have limited ways to judge nonprofit organizations.

Nonprofit groups do not face public elections and consequent reorganizations as government entities do. Nor do they have a bottom line of profit or loss determined by customers, as in the commercial sector. Nonprofit organizations are now required by law to make copies of their financial information returns (IRS Form 990) and their application to the IRS for tax exemption (Form 1023 or Form 1024) available on request by any individual. The basic financial information (Form 990) is also now available via the Internet. Nonetheless, these documents provide minimal information on the effectiveness of the organization's programs and services, and, by and large, people put faith in nonprofit organizations just because such organizations are supposed to be charitable.

The public assumes that nonprofit groups do their work with greater economy than government and with greater concern for individuals than either government or commerce. It believes they will work toward their goals in an honorable and humane way, with continuing regard for the rights and needs of individuals. The public has faith in the stewardship of voluntary and philanthropic organizations, but it also has concerns.

Clearly, abuses occur in the name of charity. The nonprofit sector has frauds and questionable operations. Unfortunately, their exposure gives the impression that the sector as a whole is losing its reliability. The public rightly demands the fullest examination of groups that ask for its support. The charitable community can expect and should welcome this greater scrutiny. Its leaders must speak out against waste, fraud, and abusive practices. The independent sector, along with government and the media, must address these violations of the public trust forcefully. Unethical and illegal practices are offensive to all philanthropic and voluntary organizations—that is the message the independent sector and its leadership must convey, individually and together.

When the institutions of the independent sector do not reflect high standards of openness, honesty, and public service, their contributors and clients are ill-served. This sector depends upon public goodwill and participation. If public support is eroded, so is the capacity for public service.

Being Responsible and Accountable

The basic means by which the independent sector can ensure confidence in philanthropic and voluntary organizations is to demonstrate the quality of its leadership. This demonstration begins with full and consistent evidence that trustees, staff directors, and all other participants habitually reflect the ethics people have a right to expect of them and that they make ethical practices part of the organization's culture.

Some trusteeship responsibilities relate to the organization's status as a formal legal entity, such as being sure that required reports are submitted to government. However, most expectations are of the higher order of Lord Moulton's "obedience to the unenforceable," such as making the contributor's dollar go as far as possible for the client and the cause. Although the higher calling of obedience to the unenforceable constitutes the larger expectations of stewardship, our duties begin with obeying the law. The most obvious scandals involve stewards who do not obey the law or who stretch it so far in the direction of self-benefit that any semblance of public benefit is obscured. Because obedience to the law is basic though not always practiced, we begin there.

Trustees are responsible for legal compliance but often do not even take the step of knowing what they are supposed to ensure is done and whether it is, in fact, accomplished. For example, trustees should know federal, state, and local requirements relating to the organization's legal status and should make it their business to be certain the organization is in compliance.

There have been several court cases in which board members were held accountable largely because they failed to exercise reasonable oversight. When these cases are reported in the media, the trustees sometimes say that they have not seen financial reports, did not know what was going on, were not aware that the organization had contracted with a firm owned by a staff or board member, or simply were not clear that they had to take responsibility for knowing what was happening.

This ignorance of legal obligations leaves voluntary organizations vulnerable to oversights that often place them in jeopardy. Being charitable is no excuse for laxity. Voluntary and philanthropic organizations need to build specific internal processes that educate trustees about their legal obligations and provide timely procedures to meet them.

Most often the legal problems faced by trustees and other stewards are not the result of malfeasance. Good people believing in good things frequently get into trouble. Yet, without checks, balances, and early warning signals, they have little hope of escaping spiraling legal difficulties.

Whether board members are called trustees, directors, governors, or something else, they are the trustees in the literal and legal sense. No matter how the organization is structured or the degree of authority delegated to staff or affiliates, the board (and therefore the trustees) is ultimately accountable for any breakdown, wherever it occurs. In a 1984 court action involving an organization called "Friends of Clinton Hill," a sympathetic judge listened to the board members' reasons for not knowing that their association had failed to pay the government income taxes withheld or Social Security taxes. He described these volunteers with such terms as "selfless, dedicated, and compassionate" but said the law left him no alternative but to hold them accountable for all taxes and stiff interest penalties. The law, however, is not punitive as long as the trustees' attention to responsibility is reasonable. Joseph Weber, former head of the Greater New York Fund, pointed out in Managing the Board of Directors that "this does not mean that a director needs to feel liability for every corporate loss or mishap that may occur. On the contrary, a director is generally protected from liability for errors of judgment as long as he or she acts responsibly and in good faith, and with a basic interest of the [charitable] corporation as the foremost objective."

It is important to acknowledge that at times some voluntary organizations knowingly disobey certain laws, for example, by illegal sit-ins or by providing sanctuary for illegal aliens. An organization may feel such abridgements are necessary to fulfill its mission, but even courageous acts of conscience do not put people above the law. As indicated by Henry David Thoreau in *Civil Disobedience*, one must believe so completely in such acts as to be willing to pay the consequences.

Unenforceable Requirements

Much more challenging than following procedures set in law and regulation, however, is obeying the unenforceable. Many ethical situations are quite clear, but often there are no procedures to disclose them. For example, it is obvious that ethical issues must be considered if an organization is doing business with a firm controlled by a staff member's spouse, but if no conflict of interest policy exists and if there is no requirement for annual review of compliance with such a policy, how can the behavior be checked?

The first level of ethical behavior is to be concerned about obeying laws. The second is composed of those behaviors where one knows the right action but is tempted to take a different course. There is also a third level of consideration where decisions are not a contest between good and evil but among competing options. These present tough ethical dilemmas. Because charitable organizations often serve interests that have scant resources, they inevitably must confront difficult choices and provide answers to ethical questions. For example, who will and will not receive scarce health services such as dialysis?

An organization must have processes by which it can decide if the law is being obeyed, if thoughtful ethics are being practiced, and if tough ethical dilemmas are being openly considered, and decided.

Organizations that routinely utilize ethical decision making practices will be much better prepared to handle a crisis when it hits.

What Organizations Can Do

We cannot anticipate every ethical standard applicable to all philanthropic and voluntary organizations. The sector is wonderfully diverse and contributes richly to society because it embodies the pluralism and the freedoms so vital to our democratic system. Without proposing limits to that diversity, however, or implying that this is the definitive listing, we present the following values and ethical behaviors as what this sector and its organizations have in common and should stand for. We believe:

- Commitment beyond self is at the core of a civil society;
- Obedience of the laws, including those governing tax-exempt philanthropic and voluntary organizations, is a fundamental responsibility of stewardship;
- Commitment beyond the law, obedience to the unenforceable, is the higher obligation of leaders of philanthropic and voluntary organizations;
- Commitment to the public good requires those who presume to serve the public good to assume a public trust;
- Respect for the worth and dignity of individuals is a special leadership responsibility of philanthropic and voluntary organizations;
- Tolerance, diversity, and social justice reflect the independent sector's rich heritage and the essential protections afforded it;
- Accountability to the public is a fundamental responsibility of public benefit organizations;
- Openness and honesty in reporting, fundraising and relationships with all constituencies are essential behaviors for organizations which seek and use public or private funds and which purport to serve public purposes; and
- Responsible stewardship of resources is a concomitant of public trust.

Beginning the Process

To begin the process, we believe every organization should adopt at least a simple organizational creed committing itself to ethical practices. The extent of each statement will depend upon the size and capacity of the organization, but it need not be elaborate. As an example:

Organizational Creed of Ethical Practices We believe that as stewards of [organization], which has been established for public benefit and has legal standing for that purpose, we have accepted a public trust to abide by high standards of performance and ethical behavior.

Adoption of a creed will be effective only if it initiates a conversation within and throughout the organization. But an organization cannot stop there. We believe we all must continue to review these principles in light of changes in the world around our organizations, and we must continue to explore the kinds of dilemmas that occur within our organizations on a daily basis. We urge persistent and consistent moral leadership by trustees and staff leaders that asks all those associated with an organization to participate in setting an ethical environment.

We also believe it is essential that every philanthropic and voluntary organization take enough time, at least once a year, for an organization's internal "ethics audit or self-evaluation." This examination would ask at least three questions:

1. Have the requirements for our legal standing been fulfilled, such as submitting all required reports and with full and honest disclosure?
2. What, if any, activities or practices of the board, staff, or organization are there that might be contrary to our organization's creed of ethical practices and articulated core values?
3. Are there changes in the social, demographic, or economic contexts of our interest that compel us to make different and/or more difficult ethical choices? If so, what changes are there that deserve notice?

Further, we recommend that independent sector organizations undertake an external ethics audit or evaluation every few years, using trained staff or personnel from other voluntary and philanthropic organizations, universities, or nonprofit consultant organizations. An outside look can prevent ethical processes from becoming so routine as to be irrelevant, introduce different perspectives and analyses, and affirm good practice.

Beyond a creed and regular examinations of practice, we believe that all organizations should voluntarily subscribe to a set of standards that reflect sound ethical behavior. The standards of the Better Business Bureau Wise Giving Alliance are one such set of standards with broad applicability to the charitable sector. The Council on Foundations has a set of standards that are applicable to grantmaking philanthropic organizations. The Donor Bill of Rights is a declaration of the rights of donors that nonprofit organizations should respect in their fundraising practices. And many subsectors, from museums to international aid groups to evangelical organizations, have standards with specific relevance to their field of activities. Where applicable standards do not exist and where a particular subsector believes that other standards do not address their needs, we recommend that specific standards be developed for that subsector. For example, the American Association of Museums has developed a series of standards that cover a number of issues specifically applicable to museums. In addition, larger organizations should develop more complete codes of ethics and/or standards or policies, which govern the organization's ethical performance. These should include a timetable and process for the evaluation of performance in accord with the codes or policies.

A model that the Committee on Values and Ethics believes incorporates ongoing attention to ethical standards is that developed by the Land Trust Alliance. Its "Land Trust Standards and Practices" contains 15 overarching statements of standards that each land trust should unarguably meet. These cover such topics as purposes and goals, fundraising, board accountability, conflict of interest, basic legal requirements, and volunteers. Each statement is followed by a series of practices that describe more specifically how the standards may be implemented.

For example, Standard #5 concerns fundraising and includes this discussion:

> A Land Trust must conduct fundraising activities in an ethical and responsible manner. Because fundraising is a critical, ongoing activity of every active land trust, it must be done not only with an eye toward how much can be raised this year, but with an understanding of how fundraising practices affect the long-term credibility of the land trust.

Practices

- Charitable Solicitation Laws: The trust complies with state charitable solicitation laws.
- Donor Notification of Deductibility: If a donor receives a premium or other substantial benefit in exchange for a contribution, the land trust's fundraising solicitation informs the donor that only the portion of the contribution in excess of the fair market value of the benefit is tax-deductible.
- Accurate Representations: All representations made in promotional, fundraising, and other public information materials are accurate and not misleading with respect to the organization's accomplishments, activities, and intended use of funds.
- Use of Funds as Specified: All funds are spent for the purpose(s) identified in the solicitation or, where not specifically solicited, in accordance with any stated wishes of the donor.

For further information on and examples of ethical codes and standards, see

- Independent Sector's web-based resource center on Ethics and Accountability at www.IndependentSector.org.
- American Association of Museums, "Code of Ethics for Museums 2000," n.d., at www.aam-us.org.
- Land Trust Alliance, "Land Trust Standards and Practices," n.d., at www.lta.org.

Reasonable Fundraising Costs   Overall costs of fundraising are reasonable as a percentage of funds raised. Who should be involved?

In developing and implementing ethical standards, organizations should involve fully all of their constituencies, internally and externally. Each needs an opportunity to shape the organization's values and ethics and the modes of compliance to them. We believe that maximum meaningful involvement is the single most important step in the process to ensure that an organization is true to its values and public trust. Leadership opens the door. The opportunity to participate depends upon the receptivity of the trustees and senior staff to making this process an open, honest, and essential mission. Organizations should do everything possible to be certain the documents and the values they reflect become part of the culture of the total organization. For example, orientation sessions for new board members, staff, and volunteers should include a review of the creed of ethical practices and other documents related to values, standards, and ethics.

Just as we believe that voluntary and philanthropic organizations should subscribe to or develop codes or standards beyond a creed of ethical practices and annual review of performance, we also recommend that trustees be involved in the process and ultimately responsible for approval of such reports.

Merely signing off on legal requirements or accountability standards is too perfunctory to fulfill our vision. The trustees' reviews should be thorough and aim beyond the mere prevention of problems. We urge that the process be seen as one that can affirm the good an organization does and help those involved with it to be proud of what they do. This is an opportunity to express respect for individuals and causes, to encourage creativity, and to create a committed community.

Illegal Acts, Unethical Behaviors, and Ethical Dilemmas   To provide more specific guidance, the following examples of illegal acts, unethical behaviors, and ethical dilemmas are related to a number of the value statements articulated above. We offer no answers to ethical dilemmas, because organizations must struggle with such decisions on their own. Rich benefits will derive from the process each organization follows in examination of its own values, ethical behaviors, and practices. We are providing these examples but encourage each organization to take hold of these, struggle with them, and find applications for their own organizations. In addition, many of the examples found below do not fit neatly into a single value statement, so they are intended simply to be illustrative of what organizations may encounter in their own situations.

Commitment Beyond Self

- Example of an illegal act: The board agrees to sell property to a board member's spouse without competitive bidding and at a price below fair market value.

- Example of unethical behavior: The CEO of a financially strapped organization continues to fly first-class on short business trips while the organization has to lay off staff.
- Example of an ethical dilemma: A board member who heads the best public relations firm in town is the volunteer chair of your publicity committee, and has a contract for some of the organization's advertising. While the organization has complied with all the requirements of the intermediate sanctions law, is this relationship acceptable and if so, under what conditions?

Obedience of the Laws

- Example of an illegal act: A solicitation indicates that contributions are tax-deductible when they are not.
- Example of unethical behavior: Trust Fund trustees are paid inflated annual fees for very few meetings and decisions.
- Example of an ethical dilemma: The organization debates undertaking an illegal sit-in to call attention to the dangers of a new nuclear power plant. Legal counsel says that even if they succeed there are likely to be arrests. What do you do?

Commitment to the Public Good

- Example of an illegal act: A private foundation does not live up to the minimum payout requirement for grants.
- Example of unethical behavior: A foundation's grant guidelines are broad and its application procedures are complicated, but most of the money goes annually to a few institutions with which foundation trustees have affiliation and which submit sketchy applications and reports.
- Example of an ethical dilemma: Should there be any compromise in your foundation's standards or procedures if you receive a request for joint funding of a project from another funder that recently responded favorably to your request for joint funding?
- In the 1991 edition of this report, this example was given as an instance of unethical behavior. However, with the passage of

the Intermediate Sanctions Law in 1996, current law prohibits excessive payments to trustees.

Respect for the Worth and Dignity of Individuals

- Example of an illegal act: Hirings and promotions that deny equal employment opportunity in accord with the law.
- Example of unethical behavior: Despite high-quality work, an employee is passed over for promotion for no other reason than a personal difference in style between the employee and the supervisor.
- Example of an ethical dilemma: What do you do when an ad hoc group of the organization's clients demand to meet with the board to present grievances and the staff says that they will quit if the board caves in to these chronic complainers?

Tolerance, Diversity, and Social Justice

- Example of an illegal act: A staff person is identified as a leader of a conservative fundamentalist sect and is dismissed from his research position.
- Example of unethical behavior: No minority persons are on a social service board serving minority neighborhoods.
- Example of an ethical dilemma: Should grants be given to a corporation's potential detractors or to causes poorly regarded by some employees?

Openness and Honesty

- Example of an illegal act: Required government reports are not filed or are filed with inaccurate information.
- Example of unethical behavior: The combination of four grants given to the organization by different donors covers 200 percent of the education director's time, salary, and space.
- Example of an ethical dilemma: Does the grantmaker tell an applicant the application was terrible and does the applicant tell the grantmaker the process was rude?

Accountability to the Public

- Example of an illegal act: Form 990 is not available to the public.
- Example of unethical behavior: For the fifth year in a row, the fundraising appeal talks only about plans and not about what's been done to date.
- Example of an ethical dilemma: Should a nonprofit that espouses full disclosure but is dealing with a very controversial cause publish its list of contributors?

Responsible Stewardship of Resources

- Example of an illegal act: A friendly candidate for public office uses the organization's copying and fax machines routinely.
- Example of an illegal act: To deal with a worsening deficit, money withheld from employees' paychecks for federal income tax is not turned over to the IRS.
- Example of unethical behavior: In lieu of salary, the staff director prefers a percentage of all funds raised.
- Example of unethical behavior: Services are targeted to clients with the least needs because the organization wants to show funders high numbers of people served successfully.
- Example of an ethical dilemma: The all-volunteer organization recognizes that to hire its first executive director will absorb all the money on hand and in sight. Half the board argues that all the time and money will go to support the position with nothing left for programs and the other half says it's a necessary investment in future growth. What should they do?
- Example of an ethical dilemma: Should a rapidly growing foundation greatly increase the size of its grants to a relatively few known and respected applicants or increase greatly the number of organizations funded, even though this means concomitant increases in its staff?

We believe the values and ethical behaviors described above represent minimal considerations for the independent sector. They form the basis for the process and the practices that should characterize all that we do. It is important for each organization to apply these to its own circumstances.

Education of the Public   Good performance is the best way to fulfill public trust, but individual voluntary and philanthropic organizations and the independent sector as a whole should help the public distinguish between effective and ineffective stewardship. The independent sector also needs to support and increase public education about the charitable community. The public should know what questions to ask, where to get information, how to interpret reports—all those skills which would enable it to make informed decisions about appeals for time and money.

We believe the sector can be proud of what it is and does. Policies and actions that enhance a trusting partnership with the public will build on that credibility. And they will do much more. An independent sector whose actions earn public confidence ultimately contributes to the integrity and strength of society as a whole.

Such an arrangement might also be an example of an illegal act, in violation of the Intermediate Sanctions Law, if the amount paid to the staff director exceeds what is reasonable for the services rendered.

Independent Sector's Role   Independent Sector has a special obligation to support and enhance this statement. Through wide dissemination, integration of such principles in its work, and collaboration on its recommendations throughout the voluntary and philanthropic community, Independent Sector can exemplify the statement's purpose.

The public is demanding greater demonstration of ethical behavior by all of our institutions and leaders. Our concerns about ethical behavior are not primarily a response to shortcomings or transgressions, but are based on our belief that the ethical behaviors and values we have articulated are the essential values for our society and it is right for us to model them.

There have always been high expectations of philanthropic and voluntary organizations, but because of recent allegations of wrongdoing in the charitable community and illegal activity in the corporate and accounting communities, the potential of eroding public trust is great.

To the extent the public has doubts about us, we shall be less able to fulfill our public service.

Therefore, each and every one of us has a responsibility to develop policies and practices that will serve regularly as guidance and checkpoints ensuring obedience to the law, ethical practices, and responsible stewardship.

In addition, we must all make far clearer to the public that this sector and its organizations practice high standards of ethical behavior. Independent Sector believes it is essential that, at a minimum, all organizations in the sector:

- Adopt an organizational creed of ethical practices.
- Conduct an ethics audit or self-evaluation every year (this is as important as an annual fiscal audit).
- Subscribe to and abide by a set of codes or standards.
- Involve all of their constituencies in the process.
- Infuse the process and the documents into the culture of the total organization.

Larger organizations should expand their efforts to develop a set of codes or standards where gaps exist.

Independent Sector will continue and expand its role to assist philanthropic and voluntary organizations to be aware of and fulfill the public's appropriately high expectations and to participate with all other institutions in society for adherence to higher standards of ethical behavior.

MODEL STANDARDS OF PRACTICE FOR THE CHARITABLE GIFT PLANNER[5]

Preamble

The purpose of this statement is to encourage responsible gift planning by urging the adoption of the following Standards of Practice by all individuals who work in the charitable gift planning process, gift planning officers, fundraising consultants, attorneys, accountants, financial planners, life insurance agents and other financial services professionals (collectively referred to hereafter as "Gift Planners"), and by the institutions that these persons represent.

This statement recognizes that the solicitation, planning and administration of a charitable gift is a complex process involving philanthropic, personal, financial, and tax considerations, and often involves professionals from various disciplines whose goals should include working together to structure a gift that achieves a fair and proper balance between the interests of the donor and the purposes of the charitable institution.

I. Primacy of Philanthropic Motivation   The principal basis for making a charitable gift should be a desire on the part of the donor to support the work of charitable institutions.

II. Explanation of Tax Implications   Congress has provided tax incentives for charitable giving, and the emphasis in this statement on philanthropic motivation in no way minimizes the necessity and appropriateness of a full and accurate explanation by the Gift Planner of those incentives and their implications.

III. Full Disclosure   It is essential to the gift planning process that the role and relationships of all parties involved, including how and by whom each is compensated, be fully disclosed to the donor. A Gift Planner shall not act or purport to act as a representative of any charity without the express knowledge and approval of the charity, and shall not, while employed by the charity, act or purport to act as a representative of the donor, without the express consent of both the charity and the donor.

IV. Compensation   Compensation paid to Gift Planners shall be reasonable and proportionate to the services provided. Payment of finder's fees, commissions or other fees by a donee organization to an independent Gift Planner as a condition for the delivery of a gift is never appropriate. Such payments lead to abusive practices and may violate certain state and federal regulations. Likewise, commission-based compensation for Gift Planners who are employed by a charitable institution is never appropriate.

V. Competence and Professionalism   The Gift Planner should strive to achieve and maintain a high degree of competence in his or her chosen area, and shall advise donors only in areas in which he or she is professionally qualified. It is a hallmark of professionalism for Gift Planners that they realize when they have reached the limits of their knowledge and expertise, and as a result, should include other professionals in the process. Such relationships should be characterized by courtesy, tact and mutual respect.

VI. Consultation with Independent Advisers   A Gift Planner acting on behalf of a charity shall in all cases strongly encourage the donor to discuss the proposed gift with competent independent legal and tax advisers of the donor's choice.

VII. Consultation with Charities   Although Gift Planners frequently and properly counsel donors concerning specific charitable gifts without the prior knowledge or approval of the donee organization, the Gift Planner, in order to insure that the gift will accomplish the donor's objectives, should encourage the donor early in the gift planning process, to discuss the proposed gift with the charity to whom the gift is to be made. In cases where the donor desires anonymity, the Gift Planner shall endeavor, on behalf of the undisclosed donor, to obtain the charity's input in the gift planning process.

VIII. Description and Representation of Gift   The Gift Planner shall make every effort to assure that the donor receives a full description and an accurate representation of all aspects of any proposed charitable gift plan. The consequences for the charity, the donor and, where applicable, the donor's family, should be apparent, and the assumptions underlying any financial illustrations should be realistic.

IX. Full Compliance   A Gift Planner shall fully comply with and shall encourage other parties in the gift planning process to fully comply with both the letter and spirit of all applicable federal and state laws and regulations.

X. Public Trust Gift Planners shall, in all dealings with donors, institutions, and other professionals, act with fairness, honesty, integrity and openness. Except for compensation received for services, the terms of which have been disclosed to the donor, they shall have no vested interest that could result in personal gain.

THE SALVATION ARMY FUNDRAISING CODE OF ETHICS[6]
Obligations of The Salvation Army

The Fundraising Code of Ethics declares those values by which The Salvation Army, as an organization, and all individuals involved in Salvation Army fundraising activities are governed.

1. The Salvation Army acknowledges the trust relationship that exists between The Salvation Army and the public to whom it appeals for financial gifts in support of its programs and services.
2. The Salvation Army will maintain governing structures, which ensure that its programs and services are faithful to the mission and values of The Salvation Army.
3. The Salvation Army will clearly communicate the purpose for which the funds are being raised.
4. The Salvation Army, in recognizing its responsibility to the donor, will make every effort to honour donor requests in the following areas: Change of name and change of address updates; Accurate update of mailing preferences; and Provide information regarding The Salvation Army.
5. The Salvation Army will strive to ensure that all representations of fact, descriptions of financial condition of the organization, or narratives about events will be current, complete and accurate, without material omissions, exaggerations of fact, use of misleading photographs or any other communication that would tend to create a false impression or misunderstanding.

6. The Salvation Army will communicate realistic expectations of what a donor's gift may actually accomplish within the limits of its ministries.

7. The Salvation Army will seek to honor the donor's intent when making a gift. The donor's intent may be related to what was communicated in a general or special fundraising appeal or to specific instruction accompanying the gift.

8. The Salvation Army will seek the consent of the donor before changing the conditions of any gift.

9. The Salvation Army will express its gratitude for support by way of clear and continued communication with donors.

10. The Salvation Army will decline a donation that would not be in harmony with its mission. The Salvation Army will not solicit a donation that would not be in harmony with its mission. It may also determine certain means of raising funds to be inconsistent with the values of The Salvation Army. When such a decision is made, The Salvation Army will communicate its limitations clearly to its fundraising personnel, and apply its decision consistently. The Salvation Army will continue to treat all persons with respect, even if their gift is declined.

11. The Salvation Army regards accountability as a fundamental principle in its relations with its supporters. Accountability is comprised of several factors, all of which exist to protect the public trust and ensure that the intentions of the donor are honored by:

Use of accurate and consistent accounting methods that conform to the appropriate guidelines adopted by The Canadian Institute of Chartered Accountants.

Adherence to financially prudent and ethical investment policies as established by The Salvation Army territorial administration.

Clear and regular communication with donors to report on how the mission of The Salvation Army has been furthered by their donations, and how the conditions of their gifts have been met.

Clear communication concerning donor recognition and donor benefits.

Disclosure of the financial status of The Salvation Army by way of independently audited statements of account.

Disclosure of fundraising costs that endorse effective management and resource development.

The Salvation Army considers names on its donor list to be strictly confidential, and under no circumstances will these lists be sold or traded.

12. The Salvation Army will respect the privacy of those who benefit directly from the fulfillment of the mission of The Salvation Army.

13. The Salvation Army will use suitably trained personnel (officers, employees, and volunteers) in its fundraising activities and will ensure that they are appropriately supervised.

14. In addition to its regular personnel The Salvation Army solicits the shorter-term assistance of community volunteers at various times of the year in connection with its seasonal fundraising appeals. Volunteer coordinators will provide orientation and guidelines to these volunteers.

15. The Salvation Army will, through its complaint policy, closely monitor complaints received from donors and prospective donors and seek to provide clarity and, where applicable, solutions to the problems.

16. The Salvation Army does not enter into contractual agreements based upon commission-based or percentage-based fundraising.

17. The Salvation Army will make available to any party a copy of its Fundraising Code of Ethics.

Obligations of Salvation Army Fundraisers

Persons involved in raising funds on behalf of The Salvation Army are expected to:

1. Act according to high ethical standards and seek to inspire others through their own sense of dedication and commitment.

2. Treat all persons with the utmost dignity and respect, valuing the privacy, freedom of choice and interests of each donor.
3. Be aware of the mission of The Salvation Army, and ensure that needed financial resources are vigorously and ethically sought for the advancement of that mission.
4. Be supportive of the mission and leadership of The Salvation Army, and seek to promote its reputation.
5. Act with integrity, fairness, honesty and truthfulness to safeguard the public interest.
6. Avoid conflicts of interest that may negatively impact the donor–Salvation Army relationship. In addition, the supplier will immediately disclose to The Salvation Army an actual or apparent conflict of interest.
7. Avoid soliciting a gift, accepting a gift, or entering into a contract with a prospective donor that would knowingly place hardship on the donor, or place the donor's future well-being in jeopardy.
8. Ensure, to the best of their ability and within the scope of their responsibility, that contributions are used in accordance with the designation of the donor.
9. Seek to improve their fundraising knowledge and skills in order to enhance service to donors and The Salvation Army, and freely share their knowledge and experience with others.
10. Recognize the boundaries of their individual competence, and in the interests of The Salvation Army and its donors, recommend the involvement of others as appropriate.
11. Comply with the spirit and letter of all applicable laws.
12. Report unethical behavior to appropriate Salvation Army personnel.

Donor Rights

The Salvation Army endorses the following Donor Bill of Rights, which has been developed by the American Association of Fund Raising Council, the Association for Healthcare Philanthropy, the Council for Advancement and Support of Education, and the Association of Fundraising Professionals (formerly the National Society of Fundraising Executives).

Philanthropy is based on voluntary action for the common good. It is a tradition of giving and sharing that is primary to the quality of life. To assure that philanthropy merits the respect and trust of the general public, and that donors and prospective donors can have full confidence in the not-for-profit organizations and causes they are asked to support, we declare that all donors have these rights:

1. To be informed of the organization's mission, of the way the organization intends to use donated resources, and of its capacity to use donations effectively for their intended purpose.

2. To be informed of the identity of those serving on the organization's governing board, and to expect the board to exercise prudent judgment in its stewardship responsibilities.

3. To receive a copy of the Fundraising Code of Ethics as established by The Salvation Army.

4. To have access to the organization's most recent financial statements, including the charity's registration number as assigned by the Canada Customs and Revenue Agency and information contained within the public portion of the annual Charity Information Return to the Canada Customs and Revenue Agency.

5. To be assured their gifts will be used for the purposes for which they were given.

6. To receive appropriate acknowledgement and recognition.

7. To be assured that information about their donations is handled with respect and with confidentiality to the extent provided by law.

8. To expect that all relationships with individuals representing organizations of interest to the donor will be professional in nature.

9. To be informed whether those seeking donations are volunteers, employees of the organization or hired solicitors.

10. To have the opportunity for their names to be deleted from mailing lists that an organization may intend to share.

11. To feel free to ask questions when making a donation and to receive prompt, truthful and forthright answers.

Appendix A

Official Minute Regarding Lottery Funds   No application may be made by any Salvation Army unit to lottery organizations for a grant from lottery funds, neither should the name of The Salvation Army be used for the promotion of any lottery.

Interpretation of Minute for Fundraising   The Salvation Army will not actively or directly participate in, or permit the use of the name and logos of The Salvation Army to promote, games of chance, raffles, bingos, lotteries and other social/recreational activities which would conflict with the mission and values of the organization.

The Salvation Army deems it acceptable to receive monies raised as a result of games of chance, raffles, bingos, lotteries and other social/recreational activities, sponsored by other organizations and offered to it for the maintenance and advance of the mission of The Salvation Army.

Positional Statement on Gambling   Gambling has become a worldwide obsession with tentacles reaching into almost every aspect of daily life. Government and private lotteries, boosted by sports betting, have served cunningly to work gambling into the very fabric of the family.

The Salvation Army deplores the fact that, with the advent and proliferation of government lotteries, legislators have encouraged the tendency to prey on the greed and weakness of human nature.

The Salvation Army continues to resist this insidious occurrence and cautions both governments and individuals of the inherent dangers in this gambling craze.

The Salvation Army warns of the selfishness in gambling in which individuals seek gain at the expense of others, and is saddened by the plight of those suffering from gambling addiction. Its social welfare experience underscores the fact that there are those who disregard the needs of family in order to indulge.

The Salvation Army asserts that gambling runs counter to Christian love, which respects and shows concern for others. Even in its simplest form gambling can lead to excess and undermine the personality and character of the individual.

Salvationists should resist participation in any scheme which would give them material advantage on the basis of chance.

Statement of Ethics and Accountability for Washington Grantmakers

Washington Grantmakers' board and staff recognize the wide diversity of philanthropic goals and resources among the Washington Grantmakers membership. We strive to respect donors' charitable intentions expressed in organizational charters and core documents as we apply our philanthropic resources to contemporary social conditions. We attend to the future through prudent stewardship of financial and other resources and we recognize that accountability calls for openness, fairness, and trust. In our actions, we commit to responsiveness to our members and the public; transparency of governance and operations; disclosure of information regarding our goals and practices; and a commitment to accessibility to those we serve.

Washington Grantmakers enhances accountability in many ways. We focus particular attention on:

- Understanding and complying with legal requirements.
- Communicating to the public our commitment to responsible and effective philanthropy.
- Communicating to the public the goals and procedures that govern our decision-making process.
- Practicing and promoting ethical behavior.
- Building respectful and constructive relationships with our diverse constituencies.

In short, we hold ourselves responsible to our members, our diverse constituencies, and those who may rely on us in the future.

NOTES

1. Adopted 1964; amended October 2007.
2. Copyright 2004 by the Association of Professional Researchers for Advancement.
3. www.ePhilanthropy.org. Approved: November 12, 2000. Revised: January 25, 2001/September 23, 2002/September 23, 2004/December 8, 2005.
4. Independent Sector. www.independentsector.org/.
5. Partnership for Philanthropic Planning. www.pppnet.org.
6. Salvation Army. www.salvationarmymyusa.org/usn/www_usn_2.nsf.

Websites for International Fundraising Codes of Ethics and Standards

Argentina: www.aedros.org/

Australia: www.fia.org.au/pages/principles-standards-of-fundraising-practice.html

Austria: www.fundraising.at

Brazil: http://captacao.org/recursos/

Canada: www.imaginecanada.ca/ethicalcode

Denmark: www.isobro.dk

Dominican Republic: World Association of Non-governmental Organizations: www.wango.org/codeofethics.aspx

France: www.fundraisers.fr/page/0072-ethique

Germany: www.fundraisingverband.de/verband/ethische-grundsaetze/19-grundregeln.html

Italy: www.assif.it/index.php/en/codice-etico

Mexico: www.afpnet.org/files/ContentDocuments/CodeofEthics.pdf

Netherlands: www.vfi.nl

New Zealand: www.finz.org.nz/Site/About_Us/Code_of_
Conduct.aspx

Nigeria: World Association of Non-governmental Organizations:
www.wango.org/codeofethics.aspx

Poland: www.fundraising.org.pl

Republic of Congo: World Association of Non-governmental
Organizations: www.wango.org/codeofethics.aspx

Singapore: www.afpnet.org/files/ContentDocuments/Codeof
Ethics.pdf

South Africa: www.saifundraising.org.za/index.php/ethics/saif-
code-of-professional-ethics

Sri Lanka: World Association of Non-governmental Organizations:
www.wango.org/codeofethics.aspx

Sweden: www.frii.se

Switzerland: www.swissfundraising.org

United Kingdom: www.institute-of-fundraising.org.uk/guidance/
code-of-fundraising-practice.

United States: www.afpnet.org/files/ContentDocuments/Codeof
Ethics.pdf

Zambia: World Association of Non-governmental Organizations:
www.wango.org/codeofethics.aspx

Association of Fundraising Professionals: www.afpnet.org/files/
ContentDocuments/CodeofEthics.pdf

World Association of Non-Governmental Organizations: www
.wango.org/codeofethics.aspx

International Statement of Ethical Principles

www.afpnet.org/Ethics/IntlArticleDetail.cfm?ItemNumber=3681.
It was adopted on October 16, 2006, by the following
countries:

Argentina

Australia

Belgium

Canada

Finland

France

Germany

Hungary

Hong Kong

Indonesia

Italy

Kenya

Republic of Korea

Netherlands

New Zealand

Poland

Singapore

South Africa

Spain

Sweden

Switzerland

Ukraine

United Kingdom

United States

Statement of Values and Standards for Excellence of the Tucson Symphony Society dba Tucson Symphony Orchestra

INTRODUCTION

As a matter of fundamental principle, the Tucson Symphony Orchestra (TSO) should adhere to the highest ethical standards[1] while striving to accomplish its mission to present live symphonic performances and music education at the highest level of artistic excellence, enriching and entertaining the people of Southern Arizona. The TSO is supported by individuals, corporations and foundations through charitable contributions and volunteer effort; by government agencies through grants; and by consumers through purchases, fees, and taxes.

The TSO must earn this public trust every day and in every possible way. Organizations are, at their core, people, and it is up to the people of the TSO—board members, executive leaders, employees, and volunteers—to demonstrate their ongoing commitment to the core values of integrity, honesty, fairness, openness, respect, responsibility, and accountability.

Adherence to the law is the minimum standard of expected behavior. Nonprofit and philanthropic organizations must do more, however, than simply obey the law. As a nonprofit and philanthropic organization the TSO must not merely embrace the spirit of the law, but go beyond legal requirements to make certain that what it does is matched by what the public understands about what it does. Transparency, openness, and responsiveness to public concerns must be integral to its behavior.

STATEMENT OF VALUES

An effective organization is built on a foundation of widely shared values. The values of the TSO include:

- Commitment to our audiences, future audiences, children and the public good;
- Accountability to the public;
- Commitment to the spirit as well as the letter of all applicable laws and regulations;
- Respect for the worth, dignity and contributions of our musicians, staff, volunteers and patrons;
- Inclusiveness;
- Respect for pluralism and diversity;
- Transparency, integrity and honesty;
- Responsible stewardship of all resources;
- Commitment to excellence and to maintaining the public trust;
- Dedication to traditional classical as well as quality innovative symphonic music.

Standards for Excellence and Guiding Principles

I. Mission The TSO maintains a clearly stated mission and purpose, approved by the Board of Trustees, in pursuit of the public good. All of its programs are evaluated to assure they effectively and efficiently support that mission. All who work for or on behalf of the TSO understand and are loyal to that mission and purpose. The mission is responsive to the constituencies and communities served by the TSO and of value to the society at large.

II. Governance   The TSO has an active governing body, the Board of Trustees, that is responsible for setting the mission and strategic direction of the organization and oversight of the finances, operations, and policies of the organization. The governing body:

- Ensures that its trustees are personally committed to the mission;
- Ensures that its trustees have the requisite skills and experience to carry out their duties and that they understand and fulfill their governance duties acting for the benefit of the TSO and its public purpose;
- Maintains a conflict of interest policy that ensures that any conflicts of interest or the appearance thereof are avoided or appropriately managed through disclosure, recusal or other means;
- Is responsible for the engagement, regular performance review and termination of the Executive and Music Directors and ensures that the compensation of the Executive and Music Directors is reasonable and appropriate;
- Ensures that the Executive and Music Directors and appropriate employees provide the Board of Trustees with timely and appropriate information so that the board can effectively carry out its duties;
- Ensures that the TSO conducts all transactions and dealings with integrity and honesty;
- Ensures that the TSO promotes working relationships among board members, staff, musicians, volunteers, and program beneficiaries that are based on mutual respect, fairness and openness;
- Ensures that the TSO is fair and inclusive in its hiring and promotion policies and practices for employees and in its recruitment and appointment of board members and volunteers;
- Ensures that policies of the TSO are in writing, clearly articulated and officially adopted;
- Ensures that the resources of the TSO are responsibly and prudently managed;

- Ensures that the TSO has the capacity to carry out its programs effectively;
- Ensures written minutes of board and board committee meetings are executed, distributed and archived;
- Ensures that Trustees practice self-evaluation on an annual basis.

III. Responsible Stewardship   The TSO manages its funds responsibly and prudently. Consistent with national norms for professional symphony orchestras, the TSO:

- Spends a reasonable percentage of its annual budget on programs in pursuit of its mission;
- Spends an adequate amount on administrative expenses to ensure effective accounting systems, internal controls, competent staffing, and other expenditures critical to professional management;
- Compensates employees, and any others who may receive compensation, reasonably and appropriately;
- Has reasonable fundraising costs, recognizing the variety of factors that affect fundraising costs;
- Does not accumulate operating funds excessively;
- Prudently draws from endowment funds consistent with donor intent and to support the public purpose of the organization;
- Ensures that all spending practices and policies are fair, reasonable and appropriate to fulfill the mission of the organization;
- Ensures that all financial reports are factually accurate and complete in all material respects;
- Annually carries out board level review of the audit in the absence of staff during a meeting with the auditors.

IV. Financial and Legal   The TSO practices sound financial management and complies with generally accepted accounting principles. The TSO is knowledgeable of and complies with all laws, regulations and applicable international conventions. Accurate financial records are kept, and the financial resources are used in the furtherance of the mission of TSO. Further, the TSO:

- Operates in accordance with an annual budget which has been approved by the Board of Trustees;
- Files a Form 990 and is subject to an audit by an independent Certified Public Accountant;
- Prepares internal financial statements monthly, that are provided to the Board of Trustees and/or its Finance Committee, identifying and explaining any material variation between actual and budgeted revenues and expenses;
- Provides employees a confidential means to report suspected financial impropriety or misuse of TSO resources;
- Maintains written financial policies governing: (a) investment of its assets, (b) internal control procedures, (c) purchasing practices and (d) reserve funds;
- Periodically assesses the need for insurance coverage. A decision to forego general liability insurance or Directors and Officers liability insurance coverage shall only be made by the Board of Trustees.

V. Human Resources   All Trustees, executive leaders, employees, musicians, and volunteers of the TSO act with honesty, integrity and openness in all their dealings as representatives of the TSO. The TSO promotes a working environment that values respect, fairness and integrity.

The TSO has a policy of promoting inclusiveness, and seeks to have its employees, Trustees and volunteers reflect diversity in order to enrich its programmatic effectiveness. The TSO takes meaningful steps to promote inclusiveness in its hiring, retention, promotion, board recruitment and constituencies served.

The TSO has written personnel policies and procedures governing the work and actions of all employees. It has a system for regular written evaluation of employees by their respective supervisors, which takes place at least annually. The TSO human resource policies are fair, establish clear expectations, and provide for meaningful and effective performance evaluation.

All employees receive a copy of personnel policies and procedures and a copy of this Statement of Values and Standards for Excellence.

VI. Openness and Disclosure The TSO operates for public purposes with public support. As such, it provides comprehensive and timely information to the public, the media, and all stakeholders and is responsive in a timely manner to reasonable requests for information. All information about the TSO will fully and honestly reflect its policies and practices.

Basic informational data about the TSO, such as the Form 990, reviews and compilations, mission, program activities, names of members of the Board of Trustees, names of administrative staff, and audited financial statements, is posted on the TSO website or is otherwise available to the public. All solicitation materials accurately represent the TSO policies and practices and respect the dignity of program beneficiaries. All financial, organizational, and program reports are complete and accurate in all material respects.

The TSO will provide members of the public who express an interest in its affairs with a meaningful opportunity to communicate with an appropriate representative of the TSO. At least one staff member is responsible to assure that the TSO is complying with both the letter and the spirit of federal, state, and municipal laws, which require disclosure of information to members of the public.

VII. Program Evaluation The TSO regularly reviews program effectiveness and has mechanisms to incorporate lessons learned into future programs. The TSO is committed to improving program and organizational effectiveness and develops mechanisms to promote learning from its activities and the field. The TSO is responsive to changes in its field of activity and is responsive to the needs of its constituencies.

VIII. Fundraising The TSO fundraising program is maintained on a foundation of honesty and responsible stewardship, and as such is truthful in its solicitation materials and keeps its fundraising practices consistent with its mission, compatible with its organizational capacity and respectful of the interests of donors and prospective donors. The TSO Board of Trustees has voted to adopt the attached Code of Ethical Principles and Standards of Professional Practice promulgated by the Association of Fundraising Professionals as well as the National

Committee on Planned Giving Model Standards of Practice for the Charitable Gift Planner. A copy of these documents is hereby incorporated by reference and made a part of these Statement of Values and Standards for Excellence. The TSO respects the privacy concerns of individual donors and expends funds consistent with donor intent. It discloses important and relevant information to potential donors.

In raising funds from the public, the TSO will respect the rights of donors, as follows:

- To be informed of the mission of the TSO, the way the resources will be used and the TSO capacity to use donations effectively for its intended purposes;
- To be informed of the identity of those serving on the TSO Board of Trustees and to expect the board to exercise prudent judgment in its stewardship responsibilities;
- To have access to the most recent audited financial reports of the TSO;
- To be assured their gifts will be used for the purposes for which they are given;
- To receive appropriate acknowledgement and recognition;
- To be assured that information about their donations is handled with respect and with confidentiality to the extent provided by the law;
- To expect that all relationships with individuals representing the TSO will be professional in nature;
- To be informed whether those seeking donations are volunteers, employees of the TSO or hired solicitors;
- To regularly be offered the opportunity for their names to be deleted from mailing lists that the TSO may intend to share; and,
- To feel free to ask questions when making a donation and to receive prompt, truthful and forthright answers.

IX. Public Affairs and Public Policy The TSO, through its membership in Arizona Action for the Arts, maintains a written policy on advocacy, defining the process by which the organization determines positions on specific issues.

The TSO ensures that any educational information provided to the media or distributed to the public is factually accurate and provides sufficient contextual information to be understood.

The TSO assures that its activities promoting public participation in community affairs are diligent in assuring that the activities of the TSO are strictly nonpartisan.

NOTE

1. Date Approved: October 4, 2006. Revised: October, 6, 2006.

References

Afterhours Inspirational Stories. *Admitting Flaws.* www.inspirationalstories.com/7/709.html.

Anderson, Albert. 1996. *Ethics for Fundraisers.* Bloomington, IN: Indiana University Press.

Anheier, Helmut K., and Lester M Salamon, eds. 1998. *The Nonprofit Sector in the Developing World: A Comparative Analysis.* Manchester, UK: Manchester University Press.

Anheier, Helmut K., Adele Simmons, and David Winder (eds.). 2006. *Innovation in Strategic Philanthropy: Local and Global Perspectives.* New York: Springer.

Armstrong, M., and D. Sappington. 2005. "Recent Developments in the Theory of Regulation." In M. Armstrong and R. H. Porter (eds.), *Handbook of Industrial Organization,* vol. 3 (Amsterdam: North-Holland, 2005). www.econ.ucl.ac.uk/downloads/Armstrong/reg.pdf.

Association Française de Fundraisers. Code of Professional Ethics.

Association Française de Fundraisers. Union pour la Générosité. www.fundraisers.fr.

Association of Fundraising Professionals. 2007. AFP Code of Ethical Principles and Standards and Professional Practice. www.afpnet.org//Ethics/EnforcementDetail.cfm?itemnumber=3261.

_____. International Statement of Ethical Principles in Fundraising. www.afpnet.org/Ethics/IntlArticleDetail.cfr?itemnumber=3681.

_____. 2005. *Ethics Leadership Guide* (January).

Aviv, Diana. 2003. "Purpose, Power, and Participation: Ideas for the Future of Our Sector." Opening Plenary Address, Independent Sector Annual Conference (San Francisco, November 2). www.independentsector.org/speeches.

Barber, Putman, ed. 2001. *Accountability: A Challenge for Charities and Fundraisers: New Directions in Philanthropic Fundraising* 31 (Spring).

Beyel, Joseph S. 1997. "Ethics and Major Gifts." *Developing Major Gifts, New Directions in Philanthropic Fundraising* 16 (Summer).

Bowman, W., and A. Bies. 2005. "Can the Charitable Sector Regulate Itself? Special issue," *The Nonprofit Quarterly* 12.

Buechner, Frederick. 1993. *Wishful Thinking: A Seeker's ABC.* San Francisco: Harper San Francisco.

Burnett, Ken. 2006. *The Zen of Fundraising: 89 Timeless Ideas to Strengthen and Develop Your Donor Relationships* (San Francisco: Jossey-Bass).

Center for Civil Society Studies at the John Hopkins University Institute for Policy Studies: www.jhu.edu/ccss.

Center for Civil Society Studies at the John Hopkins University Institute for Policy Studies. UN Nonprofit Handbook.

Charity Commission for England and Wales. www.charity-commission.gov.uk.

CIVICUS, World Alliance for Citizen Participation. www.civicus.org.

Cox, Harvey. 1995. *Fire from Heaven: The Rise of Pentecostal Spirituality and the Reshaping of Religion in the 21st Century.* Cambridge, MA: Da Capo Press.

Day, Duane L. 1998. *The Effective Advancement Professional: Management Principles and Practices.* Gaithersburg, MD: Aspen Publishers, Inc.

De Tocqueville, Alexis. 2003. *Democracy in America.* Kramnick & Bevan (eds.). London: Penguin Classics.

DiLorenzo, T. J. 1996. "The Myth of Natural Monopoly." *The Review of Austrian Economics* 9(2).

Dorff, Elliott N. 2005. Nonprofits and Morals: Jewish Perspectives and Methods for Resolving Some Commonly Occurring Moral Issues. In *Good Intentions: Moral Obstacles & Opportunities*, David H. Smith, ed. Bloomington and Indianapolis: Indiana University Press.

Dove, Kent E. 2001. *Conducting a Successful Fundraising Program: A Comprehensive Guide and Resource.* San Francisco: Jossey-Bass.

Duronio, Margaret A., and Eugene R. Tempel. 1997. *Fund Raisers: Their Careers, Stories, Concerns, and Accomplishments.* San Francisco: Jossey-Bass.

Dutch Fundraising Association. Code of Conduct for Fundraisers. www.vfi.nl.

Ebrahim, A. 2005. "Accountability Myopia: Losing Sight of Organizational Learning." *Nonprofit and Voluntary Sector Quarterly*, 34(1).

Edge, Laura Bufano. 2003. *Andrew Carnegie: Industrial Philanthropist.* Minneapolis: Lerner.

Elmore, R. F. 1978. "Organizational Models of Social Program Implementation." *Public Policy* 26(2).

Fischer, Marilyn. 2000. *Ethical Decision Making in Fund Raising.* New York: John Wiley & Sons.

Fischer, Marilyn. 1994. "Ethical Fund Raising: Deciding What's Right in Advancing Philanthropy." *The Journal of the National Society of Fund Raising Executives* (Spring).

Fogal, R. E. 2004. "Developing and Managing the Fundraising Program." In *The Jossey-Bass Handbook of Nonprofit Leadership and Management*, 2nd ed., edited by R. D. Herman. San Francisco: Jossey-Bass.

Fredericks, Laura. 2001. *Developing Major Gifts: Turning Small Donors into Big Contributors.* New York: Aspen Publishers.

Friedman, Thomas. L. 2005. *The World Is Flat: A Brief History of the Twenty-First Century*. New York: Farrar, Strauss & Giroux.

Fulda, Joseph. 1997. *The Appearance of Impropriety*. www.csulb.edu/~asc/post16 .html.

Fundraising Standards Board. www.frsb.org.uk.

Fundraising Institute of Australia Ltd. www.fia.org.au.

Fundraising Institute of New Zealand. *Promoting Fundraising Excellence*. www.finz.org.nz/.

Gaudiani, Claire. 2003. *The Greater Good: How Philanthropy Drives the American Economy and Can Save Capitalism*. New York: Times Books, Henry Holt and Company.

Gladden, Washington. 1905. *The New Idolatry and Other Discussions*. New York: McClure, Phillips Co.

Grace, Kay Sprinkel. 1997. *Beyond Fund Raising: New Strategies for Nonprofit Innovation and Investment*. New York: John Wiley & Sons.

Grace, Kay Sprinkel and Alan L. Wendroff. 2001. *High Impact Philanthropy: How Donors, Boards, and Nonprofit Organizations Can Transform Communities*. New York: John Wiley & Sons.

Greenfield, James M., and Richard F. Larkin. 2002. *Fund Raising: Evaluating and Managing the Fund Development Process*, 2nd ed. New York: John Wiley & Sons.

Greenfield, James M., and Richard F. Larkin. 2000. "Public Accountability." *Serving the Public Trust: Insights into Fundraising Research and Practice*, Vol. II. *New Directions in Philanthropic Fundraising* 27 (Spring).

Guidestar UK. www.guidestar.org.uk.

Hammack, David C. 2005. "Donors, Intermediaries, and Beneficiaries: The Changing Moral Dynamics of American Nonprofit Organizations." In *Good Intentions: Moral Obstacles & Opportunities*, edited by David H. Smith. Bloomington, IN: Indiana University Press.

Hart, Ted, James M. Greenfield, Pamela M. Gignac, and Christopher Carnie. 2006. *Major Donors: Finding Big Gifts in Your Database and Online*. Hoboken, NJ: John Wiley & Sons.

Heldt, Diane. 2007. "Faculty Says No to Naming UI College after Wellmark." *The Cedar Rapids Gazette*, July 5.

Herman, R. D. 2004. "Conclusion: The Future of Nonprofit Management." In *The Jossey-Bass Handbook of Nonprofit Leadership and Management*, 2nd ed., edited by R. D. Herman. San Francisco: Jossey-Bass.

Herman, R. D., and D. O. Renz. 2004. "Doing Things Right: Effectiveness in Local Nonprofit Organizations, A Panel Study." *Public Administration Review*, 64 (4).

Hochschild, Adam. 2005. *Bury the Chains: Prophets and Rebels in the Fight to Free an Empire's Slaves*. New York: Houghton Mifflin.

Imagine Canada's Ethical Fundraising and Financial Accountability Code. www
.imaginecanada.ca/?q=en/node/21.

Independent Sector. *Intermediate Sanctions.* www.independentsector.org/PDFs/
sanctions.pdf.

Independent Sector. 2002. *Obedience to the Unenforceable: Ethics and the
Nation's Voluntary and Philanthropic Community.* www.independentsector
.org/PDFs/publications.

Independent Sector. 2004. Statement of Values and Code of Ethics for Nonprofit
and Philanthropic Organizations. Washington, DC: Independent Sector.

Ingram, Richard T. 2003. Ten Basic Responsibilities of Nonprofit Boards (Board-
Source). Washington, DC.

Institute of Fundraising. www.institute-of-fundraising.org.uk.

Institute of Fundraising. Code of Conduct for Fundraisers. www.institute-of-
fundraising.org.uk/home.

International Center for Not-for-Profit Law. www.icnl.org.

Irvin, R. A. 2005. "State Regulation of Nonprofit Organizations: Accountability
Regardless of Outcome." *Nonprofit and Voluntary Sector Quarterly* 34(2).

Jeavons, T. H. 2004. "Ethical Nonprofit Management." In *The Jossey-Bass Handbook of Nonprofit Leadership and Management*, 2nd ed., edited by R. D. Herman.
San Francisco: Jossey-Bass.

Jennings, Marianne M. 2001. "Ideas & Society." *Meridian* Magazine. www.ldsmag
.com/1/article/4574.

Johnson, Paula D., Stephen P. Johnson, and Andrew Kingman. 2004.
Promoting Philanthropy: Global Challenges and Approaches. Paper for
International Network on Strategic Philanthropy. www.tpi.org/promoting_
philanthropy/tpi_services/international_philanthropy.aspx.

Johnston v. Koppes, 850 F.2d 594 (9th Cir. 1988).

Josephson, Michael. 2003. *Ethical Issues and Opportunities in the Non-Profit Sector.* Marina del Rey, CA: The Joseph & Edna Josephson Institute for the
Advancement of Ethics.

Kass, Amy A., ed. 2002. *The Perfect Gift: The Philanthropic Imagination and Poetry
and Prose.* Bloomington, IN: Indiana University Press.

Kearns, K. P. 1994. "The Strategic Management of Accountability in Nonprofit Organizations: An Analytical Framework." *Public Administration Review*,
54(2).

Kelley, Kathleen S. 1998. *Effective Fund-Raising Management.*(Mahwah, NJ:
Lawrence Erlbaum Associates).

Kent, Pam. 2005. "Arts, Briefly: British Charity Rejects 'Jerry Springer' Opera
Donation." *New York Times*, February 22.

Kidder, Rushworth M. 1995. *How Good People Make Tough Choices.* New York:
William Morrow.

Kirsch, Rodney P., and Martin W. Shell. "Achieving Leadership Gifts: The Investment Returns of Lasting Relationships." In *Capital Campaigns. New Directions in Philanthropic Fundraising* 231 (Fall 1998).

Lancaster, Lynne C., and David Stillman. 2005. *When Generations Collide.* New York: Collins Business.

Lang, Andrew S. 2003. *Financial Responsibilities of Nonprofit Board.* (BoardSource). Washington, D.C.

Laughlin, Rosemary. 2004. *John D. Rockefeller: Oil Baron and Philanthropist.* Greensboro, NC: Morgan Reynolds Publishing.

Lincoln, Abraham. 1846. *Handbill Replying to Charges of Infidelity.* July 31.

Lindblom, Charles. 2001. *The Market System: What It Is, How It Works, and What To Make of It.* New Haven: Yale University Press.

Marion, Barbara. 1994. "Decision Making in Ethics." In *Ethics in Fundraising: Putting Values into Practice, New Directions for Philanthropic Fundraising* (Winter).

Matten, D. 2003. "Symbolic Politics in Environment Regulation: Corporate Strategic Responses." *Business Strategy and the Environment* 12(4).

McCambridge, R. 2005. "Is Accountability the Same as Regulation? Not Exactly." Special issue. *The Nonprofit Quarterly* 12.

McGarvie, Mark D. 2003. "The *Dartmouth College* Case and the Legal Design of Civil Society." In *Charity, Philanthropy, and Civility in American History*, edited by Lawrence Friedman and Mark McGarvie. Cambridge, UK: Cambridge University Press.

McGinly, William C. Association for Healthcare Philanthropy. In November 9, 1993, news release on *Rights of Charitable Donors Reinforced.*

Metrick, L. Alayne. 2005. "Successful Strategies for Effective Stewardship." *In New Directions for Philanthropic Fundraising* 49 (Fall).

Morgan, G. 1986. *Images of Organization.* Beverly Hills, CA: Sage.

National Committee on Planned Giving. Model Standards of Practice for the Charitable Gift Planner. www.pppnet.org/ethics/model_standards.html

Nederlands Genootschap van Fondsenwervers. www.ngf.nu.

Neufeldt, Victoria, Editor in Chief, and David B. Guralnik, Editor in Chief Emeritus. 1994. *Webster's New World Dictionary of American English.* New York: Simon & Schuster, Inc.

Newsweek. 2005. "Spirituality in America." August 29–September 5.

New York Times. 2005. "Bidding Goodbye to Tainted Money." December 2.

Offenheiser, Raymond C., and Susan H. Holcombe. 2003. "Challenges and Opportunities in Implementing a Right-Based Approach to Development: An Oxfam America Perspective." *Nonprofit and Voluntary Sector Quarterly* 32(2).

O'Neill, Michael. 1994. "Fundraising as an Ethical Act." *Advancing Philanthropy* 1.

O'Neill, Onora. 2002. *A Question of Trust*. Cambridge, UK: Cambridge University Press.

Ostrander, S. A., and P. G. Schervish. 1990. "Giving and Getting: Philanthropy as a Social Relation." In *Critical Issues in American Philanthropy: Strengthening Theory and Practice*, edited by J. Van Til. San Francisco: Jossey-Bass.

Panel on Accountability and Governance in the Voluntary Sector. 1999. "Building on Strength: Improving Governance and Accountability in Canada's Voluntary Sector." www.broadbent_report_1999_en.pdf.

Panel on the Nonprofit Sector. 2005. "Strengthening Transparency Governance Accountability of Charitable Organizations." www.neh.gov/divisions/fedstate/resources/Panel_Final_Report.pdf.

Payton, Robert L. 1988. *Philanthropy: Voluntary Action for the Common Good*. New York: Macmillan.

Pettey, Janice Gow. 2002. *Cultivating Diversity in Fundraising*. New York: John Wiley & Sons.

Pomona College. www.pomona.edu/daring-minds/giving/donor-relations.

Pribbenow, Paul. 1998. "Are You a Force for Good?" *Advancing Philanthropy* (Spring).

Pribbenow, Paul. 1994. "Fundraising as Public Service: Renewing the Moral Meaning of the Profession." *Ethics in Fundraising: Putting Values into Practice. New Directions in Philanthropic Fundraising* 6 (Winter).

Pribbenow, Paul. 1999. "Love and Work: Rethinking Our Models of Professions." *Serving the Public Trust: Insights into Fundraising Research and Practice. New Directions for Philanthropic Fundraising* 1 (26).

Pribbenow, Paul. 1997. "Public Character: Philanthropic Fundraising and the Claims of Accountability." *The Professionalization of Fundraising: Implications for Education, Practice, and Accountability. New Directions for Philanthropic Fundraising* 15 (Spring).

Pribbenow, Paul. 1998. "Stewardship and Public Life: To Whom Much Is Given Shall Much Be Expected." *Advancing Philanthropy* (Fall/Winter).

Prince, Russ Alan, and Karen Maru File. 1994. *The Seven Faces of Philanthropy: A New Approach to Cultivating Major Donors*. San Francisco: Jossey-Bass.

Pulawski, Christina A. 1999. "The Effects of Technological Advances on the Ethics of Gathering Information in Support of Fundraising." *The Impact of Technology on Fundraising. New Directions for Philanthropic Fundraising* 25 (Fall).

Reich, Rob. 2006. "Philanthropy and Its Uneasy Relation to Equality." In *Taking Philanthropy Seriously: Beyond Noble Intentions to Responsible Giving*, edited by William Damon and Susan Verducci. Bloomington, IN: Indiana University Press.

Ritzenbein, Donald N. 2000. "One More Time: How Do You Motivate Donors?" *Understanding the Needs of Donors: The Supply Side of Charitable Giving. New Directions for Philanthropic Fundraising* 29 (Fall).

Rosso, Henry A. 1996. *Rosso on Fund Raising: Lessons from a Master's Lifetime Experience.* San Francisco: Jossey-Bass.

Sargeant, Adrian. 2001. "Managing Donor Defection: Why Should Donors Stop Giving?" *Understanding Donor Dynamics: The Organizations Side of Charitable Giving. New Directions for Philanthropic Fundraising* 32 (Summer).

Sargeant, Adrian, and Elaine Jay. 2003. *Building Donor Loyalty: The Fundraiser's Guide to Increasing Lifetime Value.* San Francisco: Jossey-Bass.

Sargeant, Adrian, and Stephen Lee. 2004. "Donor Trust and Relationship Commitment in the U.K. Charity Sector: The Impact on Behavior." *Nonprofit and Voluntary Sector Quarterly* 33(2).

Schon, Donald. 1983. *The Reflective Practitioner: How Professionals Think in Action.* New York: Basic Books.

Senge, Peter M. 1990. *The Fifth Discipline: The Art and Practice of the Learning Organization.* New York: Currency Doubleday.

Shakespeare, William. *All's Well that Ends Well,* Act 3, Scene 5.

Smith, James Allen. 2006. "In Search of an Ethic of Giving." In *Taking Philanthropy Seriously: Beyond Noble Intentions to Responsible Giving,* edited by William Damon and Susan Verducci. Bloomington, IN: Indiana University Press.

Stephenson, M., and Chaves, E. 2005. "The Nature Conservancy, the Press and the Social Construction of Accountability." Paper presented at the conference Boards and Beyond: Understanding the Changing Realities of Nonprofit Organizations, Kansas City, MO.

Strom, Stephanie. 2004. "Public Confidence in Charities Stays Flat." *New York Times.* www.nytimes.com/2004/09/13/national/13giving.html?.ex=119183 3729&ei=1&en=1b2773fccc4c13022.

Tobin, Gary A. 1999. "Between the Lines: Intricacies of Major Donor Communication." *Communicating Effectively with Major Donors. New Directions for Philanthropic Fundraising* 10 (Winter).

Tubbs, Sharon. 2003. "Churches at Odds Over Gifts from Gamblers." *St. Petersburg Times.* June 10.

Twitchell, James M. 2005. "Jesus Christ's Superflock." *Mother Jones.* www .motherjones.com/news/feature/2005/03/megachurches.html.

Walzer, Michael. 1982. "Socialism and the Gift Relationship." *Dissent* (Fall).

Weaver, Warren. 1983. "Pre-Christian Philanthropy." In *America's Voluntary Spirit,* edited by Brian O'Connell. New York: The Foundation Center.

Index

Abuse, 331–332
Accountability, 49, 224, 313, 345
Accountable characteristics, 6, 8, 268
The Accountable Nonprofit Organization, 128–129
Accounting, standardization, 219
Acknowledgment, 36
AFP Code. See Code of Ethical Principles and Standards (AFP)
AFP Donor Bill of Rights. See Donor Bill of Rights (AFP)
AFP Ethics Assessment Inventory (EAI), 4, 6, 10
and AFP, 274–276
alignment quest and, 269–270
building qualitative phrase, 264–266
building quantitative phrase, 266–267
critical dimensions of ethical fundraising, 267–269
ethical performance assessment, 263
findings, 276–277
frequently asked questions about, 277–279
fundraising organizations and, 274
individual fundraisers and, 273–274
origins of, 264
taking, 269–273
two step process, 264
using, 273–276
AFP Ethics Committee, 4, 10, 114
Alignment quest
individual and organizational results compared and interpreted, 272–273
individual user results, 270–271
organizational results, 271–272
American Association of Fund Raising Counsel (AAFRC), 40
The American Competitiveness and Corporate Accountability Act of 2002. *See* Sarbanes-Oxley (SOX)
American Red Cross, 143
American Symphony Orchestra League, 104
Anderson, Albert, 5, 96, 246
Annuity contract, 150
Anonymity, 66
Anonymous donor, 70

Antitrust legislation, 116
Appearance of impropriety, 197
about, 17–18
appearance of impropriety, 21–24
conflict of interest, 21–24
in defense of impropriety, 31–32
ethics vs. fiduciary duty, 18–19
rationalization, 30–31
reputation management and impropriety, 19–21
suspect behavior, 24–27
test for impropriety beyond conflict of interest, 27–30
Aristotle, 4–5
Armstrong, M., 356
Association de Fundraisers, 229–230
Association for Healthcare Philanthropy (AHP), 40, 139 n1, 246
Association issue, 100
Association of American Museums, 104
Association of Fundraising Professionals (AFP), 3, 40, 60, 79, 112, 119, 128, 139 n1, 142, 148, 196, 207, 213, 238, 246
ethical fundraising, 263
Association of Healthcare Philanthropy, 104
Association of Healthcare Professionals (AHP), 213
Association of Professional Researchers for Advancement (APRA), 246
Audiences, prioritization of, 205
Aviv, Diana, 370

Bakker scandal, 373
Bequests, 172
Berra, Yogi, 246
Berry, Leonard, 240
Bies, A., 357
Big government, 368, 371
Big institutions, 368
Bigness, 368, 371–372
Bill of Rights
Amendment I, 56
Amendment IV, 56

443